NORTHERN MEN WITH SOUTHERN LOYALTIES

NORTHERN MEN WITH SOUTHERN LOYALTIES

THE DEMOCRATIC PARTY AND THE SECTIONAL CRISIS

MICHAEL TODD LANDIS

CORNELL UNIVERSITY PRESS
Ithaca and London

This book has been published with the aid of a subsidy
from Tarleton State University, Stephenville, TX.

First published 2014 by Cornell University Press

Printed in the United States of America

Library of Congress Cataloging-in-Publication Data

Landis, Michael Todd, author.
   Northern men with Southern loyalties :
the Democratic party and the sectional
crisis / Michael Todd Landis.
      pages cm.
   Includes bibliographical references and index.
   ISBN 978-0-8014-5326-7 (cloth : alk. paper)
   1. Democratic Party (U.S.)—History—19th
century. 2. Slavery—Political aspects—United
States—History—19th century. 3. Sectionalism
(United States)—History—19th century.
I. Title.
   JK2316.L36   2014
   973.7'18—dc23   2014007808

Cornell University Press strives to use environmentally
responsible suppliers and materials to the fullest extent
possible in the publishing of its books. Such materials
include vegetable-based, low-VOC inks and acid-free
papers that are recycled, totally chlorine-free, or partly
composed of nonwood fibers. For further information,
visit our website at www.cornellpress.cornell.edu.

Cloth printing   10 9 8 7 6 5 4 3 2 1

To Whitney and Molly. For limitless love and laughs.

Contents

ACKNOWLEDGMENTS

This book has been a true labor of love. I love the topic, and I love the people who helped me accomplish it. All along the way, I relied on the advice and support of others. My wife, Whitney, read endless drafts, gave me tough feedback, and supported me, emotionally and financially, as I punched the keys in Charleston and Las Vegas. My adviser and friend Tyler Anbinder not only dissected chapters but came up with the topic in the first place. When I came to him as a wide-eyed grad student at The George Washington University, I was determined to write about "doughfaces." He had a larger vision. "Read Nichols's *Disruption*," he instructed. I rushed across the street to the Gelman Library, found the dust-covered book, and devoured it. I immediately saw what he saw—that the only work on Northern Democrats in the 1850s was woefully flawed, shockingly outdated, and entirely inadequate. I knew then what I had to do.

Encouraging me at every step of the way was Leo Ribuffo, beloved professor whose no-nonsense approach to both teaching and scholarship proved invaluable. I knew if I could win over that skeptical scholar, I was really on to something. Likewise, I've looked to Manisha Sinha as an unofficial adviser and essential ally. She has been an early and energetic supporter of my project, and she has worked tirelessly to promote my work. Thanks also go to Richard Stott and Eric Arnesen, who served with Tyler, Manisha, and Leo on my dissertation committee. Their comments and criticism have been critical to my success. Although not on my committee, my friend Eric Walther served as manuscript reader during the publication process. He meticulously combed through my manuscript not once, but twice, giving insights on everything from footnotes to interpretation. The published monograph is far better than my dissertation because of his efforts.

Of course, the book in your hand is the result in large part of my editor at Cornell University Press, Michael McGandy. His patience and enthusiasm were much appreciated. As many others can attest, Michael is extraordinarily easy to work with and possesses a keen eye for a good narrative. Along with Michael, a host of others have contributed to this book, including The George

Washington University history department office manager, Michael Weeks. Michael's unshakeable good humor and ability to defuse a crisis and find travel funding continues to make him the department's most important asset. Likewise, thanks go to Nina Silber, Dietrich Orlow, William Tilchin, and Brian Jorgensen, my advisers at Boston University, who tolerated my endless questions and guided me through the BA/MA program. Professor Silber, in particular, deserves credit for opening my eyes to the exciting possibilities of Civil War scholarship.

Speaking of funding, this book would not have been possible without the generous financial support of a variety of institutions. First and foremost, I owe gratitude to The George Washington University for granting me a five-year fellowship and full scholarship. In addition, the history department awarded me both research grants and travel money to present at conferences and scour faraway archives. Similarly, the Gilder Lehrman Institute of American History awarded me two separate research fellowships to visit the New York Public Library and the New-York Historical Society, whose archival material proved crucial. The White House Historical Association and the Cosmos Club Foundation also deserve thanks for their financial gifts.

But all the money in the world cannot substitute for devoted friends and family. My best friends, Christopher Hickman, Justin Pope, and Lindsay Moore, have been by my side since day one. They cheered my successes and helped me recover from defeats. They've never judged me, and they've always reminded me that career and life are two entirely separate realms. Other dear friends who have provided encouragement and advice include Sarah Mergel, Andrew Hartman, Pete Veru, John Quist, Frank Towers, Michael Green, and Robert Cook—each an outstanding scholar in his or her field, but, more important, marvelous, generous people. Finally, my parents and my grandma Elaine, who have been providing financial and emotional support my whole life, deserve all the gratitude I can muster.

This book has necessitated quite a bit of research, and I would be remiss if I did not thank the excellent staff of the Library of Congress Manuscripts Division, who literally had to deal with me on a daily basis, as well as the curators and archivists at the Indiana Historical Society, particularly Allison De Prey Singleton, who went far beyond the call of duty to tackle collections with me and make me feel at home in Indianapolis.

Last, but certainly not least, I wish to thank my new home of Tarleton State University; the Department of Social Sciences; my department chair, Chris Guthrie; and the dean of the College of Liberal and Fine Arts, Kelli Styron. They welcomed me to their vibrant academic community with open arms and have sustained me in my research and conference activity.

Introduction
Democrats and the Slave Power

The national capital was abuzz. So much so that young Francis Pollard, a Hoosier recruit stationed outside Washington, DC, in February 1862, quickly finished his dinner and requested a pass to spend the evening in town. A sitting U.S. senator was about to be expelled, and all Washington was eager to witness the denouement. Democrat Jesse Bright of Indiana, a barrel-chested Kentucky slave owner with a reputation for ruthlessness and physical aggression, had penned a letter to his friend Jefferson Davis, now the leader of the Southern rebellion, introducing Davis to a Texas arms manufacturer and recognizing Davis as the legitimate president of an independent Confederate States of America. The letter had been uncovered and presented to the Senate on December 16, 1861, sparking vigorous debate over how to sanction Bright for his treachery. To complicate matters, Bright's election to the Senate in February 1857 was, by all accounts, fraudulent. He had orchestrated his own election through an unlawful meeting of the state legislature and against the will of the majority of Indiana voters. When Bright assumed his seat, the Senate launched an investigation that, thanks to administration pressure and Southern power, was dragged out and quashed. By 1861, however, the Democratic Party was an embarrassing minority in the free states and had been reduced to a tiny faction in Congress. When Bright's letter to Davis was revealed, Senators jumped at the opportunity to expel their unsavory colleague.[1]

1

Completed just three years earlier, the new Senate chamber was packed with officeholders and observers. The enlarged hall was certainly more spacious but noticeably less regal, lacking the white columns and heavy red drapery that festooned the original space. Nevertheless, it was night and the new hall was illuminated by flickering gas lamps and reeked of tobacco, giving it the air of the historic old chamber. Pollard arrived in the crowded galleries in time to witness the final statements in the Bright trial, on February 6. "I heard the Senators from New York Mr. Harris, from Kentucky Mr. Davis, from Maine, Mass, Rhode Island, California, Virginia and Tennessee. And I heard Mr. Bright make his defense, which lasted two Hours pretty near," wrote Pollard to his siblings at home. Indeed, Bright's final appeal was impassioned though futile. His comeuppance had been a long time coming, and there was little doubt about his fate. When he completed his oration, he gathered his belongings and stormed out of the chamber. "He seemed to take the matter pretty hard," observed Pollard. Shortly thereafter, with Vice President Hannibal Hamlin presiding, the vote was taken and the Hoosier Democrat was officially expelled. The galleries erupted in applause.

Bright had made himself one of the most unpopular men in the North. Throughout the 1850s he had been a free state champion of slavery and Southern supremacy in Congress and had played a key role in keeping Indiana in the Democratic column until 1858. When the Civil War began, he energetically supported secession but refused to vacate his Senate seat. "Is Jesse D. Bright . . . a fit person to be intrusted with Senatorial functions?" asked the *New York Times*. "The expulsion of the traitor, while no more than an act of duty it owed itself, cannot fail to have an elevating and inspiring effect both on Congress and the country." His "complicity with the traitors," as the *Lowell Daily Citizen and News* phrased it, in 1861 was the final straw in a long career of offenses against free state voters. Jesse Bright was the quintessential Northern Democrat, and his expulsion from Congress represented Northern rejection of the old Southern-dominated Democratic Party. In the 1830s and 1840s, the organization had been nearly unstoppable and its rhetorical and political grip on the nation had been white knuckle. In the 1850s, however, the popularity of the party in the North plummeted as the thin guise of rhetoric was stripped away to reveal an aggressive agenda of slavery expansion and Southern power. The decline and demise of the Northern wing of the Democratic Party in the 1850s, and the subsequent rise of the Republicans, is the focus of this book.[2]

From its inception under Thomas Jefferson in the 1790s, the Democratic Party was controlled by Southern slave owners and energetically pursued a pro-Southern, proslavery program, often at the expense of its Northern wing. To hold the loyalty of free state voters, Democrats fashioned a compelling message of white supremacy democracy. Democracy, and its kin concept of egalitarianism, was at the heart of the political and social rhetoric of the antebellum Democratic Party. In fact, the party was commonly known as simply "the Democracy," primarily by its adherents. Democratic Party icons Jefferson and Andrew Jackson employed this rhetoric with astonishing success, claiming that the party was the sole defender of individual liberties and the laboring masses against the evils of special privilege and concentrated wealth, even though they, themselves, were wealthy, powerful, and privileged. The message masked a deeper, darker agenda that was, ironically, largely contradictory to the party's professed principles. Nevertheless, the rhetoric was potent enough to hold the loyalty of a substantial number of Northerners, even as many of them recognized the uneven nature of the coalition. The banner may have read *freedom, equality, and democracy*, but the reality was an organization dedicated to slavery, concentrated wealth in the form of land and slaves, and antidemocratic, minority rule. "This conduct in the south—I tell you in solemn & sad sincerity," lamented New York Democratic boss William Marcy in November 1849, "has, I fear, crushed their friends in the north."[3]

Southern power and slavery expansion were the fundamental principles of the antebellum Democracy. The party structure itself was designed to protect and further these objectives and was a glaring example of minority, antidemocratic rule. From the beginning, Southerners used parliamentary procedure to preserve control of the party apparatus, despite the North's fast increasing population. In the 1810s and 1820s, they employed the secret caucus, then, after widespread backlash against that practice, the "two-thirds rule," which required the consent of two-thirds of convention delegates to achieve passage of resolutions, platforms, and nominations. The two-thirds rule successfully prevented any Northerner who did not endorse slavery from gaining the presidential nomination, as well as prevent any antislavery notions from sneaking into resolutions. (Indeed, it was enough to thwart former president Martin Van Buren's bid for the nomination in 1844, despite the fact that a majority of the convention supported him. The Southern-controlled meeting instead turned to the slave-owning expansionist James Polk of Tennessee.) While a two-thirds rule might seem to ensure the will of the majority, it was, in practice, a form of minority domination. Southerners, though a numeric minority, could, with the aid of a few willing Northerners, dictate policy and candidates. Hence, the party was ruled by a cadre of Southern "bosses," who determined the outcome of conventions, the direction of legislation, the composition of administrations, the distribution of patronage, and the fate of Northern Democrats.[4]

Furthermore, subservient Northern Democrats followed the Southern lead on convention votes and repeatedly permitted Southerners to control party committees. Any Northerner who challenged Southern control of the organization was either shunned or severely punished. Likewise, any Northerner who wanted to rise within the ranks and achieve nomination to the U.S. Senate (which, since election was through the state legislature, required formidable party support) or the presidency would have to cater to Southern demands. When contemplating former vice president George Dallas's chances for a presidential nomination in 1852, longtime partisan Duff Green noted that if Dallas "goes for the rigid enforcement of the rights of the South, and in a letter or a speech does justice to Mr. Calhoun & the Southern Ultras, he can place himself before the public as the choice of the south" and thus clinch the nomination. Green's reference to Calhoun is especially noteworthy, as John Calhoun of South Carolina was a fiery champion of antidemocratic, minority rule. Bowing to the South and embracing Calhoun's doctrines would, Green knew, make the Pennsylvanian more likely to win the nomination. Future U.S. senator Richard Brodhead of Pennsylvania surveyed the 1852 field and came to a different conclusion, suggesting to a correspondent that "Mr. [Stephen] Douglas stands the best chance under the operation of the 2/3 rule." The entire party apparatus, Green and Brodhead understood, was designed to ensure Southern supremacy with the aid of but a few ambitious Northerners; the will of the Northern majority at Democratic conventions would always be thwarted by the Southern minority. It was antidemocratic to the core.[5]

The willing Northerners who tipped the scales in favor of the South and ensured continued Southern control of the party have often been called "doughfaces," meaning a Northern man with Southern principles. Though the moniker's origins are disputed, most scholars agree that it originated with a half-mad, often drunk representative from Roanoke, Virginia, John Randolph. In a speech before Congress during the Missouri Crisis of 1820–1821, Randolph expressed his contempt for easily manipulated Northerners, saying that they were so weak and cowardly that they were frightened by their own dough faces, referring to a children's game in which dough was applied to the face to create a mask. Not all doughfaces were Democrats, but most Northern Democrats were doughfaces, either explicitly championing slavery and Southern power, or implicitly aiding the South through votes and party participation.[6]

Such efforts in the name of minority, Southern rule within the party translated into minority, Southern rule of the federal government. With but two small exceptions between 1828 and 1856 (Whig victories in 1840 and

1848), Democratic dominance created a political environment where nomination usually equated to election. At a time when state legislatures elected senators and national conventions chose presidents, Northern Democrats were able to achieve election without serving the interests of their Northern voters. Once in office, these men pursued an antidemocratic agenda that outraged their constituents but pleased their Southern masters. Though small in number, these few ambitious politicos could tip the scales in the South's favor, both within the party and in governance.[7]

Moreover, it is important to recall that the Three-Fifths Clause of the U.S. Constitution gave the slave states representation in the House of Representatives beyond their voting white residents. Article 1, section 2 stated that *"three fifths of all other Persons [slaves]"* could be counted as part of the population when assessing representation in the House. Since slaves could not vote, this meant that Southerners enjoyed additional representation. This also resulted in undue influence in the Electoral College, which elects presidents and is based on state representation in Congress. Control of the executive, in turn, meant the selection of Supreme Court justices, who enjoyed lifelong terms. The more slaves the South imported, of course, the more Southern political power would grow. "Southerners demanded that any national government must agree that slavery could benefit the South in any new political arena," concludes William Cooper, scholar of Southern history. "The obverse also held; slavery must never penalize the South. Throughout the course of government making the South succeeded with its fundamental demands on slavery." Thus, the combination of the Three-Fifths Clause and the subservience of Northern Democrats gave the South almost unchallenged domination over the federal government in the antebellum era. This remarkable phenomenon, called the "Slave Power" by contemporaries and historians alike, is key to understanding the development of the nation and the causes of the Civil War.[8]

By the late 1840s, many Northerners came to realize the extent of the Slave Power and the proslavery, minority rule agenda of the Democratic Party. Jeffersonian/Jacksonian rhetoric had been sufficiently potent to keep Northerners in line for a generation, but the events of 1846–1848 alerted free state voters to the dangers of Southern power. Democratic president James Polk's invasion of Mexico in May 1846 was an unabashed grab at more slave territory, which would permit the expansion of both the "peculiar institution" and Southern control of the federal government. With the addition of new slave states, the Slave Power grew and Northern voters, though fast increasing in numbers, saw their influence in the government wane. When Pennsylvania Democrat David Wilmot boldly presented his "Proviso" in

August 1846 stating that slavery should not be permitted to spread into the territories taken from Mexico, white Southerners were enraged. Since the Whig organization had already begun to fracture, the national divide over Wilmot's Proviso spelled disaster for the Democrats. Debate turned to crisis, and Northern Democrats who opposed the expansion of the Slave Power bolted the Democracy in 1848 and formed their own partisan organization, called the Free Soil Party. In that year's presidential election, Democratic division permitted the victory of the nationalist war hero, nominally Whig General Zachary Taylor.

Over the next several years, Northern Democrats sought to heal their divisions and prove their fidelity to the Southern party leadership. This book focuses exclusively on the operations of the Northern wing of the Democratic Party in the 1850s as it simultaneously struggled to please the South and combat the rising antislavery tide in the North, a topic that has received shockingly scant attention. The machinations of Northern Democrats in this decisive decade led directly to civil war, as they helped produce the legislation and policies that tore the nation apart, yet few historians have attempted to unravel this political puzzle. There have been only two scholarly investigations into the Northern Democratic Party in the 1850s, both authored by Roy Nichols. The two volumes, *The Democratic Machine, 1850–1854* and *The Disruption of the American Democracy*, are wonderfully written but are products of the 1940s (the former was completed as a thesis in 1923 and was reprinted in the postwar period) and offer little beyond engaging stories of colorful personalities. Nichols also authored a biography of Franklin Pierce, *Franklin Pierce: Young Hickory of the Granite Hills* (1931), an important reference that, again, lacks deep engagement of the political issues of the antebellum era.

To be clear, this book is only partially concerned with antislavery Democrats, who were few in number and who were not welcome in the party after their bolt in 1848. This book addresses them only when they affected the regular Democratic organization, such as in the endless factional feuds in New York State, where proslavery "Hunker" regulars repeatedly rejected union with the generally antislavery "Barnburner" dissidents. In addition, the antislavery Democrats who returned to party ranks in 1852 promptly departed again in 1854 after the passage of the infamous Kansas-Nebraska Act. Thus, the Northern Democracy of the 1850s was effectively shorn of antislavery sentiment after 1848, and certainly after 1854. Jonathan Earle's *Jacksonian Antislavery and the Politics of Free Soil* (2004) is an outstanding study of antislavery Democrats in the 1830s and 1840s, but his narrative ends in the wake of 1848 and does not tackle the departure of Free Soil Democrats in the 1850s.

Specifically, this book argues that Northern Democrats were willful, knowing collaborators in the Slave Power agenda of slavery expansion and Southern supremacy; that Northern Democrats worked diligently and tirelessly to purge their partisan ranks of antislavery sentiment and members who sought cooperation with antislavery groups; and finally, that Northern Democrats developed and enunciated a heretofore unrecognized antidemocratic doctrine of minority rule to justify their service to the Southern grandees. By the end of the decade, this antidemocratic ideology had matured into a policy initiative at the federal level, most noticeably in the Buchanan administration's course in the Kansas Territory, where Democrats attempted to foist a proslavery, fraudulent, unrepresentative constitution on an unwilling antislavery majority.

In monographs that address the 1850s and the "coming of the Civil War," Northern Democrats are often lost in the grand narrative or deemed less significant than the rise of the Republican Party, the collapse of the Whigs, or the course of Southern secession. David Potter's *The Impending Crisis, 1848–1861* (1976) is probably the most well-known and most frequently cited of this genre, but Potter is hopelessly infatuated with Southern orators and seems bent on justifying secession and placing blame for the war on abolitionists. His work offers a useful starting point in understanding the events of the 1850s but in no way provides a fair assessment of the political issues and developments of the decade. William Freehling's masterful two-volume study of secession and antebellum politics, *The Road to Disunion* (1990 and 2007), are absolutely crucial to our understanding of the causes of the Civil War but are primarily concerned with Southerners. Likewise, *The Political Crisis of the 1850s* (1978) by Michael Holt is focused on the ethno-cultural dynamics of the sectional crisis rather than the centrality of slavery; Northern Democrats play only a supporting role in his dramatic interpretation.

In more recent years, attention has begun to shift away from the "crisis" approach to more expansive studies of prewar American politics and political culture. In 1983, Jean Baker published *Affairs of Party: The Political Culture of Northern Democrats in the Mid-nineteenth Century*. Fascinated by the concept of "political culture," Baker eschews a study of party machinery in favor of answering the question "How had some Northerners come to be Democrats?" She carefully examines schools, family life, and party iconography to discover the nature of the Democratic community, which, she concludes, inculcated party doctrine and made for lifelong party ties. While she makes some interesting observations about Democratic racism and party loyalty (determined, she concludes, by anything *but* policy), she does not address the collapse of the organization and the role of doughfaceism, nor does she explain why some Northern Democrats fled the party in the 1840s and 1850s and why some stayed.

The 2000s have seen a renewed interest in partisanship. In addition to Earle's 2004 *Jacksonian Antislavery*, there have been several excellent studies of the politics of territorial expansion and the literal "middle ground" between the antislavery North and proslavery South. Nicole Etcheson's comprehensive *Bleeding Kansas: Contested Liberty in the Civil War Era* (2004), Kristen Oertel's ambitious *Bleeding Borders: Race, Gender, and Violence in Pre–Civil War Kansas* (2009), and Stanley Harrold's exciting *Border War: Fighting over Slavery Before the Civil War* (2010) have served the historiographic debate well and have shifted attention away from Capitol Hill and onto the fight over America's border-lands, which significantly influenced popular conceptions of federal power and individual liberties. Likewise, *The Young America Movement and the Transforma-tion of the Democratic Party, 1828–1861* (2007), by Yonatan Eyal, has attempted to explore the generational gap between younger, expansion-minded Demo-cratic nationalists like Stephen Douglas and the elderly party scions like "Old Buck" James Buchanan. His observations are informative, but, in the end, the ephemeral "Young America" movement was more rhetorical than real.

The revived dialogue about Northern Democrats has also been served well by several new biographies of key politicos, such as William Lowndes Yancey of Alabama, Stephen Douglas of Illinois, Caleb Cushing of Massachusetts, and, as part of The American Presidents Series by Times Books, Millard Fill-more, Franklin Pierce, and James Buchanan. Similarly, recent scholarship on the antidemocratic nature of Southern politics, most notably Manisha Sinha's *The Counterrevolution of Slavery: Politics and Ideology in Antebellum South Caro-lina* (2000), have done much to cut through generations of myth-making to illuminate the realities of antebellum partisanship. The greatest contribution, however, has been Leonard Richards's *The Slave Power: The Free North and Southern Domination, 1780–1860* (2000). Though concerned broadly with political doughfaceism at the national level and not focused exclusively on Democrats, *The Slave Power* lays bare the nature of Southern supremacy in the antebellum era and explains in detail the role of Northern Democratic votes in the passage of key legislation. Richards's research and bold assessment of prewar politics has paved the way for scholars eager to go beyond Democratic rhetoric and understand *how* and *why* the South dominated both the party and the nation. Where Richards offers a sweeping seven-decade, multiparty overview of Southern supremacy, the present book focuses specifically on the 1850s and Northern Democratic machinations; where Richards raises broad questions about Northern proslavery sentiment, this study offers precise an-swers and explanations.

Other scholars have been more interested in ideology and expansive political trends than in the mechanics of partisanship and law-making. Sean Wilentz's *The Rise of American Democracy: Jefferson to Lincoln* (2005), for instance, examines the concepts of democracy, republicanism, and egalitarianism; he is interested in democrats, not Democrats, so to speak. This book, on the other hand, avoids the realm of ideology in order to tackle the logistics of party operation and illuminate the nuances of antebellum politicking.

Regardless of methodological differences, the vast majority of scholars have come to recognize the centrality of slavery to American political life in the early and mid-nineteenth century. This book seeks to offer a comprehensive account of Northern Democratic state and national activities in arguably the most important decade in U.S. history. This study also strives to assess events and people *in context*, meaning without an eye toward the looming disaster of disunion. The people of the 1850s did not know that war was imminent and did not make decisions based on any such premonitions. Rather, they acted in their own best interests at any given moment. Politicians, in particular, are given credit here for being cognizant of the ramifications of their actions; they were calculating, careful, and culpable, not simply "blundering," as previous historians have asserted. When Northern Democrats embraced the fraudulent, proslavery Lecompton Constitution of Kansas in 1857–1858, for instance, they well knew that the document was enormously unpopular among their free state constituents. This book will explain *why* such decisions were made and *how* they shaped the sectional crisis.

Members of Congress and observers, including young Pollard, who packed the Senate chamber on the night of February 5, 1862, were keenly aware of the symbolic importance of the expulsion of Jesse Bright, the iron-willed autocrat of Indiana Democrats. Like his party, Bright had fallen from the heights of power and influence to the depths of defeat and humiliation. He had been one of the most influential Democrats in the North, but he had long ago ceased to represent the interests of his free state constituents, the vast majority of whom opposed the expansion of slavery and the Slave Power. It would take more than the election of 1860 to finally put the nail in his political coffin—it took the onset of a bloody national civil war and the near destruction of the Union.

CHAPTER 1

"Fidelity and Firmness"

Northern Democrats and the Crises of 1850

The trouble did not begin with the convening of the Thirty-First Congress in December 1849, but the crisis did. The expansion of slavery into new territories had been a polarizing issue since the creation of the U.S. Constitution in 1787, and aggressive territorial expansion under slave-owning presidents Thomas Jefferson, John Tyler, and James Polk only exacerbated the situation. Their acquisition of more and more territory to permit the spread and growth of slavery, combined with the proslavery policies of presidents James Monroe, Andrew Jackson, and Martin Van Buren, created enormous political rifts along sectional lines, as Northerners grew to oppose the "Slave Power" and the spread of the "peculiar institution." Polk's war against Mexico, in particular, ignited a political firestorm, and debates, both at the state and national levels, raged over the fate of the new western territories forcibly taken from the United States' southern neighbor.

When the Thirty-First Congress gathered in wintry Washington City, not only had the major disputes concerning slavery and the lands forcibly taken from Mexico in the Mexican-American War (lands later referred to as the Mexican Cession) not been concluded, but other, equally contentious issues, such as slavery in the District of Columbia and the undefined western boundary of Texas, were still demanding attention. Rallied to action by the Wilmot Proviso, which sought to prohibit the expansion of slavery into the

Mexican Cession, Northern voters looked to the new Congress to take a firm stand against the Slave Power. "The disgraceful traffic in slaves brought from other quarters, and openly exhibited and sold in the national capital, ought unquestionably to be prohibited," declared one Hoosier. Such intense antislavery sentiments did not bode well for the new Congress, especially given the simultaneous movement among slave owners to usher in a new era of Southern supremacy.[1]

The undisputed champion of the South and Southern slave-owning "rights" was John Calhoun of South Carolina, onetime nationalist and full-time proslavery ideologue. Weary of growing Northern antislavery sentiment, as well as an even faster-growing Northern population, Calhoun and his followers saw an opportunity in the sectional crises of the late 1840s. If the North would not permit the expansion of slavery and submit to continued Southern control of the federal government, then the South would, as a unit, secede and forge a new slave-owning paradise. Threats of secession and disunion had been common among Southerners since the birth of the nation, but Calhoun now sought to make good on the rhetoric.[2]

With secession in mind, a Southern convention was called to meet in Nashville, Tennessee, in June 1850. There, slave state delegates would show their resolve and agree on a course for disunion if Congress did not produce legislation to their liking. Democrat James Buchanan of Pennsylvania identified with Southerners and expressed concern that Northerners no longer took secession seriously. "It is truly lamentable that the North know comparatively nothing of what is going on in the South, nor will they until after the meeting of Congress." Needless to say, the planned Nashville conference caused panic among most Northern Democratic politicians, who were still reeling from the "disastrous" electoral defeats in the elections of 1848.[3]

Democrats had reasons aplenty to be worried about the results of the 1848 presidential election, not only because they had lost, but because the episode revealed a growing sectional chasm within their organization. While Whigs had united (albeit tenuously) behind the nationalist war hero Zachary Taylor for president, Democrats succumbed to infighting over slavery. Many Northern Democrats had supported the Wilmot Proviso for policy and the New Yorker Van Buren for president, but Southerners, who controlled the party with an iron fist, would allow neither. Formerly a doughface, Van Buren had taken a turn toward antislavery by the mid-1840s, and thus was no longer a viable candidate. Instead, the Southern party bosses turned to doddering Lewis Cass of Michigan, who had built a career, as one Southerner put it delicately, in "support and defense of southern rights." "It was a fit nomination for the party of slavery," wrote Indiana politico George Julian.

"He had been thirsting for it many years, and he had earned it by multiple acts of the most obsequious and crouching servility to his southern overseers." Outraged, a significant portion of Northern Democrats bolted the national nominating convention and fashioned a new Free Soil Party, with Van Buren as the nominee.[4]

Many Northern Democrats, though, remained loyal to the regular organization and the Southern leadership, considering themselves the only "true democrats," entirely separate from Northern antislavery Democrats. The fact that Free Soilers had done surprisingly well in the 1848 election (though they won only 10 percent of the vote), and the fact that Cass and the regular Democratic Party went down to defeat, demonstrated the seriousness of the situation. Moreover, Northern Democrats sensed that antislavery sentiment was growing fast among their constituents, which made their political position all the more tenuous. "The free soil faction have the popular side of the question," admitted Democrat William Marcy of New York. Regardless, Northern Democrats entered the Thirty-First Congress determined to either destroy their antislavery associates or force them into submission, thus proving their fidelity to the Southern wing and advancing their careers. "The Democrats who were faithful in the last election," Marcy continued, "will do what they can to occupy a position which will be satisfactory to their brethren of the South." Such "faithful" Northern Democrats, commonly referred to as "doughfaces," would play a critical role in the political crises of the 1850s.[5]

The Thirty-First Congress

The divisions of 1848, still fresh in December 1849, made congressional Democrats nervous as the national legislature convened and the slavery debates resumed. Northern Democrats were still deeply at odds over slavery. The Southern wing could be counted on to act in the interests of slavery every time, and the Free Soilers were in no mood to cater to slave state demands, so the actions of the doughfaces would prove decisive. The "free soil faction do not mean to yield an inch of ground," warned Marcy. Political observers, partisan or otherwise, knew that the new session would be tumultuous, and Democrats of all stripes were keenly aware of their perilous position.

Not surprisingly, the crowded House of Representatives was the scene of the first skirmishes. As soon as the gavel brought the body to order in the semicircular, white-columned hall, debates flared over House organization, the election of a Speaker, and slavery. "The most exciting spectacle I have ever witnessed," Pennsylvania editor John Forney wrote with anticipation.

"The subject is the slave question; and there is now danger of a sectional [crisis] of the very worst character."[6] The House Democratic caucus, which was controlled by Southerners, had decided in advance to support Howell Cobb of Georgia for Speaker, but antislavery men chafed at the prospect of another slave owner in command of committees and procedure. While Free Soil Democrats refused to support Cobb, Northern Democratic regulars dutifully fell in line. In the coming weeks, a contingent of pro-Southern Northern Democrats, including Graham Fitch of Indiana, Harry Hibbard of New Hampshire, and William Richardson and John McClernand of Illinois, voted consistently with the South in support of Cobb, defying their Northern colleagues and their free state constituents.[7] For their diligence, these doughfaces would be rewarded; Richardson, in particular, was put forward for Speaker when Cobb's candidacy briefly faltered. Though the honor was symbolic and he never garnered more than twenty-nine votes, the message to Northern Democrats was clear: support the South, and you will advance in the party; oppose the South, and you will be "slaughtered."[8]

The deadlock over Speaker dragged on for weeks. Northern Democrats and Whigs alike scrambled to negotiate with their Southern wings but to no avail. The South was virtually united against Cobb's primary challenger, Massachusetts Whig Robert Winthrop, who was by no means an antislavery activist. There was almost no way that Southerners would accept a New Englander in the Speaker's chair, and there was even less likelihood of Southern Democrats accepting a Northern Whig. Time was on the side of the South, however, as federal inaction would lend credibility to the cause of disunion. The game, of course, was evident to Northerners. Representative Thomas Harris of Illinois vented to a friend: if the South wanted to end the stalemate, he fumed, why did they not vote for a Northern candidate? "The reason was he was a *Northern Man*. Why did [Southerners] not vote for Winthrop five weeks ago & end the struggle for Speaker? The reason was *he* was a northern man." "It cannot be disguised," he continued, "that . . . there is practiced an unyielding proscription of northern men. No northern man can ever be endured by them, unless he goes as far as they do in abusing the whole north."[9] Northern Democrats, perhaps for the first time, came to realize that Southern unity, particularly on the eve of the Nashville meeting, transcended party lines.

In addition to prolonging the standoff, Southern House members enflamed the crisis by intensifying their disunionist rhetoric. On December 13, obstructionist leader Robert Toombs of Georgia (considered by his colleagues the "embodiment of Slavery Propagandism") declared that antislavery Northerners were to blame for the stalemate and encouraged the South to stand firm against would-be Northern tyranny.[10] The South would not, and should not, accept a Northern Speaker. "The interests of my section of the Union," Toombs explained, playing the victim, "are in danger, and I am therefore unwilling to surrender the great power of the Speaker's chair without obtaining security for the future." As he spoke, though, Toombs dropped the facade of victim and revealed his true goals of obstruction and disunion. "We have just listened to strong appeals upon the necessity of organizing the House. I confess I do not feel that necessity. From the best lights before me, I cannot see that my constituents have anything to hope from your legislation, but everything to fear. . . . I do not, then, hesitate to avow before this House and the country . . . that if by your legislation you seek to drive us from the territories . . . and to abolish slavery in this District . . . *I am for disunion.*" Restrictions of any kind on slavery, he concluded, would be "the consummation of all evil."[11]

The declaration and the exchange that ensued threw the chamber into chaos. Now, instead of debating the Speakership and the spread of slavery, members were forced to confront imminent disunion. "Every thing here is in Confusion. . . . The extreme Southern men are becoming perfectly reckless," Senator James Shields of Illinois wrote to a rather unsympathetic Buchanan. "My deliberate opinion now is that the leaders are secretly but anxiously desirous of a secession." Southern states, observed General John Wool of New York with anxiety, were actually preparing for insurrection. "Alabama it would seem is about to arm and put herself in hostile array against the North; and the late Governor Troup of Georgia, to meet the avalanche that is to overwhelm the South, proposes 'the establishment in every state without delay military schools, foundries, Armories, Arsenals, Manufactures of Gun powder, &c,' and at once raise an army, march to Washington and take possession of the Capital." Wool's fears were well founded, as Southern mobilization and militarization was winning adherents throughout the region. "My mind is made up; I am for the fight," declared Alexander Stephens of Georgia, showing his full support for the deceased Governor Troup.[12]

Meanwhile, no Congressional business occurred. Southern obstructionism was working—the federal government appeared inept, and Southern rhetoric put Northerners on the defensive. "This is the most impracticable pettifogging Congress ever assembled in Washington or any other place," wrote soon-to-be senator Richard Brodhead of Pennsylvania.[13] Playing a key role in the crisis were the Northern Democrats who aided the South. Knowing that their only hope for advancement within the party (including election to the U.S. Senate, since control of state legislatures required formidable party backing) depended on Southern support, House Northern

Democrats dutifully provided the votes and parliamentary motions to keep the chamber unorganized.[14]

Thanks to doughfaces, the South prevailed and the eventual organization of the House favored the slave states. On December 22, after sixty-three ballots and a changing of the rules, Cobb was elected Speaker on a plurality, deciding the political character of the chamber for the coming session. Once in power, Cobb appointed committees favorable to the Southern agenda and rewarded his doughface friends with choice assignments, such as McClernand's selection for the Committee on Territories.[15] The Southern victory in the House led Southern Democrats in the Senate to consolidate their power by assailing Northern antislavery members and ousting slave owner Thomas Benton of Missouri from the chairmanship of the powerful Committee on Foreign Relations because he would not support the unrestricted expansion of slavery. With Northern Democrats in line, Free Soilers on the ropes, and the slave states once again in firm control of both houses of Congress, Southerners seized the opportunity to achieve one of their long-held goals, namely a new, more stringent fugitive slave law, one that would overcome Northern "personal liberty" laws and force free state residents to return escapees. On January 4, 1850, Senator James Mason of Virginia introduced a bill to "provide for the more effectual execution of the 3d clause of the 2d section of the 4t article of the Constitution," which was immediately referred to the Committee on the Judiciary, chaired by Andrew Butler of South Carolina, who had introduced similar bills in previous Congresses.[16]

With a new fugitive slave law before Congress, in addition to the ongoing debates about slavery in the territories and in the national capital, as well as the looming Nashville conference, the sense of calamity deepened.[17] To bring calm to the crisis, President Zachary Taylor delivered to Congress on January 21 a special message on California and New Mexico. In his remarkably brief letter, Taylor explained that he earnestly endeavored "to remove all occasion for the unnecessary agitation" concerning slavery in the territories and, to that end, had permitted California and New Mexico to form their own territorial governments as the first step toward statehood. To Congress, he left the outstanding issues of Texas's western boundary and the organization of the rest of the Mexican Cession. Taylor did, however, issue a warning to Southerners: "Any attempt to deny to the people of the State the right of self-government in a matter which peculiarly effects them [slavery] will infallibly be regarded by them as an invasion of their rights; and . . . will certainly be sustained by the great mass of the American people."[18]

"The message was wise, patriotic, temperate and firm," recorded Benton, "but it encountered great opposition." Indeed, by stating that Congress should not interfere with the formation of territorial governments and constitutions, Taylor placed himself in direct opposition to both Southern expansionists and Northern Democrats hoping to extend the Missouri Compromise Line to the Pacific. Moreover, since Californians had already voted to prohibit slavery and it was generally accepted that the climate of the New Mexican desert made slavery unlikely there, Taylor's plan was essentially a recipe for restricting slavery. This was made all the more surprising because "Old Rough and Ready," aside from being a gifted military commander and hero of the Mexican War, was a Louisiana slave owner.[19]

Not a surprise was the South's reaction to the Taylor plan: immediate attack. Southern media began trumpeting the fanfare of disunion, and Southern Congressmen raced to demand the expansion of slavery into the territories. Equally predictable, Northern Democrats continued to echo the Southern charges. Even before Taylor's message reached the Senate, Daniel Dickinson of New York, angling for the 1852 Democratic presidential nomination, declared himself ready to draw his "sword" for his "southern brethren." "I desire," he announced, "to see the South secure in the full possession and enjoyment of their constitutional rights. I have stood by them . . . regardless of peril, and will now aid in shielding them from unjust and improper aggressions upon their institutions. . . . My sympathies have been with them." Dickinson's profession of fidelity drew applause from Southern members. Shortly thereafter, Senator Cass, also with an eye on 1852, declared his willingness to defy his constituents and state legislature in defense of Southern interests. "My sentiments upon the Wilmot proviso are now before the Senate," he stated with reference to his opposition to that measure, "and will soon be before my constituents and the country. I am precluded from voting in conformity with them." It was a clear, simple declaration of his loyalty to the South.[20]

Yet even with the firm support of men like Dickinson and Cass, and avowals from doughfaces that they would defy their constituents to serve Southern interests, Southern Democrats were not satisfied. "The people of the South had been heretofore laboring under the delusion that the Northern Democrats were their friends," exclaimed Senator Jeremiah Clemens of Alabama. "God deliver me from such friends as the northern Democrats!" As more and more Northern Democrats chafed at Southern rule and fled the party, however, Southern Democrats would become increasingly dependent on their doughfaced "friends." Senator Henry Foote of Mississippi (known as "Hangman Foote" because of his threat to hang antislavery men from the "tallest trees") knew as much and gently reminded his colleagues of the importance to the party of Northern acquiescence. "There are some in this chamber who have always stood nobly by us, and who manifested even Roman firmness, and will do so yet, I know. And there are men out of this Chamber, whom I could name—such men as George M. Dallas, James Buchanan, Levi Woodbury . . . good men and true—for whose fidelity and firmness I would vouch as soon as I would for any southern man."[21] The real test of doughface dedication, however, was yet to come.

Enter "The Great Pacificator"

Amidst the swirl of legislation, perceived Whig weakness, and the aggressive posturing of Senators, energetic Stephen Douglas of Illinois acted to redeem Northern Democrats in the eyes of Southerners. As chair of the Senate Committee on Territories, and a longtime advocate of western development, he was well positioned to address the issues of California and New Mexico, as well as the Texas boundary dispute and the fate of the Mormon area dubbed "Deseret." If he could craft legislation that would please the South and be acceptable to the majority of Northerners, he would win national attention and perhaps the presidential nomination in 1852. When, on December 27, 1849, Foote introduced a bill to organize the western territories, Douglas fought to have it assigned to his committee. Unfortunately for the Illinoisan, though, his committee was slow moving and never reported the bill to the floor, which gave another, equally ambitious, man the opportunity for which had had been waiting.[22]

While Douglas's committee deliberated, Whig Henry Clay of Kentucky acted to take advantage of the legislative opportunity. Deeply aware of his reputation as "The Great Pacificator" (thanks to his successful efforts to resolve the Missouri Crisis of 1820–1821 and the Nullification Crisis of 1833) and on poor terms with the new president, Clay acted quickly to challenge Taylor's leadership and stall Douglas's initiative. On January 29, 1850, after consulting other leading Whigs, the seventy-two-year-old, called "the Sage of Ashland," introduced eight resolutions, each aimed at addressing the major issues facing the nation. The first would admit California as a state without reference to slavery (the territory had already approved a free state constitution); the second provided territorial governments for New Mexico and Deseret without restrictions on slavery; the third and fourth tried to define the size of Texas and agreed to pay its debt (amount unspecified); the fifth and sixth ended the slave trade in the District of Columbia, but reaffirmed the continuation of slavery; the seventh was Mason's more strenuous fugitive slave law; and the eighth was a denial of congressional authority over slavery.[23]

Without a doubt, Clay's measures were designed to placate the South, with the North expected to provide the bulk of the "settlement and adjustment," as it was called. California would enter as a free state, true enough, but there would be no restrictions on slavery in New Mexico or Deseret, and the slave state of Texas would get its enormous debt paid by the federal government. Also, antislavery activists had been pushing for a complete end to slavery in the District of Columbia, but Clay's bill granted only an end to the slave *trade*, a small, but critical, change, as it would permit human bondage to persist in the national capital. Even more galling for Northerners was the new fugitive slave law that would force civilians to participate in slave catching and the utter denial of congressional authority. Referring to the South Carolina victory in the nullification crisis, Benton labeled Clay's bills "a concession to the spirit of disunion—a capitulation to those who threatened secession—a repetition of the error of 1833." Yet Southerners were still unwilling to negotiate. "Mr. Clay's Compromise," noted Stephens, "satisfied very few members."[24]

To ensure a proslavery outcome for Clay's bills, Foote submitted a resolution on February 14 creating a special committee. Foote's plan was to have the committee combine the eight individual bills into one massive comprehensive bill, later labeled the "omnibus." Though Clay is often credited (and criticized) for designing the omnibus strategy, the plan was actually Foote's (and it had been Foote who originally urged Clay to take quick action and submit the eight resolutions).[25] Northern Democrats, however, were not going to sit idly by while Clay and the Whigs ran the show.[26]

In a bid to regain control of territorial legislation, Douglas instructed his lieutenants in the House, McClernand and William "Old Dick" Richardson, to make a deal with the South. On February 18, McClernand approached Stephens and Toombs on the House floor and asked for a meeting. They agreed but stated bluntly that they would not accept *any* restrictions on slavery. The following night, Northern Democrats and Southern leaders met at the Third Street residence of Speaker Cobb. McClernand and Richardson, acting as Douglas's agents, convinced Stephens, Toombs, and others to accept a free California in exchange for the protection of slavery in the national capital and payment of the Texas debt. They also agreed that Douglas and McClernand would shepherd the bills through their respective houses in the hopes of allaying Northern suspicions of a Southern plot; if Douglas and McClernand could achieve the admission of California with its current free state constitution, the rest of the pro-Southern agenda could be pushed through.[27] The meeting determined that Northern Democrats would take the lead in the creation of a "compromise."

By the end of February, the Congressional environment had taken an ugly turn. Tempers flared, and members came to the floor armed with pistols and knives. Heavy liquor consumption only made matters worse. Southerners were the more physically aggressive, convincing many Northerners that violence was imminent. Even doughfaces McClernand and Richardson, who supposedly had nothing to fear from the South, began arming themselves. Southern rhetoric, moreover, reached new heights, as they intensified their threats of disunion and claims of victimization. "Slavery slavery," exclaimed one Northern Representative, "is the eternal word in Congress and every circle of private conversation here. . . . I am satisfied that a large minority of the southern men are for Disunion per se and if the [Wilmot] proviso should [pass] a large maj[ority] are for destruction." The battle between Taylor, Clay, and Douglas for leadership on the slavery issue had thus far yielded poor results. Other voices would be heard, but the final course continued to lay in the hands of the Northern Democrats.[28]

The subsequent events of early March are fairly well known and are largely inconsequential to the legislative process. Calhoun's speech (delivered by James Mason of Virginia) on March 4 ignored Clay's bills and focused on supposed Northern tyranny, and Daniel Webster's famed three-hour pro-compromise oration on March 7 was, as a correspondent of Buchanan observed, more "a high bid to the south for the Presidency" than a serious discussion of the issues. Even William Seward's controversial "Higher Law" speech four days later, which denounced compromise and garnered a great deal of attention, only served to add fuel to the fire rather than help arrive at a settlement.[29] It was not until the Northern Democrats entered the fray that progress was made.

On March 13 and 14, Douglas drew attention back to the various territorial bills. In a forceful speech, he denied charges that he was a doughface or ever made "pledges to the slave interest," then made a vigorous plea for the admission of California. California had already created a government and a constitution, he reminded the chamber, so there should be no further need for debate. "The question is already settled," he insisted, "so far as slavery is concerned. . . . Pride of opinion is all that stands in the way of a speedy, harmonious, and satisfactory adjustment of this vexed question." Just over a week later, Chairman Douglas reported out of his committee new bills on California, Deseret, and New Mexico. His leadership in this area was part of the script decided on at the February night meeting, and he well knew that a smooth admission of California was key to paving the way for the proslavery measures to come.[30]

In the House, Richardson played the role of Douglas, but to a different audience and with a decidedly mixed message. Like Douglas, the thirty-five-year-old Illinoisan began by defending himself against charges of "truckling to the South," but then launched into a white supremacist rant about the dangers of abolitionism. Next, Richardson urged the admission of California with her present constitution, but then issued a threat to Southerners: if California was not accepted, then Northern Democrats would turn to the dreaded proviso. "I say to those now here," he stated dramatically, "that if they defeat bills for the territories, saying nothing about slavery, bills will pass Congress with the proviso." And, to make the threat real, he added, "I believe Congress has full power to pass such laws as they may think proper for the government of the territories." Richardson made it clear that if Southerners wanted to achieve their goals, they would have to accept California. In concluding, though, he combined some carrot with his stick and announced his full support for the fugitive slave law, hinting that such a law could only be achieved by accepting California.[31]

Along with the oratorical campaigns, Douglas and his lieutenants sought to kill the Foote/Clay omnibus and take advantage of the gulf between Whig leaders Taylor and Clay. Douglas sensed not only that the omnibus plan would fail (because of Southern opposition to a free California and a New Mexican territory at the expense of Texas) and lead to more sectional strife but also that Northern Democrats needed to produce a legislative outcome that would heal the divisions in their party, namely a pro-Southern "plan of adjustment" that could be sold to the North. In the coming votes on resolutions, bills, and parliamentary procedure, Northern Democrats held the balance of power. Southerners nearly always voted as a unit concerning slavery, but Northerners remained divided. Since the antislavery Free Soilers were determined to make a stand and Northern Whigs were fast turning against the measures, the decision of Northern Democrats to vote with the South was critical.[32] Anger ran deep on all sides, and at one point, an enraged Foote leveled his loaded Colt revolver at Benton. "The cowardly assassin has come here to shoot me," cried Benton. "Let him shoot me if he dares!" The dramatic scene concluded when a crowd gathered to restrain the two men.[33]

Finally, on April 19, a "Committee of Thirteen" was created to handle the omnibus. The committee chairmanship went to Clay, and the composition supposedly provided sectional and partisan balance with three more Southern Whigs, three Southern Democrats, three Northern Whigs, and three Northern Democrats. The Southern leadership knew what they were doing, however, and the three Northern Democrats selected—Jesse Bright of Indiana, Dickinson of New York, and Cass of Michigan—were dedicated doughfaces. The committee was proslavery and guaranteed to report favorably on the proslavery measures. This was not to the liking of Douglas, and he refused to participate. A successful committee report, he knew, would thwart his own legislative designs, which were to pass individually the controversial bills constituting the omnibus.[34]

The Indiana Autocrat

Douglas's absence from the committee allowed Bright, Dickinson, and Cass to chart their own course for Northern Democrats—outright participation with the Southern proslavery agenda. Bright, in particular, was eager to cast off the taint of Free Soilism from the Northern Democracy and redeem Northern Democrats in the eyes of the South. Though he represented the free state of Indiana, Bright was, in fact, a Kentucky slave owner. Bright, according to one who knew him, "in sentiment and feeling was a Southern man." He spent most of his time on his Warsaw, Kentucky, plantation rather than in his southern Indiana district and enjoyed the social and political benefits of Southern slave owning (though he once complained to a friend that he had "no other amusements than those afforded by an interchange of civilities with Niggers and Dogs").[35]

Called the "autocrat" of Indiana Democrats by contemporaries and historians alike, Bright had been a major political force in the party and on the Hill since the Polk years. His reputation as a "ruthless fighter" and manipulator served him well as he sought to crush antislavery Democrats and maintain the party's traditional pro-Southern, proslavery identity. He loved power, and he knew how to get it and keep it; he rewarded his friends and brutally punished his enemies. His Indiana political machine was more akin to an organized crime family than a partisan operation, with himself as the patriarch commanding a host of unflinchingly loyal lieutenants. "The friends I have are *my own creation*," he reminded his sister. "I was not *born* to *power station* or *wealth*, but with an energy and zeal that has never known limit." He may not have been born to wealth or station, but investments in land and slaves allowed him to amass an impressive fortune and live a life of luxury, so much so that when economic depression struck the nation in 1857 he "had no idea" of it.[36]

Bright's Southern grandee lifestyle may not have been typical among Northern Democrats, but his proslavery principles certainly were, especially by the middle of the decade after much of the Northern Democracy had withered away. His personal narrative, too, was common among doughfaced Democrats. He was born in New York State in 1812 to parents of modest

FIGURE 1. Senator Jesse Bright, Indiana (Library of Congress)

means; his father moved the family west to Kentucky, then to Indiana to start a hat-making business. Raised in Madison, Indiana, Bright early developed his trademark physical strength and aggressive personality. In the early 1830s, despite lacking formal education, he, like many of his future colleagues, began practicing law. Though law was his profession, politics was his passion, and he quickly rose to local prominence in traditionally Whig Jefferson County. Along with his older brother, Michael, Bright built up an effective Democratic organization and was soon elected probate judge in 1834. Three years later, he switched to U.S. marshal, which provided the opportunity to tour the state and gain exposure. In fall 1841, he was elected state senator, and by August 1843, his political machine had grown strong enough to make him lieutenant governor. He was a bellicose partisan, but his principal biographer warns that Bright was not motivated by any sense of public service or democratic principles but rather lust for power and office. "If the voters chose to think of him as a champion of the underprivileged," he notes, "that was all right too." Jesse Bright was many things, but "champion of the underprivileged" he was not.[37]

Despite his election as lieutenant governor, Bright's ferocious partisanship and dictatorial manner irritated Democrats and Whigs alike. When the latter gained control of the Indiana state legislature, Bright, presiding over the senate, repeatedly obstructed the election of a U.S. senator simply to prevent a Whig victory. In 1845, he managed to orchestrate his own election to the U.S. Senate, a testament to the effectiveness of his growing political family. Once in Congress, the Hoosier became fast friends with his Southern colleagues. He was a workhorse and preferred to operate behind the scenes, avoiding orations and debates; he focused on committee work and attended to the technical aspects of the legislative process. In short, he was a terrific asset to the Southern party bosses—his vote was unquestionably reliable, and he was willing to do the dirty work of lawmaking.[38]

When President Polk launched his invasion of Mexico in 1846, Bright was an enthusiastic supporter of the war, announcing that the United States could "clean out Mexico with a regiment of women, armed with broomsticks." When the gauntlet of the Wilmot Proviso was thrown down before the Senate in 1847, Bright was enraged and was one of only five Northern Democrats (along with Cass and Dickinson) to vote against it. By 1850, Bright's service to the South had earned him the position of ranking member on Douglas's Committee on Territories, and he even acted as floor leader on territorial issues in Douglas's absence. His policy agenda was entirely proslavery, even opposing the extension of the Missouri Compromise Line to the Pacific, since it would restrict slavery above the line. No restrictions of any kind could or would be tolerated. This position was even farther to the right than that of most of his Northern Democratic colleagues, such as Buchanan and Cass, who were willing to accept some kind of compromise (at least in 1850).[39]

Not surprisingly, Bright became the darling of the Southern leadership, and Polk brought him into his inner circle of advisors and agents, noting that Bright was "an honest man & one of the soundest, and most consistent & reliable democrats in the Senate." At home, however, Bright alienated voters. On hearing of Bright's reelection, one constituent gasped that "the political cauldron must have boiled its hottest to cast such scum upon the surface— Indiana must be redeemed." His unpopularity at home was not a problem, though, as his six-year Senate terms were dependent on the state legislature, not on popular votes. With an effective political machine and the firm support of the Southern bosses, Bright had little to worry about.[40]

Thus, when the Democratic Party split in 1848, Bright could wage merciless war against his Northern associates. Freed from the worries of reelection, he could attack popular Democrats and even admonish his constituents. When a township in his own Jefferson County cast forty-two antislavery votes, Bright roared to a voter: "God damn you—I wish you and they were in Hell. If I had the power I'd send you there!" He attended that year's national nominating convention, became part of Cass's "inner circle," and toured with the candidate, all the while endeavoring to punish "the treachery & base ingratitude of Van Buren." When Bright was appointed in 1850 to the Committee of Thirteen to consider the Foote/Clay bills, it provided him and Southern Democrats with an outstanding opportunity to realize their proslavery agenda.[41]

Death of the Omnibus

The committee, despite the attention it received, was intended to be a rubber stamp of sorts, simply lending legitimacy to the Foote/Clay plan, not a deliberative or policymaking body. By May 1 members had come to some basic agreements about the Texas–New Mexico boundary, the evils of the proviso, and the desirability of a new fugitive slave law, none of which significantly altered existing legislation. A week later, Clay presented the committee's report, which, to no one's surprise, endorsed his resolutions. That same day, Bright, who rarely took the floor, announced in his longest speech yet his full support of the "compromise." His promotion of the pro-Southern measures, Bright well knew, violated the will of the Indiana state legislature, which had instructed him to pursue the opposite course. Labeling his pro-Southern position "a great middle conservative course," he also admitted that he knowingly stood in opposition to the majority sentiment in the free states in general, and did not care. "There is a settled and deep feeling in most of the free States in favor of the *express* inhibition of slavery by Congress in all territorial governments," he announced to the Senate. "I have no hesitation in declaring my individual opinion against the necessity and expediency of such a course." Such disregard for the majority Free Soil sentiment would soon come to characterize Northern Democrats, but in 1850 the Northern antidemocratic doctrine was still rather novel. Northern Democrats like Bright supported the omnibus, despite Southern opposition, because they believed it to be the fastest way to achieve passage of the proslavery legislation demanded by the South and, thus, prove their loyalty to the Southern leadership.[42]

The ensuing debates throughout May and June only further sectionalized Congress. With Taylor's plan rejected and Douglas's course sidelined by Clay and the Committee of Thirteen, little was accomplished. "The political atmosphere in W. is at this time in a terrible commotion," wrote one observer from the Washington Naval Yard, "and there is no one here (in the Govt) to guide the whirlwind & direct the storm." Simultaneously, crisis loomed in the West, as Texas threatened war against a so-called Sante Fe "rebellion" that sought a state of their own free from slavery and Lone Star domination. Doughfaced Democrats followed the Southern lead and pressed for an expanded Texas border that would encompass the fledgling free state of New Mexico.[43]

By July, no progress had been made and Congress was still as divided as ever, with Northern Democratic regulars struggling to tip the balance in favor of the South. "What will Congress do with regard to the slavery question," queried one Southerner. "Will they adopt the arrangement proposed by the Senate Compromise Committee?" Earlier, Douglas, hoping to bridge the divide, had made an impassioned plea for territorial legislation that omitted the subject of slavery entirely, but to no avail. His "popular sovereignty" approach had its adherents, but Southerners were not convinced it would guarantee slavery's spread. Adding to the pressure was the threat of war in the West and the convening of the Nashville Convention, which seemed to make both sides all the more intransigent.[44]

It appeared as if a national stalemate had been reached. Yet something unexpected occurred to break that deadlock. At 10:35 p.m. on Tuesday, July 9, President Zachary Taylor died. On the Friday before, he had attended Fourth of July festivities on the National Mall and shortly thereafter developed acute gastroenteritis, to which he soon succumbed. Needless to say, the passing of "Old Rough and Ready" shocked the nation. "The death of Gen. Taylor has thrown every thing into confusion here," recorded one observer. While the confident Taylor had displayed sympathy with the Free Soil program (particularly concerning a free New Mexico) and stubborn opposition to the Foote/Clay project, Vice President Millard Fillmore of New York was deeply insecure and a known supporter of the omnibus. "The death of Genl Taylor puts a new face upon things," wrote Richardson. "It is generally believed that the whole policy of Genl Taylor will be abandoned by Mr. Fillmore." Suddenly, Southern Democrats had lost an enemy and gained an advocate.[45]

Despite Fillmore's ardent support, however, the omnibus began to fail; everyone found something in the package to oppose. "All is doubt," remarked Harris. Executive patronage was not enough to save the ailing omnibus, and Northern Democrats like Harris and Douglas were waiting in the wings for the opportunity to regain control of legislation. By midsummer, they could see Clay's failure and recognize the effectiveness of Southern obstructionism. "Things are in a very bad way here," wrote Harris. "The southern ultras say that nothing shall be done if they can get enough to call ayes and noes." An "open attempt at secession will be made," he continued, if the North did not once again placate the Slave Power.[46]

While Northern Democrats, though deeply divided over New Mexico, still clung to the omnibus as the best way to please the South, Southern extremists and Northern antislavery adherents joined forces to kill the omnibus, a feat finally achieved on July 31, after the bill was gutted by amendments. Southerners were pleased, as their proslavery measures would no longer be tied to bills designed to placate Northerners. "We have heard here the compromise bill has failed," wrote one correspondent to Senator Hunter of Virginia. "I rejoice at the fact." Douglas, too, was glad to see the omnibus fail. "By combining the measures into one Bill," he explained with a bit of boastfulness, "the Committee united the opponents of each measure instead of securing the friends of each. I have thought from the beginning that they made a mistake in this respect." With the omnibus dead, Douglas could reclaim the spotlight and initiate his own plan, thereby giving credit for a "compromise" to the Democrats. Other Northern Democrats, more seasoned and cautious than Douglas, saw danger ahead. If Northern Democrats united behind Douglas to push through the pro-Southern measures one by one, they feared, it would spell disaster for the Northern Democracy at the polls. Free state voters, some realized, would not look kindly on such violation of their beliefs. "The south will gain nothing by keeping up the agitation," wrote Marcy, "and the northern democracy will lose every thing."[47]

Daniel Dickinson, "True as Steel"

Throughout the entire ordeal, Northern Democratic regulars had proved themselves reliable advocates of Southern slavery. If they did not maintain their traditional allegiance to the South, Northern Democrats knew that Free Soilers and Southern rights proponents would battle endlessly, while the Democratic Party fractured and collapsed. To prevent this, they ignored their constituents and fought for the Foote/Clay plan, which would tie pro-Southern measures to the admission of a free California. When this strategy failed, Northern Democrats turned to their own Stephen Douglas to move the legislative process forward. Douglas, however, would have to contend with other prominent Northern Democrats who sought distinction and Southern support. Chief among these was Dickinson of New York, a fiercely ambitious partisan and fanatical champion of the South.[48]

Dickinson, born in 1800 to Connecticut farmers, migrated with his family to Guilford, New York, six years later, where young Daniel became a self-educated land surveyor and teacher. By the end of the 1820s, he had risen to local prominence as a lawyer and officeholder, prompting him to move to Binghamton in 1831 to expand his law practice. Like Bright in Indiana, Dickinson was an early promoter of "states' rights" and swiftly rose within the state Democratic organization. In 1836, he was elected to the state senate, and, after a failed run at the office in 1840, was elected lieutenant governor in 1842. Within two years, Dickinson had been appointed by the governor to fill a vacancy in the U.S. Senate. Dickinson's confirmation by the state legislature was difficult, though, as he was unpopular, and the body preferred the less conservative John Dix.[49]

In Congress, Dickinson was an ardent expansionist and promoter of the war against Mexico (in fact, he wanted *all* of Mexico), as well as a firm supporter and confidant of Polk. He was also a militant white supremacist who favored perpetual separation of races and viewed all non-Anglo-Saxons as savages. Though he fancied himself an intellectual and a poet and was considered "witty and sarcastic" by some, he lacked oratorical skill, and his speeches often cleared the chamber. In New York, he led the "Hunker" faction of proslavery Democrats, a group, one scholar notes, that was notorious for its lack of principles. Hunkers valued office, patronage, and political opportunism above all else; they *hunkered* for them. Dickinson's career would be characterized by this lack of principle as he sought to win Southern support while trying to maintain leadership of the New York Democratic organization.[50]

Equally notable is Dickinson's willingness to ignore the views of his constituents. He repeatedly violated the instructions sent to him by the state legislature by opposing the Wilmot Proviso. Indeed, popular opposition to Dickinson's course in the Senate was so intense that he considered resigning. His close friend and fellow doughface Cass came to the rescue, though,

FIGURE 2. Senator Daniel Dickinson, New York (Library of Congress)

and convinced the embattled New Yorker to keep up the fight. "I beg you," pleaded Cass, "to lay aside any thought of resigning. I beg you for my sake, for the sake of the great party to which we belong."[51] Cass and Dickinson forged a close relationship, and the two men were firm friends by 1848. When Cass won the Democratic presidential nomination that year, Dickinson served as a campaign manager, further infuriating New Yorkers who supported the antislavery Van Buren.

Dickinson could not have cared less about the feelings of the Free Soilers, however, since he viewed their campaign and platform with contempt. Along with editor and friend Edwin Croswell, Dickinson launched vicious, unscrupulous attacks on antislavery New York Democrats, known as Barnburners, who had been key to the formation of the national Free Soil Party. At the national convention that nominated Cass, Dickinson had played a leading role in preventing antislavery delegates from being seated, insisting on maintaining the party's proslavery identity. When he could not prevent a mixed Barnburner-Hunker New York delegation from being seated at the convention, Dickinson tried unsuccessfully to have the Empire State excluded from the proceedings entirely rather than permit any antislavery delegates. In fact, Dickinson, in league with the notorious Southern "fire-eater" William Yancey, was largely responsible for the split in the party that led to defeat at the polls. Better to go down to defeat, he reasoned, than tolerate any challenge to Southern supremacy. Likewise, in state elections, his hatred for the Barnburners was so intense that he chose to aid the Whigs rather than see any Free Soil victories. Though he lacked Bright's flare for the Southern plantation lifestyle, Dickinson rivaled him in his fidelity to the Slave Power. Stephens spoke for many when he called Dickinson "true as steel." When John Calhoun—symbol of Southern defiance—died in April 1850, Dickinson was one of the six Senators chosen to escort "the Cast-Iron Man's" earthly remains to the graveyard at St. Philip's Church in Charleston, South Carolina.[52]

Democratic Success

In the wake of Calhoun's death, the Nashville Convention, and the collapse of the omnibus, Clay fled the Capitol to recover his strength and lick his wounds. His gamble had failed. Southern obstructionism and Northern divisions had proved more than he could manage. But while Clay was old, tired, and disillusioned, Douglas was young, energetic, and determined. Within a month of Clay's departure, Douglas would regroup and push through the various "compromise" measures one by one—the original strategy he had suggested back in January. It was "the Little Giant" of Illinois, not the Great Pacificator of Kentucky, who was ultimately responsible for the pro-Southern "Compromise of 1850."[53]

Douglas had been working on territorial and railroad bills since his election to Congress in the mid-1840s, and he was uniquely equipped as a westerner and chair of the Committee on Territories to unravel the tangled web of legislation that remained after the collapse of the omnibus. Despite his early action after Taylor's message in January, his committee had not been able to produce a report in time to head off Clay. As has been noted earlier, Douglas sensed from the start that the omnibus strategy would fail, and he was not shy about criticizing it. Moreover, Douglas was annoyed that Clay had taken credit for the omnibus when all he had really done was take Douglas's bills and tie them together. Douglas insisted that Clay "did not write one word of it & that I did write every word."[54] The "compromise" had been his from the beginning, and it was his to bring to fruition. His political future, in many ways, depended on it. Douglas was already safely in the Senate, but if he wanted to achieve his dream of the presidency he would need firm Southern support. If he and his lieutenants in the House could shepherd the various pro-Southern measures through Congress and convince the North that it was a fair exchange for an already free California and an end to the slave trade in the capital, then he would enter the 1852 race as a strong contender. His strategy was simple: pick up the pieces of the omnibus and pass them individually, preventing factions from uniting against any one bill. "When they are all passed," explained Douglas, "you see they will be collectively Mr Clays compromise, & separately the Bills Reported by the committee on Territories four months ago."[55]

Compared with the slow, torturous life of the omnibus, Douglas's plan worked astonishingly fast. On August 1, the legislation creating Utah was passed by the Senate, and on the ninth, Douglas guided through a Texas boundary-debt bill (crafted by Senator James Pearce of Maryland). The latter had been an especially thorny issue, since it dealt with Texans' militant determination to expand their borders to engulf an infant New Mexico, and Southern intransigence concerning their fellow slave state (especially since New Mexico had produced an antislavery constitution). "The Texas boundary must be adjusted or put in the way of adjustment," observed Marcy, "otherwise we shall have civil commotion probably attended with bloodshed." The Douglas/Pearce bill, which shrunk the borders of the Lone Star State but included a tremendous ten-million-dollar bribe, pleased both groups.

With Southerners placated by the Texas debt payment and a border bill of their making, Douglas could then turn to California and New Mexico, which saw shrill, impassioned debates up to the moment of their respective passage. The California bill passed on August 13, and New Mexico (with no restrictions on slavery) on August 15. Throughout, Douglas worked tirelessly, constantly in the chamber, directing parliamentary strategy, and parrying sudden opposition moves. For the next three days, though, Douglas was conspicuously absent as debate raged over the centerpiece of the Southern agenda: the new Fugitive Slave Law. Introduced by Mason of Virginia and escorted through committee by Butler of South Carolina, it had been under consideration since January 24. Here again, Northern Democratic support was critical, for while Douglas stayed away to avoid being associated with the bill, dedicated doughfaces such as Dickinson stayed to advocate for the South.[56]

As Douglas guided his bills through the Senate, he worked closely in the House with Linn Boyd of Kentucky (chairman of the Committee on Territories and "zealous Democratic partisan"), as well as Richardson and McClernand, to ensure a speedy acceptance of the Senate bills. Though the Douglas crew in the lower chamber was well organized, theirs was not an easy task. "*Extremes* unite in the House, as they did in the Senate, but my own opinion is they will all pass," observed Bright. Throughout, Northern Democrats remained optimistic, and for good reason—by throwing their weight to the South, they could pass each bill with a (relative) minimum of fuss. On September 6, the House passed a Texas–New Mexico combination bill. The following day, the California and Utah bills saw success, resulting in citywide celebrations. "The day has been one of almost universal rejoicing," wrote an excitable correspondent to Buchanan, "bonfires, processions—serenades, speeches, suppers and drinking—and guns." Indeed, the motto of the celebration seemed to be that it was "the duty of every patriot to get drunk." Among the revelers were Douglas and Foote, who both suffered from severe hangovers the next day.[57]

While the most difficult work, that of passing a Texas–New Mexico bill that satisfied Southerners, was now complete, the remainder of the "compromise" bills still required congressional approval. The Fugitive Slave Law, which had passed the Senate on August 23, was passed by the House on September 12, returned to the Senate, and adopted on September 18. On September 16 and 17, the House and Senate together passed restrictions on the slave trade in the District of Columbia, completing the "compromise" package. President Fillmore signed the bills as they arrived on his desk, on September 9, 18, and 20, and there was a collective sigh of relief among Northern Democrats. "I believe the Union to be now safe," wrote Buchanan from his estate in Lancaster, Pennsylvania. Others, however, were not so comforted. Southern Democrats were angry at having to swallow the bitter pill of a free California and a truncated Texas, and Free Soilers were frustrated at not being able to stop Douglas and prevent the passage of the several pro-Southern bills.[58]

Of special note is the number of congressmen who skipped crucial votes. The Fugitive Slave Law is a telling example. In the Senate, final passage occurred on August 26 by voice vote to save Northerners from an embarrassing recorded vote. But two days earlier a vote was taken on a third reading of the bill, which was tantamount to passage. It is here we see that Northern Democrats knew their support for the bill violated the will of their constituents and thus declined to go on record. Bright, Dickinson, Cass, Douglas, Shields, James Whitcomb, and Alpheus Felch all skipped the August 24 vote; only James Bradbury of Maine and Issace Walker and Henry Dodge (father of Augustus Dodge) of Wisconsin took a stand against the Slave Power. (Bright, though his promotion of the bill was plain enough, later claimed, rather unconvincingly, that he had been accidentally absent.) Overall, fifteen of the twenty-one senators who went unrecorded on the issue of the Fugitive Slave Law were Northerners. If all fifteen had voted as their constituents likely desired, the bill would have failed. In addition, out of the four Senators who voted for all six "compromise" measures, two were Northern Democrats (Dodge of Iowa and Daniel Sturgeon of Pennsylvania), while seven Northern Democrats voted for five of the six. In the House, Democrats outweighed Whigs voting for the pro-Southern Fugitive Slave Law, the Texas–New Mexico combination, and Utah, but Whigs predominated in the antislavery measures (California and the District of Columbia).[59]

Northern Democrats were clearly responsible for the Compromise of 1850. Douglas was an active legislator and deal-maker from the beginning, and after the failures of Taylor and Clay, he took command and pushed the measures through. Aiding him with votes, speeches, and parliamentary procedure were a host of Northern Democrats, in particular Dodge, Dickinson, Richardson, and McClernand. On the Texas boundary issue, the crucial votes in the Senate came from Bright, Cass, Dickinson, Douglas, and Shields. Moreover, the key committees (thanks to the election of Speaker Cobb) were stacked with Northern Democrats sure to toe the proslavery line. Dough-faced Democrats aided in the election of Cobb, then proceeded to assist the Southern bosses in the passage of proslavery legislation, regardless of the method, be it omnibus or piecemeal.

Not only did these men achieve passage of the bills, but they created a political environment where pro-Southern was "Unionist" or "moderate," and any challenge to the Slave Power, let alone slavery, was considered "radical" or abolitionist. By repeatedly claiming to occupy a middle position, they cloaked their pro-Southern agenda in patriotism. This skewed political spectrum had enormous implications as the decade proceeded; Southerners and doughfaces would become increasingly intolerant of *any* hint of challenge to either slavery or Southern domination. Yet the role of Northern Democrats has been obscured by the popular fascination with "great men" and grand orations. Webster, Clay, Calhoun, and Seward have received the bulk of attention from historians, while Douglas, Dickinson, Bright, Richardson, and the like have often been reduced to supporting roles. What really mattered were *votes*, both on bills and on procedure—votes to elect a Southern Speaker, votes to kill antislavery legislation, votes to pass proslavery legislation. Northern Democrats provided those votes, and the implications were tremendous.[60]

Rewards for Firmness

The aftermath of the compromise brought mixed results for Northern Democrats. Their constituents were often furious with their pro-Southern course, but the Southern party bosses were more than pleased. Service to the South, of course, yielded rewards that voters could not affect. In the case of Richardson, his work with Douglas and Boyd in the final passage of the pro-Southern measures won him the friendship and respect of soon-to-be-Speaker Boyd, as well as the chairmanship of the House Committee on Territories. Cass, on the other hand, was already a well-known figure and leader within the party, though his embarrassing defeat in 1848 cost him dearly. His role in the crises of 1850, however, returned him to national standing and made him once again a viable candidate for the presidency. Southern Democrats had reason to be appreciative of his defense of their interests and his support for proslavery legislation. Southerners, remarked Dickinson to John Breckinridge of Kentucky, owed Cass "a debt of gratitude for his early and bold stand against the encroachments of the North."[61]

Dickinson, Bright, and Douglas, too, benefited from the events of 1850 and were catapulted to a national prominence on par with Cass. By the 1852 nominating convention, all three men would be major players in the party, with Dickinson and Douglas actual contenders for the presidency. "I have been very much gratified," wrote Buchanan to Dickinson, "with the very high standing which you have deservedly acquired in the Senate and throughout the country, during the present session."[62]

Though he won praise and gratitude from Southerners and fellow dough-faces, Dickinson faced a decidedly displeased constituency. His course in the Senate had made him even more unpopular than before in his home state. Nevertheless, Dickinson gambled that his actions would guarantee advancement within the party, regardless of reelection. Northern Democrats knew there was life beyond elected office for doughfaces: patronage appointments, diplomatic posts, party positions, and even nomination as vice president or president. "Whatever may be the result of matters in your State," Cass reassured Dickinson, "your position before the American people cannot be shaken, and you are young enough to receive the rewards of your firmness." "Rewards" for "firmness" was exactly what Dickinson was expecting.[63]

Such rewards would not likely come from his own constituents, as Dickinson's course in the Senate had made him too closely associated with slavery. His support at home derived almost entirely from the Hunkers and from New York City merchants who held important economic ties to Southern slavery. Divisions within the New York Democracy deepened as the Hunkers endeavored to foist Dickinson on an unwilling electorate, and the Barnburners fought to defeat him. Barnburners, noted one Democrat, preferred voting for Whigs to voting for Dickinson.[64]

The New York state elections in November 1850, as expected, resulted in the selection of legislators who would not elect Dickinson. His defeat, he whined to all who would listen, was the result of "partisan vindictiveness" and "malign influences, sinister efforts, and questionable combinations." His doughfaced brethren lamented his fate, as they knew that at some point they, too, would face voter retribution. "I am truly sorry for Dickinson," wrote Buchanan to Marcy. "He deserves a better fate. His boldness, ability & patriotism throughout our late abolition troubles constitute strong claims upon his country." Dickinson assuredly believed so, and he was not yet ready to give up the fight. His actions in New York in the coming years would have enormous implications for both that state and the national Democratic organization.[65]

But Dickinson's defeat did not stem the tide of voter anger. The passage and implementation of the infamous Fugitive Slave Law of 1850 created a new wave of Northern outrage and frustration with their Democratic representatives. The bill was far more inflammatory than the Wilmot Proviso, as it mandated the arrest and detention of real human beings, not the theoretical expansion of the "peculiar institution." The measure was of the utmost importance to the South, and Northern Democrats were expected to toe the line and see it through. For decades, Southern slave owners had demanded revision and augmentation of the original 1793 law, especially after Northern free states passed personal liberty laws guarding against slave catching and kidnapping. In response to those laws, Southern states implemented a series of statutes providing lucrative rewards for slave catching, leading to an overall increase in cross-border kidnapping. The cycle escalated until 1850, when Southerners finally achieved their goal of a more stringent national law.[66]

Passage of the bill was only the start, however; the next step was getting the heinous law enacted. "If the fugitive slave bill is not enforced in the north," threatened Cave Johnson of Tennessee to Buchanan, "there is no guessing what may be the consequences." The provisions of the bill were straightforward enough but would require a great deal of effort on behalf of free state officials. First, the law denied alleged fugitives any right to trial by jury or habeas corpus. Second, it permitted the case to be removed from ordinary courts and tried before a special commissioner. Third, slave owners only had to provide "satisfactory proof" of ownership in their own state, not to Northern officers. Fourth, the law was to be carried out by appointed commissioners, who would receive ten dollars for convictions, and five dollars if the alleged fugitives were set free. Fifth, federal marshals were empowered to force civilians to participate. Finally, any marshal who refused to act under the law would be fined one thousand dollars, and civilians who obstructed its implementation were liable to fines and imprisonment. All the provisions were anathema to Northern voters, but the last two were most outrageous—the commissioner fee system would reward convictions (false or otherwise), and civilians would be *forced* to participate. This was simply intolerable to conscientious Northerners, who, regardless of their politics, had no interest in becoming slave hunters. It was more than just a law to chase down escapees, it also permitted the reenslavement of blacks who had been living peacefully in the North for years; it opened the door to wholesale kidnapping.[67]

Incredibly, despite Northern indignation, Democrats did not hesitate to do their duty to the Southern bosses. Within two months of the bill's passage, Northern Democrats were "anxious" to put the law into effect, quickly appointing commissioners to enforce it. "The fugitive slave Law shall be faithfully executed," promised Buchanan. Others, like Douglas, simply misread Northern sentiment and believed the law would eventually win acceptance. "That law will never be repealed or rendered less efficient in our day," he wrote. "It will be executed at the north with the same fidelity that the several states execute their own local laws. Public opinion is becoming sound & enlightened upon this question." Combined with their overall eagerness to please the South was a spirit of vengefulness, a desire to punish Free Soilers for their antislavery stand. Free Soil counties, such as David Wilmot's in Pennsylvania, were assigned slave-catching commissioners before others—as revenge for their heresy.[68]

Public outrage was only enflamed by this rush to capture black Americans. The most famous indicator of Northern sentiment was Harriet Beecher Stowe's *Uncle Tom's Cabin* (first published in serial form in 1851), which served to mobilize public opinion against both slavery and the Fugitive Slave Law. But Northern defiance was manifest throughout the North, not just in published fiction. Mass meetings were held across the Northeast and Midwest, and huge protest rallies erupted in urban areas. New York Democrat

Horatio Seymour wrote that opposition in his state was "virulent," and in Illinois, Richardson nearly lost re-election because of it. (Fortunately for "Old Dick," his opponent did not want the office and did not really campaign, thus tipping the close election in Richardson's favor.) "A very deep excitement pervades this community in reference to the fugitive slave bill," announced the *Detroit Advertiser*. "Its terms and provisions meet with general reprobation by a majority of our citizens, independent of all party distinctions, and the utmost surprise is felt that any man could have been found arrogant enough to give his support to the measure, while *pretending* to represent the feelings and wishes of the citizens of Michigan."[69]

Throughout the North, Democrats took the lead in defending the Fugitive Slave Law. Douglas in Illinois, Cass in Michigan, and Buchanan in Pennsylvania set the tone for lesser politicos, defying angry crowds and framing the argument in terms of patriotism. Thomas Dorr in Rhode Island called it "a measure of patriotism & of high public policy," and William Bigler in Pennsylvania announced that "whatever diversity of opinion may have been heretofore entertained by individual citizens and statesmen in reference to the various elements embraced in these measures of compromise . . . [it is] the clear duty of the people of the free states, however repugnant it may be to their inclinations to maintain and carry out this as fully as another clear requisition of the constitution." Buchanan echoed, "Let us then resolve to put down agitation at the North on the slave question, by the force of enlightened public opinion, and faithfully execute the provisions of the Fugitive Slave Law. Should this be done . . . it will ameliorate the condition of the slaves, by enabling masters to remove the restrictions imposed upon them in self-defence." The "enlightened public opinion" Buchanan and his cohorts pleaded for never materialized, and Northern Democrats found themselves on the losing side of an unpopular battle.[70]

As of 1850–1851, however, they still had reason to celebrate. The Compromise of 1850, from inception to implementation, was the product of Northern Democrats' looking to please the Southern party leaders. Northern Democrats who opposed proslavery legislation had taken their stand as Free Soilers, thus leaving regular Northern Democrats to take the credit (or blame) for the so-called compromise. Because of Douglas's tactic of dealing with each portion of the "compromise" individually, because of a unified Southern bloc, and because of regular Northern Democratic fidelity to the South, Free Soilers and Northern Whigs could not muster the votes necessary to kill the proslavery bills.

The key to the Compromise of 1850, then, was not sectional negotiation or cooperation, but rather Southern aggression and Northern acquiescence;

it was Northern Democrats defying their constituency and fighting for bills that would ultimately lead to disunion and civil war; it was the young Illinois Democrat with his eye on the presidency, and his young accomplices eager for advancement. Initially, Foote and the Southern Democratic leadership did not trust Douglas to produce a pro-Southern outcome, and so they turned to Clay, the Kentucky slave owner who had made a career of fashioning pro-Southern "compromises." When the omnibus strategy failed, Douglas saw his opportunity to prove to the South his soundness on slavery and his ability to parry the thrusts of the growing congressional antislavery element. His strategy worked, and the South attained nearly all its objectives: no restrictions on slavery in New Mexico and Utah; protection of slavery in the District of Columbia; payment of the Texas debt; denial of congressional authority over slavery; and a new, far more severe fugitive slave law. Northern Democrats expected that this legislative victory would not only ensure the destruction of the Free Soilers but also unite Northern Democrats under their control, thereby returning the Northern Democracy to its traditional role as subservient to the South. They were sorely mistaken.[71]

CHAPTER 2

"Harmony, Unity, and Victory"

State Politics and Presidential Posturing

Hot off their legislative victory, leading Northern Democrats acted immediately to unite the disparate factions of the Northern Democracy behind the so-called Compromise of 1850, as well as position themselves for the presidential contest of 1852. Selling the compromise measures to their Northern constituents would not be an easy task, and they needed all the help they could get. "The friends of the constitution & the Union have much to do at the north to arouse the people to a full sense of their duty," remarked Stephen Douglas in January 1851. Northern Democrats like Douglas labored to convince voters of the "finality" of the measures, both to please the South and to achieve ever-elusive party harmony. In Congress, Northern Democrats also treated slavery as case closed and maintained an optimistic attitude about the future of the Northern Democracy. "All indications thus far are most favorable to the union of the democratic party," announced Representative Thomas Campbell of Illinois, who shared a room and writing table with William Richardson. "A good spirit prevails, and . . . peace is the motto of the democratic party, and with it will come harmony, union, and victory."[1]

It would take more than positive thinking, however, to overcome Northern antislavery sentiment and bring "harmony" to the Northern Democracy. Most Northerners were appalled by the proslavery measures passed by the Thirty-First Congress, and many Northern Democratic officeholders began having doubts about their future in the party. Indiana representative George Julian spoke for a growing segment of Northern Democrats when he fumed that "the tables seemed to be completely turned, and the time-honored rule of our slave-masters impregnably re-established." Democrats with such antislavery convictions could either bolt the party and fight the Slave Power from outside the organization, or stay loyal to the Southern leadership and pray that the proslavery agenda could be changed from within. Many, like Julian, followed their conscience and fled to antislavery ranks, but more decided to stay, at least for the time being.[2]

Indiana

"Harmony, union, and victory" would have to be achieved at the state level before it could bear fruit in national elections. Northern Democratic leaders returned to their respective states in the wake of the compromise and set to work forging consensuses and disciplining dissenters. Bright of Indiana was the first to bring his state organization into line behind the compromise and, in the process, cement his autocratic rule. Stifling the slavery debate, Bright knew, was critical to the survival of his political machine, as well as his future within the party. If he was to remain in the Senate, he would have to crush opposition and impose unity. "He was imperious in manner, and brooked no opposition from either friend or foe," observed William Woolen years later. "Indeed, he classes every man as foe who would not do his bidding, and made personal devotion to himself the test of Democracy." Verbal harangues, physical intimidation, and political attacks became the order of the day as Bright struggled to squash the antislavery movement and keep Indiana in the Democratic column.[3]

Despite his activities in Washington, as well as time spent on his Kentucky plantation, Bright kept a close eye on events in the Hoosier State. He had no tolerance for the growing antislavery movement and waged almost constant war against any who challenged his and the Slave Power's authority. But Democratic opposition to Bright did not just come from antislavery corners; his dictatorial methods created a plethora of Democratic enemies, making control of the party all the more difficult. In January 1851, for instance, as Bright was preparing for reelection, Democratic challenger Robert Dale Owen publicly accused Bright of bribery, graft, and corruption. Red hot, Bright rushed to Indianapolis in record time, found Owen, and forced him into a "secret huddle." "My opponent was a very wealthy man, and a somewhat unscrupulous one as to means and appliances," Owen complained to his diary. On January 10, the Democratic caucus voted unanimously to nominate Bright, securing his reelection to the Senate.[4]

Bright never forgave or forgot a challenge to his authority and never failed to get revenge. He fought duels, threatened friends and enemies alike, and indulged in character assassination. Bright's rule, as the Owen incident indicates, was far from unchallenged, and his course in Indiana and in Washington made him increasingly unpopular with Hoosiers. Much to Bright's consternation, a rival Democratic organization developed in Indiana, one that chafed at Southern supremacy, rejected Bright's leadership, and leaned toward antislavery. If Bright lost control of the Indiana Democracy, and the state slipped into the antislavery column, it would have enormous implications for the national party. Thus, he spent nearly two decades battling the leader of the Indiana antislavery Democrats, Joseph Wright. While Bright was a slave-owning tyrant, Wright was popular and moderate; needless to say, Bright loathed Wright.[5]

The "titanic struggle," as one historian has called it, between Bright and Wright erupted in the late 1840s when antislavery Democrats coalesced as a faction and Wright obtained the Democratic nomination and won the election for governor, despite Bright's fierce opposition. Bright's hatred only deepened when he could not prevent Wright's reelection. The battle erupted anew in October 1852, when the death of James Whitcomb created a vacancy in the U.S. Senate. Wright wanted former congressman and U.S. district attorney John Pettit to replace Whitcomb, but Bright was determined to install Dr. Graham Fitch. Fitch, a New York transplant who once flirted with Free Soilism and rejected it in favor of a strong proslavery course, was well-suited to be Bright's subordinate in the upper chamber. To accomplish this, Bright sent young William English, his protégé, to "work the wires" in Indianapolis. "Fitch's geographical position is eligible," Bright encouraged, "and above all he is a true democrat, a gentleman, a man of superior talents, *your friend, & my friend*." Regardless, on January 10, 1853, Pettit was elected by the state legislature, giving victory to the Wright clan. Bright was enraged, doubly so since Pettit was also a supporter of Stephen Douglas, Bright's primary Democratic rival in the West. "With Pettit I shall have little or nothing to do," Bright pouted. "I do not recognize him as a gentleman or as my Friend, and this you know, is enough to determine my rule of action." Instead of moderating his course, reconciling with Wright, and uniting Indiana Democrats, Bright chose to ignore the mounting antislavery sentiment and maintain control through force of will.[6]

New York

While Bright sought to impose unity on his Hoosier subjects through force, his New York counterpart William Marcy sought to achieve cooperation through persuasion, compromise, and diplomacy. It fell to him to heal old wounds and chart a new course toward unity and harmony. New York Democrats had split in 1848 between antislavery Barnburners and proslavery Hunkers. The Barnburners were in the majority, but the Hunkers were allied with the South and enjoyed recognition as "regular" Democrats. In the wake of their 1848 defeat, Barnburners, led by John Van Buren (son of Free Soil standard bearer Martin Van Buren), reached out to moderate Hunkers to negotiate reunion and reconciliation, hoping to cleanse the state party of its proslavery program. Many Hunkers, who had witnessed painful Whig victories after the split, were concerned about their party's future, and were thus eager for reunion. These Hunkers were labeled "Softs" (because they were willing to negotiate), and their leader was Marcy. Other Hunkers, however, seethed with anger over the split and loathed the antislavery Barnburners. They refused to tolerate political and philosophical dissent and remained steadfast in their loyalty to slavery and the Southern bosses. These men were called "Hards," and their champion was Daniel Dickinson. The bitterness between the two Hunker factions was destructive indeed, and Democrats North and South watched with anxiety and apprehension the evolution of the New York Democracy as the presidential election of 1852 drew near.[7]

Attention was early focused on Marcy as both well-known national statesman and leader of the Softs. There was no one better equipped to handle the crisis; he was a partisan pragmatist of the highest degree, adept at coercion, conciliation, and compromise. "In playing a political game," he once wrote, "you must . . . sometimes speculate and *finesse* deeply if you would make any thing." He was also dedicated to reunion and Democratic success, though he knew his task would not be simple. "I am ready to go all allowable lengths for harmony & conciliation," he announced to Horatio Seymour in 1851.[8] Born in 1786 to Irish Protestant parents in Sturbridge, Massachusetts, Marcy was a rebellious yet highly intelligent youth. He rejected his family's Federalist principles and was an early convert to the Democratic Party. In 1805, he was admitted to Brown University, where he developed an interest in politics but a distaste for office-mongering and dishonesty. He wrote at the time, "Men who so ardently aspire to distinction, are generally destitute of principle. They attach themselves to a party, that they may enjoy the favors it has in its power to bestow: when its fortunes change, they change also." Throughout his life, he held an abiding contempt for overly ambitious politicians and

unprincipled spoilsmen. Nevertheless, young Marcy entered the legal profession and began a long career in politics, quickly rising to a leadership position
within the Democracy Party, under the direction of Martin Van Buren.[9]

"Old Kinderhook" was attracted to Marcy's skills as both a writer and
an intellectual and endorsed him for several state offices. With the political
backing of Van Buren and the regular Democratic machine, Marcy rose to
the New York Supreme Court, then to the U.S. Senate in February 1831. In
1832 and 1836, he was elected and reelected governor, earning a reputation
as a reliable doughface and loyal Jacksonian. His defense of Jackson's policies
and attacks on abolitionism attracted significant Southern attention, so much
so that when Tennessean James Polk entered the White House in 1845, he
appointed Marcy his secretary of war. Always the dutiful Democrat, Marcy
orchestrated and oversaw the invasions of Mexico and the expansion of slavery that followed. In 1848, he opposed the Barnburner revolt and worked
with Dickinson in the Cass campaign.[10]

Yet despite his solidly proslavery career, Marcy expressed some views that
were more common to Barnburners than to Hunkers. He believed Congress had the authority to regulate slavery in the territories, and he harbored
serious doubts about the "selfish designs" of the Southern party leadership.
"The ultraism of the south," Marcy wrote in May 1850, "will not embody
the strength of the south and it will drive from their cause a considerable
part of the support it has had in the free states. It will I fear do much mis-
chief." "The south will gain nothing by keeping up the agitation," he again
wrote in August, "and the northern democracy will lose every thing." Marcy,
essentially, was a Barnburner who was unflinchingly loyal to the national
organization. Moreover, his political philosophy was one of "compromise
and conciliation," as he phrased it. His sympathy for the Barnburner cause,
his fidelity to the Democratic Party, and his political pragmatism made him
perfect for the role of unifier in 1849–1852.[11]

Marcy and the Softs knew that the fate of the New York Democratic Party
lay in their hands. Failure to achieve reunion would result in divided conventions and split delegations, not to mention electoral defeats. Furthermore, a
disorganized New York would cause headaches at national conventions and
elections. Achieving reconciliation, Softs also knew, would be supremely difficult, since the Hards were determined to stand their ground and prevent
negotiations. "I believe the mass of the democratic party are disposed to get
together," Marcy wrote, "but I fear the work is not so feasible as is generally
imagined. The leaders are much embittered against each other and those of
each section want the union should be on their particular platform." Under
no circumstances would Dickinson and his followers permit reunion, even if

it meant defeat at the polls; better to stand firm in defense of the Slave Power than to compromise; better to keep the party pure than to tolerate the taint of antislavery. Complicating matters was Dickinson's special vendetta against Marcy—Senator Dickinson blamed Governor Marcy for his 1851 electoral defeat, reasoning that Marcy's efforts at reunion permitted a coalition against him. "His opposition to you is personal," Duff Green warned Marcy. Marcy and the Softs would have to strike a delicate balance between reconciling with the Barnburners, reassuring the Hards, and soothing Dickinson's ego.[12]

In addition, Democrats outside the state had a stake in Marcy's course. The importance of the Empire State in national elections and in party conventions cannot be overstated—to control a united New York was to have a deciding influence in national affairs. If Marcy succeeded, he could perhaps enter the 1852 presidential race with a united New York behind him and the vote of grateful Barnburners; if he failed, the door was open for other leaders to court New York votes and advance their own candidacies. James Buchanan of Pennsylvania, in particular, was eager to keep New York fragmented, both so he could put himself forth as the regional leader and because he was vehemently opposed to the antislavery movement. Marcy would have to do his best to convince men like Buchanan that reunion was necessary and salutary. "I think the condition of things here is not quite so bad as you imagine," he wrote to the Keystone State boss. The road ahead was long indeed, and it would challenge Marcy's skills and patience to produce the political miracle of a united, harmonious Empire State.[13]

Luckily for Democrats, Marcy possessed a more nuanced understanding of the partisan divide than most of his colleagues, and believed that common ground could be found. "The general position of the free states," he explained to a suspicious Buchanan, "is that our territories are now free; and the essential difference between the democrats and the free soilers is this that the democrats think nothing need be done by congress to keep them so; on the other hand the free soilers say though we agree with you that they are free the south do not agree with us and the Wilmot proviso or something equivalent is necessary to guard them from the intrusion of slavery." Barnburners sought guarantees against the expansion of slavery, while "regular" Democrats (at least in Marcy's understanding) did not feel those guarantees were necessary. Aided by Seymour and John Dix, Marcy labored to convince Hards and Barnburners of their similarities, as well as the finality of the Compromise of 1850. Men like Dickinson were largely unreachable, but other Hards, like former governor William Bouck, could be reasoned with. "I consider the compromise measures as of paramount importance in a national point of view," Bouck wrote to Seymour, "and I would not yield so great a principle to satisfy the caprice of any man or set of men, be the consequences what they may. I would not abandon principle to preserve a Union with these men, but I would make liberal personal concessions." As Bouck's words indicate, there was potential for "concessions."[14]

The Compromise of 1850 only exasperated existing divisions and exposed new fissures. While Dickinson and the Hards enthusiastically supported the various proslavery measures, Marcy and friends found cause for concern. An aggressive proslavery agenda for the party would not only dramatically erode the Northern wing but also could wreak havoc in New York. Marcy found himself walking a political tightrope, balancing between fidelity to the national party and reconciliation with the Barnburners. The potential spread of slavery into California, in particular, grieved Marcy, who sympathized with Barnburners and found Southern expansionism reckless. The Southern plan for California, he wrote to Thomas Ritchie, "will evince a design to introduce slavery into that State against the expressed wish of the people. If the South become propagandist of slavery, they will put themselves where no northern man can cooperate with them. They have now, I lament to say, too few sustainers in the North." Such a move, he feared, would be "fatal . . . to the friends of the South in the free states."

But Marcy remained true to the party and joined hands with Dickinson in supporting the so-called compromise. To prevent the measures from destroying his work in New York, though, he avoided a public endorsement of them and urged both sides to consider the issues settled. By September 1850, his plan had largely worked, and Democrats of all stripes could gather that month in Syracuse to vote on the state ticket. Barnburners had been absorbed into the regular ranks with a minimum of concessions from the Hunkers; only Dickinson and the Hards remained adamant and uncooperative. "We have got rid of all negroism," Marcy reassured Buchanan, "[and] I should be encouraged to hope for good unity of action on all our candidates."[15]

Nevertheless, complete, effective reunion would not be achieved until the following year, when Democrats once again attended the annual meeting at Syracuse. The 1852 conventions and elections were fast approaching, Barnburners were still fighting against slavery, and Hards were still unyielding. If Marcy could achieve a general, even ambiguous consensus on basic Democratic principles, the state party could go into the elections of 1852 with confidence. Moderate Hunkers finally came to realize that if the Barnburner majority was not placated, they would either seize the party outright, or cause another fatal party split in an election year. Hence, they agreed to drop the endorsement of the Fugitive Slave Law and accept a vague resolution supporting the compromise. "I was of opinion that nothing was to be gained in uniting with a faction destitute of principle, and acting from selfish motives," announced Bouck, again the voice of reason among the Hunkers, "but it appeared evident to me that the largest portion of our friends desired, and many were determined on a union upon some fair principles. To have opposed this feeling or thrown obstacles in the way, might, and probably would have put the power of the democratic party in the hands of the Free Soilers." "On the whole," added Lieutenant Governor Sanford Church, "I think we did the best that could have been done." That is exactly what Marcy, Seymour, and Dix had hoped to accomplish.[16]

Pennsylvania

Equally critical to the national party were events in Pennsylvania, where, as in Indiana and New York, rival factions battled for control. There, Buchanan ran the regular Democratic machine, and Simon Cameron orchestrated a challenge. While lifelong politician Buchanan aimed to please the Southern bosses by defending slavery and opposing tariffs, businessman Cameron demanded tariff protection for Keystone State industries and leaned toward antislavery. Cameron also wisely gauged public opinion and could see the marked shift against the Slave Power. "The [fight] against slavery is yearly becoming stronger in this state," he penned in 1849, "and the more the question is agitated the stronger will become the sentiment."[17] To combat the Cameron threat, Buchanan and his lieutenant William Bigler, a former lumberman and state senator, draped themselves in the compromise and punished dissent. Support for the South, the Democracy, and the compromise was the only way to preserve the Union, they argued. But rhetoric would not be enough to maintain hegemony in the state, especially since the Cameron faction controlled much of the state patronage, and Cameron himself was determined to both regain his old seat in the U.S. Senate and thwart Buchanan's presidential run in 1852.[18]

In February 1850, Cameron took the offensive and launched a press war against Buchanan and his doughface machine. To aid him, Cameron enlisted the help of senator-elect Richard Brodhead, who believed that Buchanan had opposed his election. Their object was to undermine Buchanan's influence in Pennsylvania and erode his Southern support by making it appear that Buchanan could not unite and carry the state in a national election.[19] With this in mind, Cameron early threw his support behind Cass for the 1852 presidential nomination, dividing Pennsylvania Democrats and embarrassing Buchanan. "I am well aware," fumed Buchanan agent Alfred Gilmore, "that Cameron & that rotten part of the democracy of our State that adheres to him will endeavor to cripple you in this State, through the instrumentality of Genl. Cass." Cass was only too willing to have a friend in Pennsylvania, since a wounded Buchanan would increase Cass's chances at another nomination. Buchanan and his crew, on the other hand, had no respect for the Cameron upstarts and openly labeled the Cass-Cameron alliance "the plunderers."[20]

In December, Cass and Cameron met in New York City to coordinate against "Old Buck." Cameron's plan was to introduce and push through pro-Cass resolutions at the various county and district conventions, which would weaken Buchanan's claims to control the Keystone State. Though the plan was largely successful, and Cameron's crew was able to frustrate Buchanan men at conventions, Cameron was unable to prevent the nomination and election of Bigler as governor. Meanwhile, Brodhead used his franking privilege as senator to send copies of anti-Buchanan pamphlets to the South. Brodhead also reached out to both Marcy and Dickinson to create political confusion and cast doubts on Buchanan's strength. Buchanan men came to hate Brodhead almost as much as Cameron. "He is corrupt and selfish," wrote an angry A. H. Reeder to Buchanan, "but has a sort of foxiness which has enabled him thus far to conceal it from the democracy abroad. At home he is well known, and among other things is noted for treachery to and desertion of his friends."[21]

The victory of Bigler over antislavery Whig governor William Johnston in November 1851 boded well for the Buchanan machine and was generally seen as an indication of Buchanan's continued strength within the state, despite the machinations of his enemies. In the governor's chair, Bigler oversaw the partial repeal of the state's 1847 personal liberty law and pardoned a notorious kidnapper who had been convicted under it. Bigler's rise was regarded as a solid win for conservatives, with definite implications for the 1852 races. "The result is deeply felt through all parts of the Union," wrote Isaac Toucey of Connecticut, "& will exert a controlling influence upon the events of '52."[22] Yet, as in Indiana and New York, looks could be deceiving. Bright, Marcy, and Buchanan were, to some degree, able to unite their state organizations behind the Compromise of 1850 and reaffirm their own authority within the party, but they each continued to face determined opposition that threatened both their political machines and the national party. If Wright, Dickinson, or Cameron were able to distract or divide their states' regular Democratic voters, they could derail candidates, cause chaos at conventions, and possibly play kingmaker. If Bright, Marcy, and Buchanan wanted to rise within the party and achieve a national nomination or cabinet appointment, they would have to crush dissent, keep factions united, and convince the Southern leadership they represented and controlled the true, proslavery Democratic Party of their states.

Positioning for the Presidency

With no Democrat in the White House to offend, and thus no worry of patronage reprisals, a spate of presidential candidates had arisen almost immediately after Cass's 1848 defeat. State leaders like Bright, Marcy, and Buchanan began positioning themselves for the nomination, which was certainly up for grabs, since it was not clear if Cass could or would run again. "There is at present a good deal of *Presidential wire-working* going on here," reported Alfred Gilmore from Washington.[23]

Candidates also looked beyond their states for regional support, laboring to portray themselves as the champions of a certain section. With Cass of Michigan old, tired, and defeated, for instance, Stephen Douglas of Illinois positioned himself as the young, vigorous representative of the West. The favorite of the South was unquestionably Buchanan, who had dedicated his career to serving the Southern party bosses and openly courted the "fire-eaters." Cass, Douglas, and Dickinson were responsible for the compromise, which included a free California and an end to the slave trade in the District of Columbia, and thus were looked on with suspicion by many Southerners. Marcy was responsible for reconciliation with the Barnburners, which likewise made the Southern grandees none too pleased. Only Buchanan, who had held no office during the crises of 1850, had stood by the South and the expansion of slavery, and had no record of compromising with antislavery men. Southern support, all the candidates knew, was key to a presidential or vice presidential nomination and election. Whoever could carry both the solid South and either Pennsylvania or New York could achieve victory. That made Buchanan and Marcy the front-runners, but nothing was assured. The twenty months between the passage of the compromise measures and the 1852 Democratic nominating convention in Baltimore was more than enough time for would-be candidates to repackage themselves and convince the South that they were the most reliable on slavery and Democratic orthodoxy.[24]

Douglas, who had earned the moniker "Little Wizard of the West" after his legislative triumph in 1850, acted swiftly to capture the attention and support of Northern Democrats. Seen as the candidate of the rough-and-tumble West, Douglas, just shy of forty years old, was energetic, bold, and aggressive . . . and he desperately wanted to be president. He was also the darling of the "Young America" movement of the early 1850s, which stood for unlimited territorial expansion, militant nationalism, and technological advances. Though he saw himself as a western fighter, he was eager to appeal to the established East and to the slave states. As a slave owner, Mississippi plantation manager, and husband of the daughter of a prominent North Carolinian, he was already attractive to the South, though they were still skeptical of his devotion to slavery. Southerners were certainly appreciative of his services in 1850, but many were upset over California and the District of Columbia. Moreover, most of the Democratic elders scoffed at a Douglas candidacy at so young an age, deriding him as "that little whipster" and counseling him to wait until 1856. "He would lose nothing by keeping," according to Connecticut chieftain Gideon Welles.[25]

Nonetheless, in the summer of 1851, Douglas began his campaign for the presidency in dramatic fashion. After strategic trips to New York and Ohio to shore up his Northern support, he made a bold move to win Southern favor: he named his own running mate, Senator Robert M. T. Hunter of Virginia. Hunter was a forty-two-year-old fire-eating champion of slavery, and his selection by Douglas signaled to the South the Little Wizard's commitment to that section. The decision was truly a political bombshell. "Would you believe it? That they are trying to get up a ticket of Douglas of Ill. and Hunter of Virginia," exclaimed the governor of Virginia. "Jehosaphat! When will wonders cease!" Hunter, for his part, knew a good thing when he saw it and recognized Douglas's astute political instincts and flare for the theatrical. "He himself I think is one of the coolest observers even when he himself is concerned, that I ever saw," Hunter confessed to editor George Sanders.[26] With Hunter at his side, Douglas kicked off an unprecedented push for the presidency. He and his fans launched a letter-writing campaign, met with political leaders North and South, and gained control of a variety of Democratic publications. By November 1851, Welles could report that "within two or three months there has been an active movement for Douglas. One of his efficient and very zealous friends from Illinois called on me two or three weeks since full of zeal." Douglas also moved behind the scenes to court investors and financiers (who were attracted to his spread-eagle expansionism), and undermine Buchanan's Southern support.[27]

The only obstacles to Douglas's momentum were the controversial compromise measures and the immovable Democratic leadership. While Douglas managed to occupy a comfortable popularity with a "popular sovereignty" platform, his agents Charles Lanphier and Thomas Campbell fretted over how to deal specifically with the "immaculate" compromise, which could spell danger both above and below Mason and Dixon's line. They had to be careful not to upset Northern voters while simultaneously proving Douglas's commitment to slavery. Their solution was unimaginative: avoid the topic and keep Douglas's position flexible. "The less we say at this time about the compromise," Campbell advised Lanphier, "the better it will be for all concerned." As for the Democratic solons, the more active Douglas became, the more concern they expressed. None of them—Buchanan, Cass, Marcy, Dickinson, Bright, Welles, or Toucey—believed Douglas had a chance at the nomination, and all agreed that he would be disastrous for the party, splitting it between Young Americans and "Old Fogies." They considered him a "dangerous man" and were unnerved by his "contemptible electioneering tricks." Again and again, they counseled him to wait for 1856 and not to upset the harmony of the party. Needless to say, Douglas and his "young Roguies" were undeterred.[28]

The outcome looked far more promising for the sixty-five-year-old Marcy. He was the leading Democrat in one of the most critical states, he had just achieved the seemingly impossible by reuniting Hunkers and Barnburners, his long and distinguished career demanded respect, and he had few enemies outside New York. He was a formidable candidate, and everyone knew it. "If you can receive the New York vote there can be no difficulty," wrote John Slidell of Louisiana. As long as Marcy could keep the Empire State united behind him, he was virtually unstoppable. Buchanan and his Southern adviser, Slidell, recognized Marcy's strength and moved to woo him, hoping either to win his endorsement outright or to secure the New York delegation's support as its second choice (a favorable position to occupy, since at national nominating conventions most states voted for favorite sons first, then switched to other candidates). Buchanan, who had grown close to Marcy when they both served in the Polk cabinet, personally reached out to his rival. "And if this union [of Hunkers and Barnburners] should make you President, myself out of the way," Buchanan cooed, "I should prefer you to all other candidates." Slidell even suggested Marcy move his base of operations to Saratoga Springs, New York, where Slidell spent his summers.[29]

In the spring and summer of 1851, Marcy traveled the mid-Atlantic states to gauge his popularity and make new friends. It was on a visit to Washington that he learned of Barnburner machinations that could spoil his Southern support. Led by Azariah Flagg, several leading Barnburners increased their public praise of Marcy. Vocal Barnburner endorsement would allow Dickinson and the Hards to paint Marcy as antislavery, thereby destroying his Southern support. Marcy was displeased, writing to P. M. Witmore, "A great many national democrats are filled with suspicions and are turning their regards from me." And to an old friend in the War Department, he observed,

"I know it is the intention of some who are opposed to me to prejudice me in the south by the allegation that my support comes from those who were proviso-men & freesoilers in '48." Unfortunately for Marcy, he would have to fight a two-front war against attacks from Hards and praise from Barnburners.[30]

After the September 1851 conventions that achieved the New York Democrats' reunion, Marcy officially launched his candidacy. He established headquarters at Albany and put his agents to work: Horatio Seymour and John Stryker (of the Michigan Southern Railroad) in the upstate area; P. M. Witmore, J. Addison Thomas, and Lorenzo Shepherd in New York City; Charles Eames (of the *Washington Union*), Arch Campbell, Col. James Berret, and Congressman W. W. Snow in Washington. These men also reported from the West and the South, when they traveled there on business. Stryker, for example, had interests in Michigan and Indiana, and Thomas and his brother were native Tennesseans. Negotiations began with Cass men, and communications with Buchanan remained opened. Each candidate was eager to secure the support of the other as second choice. As for Douglas, Marcy was concerned about his increasing popularity in New York City; the merchants there liked his expansionist plans and believed him safe on slavery. Through Eames, Marcy reached out to Douglas, and Douglas reciprocated, assuring Marcy he would stay out of Empire State politics as long as Marcy stayed out of Illinois.[31]

Despite reunion, the fight with Dickinson and the Hards continued unabated. In the months preceding the national nominating convention, state-level Democratic organizations elected delegates to the national meeting. Frantic campaigning for the district elections began in November 1851, and the Marcy men were divided over the role Barnburners should play. Barnburner candidates were sure to get elected, but they might be unreliable in Baltimore; moreover, supporting Barnburners would once again raise Southern suspicions. In the end, Marcy decided to trust the Barnburners rather than leave things to chance. "I regard the mass of them as acting in good faith," he explained to a leading Hard. Meanwhile, Dickinson worked furiously to convince Southern Democrats that Marcy was both an abolitionist and unable to carry his own state. The more doubt Dickinson could plant in the Southern mind, the better his own presidential prospects would be. Marcy, the experienced partisan warrior, was not shy about defending himself. "I have in no instance or degree compromised principle," he wrote to Arch Campbell, doubtless for publication. "I have done what I did do for the common good of the party without looking to personal favor or sectional support from any quarter."[32]

Dickinson may have created doubts about Marcy's strength, but he also ended up mobilizing the majority of New York Democrats against both himself and Cass (for whom Dickinson claimed to be working). That the Hards wanted to divide the party and return to the chaotic factionalism of 1848–1849 only made the Soft-Barnburner alliance more firm. Marcy forces aimed to unite, harmonize, and avoid antagonism; the Hards sought to divide, destroy, and demand. When the district elections were held in January 1852, Marcy emerged victorious. Two-thirds of the delegates were outright Marcy men, and nearly fifteen out of thirty-four districts adopted pro-Marcy resolutions. Dickinson, though, was able to take some joy in the fact that Marcy was unable to carry *all* the districts, and thus appeared weak. Dickinson's torpedo tactics may have failed to sink the Marcy ship, but he did cause damage below the waterline.[33]

Indeed, Dickinson continued to be hard at work convincing Southerners of Marcy's heresy and New Yorkers of Marcy's duplicity. "The party is hydra headed—there are no acknowledged leaders," Byrdsall wrote to Buchanan, hoping to cast doubts upon Marcy's strength. To combat Dickinson's schemes, Marcy, in May 1852, approved the dissemination of letters to show "Southern men what sort of friend I am and have been to them." He also sent agents to meet with Southern leaders and reassure them of his reliability. Yet despite Marcy's herculean efforts to repair the damage done by Dickinson, his fate at Baltimore was uncertain, and thus the result of the entire convention was doubtful. "I really think there is a prevailing impression," Marcy confessed to Campbell, "that we are so situated that there is no horse in the stable well felled for the course and that a new one must be hunted up . . . no candidate yet brought up for consideration exactly suits the condition of things." Events would prove Marcy correct, much to the delight of Dickinson and the Hards.[34]

Central to Dickinson's plan was Cass's candidacy. Dickinson and the Hards alone were not strong enough to defeat Marcy at Baltimore, but Cass certainly was. Even if Cass could not achieve nomination, by pushing for him Dickinson could keep valuable support from going to Marcy. Moreover, once Cass and Marcy failed, the convention could possibly turn to Dickinson. This scheme was not as far-fetched as it seems, given that the traditional "two-thirds rule" at national conventions made it exceedingly difficult for a single candidate to dominate, especially after dozens of ballots (this is precisely what occurred in 1844, when front-runner Martin Van Buren was crippled by his stand against the annexation of Texas, and the convention turned to dark horse James Polk of Tennessee). And if Cass was nominated and elected, Dickinson would reap the rewards of power, influence, and patronage and could use all three to destroy Marcy, the Softs, and the Barnburners, bringing the New York Democracy under his control. For these reasons, Dickinson did everything in his power to secure the nomination for Cass. "I am for him, up and down, and round about, and diagonally, and shall sink or swim with him," Dickinson proclaimed to a friend. Any way he looked at it, fighting for Cass was his best bet.[35]

To many, though, it may have appeared an odd alliance. Dickinson was a man of passion, poetry, and purpose; he never wavered from his advocacy of Southern rights, and his driving principle was crystal clear: no union with antislavery men. But Cass's career had been built on ambiguity, appeasement, and a remarkable ability to flow with the political currents; he avoided controversy at all costs and almost never took a public stand on an issue. He had risen within the party because he held no firm principles and did whatever his superiors asked of him. Born in Exeter, New Hampshire, in 1782 to old-stock New England Federalists, Cass was a self-disciplined yet socially awkward youth. In 1800, his father moved the family to Ohio to claim bounty lands from his military service. After studying law, young Lewis was admitted to the bar in 1803 and soon began a lifelong career in politics. Motivated by political ambition, he abandoned Federalism and embraced "Jeffersonianism." (Since Democrats controlled the Ohio state legislature and the congressional delegation, if Cass wanted to succeed in politics, he had to join their ranks.) After winning election to the state legislature, he served in the War of 1812 as an Ohio militia colonel, where he was reprimanded for insubordination and was responsible for the embarrassing surrender of Detroit (although he blamed others). After currying favor with President Madison, Cass gained a commission as a brigadier general in the regular army, then, in 1813, was appointed military governor of the Michigan Territory at age thirty-one.[36]

His extended term as governor is notable only for his handling of Indian affairs and his uncanny ability to avoid controversy. He also managed to amass, like Bright, a huge personal fortune through real estate and commercial investments, so much so that he hardly noticed the panic of 1837 and the ensuing depression. He used his office to enrich himself and his friends, particularly John Jacob Astor and Astor's American Fur Trading Company, with which he had close ties. He was also fiercely Anglophobic, and was perpetually obsessed with maritime affairs. More important, Governor Cass refused to announce a party affiliation and exhibited a penchant for dishonesty. He owned at least one slave in his life, for instance, yet repeatedly lied about it. He did not, however, disguise his deep sense of white supremacy and sympathy for the "peculiar institution" and formed a warm relationship with

John Calhoun. In the 1830s, he served as President Jackson's secretary of war and dutifully carried out Indian removal, which he largely mismanaged. Even his apologetic biographer admits that Cass's insensitivity, carelessness, and racism led to untold suffering among Native Americans.[37]

In May 1836 his service to Jackson earned him appointment as minister to France. His militant Anglophobia made him an apt choice, but he spent most of his time on lavish entertainments. Because he avoided controversy and partisanship, he was left in place by Presidents Van Buren, Harrison, and Tyler. He shocked politicos when he resigned in 1842 over the Webster-Ashburton Treaty, which he believed did not deal sufficiently with protecting American ships from search and seizure (Britain had demanded search and seizure rights to curb the international slave trade, but Cass would have none of it). It was, perhaps, the first time in his life he took a bold stand on an issue. Conveniently, his resignation made him an available candidate for the 1844 Democratic nomination, since his position on the treaty was popular with Democrats. He was an inept campaigner, though, and it did not help that the sixty-two-year-old was overweight and wore an ill-fitting wig. Needless to say, his awkward public demeanor, refusal to address any issue (besides the treaty), and his ambiguous principles did not attract many voters. Numerous Democrats, in fact, were not even convinced he belonged in the party. After failing to win the endorsement of his own state of Michigan, he failed miserably at the national convention. He did manage to win some significant Southern support by expressing proslavery views, endorsing territorial expansion, and making wild claims about British invasion. When it was clear they could not carry the convention, Cass men supported the two-thirds rule, which ultimately deprived Van Buren of the nomination and gave victory to Polk. Cass's actions had resulted in another proslavery Southern candidate, and Northern Democrats would not soon forget this betrayal.[38]

Nevertheless, in 1845 the Michigan state legislature sent Cass to the U.S. Senate, where he served on the Committee on Foreign Relations and became one of the most vocal and militant expansionists in Congress. He wanted all of the Oregon Territory (which the United States shared with Britain) and all of Mexico, wholeheartedly advocating war to obtain both. His Northern support continued to erode when he violated the instructions of his state legislature and voted against the Wilmot Proviso. Given Cass's abhorrence of taking a stand on an issue, his vote against the proviso was doubtless motivated by both his sympathy for slavery and his desire to secure Southern support for another run at the presidency. Northern voters, again, were not pleased. To shore up his free state support, Cass stumbled on the vague concept of "popular sovereignty," which would allow the territories to vote on slavery, thus potentially permitting the spread of slavery above the old Missouri Compromise Line of 1820. This policy had the distinct advantage of being double sided, which Cass admired; he could tell Northern voters that popular sovereignty would prevent the spread of slavery by allowing people to vote against it, while simultaneously assuring the South that the policy would result in slavery's growth and expansion. Neither side was entirely convinced, however, and most Northerners came to believe that in practice the "Cass Doctrine" would lead to the unrestricted spread of slavery.[39]

Thus, by 1848, Cass had created a record for himself of militant expansionism, fierce Anglophobia, and commitment to slavery. These credentials were sufficient for Southern Democrats, who, thanks to the two-thirds rule, were able to push him through the national nominating convention, hoping that Cass's Northern roots would garner some Northern votes. "The South, of course, was a perfect unit," recalled George Julian, "and fully resolved upon the spread of slavery over the Territories. It had always been the absolute master of the Northern Democracy, and had no dream of anything less than the supremacy of its own will. Its favorite candidate was now Gen. Cass." When he learned of his nomination, Cass resigned his Senate seat and proceeded to run a typical Cass campaign: he avoided issues, catered to the South, and tried to focus attention on popular sovereignty. Cass, noted Marcy, was "weakened in the North because he held and openly avowed sentiments favorable to the rights of the South." Cass also had to contend with the new Free Soil Party, which ran effective campaigns throughout the free states. Unsurprisingly, Cass lost the presidential race to Whig Zachary Taylor. Many Democrats blamed the Free Soilers for the defeat, but Cass's most recent biographer has argued that the Michigander was so unpopular and so ineffective that he would have lost regardless. After the embarrassing loss, Cass returned to the Senate, a position he regained only after promising Michigan voters that he would henceforth follow their antislavery instructions.[40]

Cass was undaunted and began campaigning for the 1852 presidential nomination soon thereafter. Most Democrats, though, hoped to move on from the elderly, inept Cass and were frustrated by the Michigander's persistence. "Cass has not left a stone unturned to secure his nomination, and I believe by his eagerness to effect it, has done and is still doing himself much harm," reported J. M. Folty to Buchanan in 1850. In November 1851, Cass stopped in New York City en route to Washington and convinced many Douglas men there to switch their support to him. Simultaneously, Dickinson and the Hards did their part by waging war on Marcy. While Dickinson labored to cause divisions at home, Birdsall and Beardsley were sent to

Washington to damage Marcy's reputation among officeholders. From the Capitol, Representative Snow reported to Marcy, "The war of Dickinson and his friends is intended to defeat Your nomination. I am told Dickinson is in Confidential correspondence with his friends south and openly hostile to You." Marcy could only watch as the Dickinson-Cass alliance damaged his presidential prospects. "Beardsly, Dickinson, Croswell, Birdsall, &c. &c. have used their pens very nimbly," he admitted to Seymour. "They have addressed almost everybody—& have succeeded in bringing a few considerable men into their measure."[41]

Dickinson acted with purpose and focus, all the more so because he hoped to effect his own nomination once Cass crumbled. He knew that working openly for Cass brought him the appreciation (and possibly second choice) of Cass men across the country, and his battle with the Barnburners increased his standing with the South. The combined votes of the solid South and the Northern Cass men could prove decisive at Baltimore. "Your patriotic efforts, in behalf of the South and its institutions," wrote South Carolina representative James Orr to Dickinson, "have touched the heart of every generous, honest man, and kindled a feeling of love and confidence which will never diminish, but continue to expand and grow until your elevation to the Presidency will be the grand *finale* . . . In the heart of every Southerner you will ever live."[42]

Dickinson's plan at the national convention was complex but feasible: convince Marcy's Hunker supporters to vote for Cass on the first ballot, which would rally Cass men in other states and show that Cass could win the nomination, meanwhile telling Marcy's supporters that they could vote for Marcy on the second ballot, knowing that a rush for Cass would make Marcy's nomination less likely. Dickinson men would play along, aiming to get the nomination for him when Cass, Marcy, and Douglas failed. With Southern support, Dickinson's plan seemed foolproof. But Marcy was no fool. "*Dickinson* is for himself and fondly believes every democrat at the South will rise at his request and go as one man for him," he informed James Berret. Marcy would have to stay above the fray and allow Dickinson's duplicity to reveal itself to the convention, and thereby kill his candidacy. Unlike Marcy, Cass was clueless about Dickinson's schemes. "I know you are as true a man as ever walked the earth—I may say, the very model of true fidelity," Cass penned to his would-be friend.[43] He seemed to be equally oblivious to his own prospects, believing Democrats North and South would rally to him once again. Nothing could be farther from the truth, however, and few Democrats believed Cass had any chance at the nomination. Cass was a "*dead cock in the pit*."[44]

It was in Buchanan's interests to downplay the chances of his longtime rival Cass. Both men had been career Democrats and dedicated doughfaces, and after losing the nomination to Cass in 1848, Buchanan was determined to quash Cass's return in 1852 and seize the nomination for himself. The tall, paunchy Buchanan had been angling for the presidency for a decade and had served in a variety of federal and state offices to that end. He was an open advocate of Southern interests and never missed an opportunity to remind the South of his "numerous speeches in favor of Southern rights," "the identification of myself, humble as I am, with Southern rights," or "my long, consistent strong support of Southern rights." He was an adamant foe of the Wilmot Proviso, which he labeled "the greatest evil of all political calamities," and an ardent expansionist, envisioning ever more lands to the south where slavery could spread and flourish. Both privately and publicly, Buchanan identified more with the South than his Pennsylvania constituents. He was perpetually concerned about Southern rights, always looking to curry favor with the Southern bosses, and refused to acknowledge the growing antislavery sentiment among his own Keystone neighbors; he even preferred to read Southern newspapers. Buchanan was the quintessential doughface.[45]

And that doughface reputation served him well. It garnered him more Southern support than that of any other Northern Democrat and made him the undisputed front-runner going into the 1852 national nominating convention at Baltimore. Marcy, Dickinson, Douglas, and Cass all had claims on Southern gratitude, but only Buchanan had emerged from the events of 1850–1851 untarnished. Southern Democrats, for their part, expressed total agreement with Buchanan's pro-Southern positions on slavery, territorial expansion, the Fugitive Slave Law, and congressional authority in the territories. "You are decidedly the favorite of that section," wrote Senator William King of Alabama, and another Southern admirer exclaimed with accuracy, "You are the *fast advocate* of *Southern rights*."[46] Indeed, Buchanan not only occupied the "correct" Southern positions on all issues, he held close ties to leading Southern Democrats, particularly Slidell, King, and Henry Foote. Slidell provided news from the Deep South, as well as from his summer home in Saratoga Springs, New York, while Cave Johnson in Tennessee kept him abreast of events in the Upper South. Foote of Mississippi was in the U.S. Senate, handled Buchanan's affairs in Congress, and made sure that Buchanan's voice was heard at the right moments.[47]

Perhaps Buchanan's most important relationship, however, was with King of Alabama. Theirs was a special bond dating back years, possibly physical, certainly emotional. For a time, they shared a house on F Street in Washington, and King addressed him as a fellow Southerner. For years King served as

Buchanan's trusted adviser and defender, and whenever Buchanan's commit-ment to the South was questioned by his rivals, it was King who took the lead in defending him. The Alabamian was also remarkably protective. When Buchanan was battling Simon Cameron in 1850, King unleashed an angry rant, calling Cameron "that unprincipled intriguing fellow . . . destitute of all political principle and I would add in my opinion moral honesty." King even displayed some jealousy over Buchanan's relationship with Foote, with whom Buchanan was also close. These Southern bonds were enormously important to Buchanan's career and reputation and would play a key role at the Democratic nominating conventions of the 1850s.[48]

Despite his pro-Southern credentials and slave state friends, it was Bu-chanan's words and deeds during the crises of 1850 that earned him true respect in the South. Throughout the ordeal, Buchanan was an outspoken advocate of extending the Missouri Compromise Line of 1820 to the Pacific Ocean, thereby granting federal sanction to, and guaranteeing the spread of, slavery into the free western territories. Given the mixed assortment of plans being presented to Congress, Buchanan's position was designed to attract Southern favor and avoid a free California. As Congress debated, Buchanan, comfortable at his Pennsylvania estate, was advised by his Southern friends on which positions to take and when. "Southern members would generally prefer the Missouri compromise line with the express understanding that slave property should be protected south of that line," counseled King. Bu-chanan proceeded accordingly. Of special concern was the Nashville Con-vention, attended by Southern rights advocates, which Buchanan aimed to court. Cave Johnson, who reported to Buchanan from that city, advised him on how to win their favor. When Buchanan's position on the Line was made clear to the convention, Johnson informed him that the effect was transfor-mative and that "most of the southern members and particularly those from S. Carolina would favor your nomination." The convention subsequently endorsed the plan, thereby strengthening Buchanan in that region. Likewise, Foote made Buchanan's positions clear in the Senate, aiming to influence the compromise debates.[49]

These were bold actions, and Buchanan's Northern Democratic rivals were reluctant to follow him in such blatant disregard for Northern senti-ment. "His recent open and abandoned connection with the Jack Asses of the Nashville Convention had seriously dissatisfied the Pennsylvania Demo-crats," exclaimed one angry voter. Marcy in New York, always cautious and perceptive, noted to a friend that "Buchanan has great hopes of the south. He thinks the Secessionists will favor him because he went for the Mis-souri compromise line & in this respect he has the advantage of any other

Candidate." This might be good politics, Marcy knew, but it was a dangerous game to play, given the ever-growing antislavery movement. Marcy even warned Buchanan directly, hinting that his course could spell disaster in the near future. "Will not the man who offers this line accompanying it with such an admission be regarded as acting affirmatively in extending slavery to territory now free?" Marcy queried. "Such a line will be much less favorably received in the free states than it would have been a year or two ago." Buchanan's vigorous support of the now-infamous Fugitive Slave Law also did much to please the South and distance himself from other candidates. He spoke often of the "constitutionality & justice of the fugitive slave law," and declared openly that "the Fugitive Slave Law must be sustained; because I believe it is right in principle & in sustaining it we sustain the union."[50]

Buchanan may have played his role perfectly, but he could not control his Northern Democratic rivals. Marcy, he perceived, was his primary challenger both in the mid-Atlantic region and in the national party. To prevent any surprises, Buchanan met with him in the autumn of 1851 in New York City, where the two men expressed mutual friendship and agreed to keep communications open. Buchanan also expressed his preference for Marcy over the other candidates, especially doddering Cass and dangerous Douglas. If his own candidacy should fail, Buchanan assured Marcy, he would throw his support to him. "The friends of Buck—will back N.Y. when the test comes," reported Snow from Washington. The Dickinson-Marcy-Cass chaos in New York, however, left little room for a Buchanan movement, so Marcy had scarcely anything to fear from the Pennsylvanian until the convention. Moreover, Buchanan's pro-Southern course made him unpopular with the majority of Northern Democrats, who would most likely prefer Marcy or Douglas to Buchanan. "Buchanan has few friends among us," Marcy stated bluntly to a correspondent. That being so, the Buchanan juggernaut could not be ignored, even in New York.[51]

Giving up New York to his rivals was made far less painful for Buchanan by the addition of Virginia. Envisioning a powerful Virginia-Pennsylvania alliance, future governor Henry Wise was receptive to Buchanan's overtures and became his most vocal supporter in the Upper South. Buchanan and Pennsylvania, he came to believe, were "absolutely necessary to our [Virginia's] success." For Buchanan, the relationship made him a formidable force, increasing his clout with South and cowing his Northern competitors.[52] Buchanan was pleased to join arms with Wise, and the two politicos grew close, emotionally and professionally. "I wish I could have you here for a few days," Buchanan wrote to Wise in the spring of 1852. "We might convert my woods into the garden of the Academy & I should become your disciple in moral philosophy." Yet Wise was not prepared to throw the entirety of his considerable political weight behind Buchanan. Old Buck may be the choice of the South, but was he the choice of Pennsylvania? If he could not carry his own state, then Buchanan's candidacy was in jeopardy. Buchanan would have to prove to Wise and other would-be allies that he could survive the test of Pennsylvania district and state meetings, where Simon Cameron and Richard Brodhead were still hard at work against him.[53]

On March 4, 1852, despite the efforts of his enemies, the Pennsylvania state Democratic convention endorsed Buchanan for the presidency. This gave Buchanan the confidence and political surety to take his campaign into other states and into the national convention. To his protégé J. Glancy Jones, Buchanan chirped that with the Keystone State secure, he would have "little difficulty in obtaining the nomination." "I am truly gratified at the result of your convention," added King, representing Buchanan's Southern base, "as it so completely gives the lie to the representations made here by your malignant enemies, that you could not carry your own State." Victory at the various district and state meetings that preceded and followed the state convention signaled to Wise (and everyone else) that Buchanan held Cameron in check, and thus was a shoo-in for the nomination.[54]

Wise was certainly eager to have Virginia announce for Buchanan as well. In the Virginia state convention, which was held in March 1852, Buchanan forces were able to gain the chairmanship of the convention, elect the committees, and pass their resolutions, but Douglas devotees, in retaliation, spread rumors that Buchanan could not carry Pennsylvania. The tactic was effective, and the meeting did not instruct its delegates to vote for Buchanan. The convention did, however, make clear its preference for Buchanan and Virginia's solidarity with Pennsylvania. "*Virginia is unquestionably with us,*" noted one Buchanan lieutenant with confidence. The victories in Pennsylvania and Virginia added to Buchanan's momentum, and his agents across the country mobilized their forces and reported regularly the workings of other state parties. Alfred Gilmore carefully watched events in New England, Isaac Toucey was Buchanan's friend in Connecticut, August Belmont kept his eye on New York and the financial sector, Wise now joined Cave Johnson in working the Upper South, Slidell reported from the Gulf Coast, and King was ever vigilant in Alabama and the Deep South. With Cass expected to fail fast, Douglas alienating the party elders, and Marcy still embroiled with Dickinson, Buchanan appeared to be the most likely nominee.[55]

Few suspected much from New England. Some northeastern Democrats, though, hoped to advance the career of Franklin Pierce of New Hampshire, a handsome young man who seemed eager to please. Born to settlers in

Hillsborough, New Hampshire, in November 1804, young Franklin had been an undisciplined, below-average student whose chief characteristic was his penchant for trickery. He eventually became a mediocre lawyer in his hometown and, because of his father's repeated gubernatorial runs, flirted with politics. He served in the state legislature without distinction, and was elected to the U.S. House of Representatives because of the absence of any organized opposition. His tenure in Congress was notable only for his public drunkenness and his eagerness to please the Southern leadership. He proved a dutiful Democrat in the House, siding with the South on almost every issue, including the annexation of Texas and the "gag rule," which prevented antislavery petitions from being considered by Congress and thus violated First Amendment rights. "He found early the key to southern sympathy and friendship," notes his principal biographer, "and for weal or woe he was never to lose it." In late 1836 he was elected by the state legislature to the U.S. Senate, where he was content to follow the Southern lead and become an admirer of Jefferson Davis.[56]

Following an unexceptional Senate term, Pierce returned to his Hillsborough law practice. Always in the shadow of his more popular, more respected father, he struggled with depression and alcoholism. Nevertheless, he was a fierce partisan who refused to tolerate any challenge to the Slave Power. In the 1840s, he was an enthusiastic supporter of both Polk and the war against Mexico. As reward, Pierce received a political appointment as a brigadier general, though he was largely ignorant of military affairs. He proved a poor commander, and, in the campaign against Mexico City, Pierce fainted twice in combat because of a minor but painful groin injury. Rumors quickly circulated that he was a coward, especially after he managed to avoid any major engagements (he always claimed to be suffering from fainting spells, diarrhea, or general war weariness).

After his abortive military career, he once again returned to New Hampshire law and politics, where he enjoyed some local prominence. He soon formed the "Concord Regency" with friends to combat the rising antislavery tide. Through his infant political machine, he gained control of the New Hampshire Democracy and proceeded to purge the party of antislavery men. As chairman of the State Central Committee, he waged war against the principled antislavery Democrat John P. Hale, publicly labeling Hale's stand against slavery "factious, selfish and disorganizing," and ignoring the overwhelming public support for Hale. Though younger and less well known than Jesse Bright, Pierce proved to be his equal in achieving autocratic rule; after ousting Hale, Pierce became virtual dictator of the state organization and an attractive prospect for Democratic kingmakers.[57]

FIGURE 3. President Franklin Pierce, New Hampshire (Library of Congress)

Chief among the would-be kingmakers was New Hampshire editor and periodic officeholder Edmund Burke. Burke, who had superb political contacts and solid doughface credentials, was bent on obtaining a Senate seat through the election of Pierce. Burke had served New Hampshire in Congress, where he voted for the gag rule, and used his *Newport Argus & Spectator* to promote the Southern agenda. In 1845, he was appointed commissioner of patents by President Polk and continued to nurture his many political friendships, particularly with Polk, Cass, and Buchanan. Thanks to those contacts, Burke was elevated to the national Democratic Executive Committee, where he became the consummate insider. In his home state, he worked side by side with Pierce to punish antislavery dissent and defend the Fugitive Slave Law.[58]

Burke was a wily operator, and his support for Pierce was not evident at first. Up until March 1852, just months before the national nominating convention, Burke had been "all things to all men," simultaneously supporting Buchanan, Marcy, Cass, and Douglas. In Washington, Burke met with leading politicos, advocating Pierce as the best *second* choice and proclaiming his reliability on slavery. "You represented him [Pierce] as peculiarly acceptable to Politicians of the Virginia School," recalled Virginian James Barbour. "You said that he conformed to our notions on state rights—the tariff—public lands and internal improvements as well as upon the slavery subject. You assured me that on the slavery question . . . [Pierce] was as good as . . . any of our own representatives." By April, the Pierce movement had gained some momentum, and Pierce authorized Burke to use his name at the Baltimore convention. Burke also gained the active aid of Massachusetts conservative Caleb Cushing and Tennessee military hero Gideon Pillow, who toured the Northeast in support of Pierce. Remarkably, Burke was able to unite most of New England behind Pierce just in time for the nominating convention. The New Hampshire delegates left for Baltimore at the end of May, having agreed to scatter their strength among the various candidates and see how the balloting proceeded; if deadlock ensued and another state put forth Pierce's name, the Granite State would unite behind him and—they hoped—start a rush for their favorite son. It was up to Burke to make sure that rush to Pierce occurred.[59]

Harmony and unity of the Northern Democracy may have been achieved, but victory in 1852 was still uncertain. And who would benefit from the victory, should it come, was even more unclear. The control and discipline imposed by Bright, Marcy, and Buchanan on their state organizations was tenuous at best, and they all continued to face active, effective opponents who were determined to torpedo their candidacies and unseat them as political bosses. Wright and Cameron represented the fast-emerging antislavery faction, while Dickinson led the forces of reaction and conservatism. Moreover, Bright, Marcy, and Buchanan had to contend with the return of Cass and the sudden rise of Pierce. If the Northern Democracy was to survive and maintain its traditional loyalty to the South, Northern leaders would have to both accept the outcome of the 1852 national convention and rally their state organizations to the nominee and platform, however proslavery they may be. None of this, of course, would be easy, especially after the contentious national nominating convention at Baltimore.

CHAPTER 3

"One of the Most Reliable Politicians upon This Subject of Slavery"

The Rewards of Fidelity and the Perils of Power

Delegates to the June 1852 Democratic National Convention in Baltimore began congregating a month in advance, forty miles south in Washington, to meet, scheme, and negotiate. "The city is thronged almost to suffocation by delegates to the convention and innumerable outsiders who came along to help make the nominations," reported Representative Thomas Harris of Illinois. Thirty-one states meant thirty-one delegations, with each state casting as many votes as it had presidential electors. But many states sent far more than their voting delegates, hoping to pack the Maryland Institute Hall and influence events through sheer numbers and noise. Though each state could decide its own method of delegate selection, the system was designed to give inflated power to the slave states. Since convention voting was tied to the Electoral College, slave states, which enjoyed the electoral benefits of the Three-Fifths Clause of the Constitution, could field larger delegations than their small white populations warranted. Thus, the South expected to command the convention as it always had. "We have and can maintain," asserted future Confederate secretary of war James Seddon with confidence, "ascendancy in the Democratic party . . . and probably controlling influence on the general policy and action of the whole party in the Union."

Through their exaggerated representation and traditional Northern Democratic subservience, Southern delegates expected to control the organization of the meeting, the membership of the committees, the content of resolutions, and the nominations. If Northern Democrats wanted to influence the proceedings, or possibly receive a nomination, they would have to cater to the South and convince them of their continued fidelity.[1]

By June, Baltimore hotels were packed to capacity, with delegates and politicos sleeping where they could. Agents and representatives of all the potential candidates were in attendance, ready to make a deal or sign a pledge. Jesse Bright of Indiana led one wing of Cass supporters, while Daniel Dickinson of New York led the other. Bright was determined to thwart the aspirations of young Stephen Douglas of Illinois, his primary rival in the Northwest. Though Indiana Democrats preferred General Joseph Lane for president, Bright and his protégé William English controlled the delegation with an iron fist and kept ready to turn that fist against Douglas at the opportune moment.[2]

Unlike Bright, Dickinson sought the presidential nomination in addition to leading Cass troops from the east. His use of Cass as cover was less than subtle, and convention observers were eager to see what Dickinson would do when balloting began. "There are *Cass delegates* who are not *Cass men*," wrote John Cadwalader to James Buchanan. Despite his duplicitous game, Dickinson had reason to be optimistic. He enjoyed firm Southern support for his war against the Barnburners and his proslavery course in the Senate. "Your patriotic efforts, in behalf of the South and its institutions," wrote Henry Orr of Virginia, "have touched the heart of every generous, honest man, and kindled a feeling of love and confidence which will never diminish, but continue to expand and grow until your elevation to the Presidency will be the grand *finale*." And Alexander Stephens reassured fellow Georgian Howell Cobb that "Dickinson of New York is true as steel." But Dickinson also had a third objective: to destroy Empire State competitor William Marcy. For years, Dickinson had labored to convince Southerners that Marcy was a tool of the antislavery movement—a death sentence for any candidate. His eagerness to torpedo Marcy, however, made Dickinson appear a desperate man, perhaps even a loose cannon, someone neither Northerners nor Southerners could fully trust.[3]

In the preconvention maneuverings, none could match Douglas's energy or ambition. "Douglas is cock sure of being the nominee, and he has certainly spared no electioneering arts to advance his extraordinary pretensions," warned William King to Buchanan. Though not in Baltimore himself, Douglas's trusted lieutenant William Richardson attended the convention as wire puller. Richardson, along with Senators David Yulee of Florida and Pierre Soulé of Louisiana, managed the Little Wizard's affairs at the convention. Like Dickinson, Douglas had earned some Southern support for

his role in the so-called Compromise of 1850, and he attracted the attention and loyalty of Southern expansionists (like Yulee and Soulé) eager for
more slave states, but Democratic elders of all sections continued to doubt
his tactics and principles. More immediately, they worried about what she-
nanigans Douglas might try during the proceedings to undermine his rivals
and secure nomination. Supreme Court Justice John Catron of Tennessee,
for instance, considered the Douglas movement a "clap trap rabble seeking
parade." Wisely, Douglas instructed his managers to simply "keep cool" and
to "do nothing to irritate any body."[4]

Edmund Burke of New Hampshire was under no such restrictions in his
representation of Franklin Pierce, and indeed worked tirelessly to spread the
word about "Handsome Frank." After endless meetings with key delegates,
and distributing material on New Hampshire's favorite son, Burke intended
to wait and watch during the convention, wait for the prominent candidates
to destroy each other and watch for the right moment to bring forth Pierce
as a "compromise" candidate—a New Englander with a strong proslavery
record.[5]

While Dickinson, Douglas, and Pierce positioned themselves for a lightning strike, Cass and Buchanan were the easy front-runners. Cass benefited from residual loyalty from his abortive run four years earlier and, at
seventy years old, was unquestionably the elder statesman of the party. But
few Democrats preferred him. Many planned to cast their first votes for
Cass only as a show of respect, believing that he had been "ingloriously defeated" in 1848 and considering it a "matter of pride" to avenge their former
standard-bearer. Such sentiments, though hardly a recipe for victory at the
convention, buoyed Cass's spirits and convinced him that he would emerge
triumphant. What he failed to consider was mounting Southern skepticism
of his famously ambiguous principles. "Popular sovereignty," a vague and
untested policy of allowing territories to vote on slavery prior to statehood,
in particular, gave Southerners pause. "He has talents," admitted Virginian
Edmund Hubard, "but with all is deemed more of a demagogue than statesman. His strong proclivity to ride both sides of a sapling argues unsoundness
or over ambition—either way he is not trustworthy."[6]

Buchanan, on the other hand, had absolutely nothing to worry about
from the slave states. His Southern credentials were as unquestionable as
those of any South Carolinian. It was in the free states that "the Sage of
Wheatland" was unpopular and distrusted. "I am no partisan of Buchanan,"
confided Gideon Welles to Sam Tilden. "[His] course on all recent questions
appear to me extremely objectionable." "You alone," wrote cantankerous
James Gadsden of South Carolina, would please the South, and John Slidell

assured his friend that "you may rely upon almost unanimous support from the Southern States." Buchanan had little to fear except from Marcy, his old comrade in the Polk Cabinet. Buchanan hoped that if he could not secure the nomination in the first few ballots, Marcy supporters would flock to his ranks after Dickinson eroded Marcy's Southern support.[7]

With the South nearly united behind Buchanan, Cass sure to fail fast, and Pierce playing the waiting game, all eyes were on New York. Would the Empire State rally behind Marcy, or would Dickinson's masterly machinations successfully divide the state and kill Marcy's candidacy? Dickinson attended the convention himself and brought along acerbic editor Edwin Croswell as lieutenant, but Marcy remained aloof, allowing his interests to be handled by capable Softs Horatio Seymour, J. B. Skinner, and Erastus Corning. The Marcy men sought to maintain the coalition of Softs and Barnburners forged in New York, and Dickinson worked to undermine the coalition and spread doubt about Marcy's principles and leadership. Marcy's negotiations with the antislavery Barnburners, Dickinson insisted, made him unreliable on slavery, and thus unelectable. Moreover, Dickinson asserted that New York was *not* united behind Marcy but in fact was up for grabs by any candidate. Barnburner "odor," insisted one Dickinson agent, "is upon Gov. Marcy and it will not be pleasant in the nostrils of Southern Delegates."[8]

Marcy, for his part, instructed his managers to avoid any "entangling alliances" and allow Dickinson's secret agenda to reveal itself in due course. Simultaneously, Marcy worked to convince Southern leaders of his soundness on slavery and his support for the Fugitive Slave Law, personally writing letters guaranteeing his doughfaceism. Likewise, he instructed agents in Baltimore to distribute letters authored by him. "Their perusal," Marcy believed "will convince every southern man that . . . I have not gasconaded as much about the compromise measures as Mr. Dickinson & others. I have done much more to advance the cause in the south." "They will show Southern men what sort of friend I am and have been to them," he added. Covertly, Marcy sent Seymour to meet with Henry Wise of Virginia and Caleb Cushing of Massachusetts to make sure there was no doubt about Marcy's record. In return for these guarantees, moderate Southerners continued to give their support, seeing Marcy's coalition-building as critical to the future of the party.[9]

The 1852 Democratic National Convention

In the final days before the convention, the "noise and confusion" among the delegations was frenzied—no one could predict what would happen, and all the participants scrambled to make deals and ensure patronage for their states regardless of the outcome. On the morning of June 1, delegates, exhausted from all-night carousing, gathered in the Great Hall of the Maryland Institute to begin the work of national organization. The inflated delegations made for large crowds and a raucous atmosphere. At noon, the chairman of the Democratic National Committee, Benjamin Hallett of Massachusetts, called the assemblage to order, some initial committee selections were made, and neutral John Davis of Indiana was elected permanent chair.[10]

The second day, Wednesday, June 2, was more eventful, as candidates and their agents began showing their cards. After the appointment of anti-Marcy men to key committees, the New Yorker's agents circulated his proslavery letters, which, according to J. Addison Thomas, did "wonders to destroy the aspirations of Dickinson." Bright introduced a resolution strongly endorsing the Fugitive Slave Law, and Dickinson began to drop his facade of Cass manager. The Buchanan men, led by Wise, tried and failed to push through a motion to adopt a platform before a nominee, knowing that a proslavery platform would aid Buchanan's candidacy.[11]

Day three commenced with Dickinson launching an all-out attack on Marcy and the Buchanan band once again pushing for platform before nominee. Nevertheless, the much-awaited balloting began. There were a total of 288 delegates, and, thanks to the pro-Southern two-thirds rule, a candidate needed 197 to achieve nomination. As everyone expected, the first ballot put Cass firmly in the lead with 116, but Buchanan was close behind with 97. Marcy and Douglas trailed with 27 and 20, and Bright kept Indiana in the Lane column. Eight ballots were cast that morning, with Cass as the frontrunner, primarily as a show of respect for 1848. The round of ballots in the evening showed Cass weakening, Buchanan and Douglas gaining, and Marcy lagging. New Yorkers pressured Dickinson to unite the state behind Marcy and start a rush for him, but Dickinson was adamant.[12]

Another night of caucusing and deal-making led into a second day of voting. Cass's candidacy collapsed, while the preconvention deal-making began to take effect and Buchanan and Douglas surged. On the twentieth vote, Buchanan took the lead, with Virginia supporting him in full force. But Douglas's impressive rise made the Buchanan devotees nervous, and they begged the Marcy men to come to their aid, promising to support Marcy if Buchanan failed. Marcy's managers, however, knew that Buchanan had little support above Mason and Dixon's Line and withheld their votes. Needless to say, the Buchaneers, as Buchanan's supporters were known, were embittered.

When the meeting finally adjourned for the day, tempers ran short and tensions were high. The Buchaneers were furious with their inability to win the nomination and were determined to torpedo Douglas. That evening, they invited delegates from the slave states to their rooms at Caroll Hall to solidify their Southern base and set strategy for the next day. They agreed to allow Cass, Douglas, and Marcy to destroy each other before making a surge for Buchanan, and decided that Pennsylvania, Georgia, and Alabama would stay firm, keeping Buchanan's candidacy alive, while Virginia, North Carolina, and Mississippi tried other candidates in order to weaken Buchanan's competitors. At the same time, Cass men met with the Douglas delegates and pleaded for help. If you would support us now, they promised, we will guarantee Douglas the nomination in 1856. Douglas, observing these events from afar, instructed his agents to ignore all offers; "Make no arrangements," he wrote Yulee.[13]

Saturday dawned with Virginia delegates deep in early morning strategy meetings. While waiting to return to Buchanan, they decided to promote the candidacy of Dickinson. This move, they reasoned, would cause a rush to Buchanan by Marcy men in order to stop Dickinson. On hearing the news, Dickinson's brother-in-law ran to tell Dickinson. Back in the Great Hall, balloting resumed with no clear leader. When the Old Dominion announced for Dickinson, he surprised the congregation by declining the honor. There was method to his madness, however, as he privately planned to revive his candidacy after the others failed, or at the least, earn the gratitude of the nominee and receive a cabinet post. "Dickinson played his game to defeat you," reported H. K. Smith to Marcy, "& his speech to Virginia . . . was a bid for the Cabinet." With Dickinson temporarily out, the Virginia delegation turned to Pierce. But before they cast their ballots for this "dark horse," they required final assurances from Burke of Pierce's "perfect soundness" on slavery. Burke promptly provided letters, and Virginia re-entered the hall ready to change the game.[14]

On the thirty-fifth ballot, Virginia announced for Pierce, with Maine, New Hampshire, and Massachusetts following their lead. North Carolina and Mississippi, as per that morning's plan, came over to Marcy. Marcy gained, but Pennsylvania, recalling how Marcy men had declined to help them, "positively refused" to rally to Marcy and urged Virginia to stick with Pierce. Nevertheless, on the forty-fifth ballot Marcy took the lead, but his momentum was halted by Dickinson, who once again prevented the Empire State from uniting. All the while, Burke and his friends pressed hard for Pierce, using personal relationships to make converts; Burke also continued to emphasize Pierce's proslavery credentials, fondness for the South, and the fact there had never been a Democratic nominee from New England. The efforts paid off, and on the forty-sixth ballot Kentucky went to Pierce, bringing "Handsome Frank" up to third place. The next ballot saw Maryland join the movement, causing panic in the New York ranks. They tried to adjourn to save Marcy, but to no avail. When Douglas men tried to coax Virginia away, delegation leader John Barbour (who had roomed with Burke in Washington) remained firm and divulged that North Carolina and Georgia were switching to Pierce on the next vote. Marcy struggled to remain in the lead, and New York delegates withdrew from the meeting to dissuade Dickinson from his opposition. Dickinson refused to negotiate, leaving Marcy's managers few options. Upon returning, Seymour took the floor and withdrew Marcy's name in favor of Pierce, causing Dickinson to announce for him as well. When Pennsylvania cast for Pierce, the deed was done and the other states fell in line, bringing the candidate up to 283 and securing him the nomination.[15]

Burke had done his work well. "No man so much as yourself is Gen. Pierce indebted for his nomination," remarked one correspondent. His tireless campaigning on behalf of Pierce had turned the obscure New Hampshire doughface into the likely next president of the United States. As a consolation prize to the recognized front-runner, the convention gave the vice-presidential nomination to Buchanan's "Siamese Twin" companion, William King of Alabama. It was a nice gesture, but far from satisfactory. As for the platform, it was proslavery and quickly approved, and, despite the general surprise at Pierce's sudden rise, the convention adjourned in a happy state. The Cass crew were glad that Douglas and Buchanan had been defeated; Buchanan and Douglas were pleased to see Cass finally put down; Dickinson was thrilled at his ability to kill Marcy's momentum; "Young Americans" were glad to have young Frank Pierce as the nominee instead of an "Old Fogy"; and "Old Fogies" were happy to see Douglas disciplined. Overall, few knew Pierce well, so few could have a grudge against him. Most knew him only as a reliable Democrat and doughface. Even Marcy had to admit his approval of the nomination: "I have this moment heard of the nomination of Pierce," he wrote to a friend, "and, strange as you may think it, I really rejoice at it . . . Pierce is a fine fellow." When the news reached Mr. and Mrs. Pierce on an afternoon ride from Boston to Concord, New Hampshire, he was speechless and she fainted. "Few events," Pierce confided to Buchanan, "could have taken me more by surprise than my nomination at Baltimore."[16]

As the convention high wore-off, however, further reflection among Democrats yielded some doubts about their decision. "The strong men have been thrown over board" in favor of an unknown, lamented Georgia delegate John Lumpkin. The Buchaneers, in particular, grew "exceedingly disappointed" and "disgusted" as they realized the impact of Pierce's nomination. "No friend of yours could feel more mortification at your failure to obtain the nomination of the Baltimore Convention than I did," fumed King. "My Friends of the South felt satisfied that you were the choice of our people." To prevent another dark horse victory in the future, Buchanan supporters toyed with the idea of changing convention voting procedures. Indeed, some even advocated giving Northern states *less* representation at conventions, making Southern control of the party impenetrable. "It is true some change should be made in the mode of selecting a candidate for the Presidency," wrote Alfred Gilmore to Buchanan, "when the unanimous voice of eight democratic [Southern] states is disregarded and stifled by Federal [Northern] states, that never have, or will give a democratic vote." And Cave Johnson added, "The mode of selecting the delegates must be improved and the laws of the convention changed, so that after a certain number of ballots, the lowest should be dropped & the number of votes given be adjusted in proportion to the democratic strength of each state—the whig [Northern] states ought not to have the same weight in the selection as the democratic states." That Buchanan's Northern supporters agreed with Southern schemes to alter convention procedure reveals the depth of Northern Democratic devotion to the South and their determination to keep the party proslavery.[17]

Marcy, too, had reason to be frustrated. He had achieved a steady lead until his candidacy was almost single-handedly thwarted by Dickinson. After the convention, Marcy's supporters threw up their hands at Dickinson's obstinate obstructionism, labeling him a "scoundrel" and "the basest and most contemptible of mankind." "Had he yielded in his *stubborn* opposition to you," recalled James Berret to Marcy, "the Virginia delegation which went against you by a *single vote* would have come to our support and thereby rendered your nomination certain." Though claiming to be unsurprised by Dickinson's actions in Baltimore, Marcy nevertheless lamented his defeat.[18] Dickinson, for his part, was pleased with his work but regretted declining the nomination and betting on future opportunity. "I saw, and so did many friends, the presidency virtually laid at my feet," he wrote with typical exaggeration. His plan had nearly worked, but he believed he had been defeated by the "the enemies of the true national Democracy," a.k.a. antislavery ne'er-do-wells.[19]

Though Northern Democrats in general saw young Frank Pierce as a welcome break from the "Old Fogies" of the past, his nomination did not solve the major problems facing the party. Pierce may have been the first New England Democrat trusted with the nomination, but his principles were firmly rooted in Southern soil, keeping policy squarely in Southern hands. Moreover, the convention failed to mend the fissures over slavery that had crippled the organization since the 1840s. The Compromise of 1850 would be difficult for Northern Democrats to defend, and the divisions in the key states of New York, Pennsylvania, and Indiana were only temporarily glossed over. Overall, there was hope but little enthusiasm. "The news of the nomination was rather a damper upon the Democracy here," wrote one Hoosier; "still they [Democrats] made a faint demonstration and consumed a few old tar barrels." Most saw Pierce and the platform as simply "satisfactory."[20]

The slave states had more reason to celebrate. They had maintained control of the party and the Northern wing had remained subservient, despite the rising antislavery tide. The nominee was a tried-and-true doughface who was sure to follow Southern dictates in office. "I was a member of the Ho[use] of Rep[resentative]s whilst Gen[era]l Pierce was in the Senate and had some opportunities to observe his course," noted Robert Hunter with satisfaction. "The result of these observations was a conviction that he was one of the most reliable politicians upon this subject of slavery of all whom I knew in the non-slaveholding states." Even Buchanan's companion King allowed himself some joy at his and Pierce's nomination. "I feel perfectly satisfied that after you he is more acceptable to the South than any of the persons whose names were before the convention." Indeed, from the Southern perspective, the future looked bright and there was expectation that "we shall again navigate smooth waters."[21]

Campaigns and Elections

With resignation in the North and cautious optimism in the South, the campaigns and elections of 1852 were largely anticlimactic, especially after the exciting Baltimore convention. Whigs were divided and dismayed over their gout-stricken, elderly candidate "Old Fuss and Feathers," General Winfield Scott, while Democrats were generally united behind "Handsome Frank." And since both camps endorsed the Compromise of 1850 and both labored to appeal to the growing immigrant population, attention focused on candidate character and foreign policy, with Whigs opposing the militant expansionism of the Democrats.[22] Candidate Pierce remained, for the most part, in "dignified retirement," as one biographer phrased it, in the quiet capital of Concord, with frequent visits to Boston for meetings. Once Pierce officially accepted the nomination, orators, brass bands, and well-wishers flooded the sleepy town. But most of the country remained unmoved. "Who is Frank Pierce?" was heard throughout the land, as Democrats and Whigs alike tried to figure out the dark horse. To address this problem, campaign chiefs dubbed the New Hampshire doughface "Young Hickory of the Granite Hills" in a futile attempt to connect him to Democratic icon "Old Hickory," Andrew Jackson, and saw to the publication of syrupy campaign biographies. "Granite Clubs" were established around the country, and "Hickory Poles" were erected in town squares. Nevertheless, reports of Pierce's drunkenness and embarrassing military career surfaced quickly, and Whigs quipped about the "Hero of Many a Well Fought Bottle."[23]

In the northwestern states, the campaign was relatively uneventful. In Indiana, Bright, whose doughface course and tyrannical methods had made him enormously unpopular, could only watch as his rival (and Free Soil sympathizer) Joseph Wright was nominated for another term as governor. Refusing to help Wright and frustrated with his declining power in the state, Bright sat out much of the campaign, claiming poor health. State elections in October resulted in modest Democratic success, as Democrats had been generally united behind Wright, and his popularity essentially carried the rest of the state ticket into office. Despite respectable Free Soil gains and furious, futile efforts by the Whigs, Democrats won control of the state legislature with a two-to-one majority. Even Bright's protégé, William English, was able to win election to Congress, thanks to the predominance of Southern souls in the second district.[24]

Next door in Illinois, Democrats had to recover from the disappointment that their favorite son Douglas did not receive the nomination. Moreover, Illinoisans found it difficult to rally around an obscure New Englander. Senator James Shields had Gustave Koerner, a Protestant German, put on the state ticket to attract the vote of the growing German community of the state, and Douglas took to the stump to boost voter enthusiasm. He even ventured beyond Illinois, capitalizing on his energy and name recognition, calling for an expansionist foreign policy and condemning Whigs as corrupt and incompetent. Illinois state elections in October brought more confidence to the Democrats, as both Douglas and his trusted lieutenant, William Richardson, were reelected. The victories were deceiving, though, as they largely resulted from the mobilization of the immigrant vote rather than from the popularity of Democratic proslavery policies. Democratic state victories in Indiana and Illinois, particularly the election of doughfaces Douglas and Richardson, virtually ensured that Pierce would carry those states in the November election.[25]

Pennsylvania, more so than Indiana and Illinois, was a must-win for the Democrats, both symbolically and electorally. If Buchanan could not deliver his populous home state, then the Northern wing of the party was in far more danger than anticipated. Old Buck, however, was in no mood to help young Pierce, and he did not take an active role in the campaign until his political machine was seriously threatened by the now-potent antislavery movement. For much of the summer, he sat on his hands at his estate, fighting bilious attacks and bad teeth. Antislavery sentiment had spread dramatically in the Keystone State, and voters were angry over Buchanan's open pandering to the South. In addition, since Buchanan's failure at Baltimore, challengers like Simon Cameron were emboldened to make more aggressive attacks on the traditional party apparatus.[26]

Once Buchanan recognized the antislavery threat to his personal base, he mobilized his supporters and got to work. On the stump, though, he displayed questionable political judgment when he defended the odious Fugitive Slave Law and hailed Pierce's pro-Southern credentials. His subordinates were more practical and fretted about the large "Catholic vote" of the state, though they were confident they could better court that community than the Whigs. "There is no doubt about Pennsylvania," asserted German Democrat Francis Grund, "the victory is easy." Although they vigorously opposed the doughfaced leadership, Cameron and Democratic dissidents were brought in line for the state and presidential elections. Thanks to low voter turnout and Whig divisions, Democrats emerged victorious in October, much to the relief of Democrats across the country. Exclaimed one observer, "The returns from Pennsylvania seem to have settled the presidential contest."[27]

But New York was still the "great arbiter of the election." Marcy, once again, was expected to hold the Democratic ship together, battling both unrelenting Hards and well-organized Whigs. Not only did it fall on his shoulders to secure the state for the man who defeated him at Baltimore, but he and his allies had to maintain the tenuous coalition of Softs and Barnburners. From the moment the nomination was seemingly snatched from his hands, Dickinson was determined to bring chaos to the Empire State and defeat Marcy's candidates for state office. Such actions could be hugely destructive for both the state organization and the national party. "Dickinson and the little band of his toadies are savage and will do any thing & risque every thing to thwart me & my friends," Marcy fumed. But if Dickinson wanted to play any role in a Pierce administration, he would have to stop short of undermining the national campaign. To help bring Dickinson into line, Pierce sent New Hampshire representative Harry Hibbard and adviser Charles Atherton down to New York. Pierce also stayed in close contact with Marcy, obviously very concerned about events in the Empire State. By harnessing Dickinson and his followers behind the Pierce banner, Marcy was able to get his coalition candidates nominated and elected, most notably Seymour, who received the gubernatorial chair. When the fall elections yielded victories, Marcy was

FIGURE 4. Senator Stephen Douglas, Illinois (Library of Congress)

cool and cautious, but his friends were joyful. "I confess it gives me no pain to hear that he [Dickinson] meets with mortification and disgrace at every political step he takes," wrote Arch Campbell to Marcy. "You stand at the head," gushed Representative W. W. Snow, "and the wisdom of your council has saved the party from disgrace."[28]

Indeed, the work of men like Marcy was critical to success in the presidential race. Despite the deterioration of the state parties and the growing power of the antislavery movement, Marcy, Seymour, Dickinson, Buchanan, Bright, Douglas, and Richardson were able to deliver key Northern states and produce an electoral landslide for Pierce. Northern Democrats were also aided by the deterioration of the Whig Party, which was slowly succumbing to internal divisions over slavery. As the antislavery tide swept the free states, Northern and Southern Whigs found it increasingly difficult to work together and could not unite on "Old Fuss and Feathers."

In the end, the Democracy carried twenty-seven out of thirty-one states and crushed Scott in the Electoral College, 254 to 42. "The triumph is the most glorious of any since the days of Jackson," gushed Cave Johnson, "and I cannot doubt that our affairs will be so conducted that the great interests of the country will be promoted and the Democratic party kept in the ascendancy for the next quarter of a century." Even Whigs saw the writing on the wall. They had succumbed to divisions over slavery, while the Democrats had remained united. "Democracy, with its indomitable energy has swept every vestige of Whiggery from the land," lamented one Hoosier Whig. But perhaps financier and New York Democrat August Belmont spoke too soon when he called the "unprecedented victory" the "complete overthrow & *political extinction* of our unprincipled opponents." Democrats may have fought off the forces of reform and antislavery, but it was a tenuous, temporary victory at best. The few remaining antislavery Democrats like Wright and Cameron may have toed the line in 1852, but the unity was fleeting, and there was little excitement among the Democratic rank and file in the North to continue the proslavery course.[29]

There was also much worry about what path Pierce would take. Would he stay obedient to the Southern bosses, or would he assert independence and reach out to the dwindling antislavery Democrats? If he did not stay true to the party's proslavery foundation, Southerners vowed never to promote another doughface. "Pierce's antecedents were few, and he was nominated little known to the country generally," wrote King to Buchanan. "I myself had to answer hundreds of letters of inquiry from the Southern States in which I fully endorsed him as in every way to be relied on. Let us again be deceived, and all the powers of earth will never be able in future to secure the Southern vote for a *Northern man* with *Southern principles.*" Pierce's nomination and election had been a vote of confidence in doughfaces by Southern Democrats. They were confident that Northern Democratic leaders like Pierce and Buchanan could beat back the rising antislavery tide and produce policies and legislation that promoted slavery and Southern interests.

Northern Democrats had proved themselves safe on slavery during the crises of 1850 and the state battles of 1851–1852, and had proved themselves to be formidable political powers in their regions, despite the fact that their constituents largely disagreed with their policies. It was now up to President-elect Pierce to show his gratitude for that confidence and repay that debt of trust by choosing a cabinet that would put the South at ease and ensure four years of harmony.[30]

The Patronage Puzzle

Even before the election, cabinet appointments and patronage became the all-consuming passion of Northern Democrats, eager for the feast after the famine of the Taylor and Fillmore years. Patronage was enormously important to both policy and the party—it determined who was in charge at the local, state, regional, and national levels; who was favored and who was shunned; which policies would be implemented and which would be rejected. The public could tell a lot about an incoming administration just by the cabinet selection, since that cabinet, in turn, would administer the executive branch and dole out patronage. Every American from the top political bosses to the lowliest rural postmaster waited with bated breath to see who was in and who was out. Any perceived mistake by Pierce could cost him valuable support even before his term began; he could, if he was not careful, alienate key Democrats and cripple his infant administration. "Gen. Pierce & his Cabinet," noted future representative Norman Eddy of Indiana, "will in the end be judged neither by the foreign & domestic policy adopted than by the Appointments made."

Each faction of the party expected recognition in the cabinet, if not direct representation by the selection of their leader. Buchanan, Marcy, Douglas, Bright, Dickinson, and even old Lewis Cass expected to be rewarded for their loyalty and leadership, as well as consulted on all patronage matters. If a faction or state machine was denied patronage, it would be fatal, resulting in dramatic shifts in power at the state level, which would then affect the national organization. "I have never before seen so much solicitude among the rank and file of the Party as to the formation of the Cabinet," noted one correspondent to Buchanan. "Men who on former occasions took no thought of this subject until the result was announced are canvassing and inquiring about it with keen anxiety." As soon as the electoral votes were counted, the guessing, scheming, and maneuvering began in earnest.[31]

Pierce's chief advisor was ex-senator Charles Atherton of New Hampshire. He, too, had a long proslavery record and had even been a sponsor of the infamous gag rule in Congress. Pierce wanted Atherton returned to the Senate to be his advocate on the Hill and orchestrated Atherton's election, in the process defeating Senator John Hale, who had just run against Pierce as the Free Soil presidential candidate. With that accomplished, Pierce turned to the formation of his cabinet. Office seekers and agents flocked to Concord to press their claims, and the president-elect was forced to shift his headquarters to Boston. Surrounded by both friends and foes, advice givers and advantage takers, Pierce played his cards close to his vest. He refused to discuss his deliberations with any but a select few, causing "intense anxiety" among Democratic leaders who waited in limbo to hear their fate. "[I] know nothing of General Pierce's intentions either in regard to myself or any other person," complained an anxious Buchanan, and Cass remarked with agitation, "I have no communication, none at all, with Gen. Pierce direct or indirect, verbal or written." Even the Southern bosses were left in the dark, lest a leak lead to a premature mutiny. "Who is in the Concord Confidence?" Henry Wise asked Buchanan. "Is it you? It is not I. . . . Is Cass to predominate? Is Douglas to be allowed an inheritance? Are the Van Burens, Blairs, &c &c to be let in again to a participation of the spoils?" So many questions, so many options. But Pierce was impressively diligent. As late as February 25, just days before the inauguration, political insiders were still guessing. "Every thing is all in mystery in relation to the cabinet," wrote Daniel Jenks to an exasperated Buchanan.[32]

Pierce's guiding principle in the formation of his cabinet was unity and harmony, not favoring one faction over another. But trying to please everyone, he failed to realize, meant pleasing no one. If he recognized and rewarded the few antislavery men who returned to regular Democratic ranks, he would alienate Southerners and Hards; if he rejected the antislavery men, he would be giving that group over to the opposition (first Whigs, soon Republicans); if he favored one state faction over another, he would cause divisions and infighting that would make governing impossible. "I fear that he does not fully realize the force of his position, and the utter uselessness of trying to compromise cliques and factions," fretted one Democrat. The two most important states, of course, were New York and Pennsylvania. Both had deep, destructive divisions that threatened the national party, both had large populations that were critical in national elections, and both involved men who would have won the nomination if not for Pierce's meteoric rise.

In the Empire State, the president-elect aimed to unite the factions and reward the coalition that produced victory. Marcy was the obvious choice for the cabinet, not only because of his orchestration of the Soft-Barnburner alliance, but also because of his long, respected career in public service. Buzz for Marcy as secretary of state (considered the premier post) began even before the election results were in. Marcy's agents immediately went to work on his behalf, distributing letters and meeting with Pierce's friends. But Dickinson was the choice of the slave states, and Pierce could not ignore Southern demands. "Dickinson would be as acceptable to the South as any man we have among us," advised Cave Johnson of Tennessee. But because Dickinson had been an obstacle to Democratic unity, and thus an obstacle to Pierce's election, he could not be rewarded with a cabinet post; perhaps a plum patronage assignment, but certainly not a seat in the cabinet. Nevertheless, Dickinson was determined to be in the cabinet. In his eyes, his refusal of Virginia's nomination had led directly to Pierce's success, and thus he deserved to be rewarded with the highest honors. In October 1852, even before the election had occurred, Dickinson had traveled to Concord to meet with Pierce and press his claims, as well as dissuade the president-elect from rewarding Marcy.[33]

Perhaps sensing the unlikelihood of a cabinet appointment, Dickinson threw himself into another destructive war against Marcy. If he could not have the high honors, he would prevent his rival from enjoying them as well. His strategy was simple: create chaos in the Empire State, which would make the selection of a New Yorker for the cabinet too dangerous; the young president, Dickinson guessed, would certainly shy away from a choice that could potentially alienate entire sections of the country. "He keeps his name constantly before the public," wrote Arch Campbell to Marcy, "to the eminent disgust of your friends, and apparently to the great satisfaction of the Old Dominion and other stupid Southern people who allow themselves to be humbugged by such a small specimen of humanity." Pierce nevertheless turned to Marcy. "I desire very much to see you," the president-elect wrote simply on November 9.[34]

Two days later, the two men met in Boston for a long interview. Pierce was eager for Marcy's advice, and Marcy was happy to give it. They labored for hours to construct a cabinet that would please the South and not cause further divisions in the North, but the effort was hopeless. "I tried the experiment of making out a Cabinet for him," Marcy confessed to a close friend, "but found myself unable to hitch together a team which would work fairly well." When Pierce asked Marcy to join the cabinet himself, the New Yorker replied that his appointment would enrage the Hards, causing unnecessary drama for the new administration. Marcy's supporters were not so circumspect, however, and made sure that his name stayed before the president throughout the coming months. Governor-elect Seymour and Erastus Corning, in particular, pushed for Marcy's appointment, even traveling to

Concord to argue that if Marcy was chosen, it would strengthen Seymour's hand in New York and allow him to bring order to the state. But Pierce remained reserved and noncommittal. Privately, he decided on boyhood companion and well-respected moderate John Dix as the best representative of New York. Aside from their friendship, Dix had campaigned for Pierce, aided Marcy's effort at union, and was widely considered a "most wise and expedient" selection.[35]

The choice in Pennsylvania was similarly perilous. Buchanan was the clear commander of Keystone doughfaces, but if Pierce promoted him, he would be promoting a rival. Pierce did not want him in the cabinet, but also did not want to offend the powerful Buchaneer faction of the party. Another option was Simon Cameron or Richard Brodhead, challengers to Buchanan's machine. Representing this group, Senator Brodhead visited Concord several times immediately after the election to both advocate for his friend and turn Pierce against Buchanan. The Buchaneers, however, had been plying Pierce since the summer, and Buchanan was confident that he was the only choice for the State Department. After the election, Buchanan moved to strengthen his position by making an alliance with Cass supporters. Their conservatism was attractive, and Cass was no longer a rival for the presidency.[36]

On December 7, 1852, a month after Pierce had met and strategized with Marcy, the president-elect wrote Buchanan admitting indecision and confusion about public opinion. He asked the Sage of Wheatland for advice, but informed him that no former cabinet officers would be appointed. This immediately took Buchanan and Marcy out of the running, since both had served in the Polk cabinet. Of course, Buchanan strenuously objected to Pierce's decision to omit men with experience. He warned him not to believe "Young America" rhetoric about "Old Fogies" like himself and warned Pierce not to show favor to any antislavery men. It was no use, though, and Pierce turned away from Buchanan. The Buchaneers, in turn, threw their support behind Buchanan loyalist Judge James Campbell. When Brodhead realized he was not making headway with Pierce, he too came out for Campbell, ensuring his appointment. Regardless, the "Cameron Clique," like Dickinson's Hards, remained in determined opposition.[37]

To ensure that the Southern bosses would be pleased, Pierce consulted regularly with Senators Jefferson Davis of Mississippi and Robert Hunter of Virginia. In fact, Hunter was offered a cabinet post of his choosing, which he agreed to consider, and Davis was offered the War Department. Both were fiery proslavery leaders and, if they accepted, would give Southern nationalists a strong position within the administration. With respect to the Cass crew, who had been fighting for their candidate for nearly a decade,

Pierce selected Alfred Nicholson of Tennessee, Cass confidant and editor of the *Nashville Union*. New England was also given a nod by the consideration of Caleb Cushing, a curmudgeonly doughface who had aided the Pierce movement before and at the convention. Positions were not certain, however, and though he knew he wanted these men in his cabinet, Pierce did not know which roles he wanted them to play.[38]

Before Pierce could make final decisions, though, Southerners and dough-faces unleashed a torrent of outrage at the selection of Dix. No amount of Southerners in the cabinet, they argued, would assuage the effrontery of having even one antislavery sympathizer. Pierce was shocked. His friend Dix had always denounced abolitionism and had opposed the Free Soil bolt in 1848. He had, however, expressed support for the Wilmot Proviso and sympathy for the Free Soil movement. The fact that Dix was labeled an unacceptable radical by regular Democrats demonstrated how proslavery the party remained despite the growing antislavery sentiment among voters. Dix faced "a most determined opposition from the South," reported Charles Eames to Marcy, and another politico noted that Dix's appointment "could not be sustained in the south." In protest, Hunter and Nicholson subsequently declined Pierce's offer to join the cabinet, and the president-elect found his plans in shambles. The South expected and demanded that Pierce in no way recognize or reward antislavery dissidents, or anyone even remotely connected to them, such as Dix.[39]

The Marcy and Dickinson factions saw an opportunity in the sudden crisis, and each sent representatives to meet with Pierce and convince him to appoint their man. In the end, Pierce returned to Marcy, and the "Dickinson malignants" were bitterly disappointed. Since the Southern bosses had vetoed Dix for the State Department, Pierce decided to give it to Marcy, making him the "premier of the new administration." But Southerners were not done with Dix. To ensure that he would play no role whatsoever in the administration, and to rebuke Pierce for his poor judgment, Southern leaders launched a campaign to destroy Dix's reputation and kill his career. He was attacked with a vengeance, labeled a dangerous abolitionist and a traitor to the party. When Pierce considered making his friend the minister to France, the backlash was immediate. More impressively, the attacks crossed party lines as both Whig and Democratic Southerners joined together to crush the New Yorker. "The Whigs of Georgia are unsparing in their denunciations of General Pierce for what they are pleased to call his abolition and free soil appointments to office, and your appointment has been especially singled out by the Whig presses and itinerant orators for unsparing abuse," wrote I. P. Garvin of Augusta. "You are denounced as a Free Soiler and abolitionist."

Only pure, proslavery Democrats, Southerners made clear, would be acceptable; only proven doughfaces like Pierce would be permitted to rise within the party. There was no place for a John Dix, Simon Cameron, or Joseph Wright.[40]

Bowing to Southern pressure, Pierce constructed his cabinet with a distinct proslavery bias. Marcy would lead at the State Department; Davis would remain at war to please Southern nationalists; Campbell of Pennsylvania would be postmaster general to placate the Buchaneers; popular Southern businessman James Guthrie of Kentucky was chosen for Treasury; the impeccably dressed expansionist and proslavery militant James Dobbin of North Carolina was given the Navy Department as reward for his service at the Baltimore convention; former governor of Michigan Robert McClelland was appointed as a nod to Cass loyalists; and the attorney generalship was given to Cushing of Massachusetts, whose proslavery views made him unelectable in New England. Though Cushing and Davis were known to support Stephen Douglas's expansionist program, Douglas men were left out of the cabinet entirely. In all, the final product was heavily pro-Southern: Davis, Guthrie, and Dobbin were Southerners; Cushing and Marcy were reliable doughfaces; and Campbell and McClelland represented doughfaces Buchanan and Cass. Southerners were pleased. On Valentine's Day 1853, the president-elect left Concord for the national capital, declining all public receptions along the way. He had his inaugural address to consider—his first statement of principles and objectives.[41]

Pierce arrived in Washington on February 21, 1853, after a stop in Philadelphia to consult with some Buchanan agents. Once in the capital, the president-elect immediately met at length with his new secretary of state, doubtless to finalize cabinet selections and discuss the inaugural address. Inauguration Day, March 4, dawned dark, cloudy, and cold; relentless snow and biting wind punished the swampy town throughout the day. Five feet nine inches tall, slim, with fashionably coiffed dark hair, and wearing a new broadcloth dress coat, trousers, and vest, Pierce was delivered to the steps of the Capitol by President Fillmore and Senators Jesse Bright of Indiana and Hannibal Hamlin of Maine. Though still recovering from the gruesome, sudden death of his son Bennie in a train wreck in January, Pierce would deliver his address without notes or manuscript.

The inaugural was exactly what Democrats hoped for, a short, conservative, proslavery statement. Specifically, Pierce announced a vigorous, expansionist foreign policy, a program of fiscal retrenchment, and federal protection of slavery. "I believe," he concluded, "that involuntary servitude, as it exists in different states of this confederacy, is recognized by the

Constitution. I believe that it stands like any other admitted right, and that the states where it exists are entitled to efficient remedies to enforce the constitutional provisions." He also came out in full support for the Compromise of 1850, particularly the Fugitive Slave Law, which shall be "unhesitatingly carried into effect." This was music to the ears of Democrats. "The Inaugural is excellent," exclaimed Tennessee Representative George Jones. "It could not be better. An administration based upon that and conducted upon the principles therein declared cannot be otherwise than successful." Even later, Senator Henry Foote of Mississippi recalled Pierce's inaugural and subsequent messages as "discoursing vehemently upon the untold blessings of slavery. He extolled the Sunny South and all her peculiar modes of thought and sentiment in language of most glowing exuberance; proclaimed himself to all the world as a sort of heaven-descended champion of her slave-holding rights and interests." Pierce's statements left no doubt about his course, and Democrats could look forward to four years of territorial expansion and Southern supremacy.[42]

Once in office, Pierce had to deal with patronage before he could implement policy. There was fifty million dollars a year worth to be distributed, and Democrats were hungry after four years of Whig rule. Washington became "a seething mass of importunity," as one historian described it, as hordes of office seekers arrived to press their claims. As he had tried to do with his cabinet, the new president aimed to distribute offices evenly among the factions while still maintaining a pro-Southern administration. To help him make decisions, Pierce turned to his cabinet and proceeded to allow them to make the tough choices. The new president followed more than he led, and the dominant personalities of the cabinet—Marcy, Davis, and Cushing—were soon directing more than just appointments. In addition, Pierce permitted department heads and agency chiefs to make their own decisions, and deferred to party leaders when it came to the states. For instance, he invited Senators George Jones and August Dodge of Iowa to make all the patronage decisions for their state. To fill the vacancy on the U.S. Supreme Court, he allowed the Southern majority on the bench to make their own choice; not surprisingly, a Southerner (and future Confederate commissioner), John Campbell of Alabama, was selected. This method of delegation seemed to go smoothly enough, as long as the posts and vacancies were filled with Southerners and regular Democrats.[43]

New York, as usual, was a political briar patch. Hards mobilized behind Dickinson, but failed to overcome Marcy's coalition and relationship with the president. In recognition of his long doughface career, as well as his role at Baltimore, Dickinson was offered the most prestigious, most lucrative post in the nation—collector of the Port of New York. He declined, however, claiming the appointment was beneath him and an insult to his honor. Instead, the collectorship was given to Greene Bronson, a Dickinson loyalist. As for his friend John Dix, Pierce tried to slip him into the assistant treasurer's position, but his appointment still met resistance in the Senate. Pennsylvania received a patronage boon with the selection of James Campbell as postmaster general. Out of all the cabinet members, the postmaster general had the most offices to distribute, and his decisions could have an enormous impact on state and local organizations. "His appointing power will reach every locality and make you stronger than you have ever been," Alfred Gilmore assured Buchanan. Buchanan, for his part, was "astonished" that he had not been selected for the State Department, let alone left out of the cabinet entirely. He was also angry that Pierce had gone back on his pledge not to appoint any former cabinet men. He waited in limbo to see what offer Pierce would make him; since he was denied the honor of a cabinet position, perhaps he would be offered a high-level foreign mission. Privately, Buchanan debated whether he would even accept such a second-rate appointment.[44]

In other states, Pierce also disappointed office seekers. In New Hampshire, he infuriated Burke when he permitted patronage to go to Burke's Concord enemies. In Indiana, the popular Wright faction received the spoils, enraging Bright. But in Illinois, Pierce wisely allowed Douglas to manage his own affairs, perhaps in consolation for being ignored during cabinet formation. Though Douglas was relatively content with Illinois patronage, however, he failed to get foreign appointments for his friends.[45]

Indeed, diplomacy seemed to be the one area where Pierce took an interest. He intended to distract the nation from the domestic slavery controversies by focusing on foreign policy and territorial acquisition. To accomplish this, Pierce sent a variety of Young America expansionists overseas to the various foreign missions. The newly created mission to Central America was offered to Southern expansionist John Slidell, and George Sanders, the reckless editor who was eager to foment revolutions in Europe, was appointed consul to London. The missions to Great Britain, France, and Spain were top priority, given Pierce's agenda of expansion into the Caribbean. The latter three were offered to the quixotic Pierre Soulé of Louisiana, who would prove a disastrous choice. John Y. Mason of Virginia was sent to France, since Southerners had vetoed Dix's appointment to that post. And the Mission to Great Britain was assigned to Buchanan. The decision was a wise one: Buchanan had previously served as secretary of state and thus had diplomatic experience, it was the top foreign post and therefore would assuage Buchanan's bruised ego, and it would get Pierce's leading rival out of the country. Though eager for recognition, Buchanan was not thrilled with the offer. "I have not the least desire to go abroad as a foreign minister," he wrote to Representative J. Glancy Jones. He did not want to be removed from his base of operations in Wheatland and give up control of his state organization, nor did he relish the idea of Marcy as his superior.[46]

Factions and Frustration

In the end, the major product of Pierce's patronage decisions was dissatisfaction. Only five months into the administration, Pennsylvania Democrat Francis Grund could declare, "I am clearly, fully and unequivocally an opponent of Genl Pierce's administration." It was clear to many that trying to please everyone had left no one satisfied. Even before Pierce's term began, Marcy confessed that he had low expectations. "Too much is expected of it—too many hope to be provided for," he wrote of the incoming administration. By recognizing Softs and coalitionists in some states, particularly New York and Indiana, he had angered Democratic regulars. "Those who deserted the standard of this party in 1848 and who have done what they could to ruin its prospects since are to be rewarded and honored for defeating the party in at that time," fumed one Democrat. "A more suicidal, wicked & blind policy could not have been formed by any set of men," agreed New York financier August Belmont with disgust. Democrats simply refused to tolerate any recognition of or negotiation with antislavery men, and Pierce was expected to punish dissidents, despite the fact that their votes had aided in his nomination and election. In the eyes of Democrats North and South, there was no gray area between 100 percent loyalty to the pro-Southern party agenda and treasonous abolitionism. The attacks on men like John Dix made that abundantly clear.[47]

Thus, as his administration began, Pierce faced an already hardened, determined opposition from Hards dismayed by his apparent poor judgment. Dickinson and Bright, in particular, mobilized their factions against him and sought to drive him further to the right. "Revenge has become quite fashionable among the disappointed candidates of the Dem. party," remarked Arch Campbell to Marcy. Dickinson continued to thwart party harmony in New York. He believed he deserved to be secretary of state and was angry that the Soft Marcy was chosen for the cabinet over a Hard. He worked tirelessly to disturb party unity, damage Marcy's reputation, and achieve a reshuffling of the cabinet. To broaden their attacks on the new administration, New York Hards teamed up with the disgruntled Burke clan in New Hampshire and called on the aid of their slave state compatriots.[48]

Within the state, Dickinson refused to acknowledge the Soft-Barnburner alliance as legitimate and sought to sink Governor Seymour's agenda. To placate the Hards and show sympathy with their hatred for the antislavery movement, Pierce had appointed first Dickinson, then Greene Bronson to the collectorship. Bronson proved to be *too* Hard, however, and refused to cooperate with the state organization controlled by Marcy and Seymour. This created a major "embarrassment" for the administration, and the secretary of state was forced to attend to New York squabbling rather than international diplomacy. By the September 1853 state convention, the New York Democracy had once again split between intractable Hards, reluctant Softs, and the majority Barnburners who were no longer interested in aiding the proslavery administration. Hards created an "explosion," according to John Forney, when they nominated their own ticket and read Softs and Barnburners out of the party. "The democratic party in this state is entirely broken up, without affording at present the least prospect of ever being united," wrote W. H. Tracy of Buffalo. When representatives from the rival factions met with the president, Pierce expressed his anger at their pettiness and sided with Marcy, declaring Hards the bolters.[49]

Pierce's betrayal was too much for Dickinson, and he declared open rebellion in the Empire State. Collector Bronson proclaimed his opposition to the administration and, knowing the Hards had full Southern support, dared the president to punish them. Marcy hurried to Albany, investigated the situation, and reported to Pierce—not surprisingly—that Bronson needed to be removed. "I went zealously for his decapitation," Marcy explained to Seymour. Bronson was ordered to recognize all factions of the party in his distribution of offices, but Bronson was adamant. On October 13, he wrote to Secretary Guthrie that he and the Hards, the true Democrats, would not be dictated to by the "free soil" Pierce administration. In Congress, Hards Francis Cutting and Mike Walsh joined in the attacks on Pierce, aiming to punish him for his poor judgment. It was truly a disaster for the new president.[50]

While the administration was "fast falling" into "disrepute," according to Marcy, Hards hoped to gain control of the state organization, purge it of antislavery sentiment, and achieve Marcy's removal from the cabinet. Though he favored their proslavery principles, Pierce refused to relent. In addition, he replaced Collector Bronson with Soft Heman Redfield, a naval officer and Marcy man. This did not improve matters, and at the state convention in November, the split deepened, resulting in antislavery Democrats finally abandoning the party once and for all. "The hards," wrote Marcy to Seymour, "are now discovered to be what sagacious men knew they were even before this bolt at Syracuse—enemies to the administration. Soon after the Cabinet was formed, they connived the plan of breaking it up, and getting one to suit their purposes."

This dramatic new split in New York had immediate national implications. The tenuous unity of 1852 that had resulted in Democratic victories was now shattered. Pierce's young administration appeared weak, vacillating, and incompetent. Democrats across the country criticized Pierce for getting involved in state affairs, especially on the side of the Softs. "The feeling of dissatisfaction at the course pursued by the administration in New York politics was general, I may say universal throughout the country," Slidell wrote to Buchanan. The split made defeat at the November state elections inevitable, and, considering the impressive growth of the antislavery movement, the future of the Empire State was far from certain. Equally important, Pierce's decision to take sides against the Hards wrought frustration and suspicion in the slave states. Was Pierce the man they had expected? Had the South made a terrible mistake permitting his nomination and election? "The position of the Administration on the New York question, gives us great trouble in the South," wrote Cave Johnson to Buchanan. "We thought Pierce to be sound on all the questions & through his influence mainly expected the question connected with slavery in the North to have been quieted but Dickinson & Bronson &c are not less true & have ever been so."[51]

Working closely with Dickinson was Burke of New Hampshire, previously Pierce's friend and promoter. Burke had aimed for the U.S. Senate when he took command of the Pierce movement back in 1851, and he resented the installation of Atherton in that chamber, as well as the favoritism shown toward Burke's Concord enemies. Moreover, Burke felt that Pierce's appointment of Softs and former Free Soilers was a betrayal of the pledges Burke had made on his behalf at the Baltimore convention. When Pierce ignored Burke entirely after his election, Burke declared open war on Pierce's "Concord Clique." At the June 9, 1853, Democratic state convention, Burke marshaled the opponents of the clique and gained control of the proceedings. He was made president of the meeting and chairman of the Committee on Resolutions, which he used to produce a series of resolutions condemning the administration. This caught the attention of anti-Pierce men throughout the region. "I have been intending for sometime to write and express to you," wrote one admirer, "my respect for the bold and open stand you have taken in regard to the appointments made by the present administration." The battle spread to the press, and Democratic newspapers attacked each other and the administration. When Burke and his *State Capitol Reporter* charged the administration with corruption and abolitionism, Pierce authorized the *Washington Union*, under the direction of Alfred Nicholson of Tennessee, to publish "villainous libel" against Burke's character and career, essentially removing him from party leadership. This left Burke no choice but to reach out to men like Dickinson and Francis Grund, who were now entirely focused on bringing down Pierce. "*Fight it out*," encouraged Dickinson to his new friend in the Granite State.[52]

Grund was a newcomer to the struggle in Pennsylvania. As a Protestant German, he had led the party's efforts to woo immigrant voters during the presidential election. But by the summer of 1853, disappointed with his failure to achieve appointment, he had turned against Pierce, and joined forces with Cameron and Brodhead. Buchanan's defeat at Baltimore and his banishment to England meant that the regular Democratic organization in the Keystone State was weakened. Combined with the ever-growing antislavery movement and the general outrage over Pierce's proslavery agenda, Pennsylvania was in real danger of moving out of Democratic ranks. As soon as Buchanan sailed for London, his lieutenants, especially Governor Bigler, came under attack and his party machine was threatened. Cameron and Brodhead led the challengers, and the addition of Grund brought along a key voting bloc. Buchanan could only watch from afar as the chaos of New York spread south into Pennsylvania. "We have now *no leader* in Pennsylvania, it will require a great effort to prevent Cameron from carrying all before him," worried Forney. Another dynamic at play in the Keystone State was religious bigotry, as Pierce's appointment of Catholic James Campbell to the cabinet stoked smoldering nativist fears. The idea of Papists being installed in post offices across the country was too much for some, and they gladly joined with the antislavery men in the anti-Pierce, anti-Buchanan movement.[53]

Affairs were no better in the Hoosier State. Though Bright had delayed the rush for Pierce at the Baltimore convention by holding firm for Joseph Lane, then Cass, he still expected to control Indiana's patronage and be offered a cabinet post. When he was denied both, then witnessed the patronage given to his rivals, Bright seethed with anger. "The administration of 'franklin pierce' is being understood and appreciated," he wrote coyly to close friend and Washington banker William Corcoran. In the Senate, Bright took the lead of the anti-administration forces, and, in April 1853, led nine Democrats in giving the congressional printing contract to Beverly Tucker, editor of the recently established anti-Pierce *Washington Sentinel*, rather than Pierce's choice of Robert Armstrong and the *Washington Union*. Later, he introduced a bill that would require the president to submit to the Senate his nomination for assistant secretary of the treasury, a direct attack on Pierce's authority and a not-so-subtle message about Pierce's choice for that office, John Dix.

As the months progressed, and Pierce appeared to favor Softs like Wright, Bright's hatred grew, and his vendetta became personal. In June 1853, he vowed to John Breckinridge of Kentucky that he would wrest control of the Indiana Democracy from Wright "or die trying." Such reactions to Pierce's patronage decisions reveal a startling strain of hypocrisy in Bright. He had spent his career attacking and punishing any who would dare challenge a Democratic administration, but here he was in 1853 leading the charge against Democrat Franklin Pierce. "I never for one moment, dreamed of such a thing," Bright confessed in January 1854; "I would not know how to go about opposing a democratic principle or a *sound* Democrat that was an honest & qualified." This indicates that Bright, now largely divested of his power within his state, would stop at nothing to destroy those he blamed for his downfall. Moreover, like his fellow slave owners, Bright became increasingly protective of Southern power and the expansion of slavery. With his Indiana machine rejected by voters and a formidable antislavery movement sweeping the North, Bright was getting desperate and dangerous. He began to lay plans that would ensure the survival of the Slave Power and lead to the defeat of his enemies, even if it destroyed his beloved Democratic Party.[54]

Key to Bright's plan was the advancement of the thirty-one-year-old Kentucky slave owner John Breckinridge, a favorite among doughfaces. If Bright could secure Breckinridge's rise to party leadership and national office, he would have a protégé in a position to right the wrongs of the Pierce administration. A veteran of the Mexican War, a two-term member of the U.S. House of Representatives, and a Southern slave owner, Breckinridge was poised for party advancement. The two became close in 1852, when Breckinridge invited Senator Bright to campaign with him in the Bluegrass State, and Bright, in turn, invited Breckinridge to join him across the border in Indiana. Bright's hatred of Pierce brought him closer still to his young friend, especially when Breckinridge attacked Pierce in Breckinridge's reelection campaign.

To ensure his friend's success, Bright put him in contact with banker William Corcoran, who offered advice, support, and, most important, money. Next, Bright introduced Breckinridge to other Northern Democratic leaders, such as Richardson of Illinois and George Jones of Iowa. "If I can do anything for [you] I would be glad to do it," Richardson penned to Breckinridge. "You have my prayers for your success." Breckinridge's rising-star status brought him the attention of the administration, and some have suspected that he successfully pressured Pierce to appoint the unpredictable George Sanders to the consulship at London. Breckinridge, noted one Democrat, was "one of the shrewdest politicians in America." Bright continued to mentor the Kentuckian and groom him for advancement. He repeatedly secured financial assistance for him from Corcoran and offered advice and encouragement at every turn. "Your friends, in every direction, are watching your progress with great interest," he wrote in a typical letter to Breckinridge. By the time the new Thirty-Third Congress was ready to convene, Breckinridge was considered a leading contender for Speaker.[55]

President Peirce doubtless understood the forces now arrayed against him, namely, mounting Southern suspicion and mobilized Northern opposition, both from antislavery activists and battle-hardened doughfaces. He perceived that his administration was off to a bad start. Observed Pennsylvania representative J. Glancy Jones: "Pierce, poor fellow, has no hold on the nation; he is the accidental head of an organization, without any cohesive power, individually or upon principle . . . no one fears him no one feels much interest in his personal welfare." "He is the 'de jure' not the 'de facto' head of the party," added disgruntled Slidell. Pierce's only hope was to rally the nation (and the party) around an aggressive foreign policy, anticipating that going head to head with Britain, France, Spain, and Mexico over territory and maritime rights would unite disputing factions and keep the Democrats in ascendancy. To atone for the sins of his first months in office, Pierce would have to pursue a solidly pro-Southern, unassailably proslavery course, and he would have to rely on the strength of his cabinet to carry his measures into effect.[56]

CHAPTER 4

"Pandora's Box"

Northern Democrats in Command

With the Hards openly hostile in key Northern states, party bosses suspicious in the South, and antislavery men across the board in adamant opposition, President Franklin Pierce faced a herculean task in his effort to craft a domestic and diplomatic program that would please the Slave Power and distract Americans from divisions over slavery. He owed his nomination and election to the South, yet if he hoped for continuing support from that section, he would have to somehow bring about an expansion of slavery.

The key to the Pierce agenda was thus an activist foreign policy based on unbridled nationalism and territorial acquisition. Indeed, in his inaugural he had announced that he would not shrink from "timid forebodings of evil from expansion" and vowed to acquire "certain possessions not within our jurisdiction." This had been an early goal, and he had selected men as his chief advisers who were well qualified for the task: William Marcy at State had overseen the invasion of Mexico as Polk's secretary of war; Jefferson Davis at War was a martinet, an aggressive expansionist, and a hero of the Mexican War; and James Buchanan in England had been Polk's secretary of state and was eager to acquire Cuba and assert U.S. dominance in the Caribbean. The foreign posts, too, were stocked with proslavery expansionists: John Y. Mason of Virginia in France; Pierre Soulé of Louisiana in Spain; George Sanders of New York in London; John L. O'Sullivan (coiner of the phrase "manifest destiny") in Lisbon; and James Gadsden of South Carolina in Mexico. Moreover, the Pierce administration's public call for expansion unleashed a flood of private military operations, ushering in a golden era of "filibustering." In a variety of high-profile instances, Pierce and his cabinet either openly sanctioned illegal expeditions into foreign countries or failed to take sufficient steps to prevent them.[1]

Foreign Policy

Not all endeavors, though, would involve swashbuckling conquests. In fact, Pierce's first diplomatic effort was conducted rather covertly and had immediate domestic implications. While Buchanan, Sanders, Soulé, and Mason were to see to the United States' varied interests on a grand scale, James Gadsden had a special, specific mission. The acerbic South Carolina railroad promoter had been handpicked by Davis to acquire more Mexican land. Though seemingly an innocuous mission, the objective was purely proslavery. Pierce, Davis, and Gadsden aimed to purchase a chunk of northern Mexico in order to ensure a southern route for the first transcontinental railroad. Such a path would bring people and money to the slave states and territories of the Southwest, thus depriving competing lines to the north of such potential growth. It was imperative that Gadsden complete his mission quickly and quietly, so as not to alert Northern businessmen and antislavery activists.

In October 1853, Gadsden reported to Pierce, Davis, and Marcy that Mexican president Antonio Lopez de Santa Anna was in dire financial straits and open to negotiations. Marcy secretly sent land speculator Christopher Ward of Pennsylvania down to meet Gadsden with instructions to offer fifty million dollars for the land and railroad rights. Cash-strapped Santa Anna was happy to oblige, and accepted fifteen million dollars for thirty-nine million acres and U.S. right of transit across the Isthmus of Tehuantepec. The Treaty of Mesilla was signed in January 1854, but Pierce was disappointed; he had wanted much more and had hoped the fifty million dollars would be used to full effect. On February 10, the president reluctantly submitted the treaty to the Senate, and the United States acquired what is now southern New Mexico and Arizona. Although a significant diplomatic victory, Pierce's plans for a southern railroad were not to materialize.[2]

Another area of interest for Pierce and his cabinet was the Caribbean, especially that elusive prize Cuba. Spanish, slave-owning Cuba had been coveted by proslavery administrations since Thomas Jefferson and was a major goal of Democrats in the 1850s. Southerners hoped to make at least one slave state out of the island, which would increase their electoral power and permit the growth of their "peculiar institution." Previous efforts had failed, and Spain maintained stubborn possession. Rather than negotiate with Cuban officials, the Pierce administration had to work with the Spanish government in Madrid, through official channels, resulting in what Pierce considered "irritating and vexatious delays." Great Britain and France were also part of the equation, as they were determined to prevent further territorial gains by the United States. Achieving acquiescence from London and Paris were the tasks of Buchanan and Mason, respectively. Leading the negotiations in Madrid was the flamboyant, unbalanced Soulé. The swarthy former French national was militantly proslavery and exceedingly reckless, and his vocal support for revolution in both Cuba and Spain made him anathema to the royal court. He engaged in duels, disobeyed diplomatic instructions, and plotted with dissidents to overthrow the Spanish government; he even shot the French minister to Madrid in a quarrel over a woman. In short, his "hyperthyroid personality and his penchant for pyrotechnics," notes David Potter, hampered diplomacy and offended Spanish officials. Marcy begged Pierce to replace Soulé, but Pierce was unwilling to discipline the popular Southern expansionist.[3]

Perhaps knowing that diplomatic negotiations would fail, Pierce gave his blessing to the efforts of General John A. Quitman, who was working with a Cuban junto on a plan to conquer the island. Such private enterprises of conquest were known as "filibustering," and their perpetrators "filibusters." Though they violated a variety of international treaties, as well as the U.S. Neutrality Act of 1818, filibustering was a popular means of acquiring more territory without the inconvenience of legality. Quitman, for his part, was an experienced filibuster with friends in high places, including Secretary of War Davis and Attorney General Cushing. A New York transplant to Mississippi, he had risen to become that state's governor, as well as a member of Congress. He was also enormously wealthy, fanatically proslavery, and an ardent Southern nationalist. As for Cuba, he had been involved in invasion schemes since at least 1850 and was waiting for a friendly administration. In the summer of 1853, Quitman received word of administration support and set his plans into motion. When the Spanish government threatened to free the slaves on the island to prevent annexation to the United States, pressure mounted for Quitman to act fast, before the South could lose its potential prize. We must start a revolt in Cuba and seize control, declared doughfaced Pennsylvania editor John Forney, "before every slave is set free."[4]

Headquartered in New Orleans, Quitman assembled a private armada, receiving money and men from across the South. To aid the Quitman expedition, Pierce appointed Quitman intimate Alexander Clayton Consul at Havana and informed Congress that so-called Spanish outrages on American ships demanded action. On April 3, 1854, Marcy authorized Soulé to offer up to $130 million for the island. If this could not be arranged, then Soulé was to work toward detaching Cuba from Spain by other means (instigating rebellion on the island so that Quitman would have an easy conquest). With Europe on the verge of the Crimean War, the time seemed right for Democrats to seize the island. "We are on the eve of a great issue with Cuba," wrote Georgia Whig-turned-Democrat Alexander Stephens. "England and France have set their heads against the policy of that island towards us. We must and will have it." Soulé's antics in Madrid only enflamed the situation, creating much "mischief," according to Democratic financier August Belmont, and putting the Spanish court on guard. Instead of respectfully offering to purchase Cuba, Soulé obnoxiously gave the Spanish government an ultimatum and demanded relinquishment of the island within forty-eight hours.[5]

With Spain awake to his plans, and Americans embroiled in a crisis over slavery in Kansas, Pierce decided to proceed more cautiously. At first, Pierce, Cushing, and Marcy had been willing to violate international treaties and permit the seizure of foreign territory, but now they thought it wise to abide by the law and prevent a potential diplomatic and domestic crisis over Cuba. The administration backed away from the Quitman expedition and put a new minister on a ship to Spain. But this did not mean that Democrats would suddenly agree to give up their dreams of a Caribbean empire. "The Administration is vacillating about Cuba," penned Stephens. "They are not worth shucks." When the Democratic members of the Senate Foreign Relations Committee announced they would support motions to change neutrality laws to help filibusters, Pierce called them to the Executive Mansion and convinced them to pursue diplomacy before invasion. The very next day, May 31, 1854, the president issued a proclamation stating that the administration would prosecute all violations of neutrality laws, a declaration understood to be aimed at Quitman and his supporters.[6]

Nevertheless, Democrats were unwilling to give up hopes for Cuba. Pierce had every intention of continuing negotiations with Spain and cleaning up the mess caused by Soulé. He wanted to send a commission to Madrid to secure purchase of the island, but Northern outrage over the expansion of slavery sapped support for such an initiative. When Congress refused to appropriate money for the commission, Pierce had to find a new route to acquisition. Buchanan provided the map. He and Belmont, agent of the Rothschilds and leading New York banker, had been scheming for quite some time to work behind the scenes, outside of regular diplomatic channels, to use financiers and bondholders to pressure the Spanish throne to give up Cuba. With this in mind, Buchanan had Belmont appointed to The Hague, where he would have access to Spanish royalty residing in the Netherlands. In London, Buchanan wrote to Secretary Marcy that the plan would work and that Britain would not object. With Spain once again threatening the abolition of slavery in Cuba, Pierce gave Buchanan the green light to implement his plan with Belmont.[7]

While Quitman readied his expedition, Buchanan's secretary of legation in London, New York Democrat and wild-eyed expansionist Daniel Sickles, met at length with Pierce at the Executive Mansion and gave him the details of the Buchanan-Belmont plan. Pierce, eager for a less public course, was enthusiastic. "The President had a great deal to say about Cuba and Spanish politics," Sickles penned to Buchanan. "He is determined to refer the subject, with large powers, to yourself, Mr. Mason, & Mr. Soulé." In August 1854, after Pierce withdrew his support for Quitman, the president directed Marcy to allow Soulé (still in Madrid), Mason, and Buchanan to meet in Paris to discuss and implement the scheme. Marcy's August 16 instructions to the three diplomats reveal the work of Buchanan: "I am directed by the President to suggest to you a particular step from which he anticipates much advantage to the negotiations with which you are charged on the subject of Cuba," wrote the secretary. "It is not believed that Great Britain would interpose in any hostile sense to prevent the cession of Cuba to the United States. . . . But the government of France is less responsible to the public opinion than that of Great Britain . . . and it has already indicated a tendency to intermeddle in the affairs of the American Continent. These and other considerations which will readily occur to you, suggest that much may be done at London and Paris either to promote directly the great object in view, or at least to clear the way impediments to its successful consummation." The "great object in view" was the acquisition of Cuba, now to be achieved through the secret Buchanan-Belmont plan. But Sickles was a gossip, and news of the plot spread quickly. Moreover, Buchanan did not want to work with Mason and Soulé; the plan was intended for only Buchanan and Belmont.

Nevertheless, Soulé arranged a meeting at Ostend, Belgium, for the second week of October 1854. The diplomats and their aids congregated at that town but, after only three days of discussion, were forced to flee to Aachen (or Aix-la-Chapelle), Prussia, to escape reporters. They met for another six days in Prussia, with Soulé taking notes. In brief, the final report stated the following: (1) Cuba rightfully belonged to the United States; (2) the United States would acquire it by any means, including paying up to $120 million, which they imagined would be a boon to the failing Spanish economy; and (3) if Spain refused to sell, the United States would be entirely justified in taking Cuba by force. The report also revealed its proslavery motives by expressing fears that Cuba would be "Africanized" (abolition would occur) before the United States could seize it. The document, once leaked to the press, became known incorrectly as the "Ostend Manifesto."[8]

The meeting and manifesto caused another crisis for the Pierce administration. Marcy had intended the memo to be exclusively for State Department consideration, but, mismanaged by his diplomats, it became a global declaration of American imperialism. "The President is much annoyed as I am myself at the unfortunate notoriety given to the conference," Marcy wrote to Buchanan. One phrase, in particular, caught the attention of readers: "But if Spain, deaf to the voice of her own interest, and actuated by stubborn pride and a false sense of honor, should refuse to sell Cuba to the United States, then the question will arise, what ought to be the course of the American Government under such circumstances? . . . We shall be justified in wresting it from Spain." "Wresting" Cuba from Spain was exactly what Democrats had been trying to do, whether through filibustering or behind-the-scenes machinations. Combined with the proslavery statements in the document, there was no concealing Pierce administration objectives and methods.[9]

Northern voters were once again outraged by another manifestation of the Slave Power. There seemed to be no end to the greed of the slave states and their willingness to embarrass the nation in attempts to "wrest" new slave territories from Spain, Mexico, and others. Pierce did what he could to contain the situation, but the damage had been done. Documents (edited to protect the administration) were submitted to Congress, and Soulé was finally removed. His replacement was dutiful doughface and ardent expansionist Augustus Dodge of Iowa. Like Soulé, Marcy instructed Dodge to continue negotiations with Spain over Cuba and commerce, hoping that a change in personalities would affect a breakthrough. Even when Spain refused to discuss Cuba, though, Pierce was relentless with offers and incentives; he was determined to achieve the long-held Democratic goal of Cuba as an American slave state.[10]

The Pierce administration's proslavery missteps continued in Latin America, where filibuster William Walker attempted to create a slave-owning republic and prepare it for admission to the Union. Taking advantage of domestic upheaval in Nicaragua, young Walker, a slight and slim Tennessee doctor turned lawyer turned journalist turned filibuster with piercing gray eyes, led fifty-six men in a successful overthrow of the Nicaraguan government in May 1855, prompting the British government to dispatch a mighty squadron of warships to the area. With diplomatic crisis looming, Marcy was caught between enthusiastic Southern support for Walker and war with Britain. Within five months, "the Grey-Eyed Man of Destiny," as Walker came to be known, had established his own regime and made himself "complete master of the country." He received support from Southerners applauding his boldness and from businessmen seeking an isthmian transit route. Money, men, and supplies poured in from the United States, with administration officials observing. Privately, Marcy called Walker "a pirate and an assassin" but did not take action against him.[11]

As expected, Pierce extended recognition to the Walker regime, but because of Northern outrage against the expansion of slavery, he was forced withdraw it soon thereafter. But when Walker moved to undermine the Nicaraguan designs of the American steamboat magnate Cornelius Vanderbilt, and Vanderbilt asked the administration to punish him, Pierce sided with Walker and left the young conqueror in power. Recruitment in U.S. cities proceeded with only sporadic federal interference, and men and supplies made their way to Nicaragua. The Southern bosses, meanwhile, instructed Pierce to restore recognition and send a symbolic message to the British about American resolve. The president obeyed and in May 1856 restored official recognition of the Walker regime. The next month, as planned, Walker declared himself president and announced the reinstitution of slavery in Nicaragua. Pierce was pleased, hoping that his decision in favor of Walker and slavery would secure his renomination at the upcoming national convention in Cincinnati.[12]

Pierce hoped, too, that a strictly proslavery domestic policy would earn him Southern plaudits and enough support for another term. He had filled his cabinet with Southerners and doughfaces, intending to cut back internal improvements and energetically enforce the Fugitive Slave Law of 1850, despite Northern resistance. To carry out his domestic agenda, Pierce turned to Attorney General Cushing, who became the man most responsible for the enforcement of the Fugitive Slave Act. Cushing made it clear that the entire power of the government, including the armed forces, would be put to use in the enforcement of the Fugitive Slave Law. Cushing had been a Democrat for only a short time, however, and many Democrats North and South distrusted him.[13]

Caleb Cushing

Born to prominent New England jurists and businessmen in 1800, Caleb Cushing grew up in the sleepy harbor of Newburyport, Massachusetts. While fellow doughfaces like Bright early developed confidence and aggressiveness, Cushing was an apprehensive, insecure youth, prone to hypochondria. He was an introspective intellectual, and though he excelled in his studies at Harvard, he was a loner and unpopular. In the summer of 1821, after completing college, he entered the legal profession and earned local prominence as a man of learning and oratory. Although fascinated by the Haitian Revolution (1791–1804), Cushing quickly developed conservative, pro-Southern beliefs and took a dim view of blacks and emancipation. In November 1824, he was elected representative to the state General Court from Newburyport, largely

FIGURE 5. Attorney General Caleb Cushing, Massachusetts (Library of Congress)

because of his falsely claiming that he was a "workingman." By the fall of the following year, he was elected to the state senate and began taking an active role in regional Federalist politics. In 1826, he received the Federalist nomination for the U.S. House of Representatives, but was defeated in the election. Voters, it seemed, were disgusted by his "reach after popularity and preferment," as the *New Hampshire Statesman and Concord Register* phrased it.[14]

In the early 1830s, he grew bitter and frustrated at his inability to achieve elected office, and when his wife died in 1832, he turned inward, becoming even more self-absorbed and cold. Politically and philosophically, his evolving principles took him away from the Federalist/Whig camp and toward the Democrats. He developed a strong sense of Anglo-Saxon superiority and white racial supremacy and formulated theories about the nature of black baseness; he began to defend Southern slavery, attack abolitionism, and champion territorial expansion. His switch to the Democracy, though, was long and tortured. Throughout the 1830s, he remained loyal to the Whig organization, particularly to Daniel Webster. In November 1835, Cushing finally won election to the House and pursued a strict Whig course on financial matters. His advocacy of Indian removal and aggressive territorial expansion, as well as his rants about white supremacy, however, brought him steps closer to the Democrats, but the switch did not come until the administration of Virginian John Tyler.[15]

When Whig president William Harrison died thirty days into his term, vice president Tyler assumed the office, becoming known as "His Accidency." War erupted among Whigs, as Tyler was a slave-owning Democrat who had been placed on the Whig ticket of 1840 to attract Southern votes. In the battle for party leadership, Cushing sided with Tyler over "Harry of the West," Henry Clay. Cushing found himself a loner once again, as his defense of Tyler alienated his Whig colleagues. A doughfaced New Englander could prove useful to the new president, though, and it did not take long for Cushing to join Tyler's group of intimates and advisers. When his own constituents turned against him, Cushing lashed out at them as ill informed and wrongheaded. To avoid embarrassing defeat, he decided not to run for reelection. Now free from Whig restraints and with one foot in the Democracy, he made a distinct turn against antislavery in the House and supported the Democratic proslavery agenda. To reward his loyalty (and because elective office was now out of the question), Tyler appointed Cushing to a special mission to China where he negotiated the Treaty of Wanghia, which was a milestone in Chinese-American relations.[16]

When Cushing returned to the United States, he was firmly in Democratic ranks. He energetically supported Polk's invasion of Mexico and, at forty-six years old, rushed to join the fight. Driven by his sense of racial superiority and dreams of adventure, he raised a Massachusetts regiment and rose to brigadier general of the First Massachusetts Volunteers. But, like Franklin Pierce, he was a poor commander and an inept leader. He also shared Pierce's experience of an embarrassing wound (a double fracture of the ankle, incurred when he slipped on some stones in Matamoros), which made him the butt of jokes back home. Few voters could take Cushing the general seriously, as the idea of the long-winded lecturer playing the martinet was comical.[17]

By the time he returned to Massachusetts, the Democratic Party in that state was nearly defunct because of the antislavery movement. With no prospect of political advancement, Cushing withdrew from public life, giving periodic orations on Southern rights and American righteousness. During the crises of 1850, he defended the Fugitive Slave Law and became convinced more than ever that the antislavery movement aimed to destroy the country. "Niggerism is our present phrency," he warned his listeners; "socialism will come next." He had become a man utterly fearful of change. His conservatism ran deep indeed, and he saw danger in *any* reform, including women's rights, which he believed would lead to social calamity. "He was regarded by the people of Massachusetts as a man without moral convictions and as utterly subservient to the slave power," observed contemporary George F. Hoar. To get this "unprincipled politician," as the *Boston Daily Atlas* labeled him, out of politics, Governor George Boutwell (a former Democrat who had yet to make his way into the opposition) appointed him to the Massachusetts Supreme Court in 1852, where he served until his promotion to the cabinet. At the 1852 Baltimore convention, he played a key role in Virginia's decision to switch to Pierce, which earned him "Handsome Frank's" appreciation. Pierce chose Cushing for attorney general partly for his role at Baltimore, but mostly to please the South and reward a lonely New England doughface.[18]

As attorney general, Cushing vastly expanded the powers of the office in order to thoroughly enforce the Fugitive Slave Law. He rivaled Davis and Marcy for prominence in the cabinet, and Pierce consulted him regularly about the legality of his proslavery agenda. His primary focus became an undisguised war against the antislavery movement. "If there be any purpose more fixed than another in the mind of the President and those with whom he is accustomed to consult," Cushing stated in a published letter, "it is that the dangerous element of Abolitionism, under whatever guise or form it may present itself, shall be crushed out." Such declarations undoubtedly drove more Northerners out of the party, but certainly won Southern approval.

On hearing Cushing's announcement, the militia of Quincy, Florida, for instance, fired a volley in Cushing's honor.[19]

In order to more effectively use federal agents to aid in the hunting and kidnapping of purported slaves, Cushing had to expand federal authority and create new guidelines for federal action. Immediately, he asserted that alleged runaways could be caught and returned from both free states and territories, that habeas corpus would not be recognized when someone was arrested in a duly obtained warrant, and that legal expenses incurred by slave catchers would be paid by the federal government. In March 1854, Cushing ruled that any citizen had the right to capture alleged fugitives, and in areas where no federal commissioners had been appointed, blacks could be captured without due process of law. When, in May of that year, U.S. marshals were opposed by local residents in counties across the North, Cushing granted the marshals the power to summon a posse. He also empowered them to call on *any* military person, whether militia, sailors, soldiers, or officers, to achieve capture. When violence erupted in Boston over the detention of Anthony Burns in May and June 1854, Pierce and Cushing gave the local marshals authority to carry out the Fugitive Slave Law by any means necessary. The president and his attorney general vowed to pay all expenses (estimated at one hundred thousand dollars), ordered marines and an artillery company to the scene, and even had a navy cutter waiting off shore to whisk Burns away to Virginia.[20]

The sum of Cushing's actions and rulings was that the capture of black Americans and the sanctity of slavery surpassed all other considerations of personal liberty and governmental restraint. Previous conservative notions of limited government espoused by Democrats were swept aside in the rush to please the South. Cushing did not expand the law, but rather devoted more resources to its enforcement, and his dim view of black humanity and legal status foreshadowed the *Dred Scott* decision of 1857. Such diligence permitted the kidnap and capture of hundreds of black Americans in the free states. In fact, more purported runaways were returned to slavery from federal tribunals during the Pierce administration than at any other time during the 1850s. This further endeared Pierce and Cushing to Democrats, although it guaranteed that Northern voters would not return to the party as they had in 1852. Southerners, announced Cave Johnson, have "unwavering confidence in his [Pierce's] fidelity." Indeed, by 1856, the Pierce administration's actions had even convinced leading fire-eater William Yancey of Alabama to return to Democratic ranks.[21]

But while Southerners cheered, Northerners jeered. Personally and politically, Cushing was deeply disliked in the free states. Biographer John Belohlavek admits Cushing was "the most unpopular man in New England," and contemporary Francis Grund of Pennsylvania called him "the most dangerous man in the country," since he had at his disposal a host of federal marshals and agents. Most Northerners may have loathed the pro-slavery Pierce administration, but Southerners applauded its diligence; and since the South controlled the party, Pierce had reason to be pleased. As Henry Wise's son recalled years later, "It is true that he [Pierce] was often reproached for leaning too strongly to his Southern supporters, but why should he not have done so? They nominated him and supported him in opposition to a Southern man. They were unquestionably the dominant influence in the national politics of that day. All that he was he owed to them." Indeed, Pierce labored to placate Southern demands and make the federal government a more active agent in the protection and expansion of slavery. If his administration were measured solely by his intentions, it might be labeled a modest success (with the exception of the failure to acquire Cuba). But administrations are never judged by intentions alone, and in the case of the Pierce presidency the defining event of his term was largely a surprise.[22]

Popular Sovereignty

That surprise came in the form of a bill in Congress aimed to permit the expansion of slavery into the then-free western territories. Such bills were not new, nor were bills to organize territories and put them on the path to admission. It was the *process* of organization that suddenly became the chief source of sectional animosity in 1854. The Missouri Compromise of 1820 had created an imaginary line across the continent (at 36° 30′) and had stipulated that territories located above the line would prohibit slavery, while those below would permit it. Though it was labeled a "compromise" and sanctified in the minds of politicians eager to avoid sectionalism, neither section was placated: Northerners balked at the federal guarantee of slavery below the line, and Southerners were outraged at the outright restriction on slavery north of the line. Southerners labeled the line unconstitutional and spent the next thirty years scheming to erase it. Meanwhile, settlement of the western territories proceeded rapidly (especially after the Mexican Cession in 1848 and the discovery of gold in California later that year), and the question of slavery in the territories reached a head by 1850. A second "compromise" that year had soothed Southerners, but it had not settled the issue of the 1820 Line or how territories should be organized.

The U.S. Constitution was vague on congressional power, and Democrats had always argued that the federal government had little to no authority over slavery and the territories. Until the 1850s, new states had been admitted through a multistage process of meeting population requirements, organizing as a "territory," and creating appropriate state governments and state constitutions, then applying for statehood, which would be granted by Congress. Between 1820 and 1850, new states had been either clearly above the line and thus free (such as Iowa in 1846), or below and slave (as Florida in 1845). The admission of free California, which straddled the line, was achieved, as recounted in chapter 1, through extraordinary legislative efforts and massive concessions to the South.

The admission of California in 1850 was a political truce, not a solution to the territorial problem. When bills for transcontinental railroads calling for the organization of the remaining territories appeared in Congress in 1853–1854, crisis erupted anew. Northern Democrats were once again caught between their proslavery party and their free state constituents, and they searched desperately for a way to serve the Slave Power without further enraging Northern voters. Between 1847 and 1853, they developed a remarkably ambiguous policy, labeled "popular sovereignty," aimed at achieving the spread of slavery by allowing territorial settlers to vote on whether or not to allow slavery in each territory.

Popular sovereignty was a new version of the old denial of congressional authority championed by John Calhoun. What Northern Democrats did not mention was *when* that voting would occur, leaving the answer to the public imagination. Would voting take place at the start of territorial status, before slavery could be firmly established? Or would it occur later at statehood, when slavery would already be a powerful reality? Northerners, Democrats hoped, would imagine the former, while Southerners could expect the latter. Popular sovereignty thus offered, as historian David Potter notes dryly, "tactical attractiveness." Northern Democrats could sell the same policy to two opposing groups, but what Northern Democrats and Southerners knew was that slavery would spread regardless of when voting occurred. The implementation of "popular sovereignty" would thus mean the effective nullification of the 1820 Line, since voting would be the new determinant. All that was required to put popular sovereignty into effect was the repeal of the Missouri Compromise.[23]

Southerners were eager for repeal, and though they controlled both the Democratic Party and the federal government, they still needed the traditional obedience of Northern Democrats (especially in the House of Representatives) to accomplish it. Pierce's administration was proslavery enough, but Congress had yet to endorse the spread of slavery into the territories, and many Southerners were still chafing at having to accept a free

California. Thus, pressure mounted for Northern Democrats to put popular sovereignty into action and begin the process of repealing the 1820 Line. Reliable Daniel Dickinson of New York was the first to enunciate what would become "popular sovereignty." On December 13, 1847, as debate raged over the fate of the lands wrested from Mexico, Senator Dickinson introduced a resolution denying congressional authority over slavery in the territories, leaving the issue to the settlers. Neither in territorial acquisition nor organization "can any conditions be constitutionally imposed," he asserted, conveniently forgetting that the Northwest Ordinance of 1787 had forbidden slavery in the Northwest Territory. Dickinson's resolution caused a stir, inspiring Senator Cass to stand in Dickinson's defense, perhaps recognizing the political potency of Dickinson's ideas. Instead of outright endorsing popular sovereignty, however, Cass exhibited his characteristic fear of commitment and urged the chamber to drop the issue. "It is exceedingly unwise," intoned Cass, "at this stage of the prosecution of the war, in either branch of Congress to say what we will do, or what we will not do."[24]

But Dickinson's resolution garnered little attention. It was not news that the New Yorker was a doughface, and his resolution was quickly overshadowed by debates over the Wilmot Proviso. It would take the likes of elder statesman Cass to turn Dickinson's vague resolution and Calhounite interpretation of the Constitution into a legitimate policy option. Aiming for the 1848 Democratic presidential nomination, Cass was desperate to convince the South of his loyalty, while simultaneously courting free state voters. Popular sovereignty seemed to be just the vehicle he needed.

In a much-publicized December 1847 campaign letter to Tennessee editor and friend Alfred Nicholson, Cass gave popular sovereignty its most public expression. Published at the behest of Dickinson and Henry Foote of Mississippi, Cass's Nicholson letter provided the ideological framework of popular sovereignty and gave Cass a clear platform on which to run for president. After warning of the dangers of the Wilmot Proviso, he stated simply, "I am opposed to the exercise of any jurisdiction by Congress over this matter [slavery], and I am in favor of leaving to the people of any territory which may be hereafter acquired, the right to regulate it for themselves under the general principles of the Constitution." Like Dickinson, he believed that any regulation of slavery, including the Northwest Ordinance of 1787 and the 1820 Line, were unconstitutional and unenforceable. And like Dickinson, he left the process of popular sovereignty entirely ambiguous. It was "a clever piece of work," according to a Cass biographer, which won Cass the Democratic nomination.[25]

But Cass did not win the presidency, and popular sovereignty languished in the intraparty feuds of 1850–1852. Northern voters were hardly fooled by the policy, and it became inextricably linked to Cass's 1848 defeat. "This new doctrine of Gen. Cass put forth possibly to please the faithful in certain parts of the country," exclaimed Representative Charles Hudson of Massachusetts, "is entirely superficial, and will not bear the test of examination for a moment." Regardless, the "Cass doctrine," as some labeled it, persisted throughout the early 1850s, as Cass continued to rail against the evils of the Wilmot Proviso and the "unlimited political jurisdiction" of Congress. It was Stephen Douglas of Illinois, however, who revived the scheme and created legislation to put it into effect. Since Dickinson had been denied reelection, and the aging, obese Cass became increasingly inactive, Douglas was left as its primary promoter.[26]

Believing he could achieve another legislative triumph and make himself the unchallenged hero of the Democracy, Douglas labored to put popular sovereignty into practice. Northern voters, he was convinced, would accept the policy as effectively antislavery, while the South would realize its merits as an instrument of slavery expansion. Likewise, he hoped to achieve a long-held goal of a transcontinental railroad, which would originate in Chicago, where Douglas would profit from land sales. To accomplish this, he would have to organize the land west of Iowa, which would garner both western enthusiasm and Southern frustration. The Southern grandees, it should be recalled, demanded a southern rail route, and Gadsden's successful purchase of northern Mexican lands was a means to that end. If Douglas intended to pursue a Northern route out of Chicago, he would have to ensure the spread of slavery north of the 1820 Line to win the South's support for his plan.[27]

To distance himself from the failures of Dickinson and Cass, Douglas called his version of popular sovereignty "non-intervention," in reference to Congressional activity in the territories. His would not be a bold denial of congressional authority, as Calhoun, Dickinson, and Cass had preferred, but rather a pledge against interfering with the rights of settlers. "I think the safest and wisest position for Illinois democrats in regard to slavery is this," wrote Douglas's lieutenant John McClernand, "non-interference in the Territories for the reason that the people of the territory ought to be left to judge for themselves."[28] Furthermore, Douglas was eager to redeem himself in Southern eyes after orchestrating the admission of a free California. Though himself a plantation and slave owner, with about 150 slaves on 3,000 acres along the Pearl River in Lawrence County, Mississippi, Douglas was still viewed with suspicion by Southerners. His ability to organize the territories and pioneer a transcontinental railroad, not to mention advance to the presidency, hinged on Southern support, which could only be assured through a repeal of the 1820 Line. "My plan now," he confided to one Tennessean, "is to bring forward a Bill to repeal altogether that Compromise [of 1820]." If he could achieve repeal, Douglas believed, his dreams of western development and the presidency would finally be realized.[29]

It was not only the mantle of popular sovereignty that fell upon Douglas's willing shoulders but also national party leadership—President Pierce was focused on foreign affairs, Buchanan was out of the country, Marcy was occupied with diplomacy and perpetual Empire State drama, and Cass was growing more lethargic by the month. Moreover, Douglas's defeat at the Baltimore convention did not diminish his standing within the party, but rather it "added greatly to his fame," according to Alexander Stephens, because it had proved that the young senator was a formidable force. Douglas, intent on both western development and the spread of slavery, made territorial organization the centerpiece of his legislative agenda. Long frustrated by Congressional foot-dragging, Douglas saw promise in the new Thirty-Third Congress, which convened in December 1853. Democrats had majorities in both houses, and the South was in firm control. Indeed, Southern strength in the Senate seemed impenetrable, especially after Jesse Bright arranged an increase in committee membership from five to six, with a corresponding increase in the Democratic majority on each committee. In addition, when Vice President William King died on April 18, 1853, the proslavery firebrand David Atchison of Missouri assumed the presidency of the Senate. If Douglas wanted to repeal the 1820 Line, now was his chance.[30]

Yet it was not Douglas who introduced the first bill of the Thirty-Third Congress to organize the Nebraska Territory. That honor fell to Augustus Dodge of Iowa, a stern, balding fellow of old Dutch stock. Born in January 1812 in St. Genevieve, Missouri (then the Territory of Louisiana), Dodge grew up in a slave-owning family and was raised by a "mammy" named Leah. His father Henry was a local politician of note, who, in the 1840s, rose to the Senate from the new state of Wisconsin. After fighting in the Indian wars of the 1830s, Augustus married and moved to Burlington in the Iowa Territory, which had separated from Wisconsin in 1838. There, thanks to his father's growing political influence, Dodge was appointed one of two land registers, a lucrative post. The office brought young Dodge political clout as well, and in October 1840 he was elected territorial delegate to Congress, where he focused his attention on internal improvements, western development, and Iowa boundary disputes.

In December 1846, Iowa entered the Union as a state, and thirty-five-year-old Dodge became the political boss of the new state's Democratic

Party. Charges of a "Dodge Dynasty," however, thwarted his plans for election to the U.S. Senate until the following year, when he became the first
senator born west of the Mississippi River (remarkably, his father Henry had
taken his seat in the Senate in June 1848, and the two men found themselves
side by side in Congress).[31] In the debates of 1850, Dodge sparred with antislavery men and moved distinctly into doughface ranks, becoming an avid
defender of slavery and the South. He supported the Fugitive Slave Law,
worked energetically to enforce it, and bragged about Iowa's record of returning escaped slaves. "He was not the friend of the blacks," explains biographer Louis Pelzer in something of an understatement. By the mid-1850s,
Dodge had emerged as a leading doughface and a rabid white supremacist.
In the new Thirty-Third Congress, Dodge presided over the critical Committee on Public Lands, ready to once again tackle territorial issues.[32]

The Kansas-Nebraska Act

On December 14, 1853, Dodge introduced a bill to organize the Nebraska
Territory, which was sent to Douglas's Committee on Territories. From the
start, the bill encountered Southern opposition because it did not repeal the
1820 Line and thus would prohibit the spread of slavery in the newly organized district. Senate President Pro Tempore Atchison led the opposition
to Dodge's bill. He and his "F Street Mess" housemates, Andrew Butler of
South Carolina and James Mason and Robert Hunter of Virginia, made it
clear to Douglas that no bill would receive their blessing that did not explicitly repeal the Line. Douglas, on the other hand, had hoped to push through
a bill that would achieve popular sovereignty without an explicit repeal. He
took Dodge's bill and went back to the drawing board, creating, alone at his
Washington residence, without consulting the president or his committee, a
new bill that employed the language of popular sovereignty but still lacked
explicit repeal.[33] The revised measure, not surprisingly, was still not to the
liking of the Southern bosses. On January 16, Archibald Dixon of Kentucky
rose in the Senate and added an amendment to Douglas's bill repealing the
1820 Line. It was a line in the sand for all to see—if Northern Democrats
wanted western development, transcontinental railroads, and the presidency,
they had to accept the unfettered spread of slavery. Douglas accepted the
amendment, but his Northern colleagues immediately saw danger, since supporting a repeal of the Line would be political suicide in the free states.[34]

Thus far the most prominent Northern Democrat, President Pierce, had
played no role in this legislative showdown. He was understandably reluctant
to get involved in such an explosive issue. If Southerners were not appeased,

the Democratic Party would fracture and threats of secession would be hurled anew; and if slavery was permitted to spread above the Line, free state voters would leave the party in droves. Before deciding on a course of action, the president consulted Cass and Marcy. Both men cautioned him to stay out of the impending congressional fight on the issue. Pierce decided to ignore their advice and instead convene a meeting of his full cabinet to agree on a public course of action. On Saturday, January 21, they drafted an alternative to repeal. Instead of congressional action, Pierce looked to a judicial solution (meaning that a federal court would rule on congressional power over slavery in the territories), hoping that passing the buck to the courts would prevent a sectional and partisan crisis.

The plan was sent to Douglas and the F Street Mess that night via Representative John Breckinridge of Kentucky, who had close ties to both doughfaces and the Southern bosses. Not surprisingly, the bosses rejected Pierce's plan and instructed Douglas to proceed with outright repeal. Douglas wanted a commitment of support from the president, however, knowing that he would need executive assistance to push the measure through the unruly House of Representatives. Since he was scheduled to introduce a newly revised Nebraska bill (including repeal) on Monday, time was short for the Illinois senator. The next day, Sunday, January 22, Douglas, Atchison, Davis, Mason, Hunter, Breckinridge, and Philip Phillips of Alabama met Pierce in the White House library. Confronted by Douglas and the united party leadership, Pierce relented and agreed to support repeal of the Line.[35]

But Douglas and the Southern bosses demanded more from Pierce than his consent—they demanded a written pledge. Douglas handed the president a pen and paper and instructed him to write the fateful words in his own hand: the 1820 Line, Pierce scrawled, "was superseded by the principles of the legislation of 1850, commonly called the compromise measures and is hereby declared inoperative and void." Those words, penned by the president, made the bill an official administration measure and a test of party loyalty. Every Northern Democrat would have to rally to the expansion of slavery or be read out of the party. "The administration is committed to the Nebraska Bill & will stand by it at all hazards," announced Douglas days later. "The principle of this Bill will form the test of Parties, & the only alternative is either to stand with the Democracy or to rally under Seward, John Van Buren & co." The die was cast, and the bill instantly became a dividing line between moderate Northern Democrats who saw disaster in repealing the Line, and the zealous doughfaces who were eager to cleanse the party of its remaining antislavery elements. When the news reached Marcy, he expressed disappointment, knowing that the measure would cripple the Democratic

Party in the free states. "I am . . . unwilling to do an act which will look like making the support of that bill a test of democracy," wrote the New Yorker with concern. "Though I go for it myself I would not withhold my confidence from those who honestly oppose it. I sincerely wish the measure had not been thrown upon us." He even considered resigning, but decided against it.[36]

On Monday, January 23, as scheduled, Senator Douglas introduced the new bill, now called the Kansas-Nebraska Act, creating two territories, repealing the 1820 Line, and providing for effective implementation of the Fugitive Slave Law. Douglas was confident, and Southerners were pleased. Wary that the bill would get buried beneath other pending legislation, though, Douglas pleaded for swift action. "I find it generally to be the case with my territorial bills," he explained to the Senate, "that if I do not get them acted on early in the session, they are crowded over by other business." To add to his concerns, Douglas also found himself confronted with a well-organized, well-publicized Northern opposition. Five former Democrats and a former Whig had banded together to publish "The Appeal of the Independent Democrats," a condemnation of the Kansas-Nebraska Act and the Slave Power. The authors, Senators Salmon Chase, Charles Sumner, and Joshua Giddings and Representatives Edward Wade, Gerrit Smith, and Alexander De Witt, indicted Douglas for putting his personal ambition ahead of national interest, morality, and his free state constituents.[37]

The "Appeal" was a powerful, impassioned proclamation against the expansion of slavery and Southern power, and it unleashed antislavery fury against the Kansas-Nebraska bill. Regardless, the Southern leadership remained unfazed and held Northern Democrats in line. On January 30, Douglas took the floor to support the controversial bill. The Senate galleries were packed to capacity, and so many Representatives came to witness the spectacle that the House was left without quorum. Infuriated by the "Appeal" and struggling to maintain his composure, Douglas proceeded to defend popular sovereignty and argue against the 1820 Line. The "great principle of self-government," Douglas declared, "[is] that the people should be allowed to decide the questions of their domestic institutions for themselves, subject only to such limitations and restrictions as are imposed by the Constitution of the United States." The 1820 Line prevented Americans from making decisions about their own property, he reasoned, and thus was unconstitutional and "inoperative." As for the "Appeal," it was an abolitionist trick by dangerous Sabbath-breakers, plotters, and slanderers—"a combination of men who have assembled in secret caucus upon the Sabbath day, to arraign my conduct and belie my character" (a disingenuous accusation, given that

Douglas himself had caucused secretly on the Sabbath.) If you believe in the principles of self-government found in the U.S. Constitution, he exhorted his listeners, then you *must* support the Kansas-Nebraska bill. The bill not only best represented the principles of the Constitution, Douglas concluded, but was the only hope for saving the country from fanatics.[38]

Douglas's speech set the tone of debate among Northern Democratic defenders of the bill, focusing on the virtues of "non-intervention" and the iniquities of antislavery activism. As free state opposition grew, however, opponents were emboldened, and Northern Democrats increasingly found it difficult to maintain party discipline. When a Senate discussion of Wisconsin railroads deteriorated into a debate on the Kansas-Nebraska bill, Douglas lost his temper and, after a nasty exchange with Chase, was ruled out of order. It became apparent to most observers, particularly those in the South who saw Northern Democrats scrambling for cover, that reaction to the repeal of the Line would cross the partisan divide. As in 1850, Southern Democrats and Whigs began to set aside party labels in favor of their shared interest in slavery. On the morning of February 3, a bipartisan caucus of Southern Senators "unanimously determined to carry the bill as it stands on the slavery issue," according to Senator Robert Toombs, who attended. The South would advance united, while Northerners remained divided and disorganized.[39]

Fear grew on both sides. Threats of secession were heard once again in the halls of Congress, and Northern Democrats were as frantic as ever to save their party and themselves. If the bill did not pass, promised Toombs, "dissolution will surely come, and that speedily." The "Nebraska question," Marcy wrote to New York's governor Horatio Seymour, was a "Pandora's box" for the Northern Democracy and the nation. The Senate bill was debated almost daily in February, with its defenders hammering home their view of limited congressional power and the treason of antislavery sentiment. Slavery was a positive good, they insisted; ownership of slaves was a Constitutional right that must be protected at all costs.[40]

In oratory, Northern Democrats presented a paradoxical combination of fierce protection of personal liberties and fanatical defense of slavery. Augustus Dodge and Richard Brodhead, in particular, offered forceful proslavery arguments aimed at advancing Southern power and aiding the Kansas-Nebraska bill. Dodge took the floor on February 25 and announced, after a grandiloquent homage to Douglas and Cass, that the bill was "the noblest tribute which has ever yet been offered by the Congress of the United States to the sovereignty of the people" and that the "Missouri restriction of 1820" and the Wilmot Proviso were "dangerous assumptions of power." But the thrust of the oration was an expression of Dodge's deep concern for the

minority rights of slave owners in the territories (a glimpse of an antidemocratic ideology that would come fully to fruition during the Lecompton
Constitution debates of 1857–1858) and his virulent sense of white racial
superiority. Slavery, he argued, was a blessing that rescued Africans from "a
dark and heathenish land; from the worship of filthy reptiles; from cannibal-
ism." Africans were meant to be slaves, and it was by the "decrees of God"
that they were brought to "a land of gospel light." The villains in the present
crisis were not slave owners, slave traders, and slave catchers, but abolitionists,
who intended to put wild African savages in the arms of innocent white
girls to produce "mixed offspring" and racial chaos. Sounding strikingly
like a Southerner, Dodge added that abolitionist propaganda actually hurt
the slaves, as it forced kindly masters to restrict their freedoms. Antislavery
sentiment, in all its forms, he concluded, was a sin against God, truth, and
the United States.[41]

Three days later, Brodhead formally abandoned his dissident status in the
Northern Democracy and threw his lot with the proslavery party majority. "It is said that the passage or defeat of this bill will raise a storm at the
North which will overwhelm every man who supports it," he stated. "Sir,
I am somewhat accustomed to these storms, and they have no terrors for
me. I was a member of the House of Representatives when . . . the Wilmot
proviso was brought forward, and nearly every State north of Mason and
Dixon's line, including my own, instructed their members for it. I was one
of the few who took ground against it." Opponents of the bill, he added,
were lazy and godless sectionalists who held no influence in the Democratic
Party. Indeed, it was the Northern Whigs who had the most to fear from
the bill, as Democrats were united in protecting slavery. "The fact . . . that
every Whig from the North is against the bill, and a large majority of the
Democrats for it, is quite significant," he concluded. "If it does not work
a dissolution of the Whig party, it proves that the Democratic party is the
great national party of principle, with the Constitution for a text-book."
Northern Democrats, Dodge and Brodhead made clear, would do their duty
to the Slave Power.[42]

As debate dragged on, however, Douglas began to worry that his bill would
be talked to death, even by its supporters. Defenses of Southern power were
repeated ad nauseam, and orations became tedious, unproductive exercises in
rhetoric. But despite endless delays, Douglas remained optimistic. He knew
the South controlled Congress and that all the bombast would mean little
when the final vote arrived. "We shall pass the Nebraska Bill in both Houses
by decisive majorities," he wrote to Illinois editor Charles Lanphier, "& the
party will then be stronger than ever, for it will be united upon principle."[43]

Douglas's confidence and patience were soon rewarded. At 1:00 p.m. on Friday, March 3, the Senate approved the bill's third reading, the final procedural requirement before a formal vote on enactment. Cass announced his enthusiastic support one last time and called for yeas and nays. Douglas then took the floor, at 11:30 p.m., to make the closing speech. For three hours, the Illinois senator lashed out at antislavery opponents and denied being a tool of the Slave Power. He scarcely touched on the issues of Southern power and slavery expansion, choosing instead to defend his personal character and career. At 4:50 a.m., after seventeen hours of continuous debate, and with Dodge presiding, the question was called. The South was triumphant once again, and the bill passed by a vote of thirty-seven to fourteen. Fourteen Northern Democrats and all Southern Democrats voted in favor, while all Northern Whigs opposed it. As in 1850, Northern Democrats had provided the crucial, deciding votes, choosing to side with the united South. Douglas, Cass, Brodhead, Dodge of Iowa, Jones of Iowa, Pettit of Indiana, Shields of Illinois, Toucey of Connecticut, and Thomson of New Jersey all cast their votes in favor of repealing the 1820 Line and opening the northwestern territories to slavery. Noticeably absent was Bright of Indiana, who by now was renowned for skipping controversial votes. The exhausted senators now looked to the House of Representatives to see if Northern Democratic discipline would hold in that unpredictable body.[44]

Democrats were far less certain of the result in the House, where the fast-growing population of the free states made the chamber more likely to reject Southern domination. Democrats were in the majority, but the antislavery revolt was more extensive, and there was no guarantee, even with executive pressure, that Northern Democrats would not yield to the demands of their constituents. Ninety-two of the 158 Democrats were from free states and would be in serious trouble with their constituents if they supported repeal of the Line. But the Democratic leadership remained confident nonetheless. "It will pass the House by at least a majority of 20—perhaps by twice that number," Pierce wrote to Buchanan. Even Marcy, who was always more cautious and realistic in his political assessments, admitted the likelihood of Southern victory. "In the House, there will be a vigorous opposition to it, but those who pretend to skill in counting noses say that it will pass there also." Much depended on the power and ruthlessness of the House Democratic leadership.[45]

Douglas's man in the lower chamber was William "Old Dick" Richardson, who had worked closely with Douglas and the Southern bosses in the Compromise of 1850. Douglas and Richardson were longtime friends, and Richardson was perhaps Douglas's closest confidant. "A large man with a full head of black hair, a Roman nose, shaggy brows, and swarthy complexion," according to a biographer, Richardson was a force to be reckoned with in the House of Representatives. Like Bright in the Senate, Richardson was a Kentuckian in a free state and a man of aggressive tendencies. Born, raised, and educated in the Bluegrass State, he moved to Shelbyville, Illinois, in 1831 after passing the bar. In central Illinois, he immersed himself in a community of like-minded Kentucky settlers, sheltered from the growing antislavery sentiment around them. When his Kentucky community moved west to the promising mercantile center of Rushville, Richardson followed and continued his law practice. He soon entered politics, served as state's attorney,

FIGURE 6.　Representative William Richardson, Illinois (Library of Congress)

rode the circuit, and achieved election to the General Assembly in 1836. He developed a reputation for physical aggressiveness, no-nonsense politics, and a willingness to defy the voters. When some internal improvement projects came before the Assembly, for instance, he ignored the wishes of his mercantile constituents and opposed the bill. "In his mannerism he was unguardedly rough, almost crude at times," explains another biographer; "to his enemies he was unmerciful." His time on the circuit, though, earned him statewide prominence, and in 1838 he was elected to the Illinois State Senate.[46]

As Richardson rose in the ranks of the Illinois Democratic Party, he revealed a ferocious hostility to antislavery sentiment, often equating abolitionism with treason. This stance could be difficult for Illinois voters to swallow. He failed to win election as lieutenant governor and U.S. representative and was forced to return to the General Assembly. When Polk invaded Mexico, Richardson joined his fellow Democrats in calling for continental conquest and rushed to take part in the adventure, eventually leading a regiment of Illinois volunteers into battle. Richardson's big break came in 1847 when Douglas moved from the House to the Senate, creating a vacancy in the lower chamber. A special election was held, and Richardson was "hand picked by Douglas" to succeed him, according to Douglas scholar Robert Johannsen.

Once in the House, Richardson was surprisingly inactive. He became known more for his liquor consumption and incessant tobacco chewing than for legislative activity. Regardless, his votes placed him squarely in doughface ranks, and his fidelity to the Slave Power impressed the Southern bosses. He enthusiastically supported the war against Mexico, opposed the Wilmot Proviso, and advocated for the spread of slavery. He worked closely with Southerners to achieve passage of proslavery measures and participated in that fateful February 19, 1850, meeting between Northern Democrats and Southern Whigs that helped produce the "Compromise" of that year. His association with Douglas was so close that the *Quincy Herald* quipped in September 1850 that "every time Douglas takes snuff, Richardson sneezes," and Abraham Lincoln recalled in April 1860 that Richardson "sticks to Judge Douglas through thick and thin—never deserted him, and never will." When it came time for House Democrats to push through the Kansas-Nebraska bill in 1854, Richardson was unquestionably its floor manager.[47]

Richardson did not wait for the bill to work its way through the Senate and reported it out of his Committee on Territories on January 31, 1854, just eight days after Douglas did the same in the upper chamber. Freshman Representative William English of Indiana, a member of the committee, gained the floor to make a statement. Much to the surprise of Democrats, young English, the protégé of Jesse Bright, declared his opposition to the bill and admitted he voted against it in committee. I am not afraid to "face the music," he explained. "I am a native of a free State, and have no love for the institution of slavery. I regard it as an injury to the State where it exists, and if it were proposed to introduce it where I reside I would resist it to the last extremity." His problem with the bill was not only that it would permit the spread of slavery but also that it would prevent territorial residents from voting on the issue until statehood, when slavery would already be firmly established. "I am opposed to admitting slavery into these Territories, and placing it out of the reach of the people until the formation of a State government. And it is, in part, because the bill is not explicit on this head, that I dislike it." English boldly confronted the lie of popular sovereignty, openly avowing on the floor of the House that it was a recipe for the expansion of slavery. To remedy the situation, he proposed an amendment striking out the section of the bill voiding the 1820 Line.[48]

This was heresy indeed! Richardson had not expected an oration from his committee subordinate, let alone a challenge to the bill. Several times he tried to cut English short and bring him into line, but English persisted and offered his amendment. Democrats were shocked, and Bright was infuriated. Suspecting that his young acolyte had fallen under the influence of radicals, Bright penned a note to him. "You will pardon me for venturing to advise you not *at this time* to go into caucus or make any committals against the Bills now before Congress for the organization for Territories," wrote Bright with all the politeness he could muster. "I *know* the value of the advice I give; go to your *friends* for council always, not your *enemies*." To deal with this mini-revolt, Richardson took the floor, moved to refer the bill to his committee, and acted to prevent debate. There was "considerable excitement," according to the *Congressional Globe*, as Richardson refused to yield the floor and allow a response to English's amendment. Richardson's motion blocked consideration of English's amendment, and the Hoosier representative, recognizing his temporary defeat, announced he would introduce it again at a later date.[49]

Turmoil over English's amendment and Richardson's tactics caused business in the House to be halted until order was restored. "I do not know who has the floor, or what is going on, there is such noise and confusion in the Hall," yelled Elihu Washburne of Illinois from his seat. Eventually, the House, despite fierce opposition from the South, voted in favor of referring English's controversial amendment to the Committee of the Whole (all House members), where it would receive a more favorable hearing than in one of the Southern-controlled committees. Despite English's bold stand, though, Northern Democrats knew they could never defeat the repeal of the Line. In order to stay in office, Northern Democrats would have to fashion an interpretation of popular sovereignty that emphasized extending democracy to the territories, rather than expanding slavery. This, they prayed, would make repeal more palatable to their constituents.[50]

Failure to get English's amendment sent to Richardson's proslavery Committee on Territories was only the first of several setbacks for Democrats. English's revolt opened the floodgates to antislavery petitions and motions of all kinds. On March 21, Richardson failed again to get the bill sent to his committee, and it remained on the schedule for the Committee of the Whole, albeit buried under fifty other measures. "The fate of the Nebraska & Kansas bill in the House is doubtful," remarked John Slidell. At this point, Pierce entered the fray. Keenly aware of the bill's importance to both the South and his administration, Pierce used the full force of the executive throughout March and April to compel reluctant Northern Democrats into line. "The result is doubtful," reported a correspondent to Buchanan, "but the President and Douglas are hand in hand. . . . Whether it is to be a Waterloo to either of them remains to be seen."[51]

Pierce did everything he could to aid the bill. He instructed party editors to defend it and attack its opponents; he met and strategized with key congressmen; and, most important, he used party patronage to full effect. Anyone who challenged the bill would be denied patronage requests, their friends and relatives removed from office, and their reelection contested. But Pierce was also a liability. New York Hards, still sore at the president's patronage decisions, were as eager as ever to punish Pierce and the united Democracy. Led by dour Francis Cutting, Hards in the House fought Richardson for control of the Kansas-Nebraska bill. They supported the measure in principle, but wanted to see Richardson, Douglas, and Pierce squirm. It had been Cutting, in fact, who had thwarted Richardson's attempts to have the bill sent to the Committee on Territories and instead had it sent to the Committee of the Whole, where it would cause endless headaches. This created an almost comical alliance between antislavery men and their archenemies, the Hards. The Kansas-Nebraska bill, wrote Representative John Robbins, "has broken the Democrat ranks in the House, and knocked our men in all directions."[52]

Looks were deceiving, however, and Richardson and the Southern bosses were firmly in control. By early May, Richardson and Pierce had secured enough votes to bring the bill to the floor for debate. "Tomorrow I think we shall get the Nebraska bill up in committee," wrote Stephens in anticipation. "The contest will be hard and the vote close, but we have the count. . . . I feel a deep interest in the success of the measure as a Southern man." Indeed, final passage of the Kansas-Nebraska bill and the repeal of the 1820 Line would be a tremendous victory for the Slave Power, and would dramatically change the political landscape.

On May 4, Richardson's legislative and leadership skills were on full display when he deftly laid aside eighteen other measures, one after another, to get to the Kansas-Nebraska bill. Administration pressure yielded results, as last-minute converts, including the New York Hards who ultimately wanted repeal, gave Richardson the votes he needed to shepherd the bill through the queue. When the Illinoisan finally reached H.R. 236, he successfully substituted the Senate bill for the House version and scheduled debate for May 9, 1854.[53]

The opening speech was given by English, who, pressured by Bright, Pierce, and the party leadership, had since abandoned his opposition and come out in full support. Eyeing upcoming elections, English tried to paint popular sovereignty as a policy to spread democracy. He also tried to argue that even if the bill resulted in the spread of slavery, slave owners had no desire to go west anyway, and thus Northerners had nothing to fear. "The bill is just to all sections of the country," he concluded, somewhat befuddled. English's attempt to atone for his previous heresy pleased Democrats, but did not allay fears of an antislavery revolt. English's confused conversion, though, was symptomatic of the obstacles facing Democrats in the House. Northern Democrats like English might be cowed into submission, but would they be able to sell the bill to their constituents? Repeal of the 1820 Line and implementation of popular sovereignty would prove a Pyrrhic victory if the Northern Democracy went down to defeat at the polls.[54]

Though Richardson ran the show on the House floor, Douglas was in command behind the scenes and was in the lower chamber almost daily. The two Illinoisans needed all the help they could get to keep Northern Democrats like English in line. Moreover, Democrats were pressed for time, as the House was scheduled to begin consideration of a Pacific railroad bill on May 16. On the night of May 11–12, the bill's enemies forced the House into late night session, aiming to stall debate until it was time to take up the railroad bill. Representatives brought pillows and personal items into the chamber, preparing to sleep and work at their small desks. Opponents of the bill repeatedly defeated votes to adjourn, causing the session to drag into the wee hours of the morning. "We have had no vote on Nebraska yet. How long we shall be occupied with preliminary questions I cannot tell," wrote Stephens. "I am growing insubordinate, and losing my self-respect."

Many members resorted to alcohol to pass the time, some becoming quite drunk and belligerent, so much so that it became a problem unto itself. Large numbers of drunken, heavily armed, angry, exhausted Southerners, in particular, made for an explosive environment. Henry Edmundson of Virginia, for instance, tried to start a fight with Lewis Campbell of Ohio on the House floor. For thirty-six hours, debate continued without decision. In the end, antislavery men ultimately met defeat when the Democrats marshaled enough votes to postpone consideration of the railroad bill and bring debate on the Kansas-Nebraska bill to an end. Throughout, Richardson had been ruthless, earning comparison to a "slave driver" by the Northern press. His task was made the more difficult by the presence of "the Little Giant," who violated etiquette by haranguing and harassing representatives. When the House finally adjourned, representatives North and South were furious at the protracted, pointless session.[55]

Eight days later, Richardson rose to address the House in one of the final orations on the bill. He declared passage inevitable and focused attention on rights rather than slavery. "A proposition that secures equality to the States, and the rights under the Constitution to all the people, must ultimately triumph," he began. He then launched into a personal defense of his career in Congress, denying that he was a servant of the Slave Power but boasting of standing by the South upon "great questions." As for the bill's enemies, they were profoundly wrong about its origins, aims, and effects. "Opponents of the bill say the people will condemn us forever," Richardson expounded with authority. "I have heard the same sort of talk before. Why, they have told me some years ago here, that I might look for some green spot by the side of some gentle stream, where I might find my political grave. Sir, instead of that, they have found their political grave." Political death is what antislavery men deserved, especially those within the Democracy. "We shall pass the bill, settle a great principle, and so settle it that in all future time we can sustain it; the country will approve it, and these [antislavery] gentlemen, now so clamorous, will acquiesce."

Richardson concluded with an impassioned call for Democratic unity and a vehement rejection of antislavery sentiment. "Our danger, and our sole danger, consists in our division." He urged a purification of party ranks by the elimination of remaining antislavery Democrats. "I am glad to get rid of you," he declared to them with disdain. But for regular Northern Democrats, he had compassion and emotion. "Our fortunes are linked up with this bill," he insisted. Democrats must be united behind the measure and united at the polls to survive—any dissent or division would be fatal. "Fight it out, and fight it ever. Our safety consists in standing together." It was truly a remarkable speech, laying bare Northern Democratic desperation.[56]

The next two days saw high drama, as supporters and opponents of the bill united behind their banners and battled for their cause. Weapons were drawn by congressmen, arguments flared, and bloodshed seemed imminent. Southern slave owners would stop at nothing to pass the bill, and Northern Democrats, inspired by Richardson's warnings, rallied to their aid. On May 22, Richardson, acting with Stephens, won a significant victory when the House agreed to consider the Kansas-Nebraska bill without the nativist Clayton amendment, an addition proposed by Delaware Whig John Clayton that had excluded foreigners from the would-be territories and was aimed at undermining Democratic strength among immigrants. The hours that followed saw a furious round of delaying tactics, last-minute amendment attempts, and motions to adjourn, as opponents of the bill frantically tried to prevent a final vote. "I took the reins in my hand, applied whip and spur, and brought the 'wagon' out," recalled Stephens. With the aid of the determined Georgian, Richardson effectively parried all enemy thrusts, disciplined his Northern Democrats, and achieved a vote at 11:00 p.m. The result was a narrow Democratic victory, 113 to 100. The bill, slightly different from the Senate version, was quickly sent to the upper chamber, which promptly endorsed the House measure at 1:00 a.m. on May 26. Bright once again skipped the vote, leaving Douglas, Cass, Brodhead, Jones, and Thomson to provide the decisive Northern votes. Four days later, Pierce signed the bill, genuinely believing he had ended the slavery debate forever. He could not have been more mistaken.[57]

Much to the surprise of Pierce and other naive Northern Democrats, the Kansas-Nebraska Act unleashed a political firestorm of unprecedented ferocity that would soon lead to civil war. It was tremendously unpopular in the free states, and Northerners instantly recognized the duplicitous nature of popular sovereignty. Historian Nicole Etcheson has aptly labeled the act "the greatest attack on political liberties that nineteenth-century Americans had experienced." But that mattered not to doughfaces and Southerners, who were jubilant at the passage of the bill. The bill would accomplish their two main goals, regardless of Northern outrage: the unrestricted spread of slavery into the western territories and the cleansing of the Democratic Party of its antislavery elements. "Nebraska is over," wrote a relieved Forney to Buchanan. "You will read all about it. . . . The struggle has done us good. It has been like a . . . storm that clears up . . . and purifies the atmosphere." "*I am glad that the thing is over*, and I hope that the south will now be satisfied," added Senate Chaplain Henry Slicer. Southerners were just as pleased. Declared Stephens in reference to Northern opposition, "Let them howl."[58]

And howl they would. Northern Democrats had once again produced a significant legislative victory for the Slave Power. Southern control of the federal government and the Democratic Party continued to rest on the ever-shrinking Northern Democracy, and without the discipline and votes of Northern Democrats, the Southern bosses could never have achieved repeal of the 1820 Line. Douglas, Richardson, and Pierce were the men of the hour, the generals who rallied the troops and browbeat their Northern Democratic colleagues, like English, into obedience. Like the "Compromise" of 1850, however, the Kansas-Nebraska Act brought only misery to Northern Democrats. With their loyalty to the Slave Power now obvious to every voter, Northern Democrats would be cut down at the polls. The Northern Democracy would barely survive the 1854 elections and would be confronted by terrific challenges hardly anticipated.[59]

CHAPTER 5

"Leave Us of the North to Fight the Great Battle"

Party Punishments and Purges

The passage of the Kansas-Nebraska Act produced dramatic shifts in Northern public opinion and had dire consequences for the Northern Democracy. Free state voters were appalled at the bravado of the Slave Power and the blatant disregard by Democrats for Northern antislavery sentiment. A majority of Northerners suddenly became "anti-Nebraska," meaning opposed to the repeal of the 1820 Line and the spread of slavery into Kansas. And since the bill had been a product of the Democratic Party, anti-Nebraska quickly came to imply anti-Democratic. As the bill snaked its way through Congress, anti-Nebraska meetings and rallies were held across the North, and Northern Democrats were rightly held responsible by the voters. "Douglas was hung in effigy in Boston Common—and [Connecticut] Senator [Isaac] Toucey was burned in effigy in New London Con. for voting for the bill," reported John Robbins to James Buchanan in London. "We shall have a terrible time in the North before we are through," lamented Democratic editor John Forney.[1]

Indeed, most Northern Democrats had knowingly disregarded the wishes of their constituents to vote for the bill and should not have been surprised when public sentiment turned sharply against them. "Many who voted for it will never see those halls again," predicted one Indiana observer in March 1854. "The bill will not merely kill the men who vote for it. It will utterly defeat the democratic party in the North & West." Truer words were never spoken, as Northern Democrats would suffer punishing defeats at the polls. Moreover, many Northern Democrats fled their party when it became clear that free state voters opposed the Southern agenda. Even tried-and-true Democrats who had supported the "Compromise of 1850," the Fugitive Slave Law, and Pierce's proslavery expansionism found themselves seeking cover in new anti-Nebraska organizations, such as the Know-Nothings and Republicans. "Many of our best democrats had gone into the new organization[s]," George Houston recalled with dismay in August 1855, "and I regret to say that some in my opinion are likely to remain there."[2]

Before the Kansas-Nebraska bill was even reported out of committee, it had become a profoundly polarizing issue. The repeal of the 1820 Line not only allowed the spread of slavery, but would potentially create new slave states to augment the already formidable electoral power of the South. Opposition to the bill was immediate but was not energized until the publication of the "Appeal of the Independent Democrats" on January 24, 1854. The "Independent Democrats" may not have been Democrats themselves, but the "Appeal" was nonetheless aimed at Northern Democrats whose votes were critical. Taking their cue from the "Appeal," free state presses spared no ink condemning the Kansas-Nebraska bill. Across the North and West, antislavery activists rallied and mobilized, while in Congress antislavery members employed passionate pleas and parliamentary procedure to stop Douglas and the Slave Power. In addition, almost every Northern state legislature passed resolutions against the bill, sent messages to Congress, called for the repeal of the Fugitive Slave Law, and passed personal liberty laws designed to thwart the enforcement of the Fugitive Slave Law. The Northern backlash was so ferocious, in fact, that two new antislavery, anti-Democratic political parties sprang to life in 1854 and 1855.[3]

After the crippling defeats of 1852, the Whig Party was dealt a death blow by Kansas-Nebraska. Whigs had survived for a generation as the sole challengers to Democratic supremacy but had finally succumbed to internal divisions over slavery. Northern "Conscience" Whigs ceased to tolerate their Southern colleagues and sought to build new antislavery coalitions, and Southern Whigs slithered into Democratic ranks, where their proslavery principles found a more appropriate home. The dissolution of the Whigs left a considerable void in national politics, which a dizzying array of groups sought to fill. In the political chaos following Kansas-Nebraska, single-issue advocates, such as teetotalers and nativists, vied for national attention, hoping to forge new alliances that would implement their policies and bridge the divide over slavery. Eventually, disgruntled Whigs, temperance crusaders, angry nativists, and antislavery activists would coalesce into the new Republican

Party, but only after Northern Democrats purged their ranks of all remaining antislavery sentiment.[4]

The first new organized challenge to Democrats were the Know-Nothings, or the American Party. Dedicated to curtailing the political and social influence of immigrants, the Know-Nothings had their roots deep in American nativist (anti-immigrant) sentiment. From its earliest days, the United States had enjoyed robust immigration of western European Protestants, but in the 1840s and 1850s, new waves of immigrants, this time Catholics primarily from Ireland and Germany, created suspicion and fear among many "native" Americans. Catholics, some Americans believed, were minions of a monarchical, malevolent pope and were thus incapable of republican government. Catholic Irish and Germans also indulged in religious rituals and social celebrations that struck their Protestant neighbors as offensive.

Moreover, many of these new immigrants liked to drink, gather in grog shops, and violate the Sabbath with their carousing. Protestant "native" Americans came to see them as degraded, dirty, drunken criminals and ne'er-do-wells who were more likely to overthrow the government than do an honest day's work. Nativists blamed Catholic immigrants for everything from lower wages to pauperism to political corruption. The last, at least, had some validity, as both Democrats and Whigs shamelessly courted the immigrant vote in the 1852 presidential election. The Democrats, however, had perfected the skill, and Pierce's victory in the North owed a great deal to new immigrant voters. Even more disturbing to nativists were the corrupt political machines erected by Democrats to mobilize immigrants and dole out patronage. By the 1850s, nativists believed the United States stood on a precipice, and it was their duty to stem the tide of immigrants, curb their political power, and cleanse the country of Catholic filth-mongers and rum-bums.[5]

The nativist impulse first organized in the 1840s, in the form of semi-secret fraternal societies. By 1854, they had coalesced into a national organization called the Know-Nothings, because of their tight-lipped reply when questioned about their activities. As can be imagined, this was enormously frustrating to Democrats and Whigs alike, since both parties courted immigrants and found it impossible to uncover Know-Nothings in their ranks. "Have you heard of the new Political Combination called the 'Know nothings'?" queried one correspondent of Buchanan. "Their operations, in the few instances in which they have acted, were secret & sudden, and very successful. . . . These 'Know nothings' act in perfect concert, it would seem; but where they meet, or how they are organized, no one can tell." Democrats, though, had the most to fear. Northern Democratic strength had come to depend on the immigrant vote, and the Southern bosses still required a Northern wing to advance their agenda. An effective nativist party not only threatened to reduce the political power of immigrants (and hence erode the Northern Democratic base) but also could draw away Northern Democratic voters who harbored nativist feelings. In addition, Northern Know-Nothings were solidly antislavery and offered a home to free state voters sick of two-party squabbling. While the Whig Party imploded over slavery, the Know-Nothings arose as a substantial challenge to the Democrats.[6]

At the same time the Know-Nothings were making impressive gains, another antislavery, anti-Democratic organization was being forged. Many Northern Democrats who bolted their party in 1854 sought refuge with Northern Whigs and determined Free Soilers. The resulting antislavery, anti-Democratic coalition offered yet another option for frustrated Northern voters. In May 1854, after Kansas-Nebraska passed the House, thirty anti-Nebraska representatives from across the political spectrum gathered to discuss forming a new party dedicated to stopping the spread of slavery and limiting the Slave Power. Though they adopted the name Republican, they fell short of declaring a new party. Soon after, however, they met again and issued a formal address that was published on June 22. On July 6, antislavery men in Michigan held the first Republican Party convention and then went on to victory in the fall elections. Growth for the new party was slow and sporadic, especially since the Know-Nothings garnered so much attention, but progress was made as the issues of slavery and Southern power overcame disputes over temperance and immigration. Those who oppose the "rights of the South," wrote a frustrated Pennsylvania Democrat, have united under the name Republican. "This party will be combined of the whole Know nothing and Whig organizations of the North," he explained. Nevertheless, it would not be until the spring of 1856, after more Slave Power outrages, that Republicans would emerge as the primary threat to Democratic hegemony.[7]

1854 and 1855 Elections

To complicate matters, Whigs, Know-Nothings, and Republicans often worked together to defeat Democrats. Until the slavery issue drove all antislavery men into the Republican Party, fusion was the order of the day. In 1854 and 1855, "wild scenes of confusion and fusion," as William Marcy phrased it, reigned as Northern voters grappled with slavery, temperance, immigration, and party labels all at the same time. It was not clear before 1856 that Republicans would arise as the new rival to the Democracy, and Whigs and Know-Nothings vied for Northern votes. But despite the muddle, all three parties enjoyed common ground: they were determined to stop the spread of slavery, and they were eager to defeat Democrats. These two basic principles permitted fusion candidates and slates at all levels of governance. Especially at the local level, where partisan labels were less important than real-life issues such as schools, taxes, and public projects, fusion was enormously successful. Called Anti-Nebraska, Anti-Administration, Fusion, Independent, or People's Party, it did not really matter what the name was, as long as Democrats and the Slave Power were defeated. Facing this "combination of Know-Nothings, free soilers, abolitionism, and I may say niggerdom," as one Pennsylvanian saw it, was truly the Democrats' worst nightmare.[8]

To counter the threats from "niggerdom," Northern Democrats employed three arguments. First, the Kansas-Nebraska Act and the subsequent spread of slavery was a positive good. Second, all who opposed Kansas-Nebraska and the expansion of slavery were fanatics and traitors who wanted to destroy the country and inaugurate race war. And third, the Democratic Party was the only true national party, and thus a vote for the opposition was a vote against the United States.

Armed with this reasoning, Northern Democrats entered the 1854 and 1855 state elections ready to stand their political ground, as well as purge the party of any remaining antislavery members. Voting in August, Iowa was the first test of Democratic strength. As expected, Whigs joined with Free Soilers and former Democrats to wage war on the Democracy. All three Iowa Democrats in Congress had supported Kansas-Nebraska, including Senator Augustus Dodge, which allowed fusion forces to present a clear-cut choice to the voters between Free Soil and the Slave Power. The outcome was a surprise to no one. "Dodge stands not the least chance of a reelection," admitted Jesse Bright, observing from Indiana. With little fuss, antislavery candidate James Grimes was elected governor and the state legislature went solidly anti-Nebraska, which, in turn, meant Dodge's defeat by the young antislavery activist James Harlan. "Our Southern friends have regarded Iowa as their northern stronghold," wrote Grimes to editor James Pike. "I thank God it is conquered." Indeed, it was the first step to bringing down the Slave Power, and antislavery, anti-Democratic voters across the North looked to their own states to continue the trend.[9]

Widespread voter outrage was just as virulent in Indiana, where seven of ten Indiana Democrats had voted for the bill. Hoosier Democrats were flooded with angry letters from their constituents, many of which included outright accusations of deceit and dishonesty. "A man like you and old [Senator John] Pettit that will barefacedly and knowing sell the will of their constituents for I presume the prospect of licking some one of Frank Pierce['s] plates—ought to be sold in the south and there expiate their sins under the Slave Driver's lash," wrote an infuriated William Kennedy to Representative John Davis. "You well know that [Representative] Ed McGaughey's vote on the fugitive slave bill was what killed him and elected you," he continued, hardly able to contain his rage, "and knowing all this you would be so base as to unite with old Pettit and other Dough faces of the North and betray your constituents in your vote on the Missouri Compromise and Nebraska bill—but we may expect no better of such as Douglas and Pettit and all the Northern Doughfaces that Followed in their wake they have made themselves far beneath Judas he got thirty pieces of silver for betraying his lord and master but they have betrayed him in his ministry." Hoosiers wanted no part in the Slave Power plot to spread slavery, and their passionate pleas to their congressmen bore out their sincere sense of urgency.[10]

Meanwhile, Bright continued to battle Joseph Wright for control of Indiana Democrats. Those who opposed Kansas-Nebraska fell in line behind Wright, and those who supported it sustained Bright. But the party split was based on more than just legislation. Bright's tyrannical methods had alienated many Democrats, even those who agreed with his proslavery principles. He held the reigns of power in a tight grip and refused to allow anyone, especially his nemesis Wright, to take them from him. "Is this thing never to end? It would seem not," asked one observer. On May 25, 1854, Indiana Democrats convened at Indianapolis to decide on candidates and platforms. From the start, Bright was in control and rigged the meeting to prevent any antislavery resolutions. Anti-Nebraska Democrats were swiftly denounced as abolitionists and expelled from the party, leaving the Indiana Democracy purely proslavery and entirely under Bright's command. To follow through, Bright made support for Kansas-Nebraska a test of party loyalty, driving even more Democrats into the opposition.[11]

Bright was not alone, however, as Northern Democrats had been working for years to purge the party of antislavery members. In the months following the May convention, Indiana Democrats spoke proudly of opportunities to "clean away the rubbish" and reproduce the "good old undefiled democracy." "Cut off a thousand or two thousand heads if you please and give us firm, consistent, working old line democrats," encouraged Ezra Read to John Davis. Rather than diminish Bright's machine, the exodus of anti-Nebraska Democrats actually strengthened his position, yet it also created an effective anti-Democratic opposition party in the state.[12]

On July 13, 1854, just weeks after the Democratic meeting, a huge People's Party convention was held in Indianapolis that brought together all the various groups opposed to Democrats and the expansion of slavery. The resulting fusion put Indiana Democrats on the defensive for the first time. Democrats feared being "slaughtered" at the polls and complained bitterly that the alliance against them was unholy and un-American. "We have a hard battle to fight with fanatics," penned one Democrat. Years later, Indiana politico Lew Wallace remembered the turning of the political tide: "The old party was like a whale assailed at the same time by many boats harpooning it from every direction; the best it could do was to fluke the water and blow." Even Bright admitted defeat a month before the elections. "I am afraid my friend from the signs," he wrote to Senator Robert Hunter of Virginia, "that the Free States (Indiana included) are lost for the time being to our Party."[13]

Bright was right, and in the October elections, Indiana Democrats were crushed. The People's Party won nine of eleven congressional seats and elected their entire state ticket. Proslavery candidates like Norman Eddy and John Davis went down to defeat, but, thanks to Bright's personal influence and the Southern constituency of his Second District (right across the river from Louisville, Kentucky), William English survived, albeit narrowly. "I had long since given up all hope of your success, and had indeed," wrote a relative to English. Democrats were demoralized; their proslavery principles had been rejected by the voters. "I regret deeply regret the defeat of the true democracy in this my own beloved Indiana," lamented one Democrat bitter at the overwhelming success of the antislavery movement. "And I regret that among the playmates of my childhood days—among the college mates of my boyhood days—and among the associates of my manhood are to be found those who for the sake of a 'nigger' who do injustice to their equals." And another observer remarked with less rhetoric, "We are pretty well up salt River."[14]

But Democrats would not go quietly into the night, and Bright had no intention of giving up control of his state. When the Indiana legislature met in January 1855 to elect a U.S. senator, Democrats, now in the minority and determined to prevent the election of an antislavery man, refused to go into a joint session to hold the election. "And as for Senator," assured one state legislator to Davis, "you may set your mind at ease on that subject—*There will be no one elected*—And I would set here from January to June, before I would let one of the damned *persian* [Know-Nothing] *rascals* misrepresent our State for the next six years." The result, doubtless to Bright's liking, was no election; Bright would be the sole representative of his state in the U.S. Senate until 1857.[15]

Next door in Illinois, Stephen Douglas and William Richardson were on a personal crusade not only to save the Illinois Democracy but also to save their careers. Douglas, the author and architect of the Kansas-Nebraska Act, was assailed by voters across the North the moment he introduced the bill into the Senate. Once the bill passed and was signed into law, the attacks became even more virulent. His likeness was burned in effigy in almost every free state, and in Illinois voters congregated in mass rallies to denounce Douglas and the spread of slavery. The fact that Douglas was himself a slave owner did not escape voters and the press, and some claimed that the bill was designed to increase the value of his personal human property. One hundred women sent him thirty pieces of silver, referencing Judas's betrayal of Jesus, and clergymen spoke out against the immorality of slavery and Douglas's role in its expansion. All Douglas could do was fire off angry written rebuttals from Washington and give impassioned speeches defending his actions. Perhaps Douglas did not do more to sway public opinion because he assumed people would eventually come around to his position. He sincerely believed that "popular sovereignty" would satisfy Northern voters and that Democrats would see victory in the fall elections. *"We shall carry the State with a majority in the Legislature & of the Congressmen for Nebraska,"* he assured John Breckinridge of Kentucky. Writing to Georgian Howell Cobb in April 1854, Douglas explained, "The storm will soon spend its fury, and the people of the north will sustain the measure when they come to understand it. In the meantime our Southern friends have only to stand firm & leave us of the North to fight the great Battle." The Northern Democracy, Douglas was convinced, was both strong and popular, and Northern voters needed only a sober second look at Kansas-Nebraska to see that it served their best interests.[16]

Until voters came around, though, Douglas spent his free moments defending the bill. Appearing at events in New York and Pennsylvania, he connected popular sovereignty to God's law and likened it to colonial defiance of British tyranny. But while Douglas was back east, the task of defending Kansas-Nebraska in Illinois fell to his lieutenants. Editor and close friend Charles Lanphier was in the vanguard, using his *Illinois State Register* to praise Douglas, defend slavery, and spin popular sovereignty as the "doctrine of domestic independence." Most Democratic papers followed Lanphier's lead, but when the *Chicago Tribune* dared to challenge Douglas's authority, "the Little Giant" established his own *Chicago Times* in September 1854. The paper, managed by Washington, DC, reporter James Sheahan, was designed to be Douglas's mouthpiece, dedicated to shifting focus away from slavery onto nativism. Simultaneously, Douglas ordered proslavery, pro-Nebraska resolutions introduced into the Illinois state legislature, to make it appear that his home state was united behind him. After the adjournment of Congress, Douglas rushed home to manage his affairs in person. All along the way, however, he encountered demonstrations of voter anger. "I could travel from Boston to Chicago by the light of my own effigy. All along the Western Reserve of Ohio I could find my effigy upon every tree we passed," he said famously of his westward trip.[17]

Once in the Prairie State, Douglas found himself faced with a variety of anti-Democratic fusion movements. Know-Nothings and Whigs had no trouble banding together against the Democrats; plus the large German population, which opposed the expansion of slavery, was leaving its traditional home in the Democracy. When Lieutenant Governor Gustav Koerner, who had previously been a strong supporter of Douglas, announced his opposition, James Shields exclaimed to Lanphier, "All is perfect chaos, and the feeling is such that no effort can accomplish any thing. . . . The Anti-Nebraska feeling is too deep, more than I thought." A new low point came in September, when Douglas addressed an angry crowd of ten thousand in Chicago. Douglas, who believed he could talk his way out of trouble, was drowned out by boos and hisses. Enraged, Douglas screamed at the crowd, spending the next two hours trying to shout them into submission. Finally, he lost his temper and stormed off the stage, yelling, "Abolitionists of Chicago! It is now Sunday morning. I'll go to church and you may go to Hell!" Undaunted, Douglas took to the stump in the fall campaigns with characteristic energy. Encountering unfriendly crowds at every turn, he did his best to avoid the topic of slavery and focused attention on the Know-Nothings and temperance, labeling all anti-Democratic candidates nativists.[18]

Douglas and his Democratic cohorts had a daunting uphill battle, to say the least—they had to convince voters that the expansion of slavery was good and that Democrats represented the last, best hope for the Union. "Let us look at this question of slavery in a practical and patriotic point of view," wrote former U.S. senator Sidney Breese to one Illinoisan. "How can its extension into Nebraska or any other territory affront us? Will it make one more slave? Will it increase the bondage of those who are slaves? Will it make their condition worse? Far from it. . . . I believe it is the providence of God which requires that a certain portion of mankind shall go [into] slavery." Such proslavery sentiments, though an honest expression of their principles, only hurt Northern Democrats, further convincing voters that they did not have the best interests of their free state constituents at heart.[19]

Douglas's top lieutenant, William Richardson, faced equally daunting odds, though unlike his chief, Richardson was fighting for reelection. While Democratic presses did their part, labeling Richardson a hero for his role in the House, it was clear that Illinois voters thought otherwise. The contest wore his nerves thin, and when he engaged in a heated debate with a politico in Chicago, Richardson lost his temper and declared his preference for Southerners over Northerners. When his district dumped him in favor of an anti-Nebraska man, Richardson snorted that he had not wanted reelection in the first place, but then gladly accepted the nomination when the anti-Nebraska candidate withdrew his name. Knowing that the election was a referendum on Kansas-Nebraska and Douglas's leadership, Richardson took every opportunity to praise his boss, defend slavery, and denounce his opponents as abolitionist-disunionists. Nevertheless, the campaign went poorly and Richardson expected to lose. In the end, the Democrats went down to defeat as in Indiana and Iowa. The antislavery, anti-Democratic coalition carried five of nine congressional districts and carried both houses of the state legislature, a damning, personal rebuke to Douglas. The one bright spot, however, was the surprise reelection of Richardson, who lacked much of a challenger.[20]

Even in the face of unmistakable voter anger, Illinois Democrats refused to admit the unpopularity of the Kansas-Nebraska Act. They blamed abolitionists, nativists, and all their fusion variations, never stopping to question Douglas's command or the Southern agenda. "It is amazingly surprising how these Whigs Freesoilers & Abolitionists have hoodwinked the Democrats on this Nebraska question," remarked a relative of Sidney Breese, who seemed to believe the election had been stolen. Similarly, newly elected antislavery Representative Lyman Trumbull was struck by Democratic hostility. "I am really astonished at their bitterness," he wrote to a correspondent. "They have cried out *abolition* so much that if I was really a [William Lloyd] Garrison or a [Wendell] Phillips they could not think worse of me than they do."[21]

Democratic "days of peril," as one observer phrased it, continued into 1855, when the state legislature, now in the hands of anti-Nebraska, anti-Democratic forces, elected Trumbull to the U.S. Senate instead of Douglas's handpicked choice, Shields, who had voted for the Kansas-Nebraska Act. Douglas had hoped that Shields's Irish Catholic heritage would allow him to paint his opponents as intolerant nativists, but the plan failed, and the antislavery Trumbull was sent to Washington to sit beside the Little Giant. Douglas, who was eyeing his own reelection in 1858, was doubtless disturbed by this turn of events.[22]

The shellacking continued on the East Coast. President Pierce was personally mortified when his home state of New Hampshire elected two staunch antislavery men to the U.S. Senate, James Bell and Pierce's Granite State rival, John Hale. But, electorally, Pennsylvania and New York were of far more consequence. Because of the economic prosperity of the early and mid-1850s, nativism and slavery had replaced the perennial Pennsylvania topic of tariff protection. Moreover, nativism had always been extraordinarily potent in the Keystone State, and the Know-Nothings had won their first victories there. Two events, in particular, enflamed nativist passions in Pennsylvania. The first was the elevation of the Catholic James Campbell, first to Governor William Bigler's cabinet then to postmaster general, after his rejection by Pennsylvania voters in 1850. The second was Monsignor Gaetano Bedini's visit to Pittsburgh in 1853. As he was the personal agent of the pope, his presence in the Keystone State stoked nativist fears of a nefarious Catholic plot.[23]

In addition to these outside forces, Democrats were suffering from serious internal divisions, especially after the passage of the Kansas-Nebraska Act. Twelve Keystone Democrats, including wild card Senator Richard Brodhead, had voted for the bill despite voter opposition. When the March 1854 Democratic state convention in Harrisburg failed to address Kansas-Nebraska, both sides left frustrated; the regular Democrats had demanded a firm endorsement, and anti-Nebraska Democrats (in the majority) had wanted a rejection. The latter subsequently bolted the party for the opposition, simultaneously cleansing Democratic ranks and giving a boost to anti-Democratic forces. The split was made official when the state committee endorsed Kansas-Nebraska and read the bolters out of the party. "We are in a strong mess politically in Pennsylvania," noted Buchanan agent George Sanderson in June.[24]

To make matters worse for the Democrats, Governor Bigler had made himself enormously unpopular by his ill-conceived appointments and flip-flopping on temperance. When it came to Kansas-Nebraska, he tried to avoid the subject entirely, then finally announced his support months after it had been made party policy. "Bigler has behaved with great weakness and cowardice on the Nebraska question," observed Forney. His pussyfooting on slavery deeply frustrated Democrats and further demoralized them before the October elections. Their only chance of success lay with the collapse of the fusion forces arrayed against them, a distinct possibility given the potency of nativist sentiment. "Prospects in Penna. are decidedly gloomy," explained Representative J. Glancy Jones to Buchanan. "In fact our only hopes are in the want of cordial fusion in the elements of opposition to the democracy." In the end, fusion candidate James Pollock crushed Bigler, and anti-Nebraska candidates carried the congressional races. "Many prominent men have been swept out of sight by the late Tornado, I will not run over the whole list of the '*dead and wounded*,'" reported politico Daniel Jenks. But, as with English and Richardson, a protégé survived—J. Glancy Jones, Buchanan's trusted lieutenant. Unlike many of their associates, these three men enjoyed the full support of the party machinery and the significant influence of their mentors, Bright, Douglas, and Buchanan, respectively.[25]

Regardless, the Pennsylvania Democracy had been defeated, and Democrats consoled themselves with the thought that their party was now completely free of antislavery sentiment. "It has severed many rotten branches from the tree of Democracy, whose places will be more than supplied by fresh . . . & vigorous branches," wrote Buchanan. The Democracy, agreed Sanderson, had been "purified in the furnace of affliction." In a remarkably similar situation to Indiana, the Pennsylvania state legislature, now controlled by the anti-Democratic fusionists, was unable to elect a new senator. Former Democrat Simon Cameron had received the most votes but fell short of a majority. Instead of pushing through the deadlock, the legislature postponed the election until 1856. The unpredictable Brodhead would serve as the only senator from Pennsylvania for the next year.[26]

In the Empire State, longtime divisions between Hards and Softs had weakened the Democracy even before the tempest of Kansas-Nebraska. Intractable Daniel Dickinson continued to lead the proslavery Hards, while the Softs, who were willing to work with antislavery groups, were led by Secretary of State Marcy and Governor Horatio Seymour. Hards, as always, denied the legitimacy of the Softs and worked tirelessly to keep the state party divided in order to prevent the antislavery majority from gaining control of the party machinery. They "appear to be determined to prevent the union of the Dem. party," wrote Marcy to Seymour, "& I fear that they will have sufficient success to accomplish their object." The Kansas-Nebraska debacle only deepened divisions, and it created an impossible situation for New York Democrats. The Hards were energetic defenders of Kansas-Nebraska, and enjoyed recognition as "regular" Democrats, but they had battled with the Pierce administration and caused consternation among party leaders. "There is great sympathy felt here for the New York *hards*, who are believed to be good democrats," wrote one Kentuckian to his Representative. The Softs, on the other hand, had supported Pierce and been rewarded with patronage, but opposed the Kansas-Nebraska Act (some even suspected the bill to be a cunning ploy by Douglas to kill Marcy's candidacy in 1856). Added to the mix were debates over immigration and temperance, which crossed factional and partisan lines.[27]

In July 1854, the Hard convention officially endorsed the Kansas-Nebraska Act and nominated for governor that notorious foe of the administration Greene Bronson. This perpetuated their war with Pierce, but it pleased the Southern bosses. The Softs, conversely, were not so unified. When their convention avoided any statement on Kansas-Nebraska, Preston

King led the anti-Nebraska majority out of the hall and out of the party. "I am myself opposed to the Nebraska bill for the same instinctive reason that makes the great mass of the community opposed to it," wrote King to Hard Samuel Tilden. "The design and scope of the bill is by judicial construction and decision to change the constitution and the common law of the United States—from freedom as the fathers of the Republic understood it to slavery as the modern Slave propagandist proclaims it." The remaining Softs renominated Governor Seymour and did their best to avoid discussions of slavery, neither condemning nor affirming Kansas-Nebraska. To woo some Hards, though, Softs did adopt a proliquor ("wet") platform, hoping that Hards valued alcohol more than slavery. If the Hards wanted to fight temperance and keep drinking, they would have to join with the Softs—a prospect that did not sit well with them. It was a smart move by the Softs, and the Hards knew it; temperance and nativism were powerful, intertwined issues that could divert attention away from slavery.[28]

While the Hards and Softs battled each other in the fall elections, the antislavery exodus led by King had enormous implications for the state party overall. Henceforth, there would be no antislavery, Free Soil faction of the New York Democracy, and no attempts would be made to woo their votes (as there had been in 1851–1852). Like Indiana and Pennsylvania, New York Democrats were finally free from antislavery carping and complaining, while their former colleagues flocked to anti-Nebraska fusion tickets. In fact, some Hards, including Dickinson, even encouraged the formation of fusion parties in order to get rid of anti-Nebraska Democrats. Dickinson was eager to cleanse the party, rally the "Old Guard," and "Defeat 'administration' traitors at all hazards." With this accomplished, Softs and Hards could work together more effectively and court conservative Whigs.[29]

When the anti-Democratic fusion party met at Saratoga Springs and adopted a temperance platform, Democrats saw victory within their grasp. Democratic chances looked even brighter when the fusion party faltered, and the Know-Nothings nominated their own gubernatorial candidate and congressional slate, creating three-way races that could benefit the Democrats. "Our only hope this fall," penned young William Tweed, "is in having the K-N fight among themselves otherwise we are a used up party for the present." Nevertheless, the antislavery, anti-Democratic wave was too strong for Democrats to overcome, and they went down to defeat. Whig-fusion candidates carried twenty-seven of thirty-three districts, and antislavery candidate Myron Clark became the new governor. Of the three Democrats elected, only one was an avowed Hard, and not one of the nine Democrats who had voted for the Kansas-Nebraska Act survived.[30]

Overall, the fall elections were a crushing national blow to the Democratic Party, and many Democrats, though pleased to be rid of anti-Nebraska partisans, were disconsolate. "We are a beaten party. The tide of proscription rolls over the land like a flood of fiery lava, burning up," wrote Forney, waxing poetic. And from Georgia, Cobb lamented, "The democratic party has been literally slaughtered." More specifically, it was a direct rejection of the policies of the Pierce administration, as voters were energized by the Kansas-Nebraska Act more than any other issue. All but four of the sixty-seven Southern Democrats won reelection, but only seven Northern Democrats, including English, Richardson, and Jones, saw the next Congress. Put another way, in the fall elections of 1854, Democrats lost twenty-one of twenty-two Northern districts where Democrats had voted for the Kansas-Nebraska bill.[31]

The implications for the national Democratic organization cannot be overstated—the Northern wing had been decimated, and the South was now more dependent than ever on faithful doughfaces. Perhaps just as upsetting for Democrats was that the men chosen to replace them were often fiery antislavery leaders, such as John Hale, who would oppose the Slave Power at every turn. When the Michigan legislature, now solidly Republican, instructed its congressmen to oppose the spread of slavery and vote for the repeal of the Fugitive Slave Law, Senator Cass refused to resign as he swore he would in 1849 if his state ever became antislavery. Since the legislature was no longer Democratic, he reasoned, he was not bound to keep his pledge. As Northern Democrats groped for meaning in the months that followed, the most common metaphor employed was that of a tempest-tossed boat. The Democratic ship, they imagined, had encountered a severe storm that had smashed it against the rocks, but was still afloat. All that was needed was some new rigging, new sails, and perhaps a new captain. The damaged vessel, wrote a correspondent of Lanphier, "will be ready for another cruise in 1856 with the old *chart* and *compass* and Commodore Buchanan, an old seaman, for commander."[32]

James Buchanan was indeed a leading contender for command, but in 1854–1855 he was in distant London, seeing to Pierce's diplomatic agenda. More pressing than possible presidential candidates was the impending collapse of the Northern Democracy. The Southern bosses acted quickly to show their support for loyal doughfaces and reward them with choice offices and patronage appointments. Senator Dodge, for instance, was given the mission to Spain for his vote on the Kansas-Nebraska Act. Eddy of Indiana was saved from complete political obscurity by an appreciative Pierce, who appointed him attorney general of the Minnesota Territory in 1855. His

Hoosier colleague John Davis was appointed to the General Land Office, a lucrative post. For his service in purging the Democracy of antislavery heretics, Bright was elected Senate pro tempore in December 1854, a position all the more powerful since the vice presidency had never been filled after the death of William King in April 1853. Not surprisingly, Bright

FIGURE 7.   Representative Jehu Glancy Jones, Pennsylvania (Library of Congress)

used his control of the Senate to punish his enemies and initiate changes in committee membership and voting that benefited the South. He even refused to grant committee assignments to antislavery leaders Charles Sumner, Salmon Chase, and John Hale and denied the existence of the new Republican Party.[33]

J. Glancy Jones's vote for the Kansas-Nebraska Act and his leadership of the Keystone Democracy in Buchanan's absence also required reward. In the spring of 1855, he was considered for the critical post of governor of the Kansas Territory, but he declined—as a dedicated doughface, he was much needed in Congress and was working hard to promote Buchanan's presidential candidacy. Known simply as Glancy, Jehu Glancy Jones was born in October 1811 to a family of wealthy landowners and clergymen in Berks County, Pennsylvania. Raised in the beautiful Conestoga Valley, he early displayed a fondness for learning and reading and soon decided on a life in the church. He attended the Episcopal Kenyon College in Gambier, Ohio, then, at age twenty, went to bustling Cincinnati to complete his theological studies. He was ordained a deacon in the Episcopal Church and was assigned to two small churches south of Camden, New Jersey. In 1838, after some success, he moved to the wilds of north Florida, to St. Paul's Church in Quincy. He quickly grew tired of his duties, however, and decided that his future and fortune lay in law. At twenty-nine years old, he withdrew from the ministry and moved to neighboring Georgia for legal training.[34]

After significant time in two slave states, he moved to a third—Maryland—to start a practice. Finally, he returned to the Keystone State, where he established residence and a lucrative practice in Easton. In short order, he rose to prominence in Democratic politics and became the protégé of Buchanan. By 1844, the two men were close, and Buchanan could call him a "true hearted & faithful friend." After energetically supporting Polk and expansion in 1844, Jones relocated to Reading, where political opportunities seemed brighter. From Washington, Buchanan watched the rise of his pupil with delight, offering encouragement and advice at every opportunity. "With the support of the Democracy of old Berks, & with your ability & energy," Buchanan penned in 1847, "you can choose your time for coming to Congress which would open to you the appropriate field for distinction & future honors." Berks County was thoroughly Democratic, and with Old Buck's guidance, Jones had no trouble climbing the political ladder. In 1847 he was appointed district attorney; in 1848 he was a delegate to the national convention; in 1849 he served as the chair of the Democratic state convention and in 1850 was elected to the U.S. House of Representatives (a remarkable feat, since he had lived in the area for only six years).[35]

In Congress, Jones was a reliable doughface, supporting the Fugitive Slave Law and aggressive territorial expansion. He was recognized as Buchanan's agent in the House and was appointed to the Committee on Ways and Means. Leadership of Buchanan's state machine, however, soon took precedence over his congressional career, and Jones declined renomination in June 1852. He turned his entire attention to the promotion of Buchanan to the presidency and the advancement of the Pennsylvania Democracy. By 1853, he had become Buchanan's chief advisor and a major force in the national party. "I am perfectly at your command," Buchanan wrote to Jones in a letter seeking advice. "You are on the spot & you can best inform me when & how to act." Nonetheless, Jones found himself back in the House when his successor died suddenly in January 1854. Jones returned to Congress just in time to cast a crucial vote for the Kansas-Nebraska Act, which further endeared him to the party leadership. By his reelection in October 1854, Jones had earned unquestioned doughface credentials and the trust and affection of the Southern bosses. Jones had so much clout, in fact, that when he invited Pierce to accompany him to a rally in Harrisburg, Pennsylvania, the president happily complied—an unusual favor for a second-term House member.[36]

When the Democratic House caucus met on December 1, 1855, they voted to make Jones floor leader and Richardson Speaker (a nod to party chieftains Buchanan and Douglas, who were positioning themselves for the 1856 nomination, as well as Richardson's key role in the passage of the Kansas-Nebraska bill). The caucus also adopted a resolution specifically endorsing the Kansas-Nebraska Act, a show of support for the embattled Pierce administration. "We passed, as you will see from the papers, a resolution endorsing the Kansas Nebraska Bill in all its length and breadth," wrote Representative A. Gallatin Talbott of Kentucky to Breckinridge. "We may not get Richardson for Speaker, although we are not without hope—but the resolution *will make the next Presdt. mark what I say.*" Considering Democratic defeats, Richardson's chances for Speaker were slim, but Democrats were far more united than their fractious fusion opponents.[37]

The Thirty-Fourth Congress convened on December 3, and balloting for Speaker began almost immediately. Partisans and civilians alike anxiously observed the proceedings, eager to see how the new opposition parties would fare in the face of the Slave Power. The new Congress was, historian Tyler Anbinder explains, "as unpredictable as Washington had ever witnessed." Richardson led from the start, receiving seventy-four of seventy-eight Democratic votes, and over the coming weeks, floor leader Jones kept Democrats in line and defended Richardson from attacks. Luckily for Richardson and Jones, the opposition had difficulty uniting on a candidate, first turning to Lewis Campbell of Ohio then to Nathaniel Banks of Massachusetts, who could garner more Know-Nothing votes. Banks's position was boosted when, on December 14, he received the endorsement of the anti-Nebraska caucus.[38]

Banks was unable to gain the necessary majority, though, and deadlock turned to stalemate throughout December and January. Banks held the lead around 105, with Richardson in second near 74. All-night sessions produced no results, and House members became angry and impatient, reminiscent of the Speaker crisis of 1849. Under Jones's leadership, Democrats remained a unit and refused to compromise or negotiate with the opposition. "Last night the Richardson men had a meeting, and we resolved to *sit it out*," wrote Alexander Stephens on January 8. Antislavery forces, too, remained adamant, refusing to give in to the Slave Power again. At one point, Richardson approached abolitionist Joshua Giddings and asked when the antislavery men would give up. When Giddings replied they were prepared to fight until the end of the session in March, Richardson yelled, "*You be d—-d!*" and stormed off. "It is a point of honor with us who have thus sustained Mr. Banks, and identified him as *the* Anti-Nebraska candidate for speaker, not to yield," explained former Democrat John Dix. "He has borne himself gallantly in every assault made on him, by the slaveocracy thirsting for his defeat, and if we desert him, we ought to be deserted by hope in our hour of trial."[39]

Eventually, Democrats dropped Richardson in favor of James Orr of South Carolina, betting that he would be able to get the votes of Southern nativists, but the switch yielded no change. Finally, on February 1, Stephens convinced the Democratic caucus to adopt the plurality rule that would give victory to the highest vote-getter, and to replace Orr with William Aiken, also of the Palmetto State. But the plan failed, and on the following day the opposition triumphed. Banks, a Democrat turned Republican, won on the plurality rule, and the infant Republican Party achieved its first national victory. When the votes were announced, the House galleries, packed with onlookers, erupted in cheers and "wild excitement." The decision had taken nine weeks and 133 ballots and had resulted in another crushing defeat for the Democrats. "The work is begun," scribbled an angry correspondent to Lanphier. "Hell is uncapped & all its devils turned loose—to howl until next November. The Election of Banks was an infamous fraud." "The election of Banks has given great hopes to our enemies, and their policy is dangerous in the extreme to us," observed Robert Toombs of Georgia, doubtless aware of the symbolic importance of the win for Republicans and the very real danger for Democrats.[40]

Crisis in Kansas

Equally worrisome was the crisis in Kansas, which only added to the strength of the Republicans. After the passage of the Kansas-Nebraska Act, it fell to the Pierce administration to create a territorial government and make "popular sovereignty" a reality. Northern Democrats had promised voters that popular sovereignty would produce free states in the West, but Southerners knew that its ambiguity worked in their favor. As soon as the territory was opened to settlement in May 1854, Southerners poured into the area with their human property, determined to make Kansas the next slave state.

The rush to settle Kansas was incredible. Before May 1854, there were fewer than eight hundred white settlers in the territory, but within the next nine months that number increased tenfold. Many of the new arrivals came from neighboring Missouri, whose fanatical proslavery Democratic senator, David Atchison, made it a personal crusade to control events in the territory. Under his guidance, heavily armed, proslavery "border ruffians," as the Missourians were called, entered Kansas purely to manipulate its elections, not to settle. Once in Kansas, they terrorized legitimate free state settlers, illegally influenced elections, and established proslavery organizations designed to thwart the will of the territorial majority. The entire mission of Atchison's Missourians was to use violence and fraud to prevent the free state majority from establishing an effective government. "Let the Southern men come on with their slaves 10,000 families can take possession, of and hold every acre of timber in the territory of Kansas, and this secures the prairie," declared Atchison to Senator Hunter in March 1855. "Missouri will furnish 5000 of the 10,000; and the whole State will guarantee protection. . . . We are playing for a mighty stake, if we win we carry slavery to the Pacific." When news of events in Kansas reached the Northern states, antislavery societies quickly mobilized to send free state settlers to the area. Led by the New England Emigrant Aid Society, antislavery groups sent people, supplies, and money to Kansas homesteaders, who were easily overwhelmed by the proslavery terrorists. By the end of 1854, civil war had erupted in Kansas and the violence became a national crisis. Northerners and Southerners watched anxiously to see which side, slavery or freedom, would emerge victorious.[41]

The Pierce administration was clearly on the side of slavery. The president appointed no free staters to territorial posts and considered all who opposed the Kansas-Nebraska Act traitors and subversives. At Senator Douglas's request, Pierce appointed John Calhoun of Illinois, a strong Douglas ally, to the post of surveyor general of Kansas, perhaps the most powerful position in the territory, given its control of patronage. For the territorial governorship,

Pierce turned to inexperienced Pennsylvania attorney Andrew Reeder, who, as a Buchanan man, was avowedly proslavery. Reeder was more interested in making money than he was policy, however, and was wholly unqualified for the task of bringing order from chaos in Kansas.

When Reeder arrived in the territory in October 1854, he found that widespread proslavery terrorism and electoral fraud had produced an unrepresentative, proslavery legislature. In June 1855, he watched as outraged free state voters held a convention in Lawrence, Kansas, and voted to reject the territorial legislature. Reeder did his best to mediate, but the proslavery legislature refused to cooperate with either the governor or the free-state majority. The legislature then inflamed the situation by passing a series of laws and codes that officially established slavery in Kansas, implemented stringent fugitive slave laws, and forbade antislavery activity. Reeder, meanwhile, became embroiled in petty squabbles with the proslavery legislature, even getting into a fistfight with one member over a personal insult. In addition, his inability to produce a proslavery, Democratic Kansas earned him the ire of Southerners, and the party chieftains, led by Atchison and Jefferson Davis, called for his removal. Pierce complied, of course, and removed Reeder on August 15, 1855. "[The] President is most interested to have the cause of slavery prevail in that new State," observed Georgian Thomas Thomas. "He has cast his lot with the South and he must sink or swing with us."[42]

To replace Reeder, Pierce selected William Shannon of Ohio, who had served one term in the House of Representatives and been ousted by his constituents for his vote in favor of Kansas-Nebraska. It became immediately apparent, explains historian Nicole Etcheson, that Shannon possessed an "ineptitude for any post of delicacy." More so than Reeder, Shannon was a Southern lackey who was committed to the spread of slavery. Unwilling to trust either the new governor or the Pierce administration, the free state majority in Kansas created its own territorial government at Topeka. In the name of "law and order," proslavery gangs attacked free state settlements, leading to the "Wakarusa War" in November 1855 and the commencement of "Bleeding Kansas." Pierce, dumbfounded at the perpetual violence, sent a special message to Congress on January 24, 1856. Heavily influenced by cabinet members Davis and Caleb Cushing, the president blamed the crisis on Northern antislavery societies and condemned the new Topeka government as illegal and treasonous. To follow up, on February 11 he issued a proclamation supporting proslavery forces in Kansas and putting federal troops at the disposal of Governor Shannon, ostensibly for stifling the free state majority.[43]

Southern violence against antislavery men even appeared in the halls of Congress, when, on May 22, 1856, Democratic Representative Preston

Brooks of South Carolina brutally assaulted Senator Charles Sumner of Massachusetts, nearly killing him. Sumner had just delivered a lengthy oration titled "The Crime Against Kansas," in which he denounced the repeal of the 1820 Line, indicted proslavery militants, and responded to personal attacks by Senators Douglas and Andrew Butler of South Carolina. When young Brooks, a slave-owning planter-politician, heard of Sumner's speech, he carefully planned his attack. Two days later, Brooks entered the Senate chamber, approached the seated, unsuspecting Sumner and beat him over the head with his cane, while his colleague South Carolina secessionist Lawrence Keitt ensured that no one interfered. Nearby, Douglas and Glancy Jones were aware of the attack but did not rise to stop it. The overwhelming majority of Northerners, however, were outraged. Republicans seized on the opportunity and used the assault to their advantage, explaining to voters the obvious connection between "Bleeding Kansas" and "Bleeding Sumner." The scandal intensified when Southerners feted Brooks like a hero, and Democrats fought his expulsion from the House. Even when English of Indiana called for both Brooks and Sumner to be censured, Southerners withheld their votes, refusing to acknowledge that Brooks had erred. English, who had been strong-armed by the bosses into voting for the repeal of the 1820 Line, now came to realize that Northern Democrats would never be able to please the South.[44]

At the same time Northerners were reeling from the caning of Senator Sumner, they learned of the proslavery attack on the free state town of Lawrence, Kansas. On May 21, 1856, a proslavery posse, five hundred to seven hundred strong and led by a local sheriff, surrounded Lawrence, forced the inhabitants to give up their arms, and burned the prominent Free State Hotel—another propaganda boon for the rising Republicans. But proslavery men were not the only perpetrators of violence. When militant abolitionist John Brown learned of the "Sack of Lawrence," he and his sons went on a killing rampage, murdering five suspected proslavery settlers. While the attack on Lawrence had been led by local law enforcement and was thus clothed in legality, Brown's extralegal actions gave the Pierce administration an excuse to unleash federal troops on antislavery "criminals." Yet the Pierce administration still appeared weak in the eyes of the South, and the president's influence was at rock bottom. Two and a half years of Pierce had produced nothing but legislative crises, chaos in Kansas, patronage wars, and foreign policy embarrassments. "His administration, I regret to say, is an utter and entire failure," confided a Buchanan correspondent.[45]

Indeed, "Handsome Frank" was an embattled president and by 1856 was ignored by party leaders looking forward to the election of that year. Still mourning the death of his son and unhappy with life in the White House,

Pierce often sought solace and comfort with Southerners. Nevertheless, he was still determined to implement Democratic policy and bring about peace in Kansas. In fact, he was so incensed at antislavery victories at the polls and in the press that he decided to run for another term. Marcy and the Softs, whose fate in the Empire State depended largely on the fate of the Pierce administration, had been urging Pierce to announce his candidacy, and Pierce's friends had been moving in that direction at least since the summer of 1855.[46]

To make Pierce's candidacy official, Charles Peaslee, the president's agent in Concord, forced pro-Pierce resolutions through the New Hampshire state legislature. "The President is unequivocally in the field as a Candidate and he expects all his friends to stand by him," Forney wrote to Breckinridge on November 15, 1855. Immediately after, A. O. P. Nicholson of Tennessee, acting on behalf of Pierce, reached out to Buchanan lieutenant Glancy Jones in the Keystone State. Nicholson coyly suggested a rapprochement between the rival camps: Pierce would accept Pennsylvania's nomination of Buchanan as long as Buchanan did not take an anti-administration position that might prevent Buchanan delegates from supporting Pierce at the national convention. Jones agreed. Forney, too, moved to smooth relations between Pierce in Washington and Buchanan in London; Forney knew that Buchanan was unhappy with his assignment, as well as with Pierce's handling of Cuba.[47]

Unwilling to let his fate be determined by others, Pierce used his December 1855 annual message to Congress to rally Southern support for his candidacy and shore up his proslavery credentials. In no uncertain terms, Pierce denied federal authority over slavery and downplayed the sectional crisis as an "imagination of grievance." If there are troubles in Kansas and Congress, he asserted, they are entirely the work of antislavery fanatics. "While the people of the Southern States confine their attention to their own affairs, not presuming officiously to intermeddle with the social institutions of the Northern States, too many of the inhabitants of the latter are permanently organized in associations to inflict injury on the former by wrongful acts." Southerners were innocent victims, and they had every right to be angry and defensive; Northerners, Pierce declared, had given them "cause of war." As for events in Kansas, charges that the Kansas-Nebraska Act was responsible for the chaos and violence were "utterly destitute of substantial justification." Those who opposed slavery and the Slave Power, he concluded, were enemies of the Constitution who would be punished.[48]

Pierce's message seemed a complete departure from reality and an unabashed grab for Southern support. Moreover, his assessment of recent events was so profoundly misleading that he either knowingly lied to Congress and the American public or was not in control of his own administration. Regardless, it won the hearty support of Democrats. "Mr. Pierce's message of '55," recalled Mrs. Virginia Clay, "fell like a bombshell on the Black Republican party. It's bold pro-slaveryism startled even his friends." The message did wonders for the Republican Party, which pointed to it as another example of the Slave Power. "The message is pro-slavery enough," observed Lyman Trumbull. "It is full of misrepresentation and false reasoning but I think it will do good in the North by showing the people clearly whither the government is tending."[49]

But despite his "bold pro-slaveryism," Pierce was unlikely to win renomination. "[He] has made a bold bid for the South in his late message . . . but it *won't save him*," remarked the U.S. minister to Belgium, J. J. Seibels. Pierce's course had been sufficiently proslavery in intent, but not proslavery enough in product. Kansas was a mess, and not the slave state that had been promised; slave-owning Cuba was no closer to being a state; the Ostend report had been swept under the rug instead of being sanctioned as official policy; patronage had been distributed to Softs and recalcitrant Free Soilers; and the Northern Democracy had been cut down at the polls. "The administration has lost the confidence of the country," complained a disgruntled Pierre Soulé, "and done more harm to our party in two years than all the efforts of its worst enemies would have effected in a quarter of a century." Even if they admired Pierce's persistence and sympathized with his plight, Democrats realized that their ship needed a new captain. Moreover, his unpopularity in the free states was staggering. His candidacy in the general election was sure to result in Republican victory, especially if the antislavery tide continued to rise. "The renomination of Genl. Pierce" would mean "certain and inevitable defeat," predicted Cobb.[50]

The 1856 Democratic Nomination

Southern Democrats were not foolish enough to think that a Southerner could win the presidency now that the North was effectively antislavery. To retain the executive, Democrats needed a Northern man who could win in Pennsylvania, New York, Indiana, and Illinois. Furthermore, many Southerners felt that they owed the nomination to a Northern Democrat as reward for their loyalty in the face of the antislavery wave. "I fully concur with you in the justice of first consulting the wishes of the gallant National democracy of the North, and, considering their late defeats and discouraging prospects, would be willing to concede to them the right to select the candidate, as a reward for their fidelity to principle," explained Charles Wheatley of Kentucky to Breckinridge.[51]

The nomination would have to go to either Buchanan or Douglas. The former was the elder statesman and quintessential doughface, and the latter was the legislative titan responsible for the Compromise of 1850 and the repeal of the 1820 Line. Other contenders from 1852 were no longer available. Cass was far too old and reeked of defeat; Marcy did not want to run, and he knew that his leading role in the Pierce administration made him unelectable; and Dickinson, languishing as a private citizen, was still seething with anger at Pierce's patronage decisions and cared more about thwarting Pierce than getting on the national ticket.[52] Control of patronage and lingering Southern support, however, still made Pierce a formidable contender. "The strength of Pierce consisted in 'possession,'" explained Cincinnati reporter Murat Halstead, "in the enormous amount of patronage at his disposal, in the fact that he presided in the grand central office of the wireworkers of the best drilled party in the country, and was commander-in-chief of office holders." Pierce, suspicious of Buchanan's machinations in London and aware of the Pennsylvanian's political clout with the South, reached out to Douglas, hoping he would remain loyal to the administration and help him against Buchanan's challenge. If Pierce could not win the nomination, at least he could play kingmaker.[53]

While Pierce had the power of the executive, Old Buck was the perennial favorite of the South, the all-important attribute in the Democratic Party. "Our opinion is that Buchanan is first choice for President," wrote a Kentuckian to his representative. Furthermore, Buchanan's time at the head of the U.S. Legation in London had kept him away from the political crises of the Kansas-Nebraska Act and Bleeding Kansas. Though his authorship of the Ostend report made clear his role in the Pierce administration's proslavery policies, Buchanan appeared above the political fray, a fact his friends did not fail to exploit. "*I rejoice at your absence in the present excitement,*" penned an excited Forney during the stormy passage of the Kansas-Nebraska bill, while a Southern correspondent was confident of Buchanan's record: "Your Ostend dispatch should satisfy every Southern man as to what would be your course, if President." Buchanan also seemed mercifully free from blame after the electoral defeats of 1854 and 1855. "It is a matter of great rejoicing that you are at this moment happily out of the country," wrote George Plitt. "One State after another is dropping off from us, and unless something be done to stop the panic, the Administration will be in a miserable minority in the next Congress."[54]

Along with undiminished Southern support and an untarnished proslavery reputation, Buchanan could boast the best personal organization. His

Pennsylvania political machine was under the capable direction of Jones, who also promoted Buchanan in Congress. The alcoholic but talented Forney quit the editorship of the administration *Washington Union* and redirected his considerable energy to electing Buchanan. Overall campaign management, though, was left to the ever-reliable, ever-ready John Slidell of Louisiana. On the eve of the 1856 national nominating convention, Buchanan sent Slidell a letter to be shown to key delegates and Southern leaders, a letter that would remove any doubt (if any existed) of the Sage of Wheatland's doughface principles. "I have written and spoken more than any man now alive in favor of the just Constitutional rights of the South over their slaves," explained Buchanan. "In fact a number of years of my life were, in a great degree passed, in sustaining their rights in the Senate and during the recess of Congress in advocating them before the people of my own state. . . . Truly the Democrats of Pennsylvania, who have witnessed my exertions for nearly a quarter of a century, in behalf of the rights of the South, will be greatly astonished to learn that I am now distrusted by any Southern man." Buchanan's letter also described his efforts in London as being entirely dedicated to promoting slavery and Southern interests, so much so that "the *Morning Advertiser*, a British liberal paper . . . more than once expressed its regret that I was such 'a strong pro slavery man.'" Such pronouncements, though hardly news to Southern ears, made Buchanan the unquestioned front-runner.[55]

Buchanan was in London until April 1856, however, and much of his maneuvering had to be done through back-room deals and well-placed letters. Slidell did his best to sell Buchanan as a political outsider at the head of a conservative people's movement, Democratic in principle but divorced from the unpopular administration, but few were fooled. Slidell, Jones, and others counseled their chief to stay in London as long as possible and to not take any stands on issues—his candidacy would be much easier to handle if he remained mum. In addition, Buchanan's agents revived the Pennsylvania-Virginia plan put forth by Henry Wise in 1852. Wise was still an ardent supporter of Buchanan and a leading Southern Democrat. His election to the governorship of the Old Dominion in May 1855 was seen as a good omen for Old Buck, and Wise was considered by some to be the ideal running mate. After his victory, he resumed his correspondence with Buchanan and gave him advice. "You must rally Penna & unite her with Virginia in your name," he counseled. Together we can "rule 'em." Armed with Wise's guidance, clout, and support, as well as a well-disciplined political machine ready to make him president, Buchanan arrived back in the United States in April 1856, just in time to take his place as the leading candidate.[56]

Nevertheless, Douglas considered himself the best man for the job. Unlike Buchanan, he had fought the hard battles and produced results, most notably the Kansas-Nebraska Act. His ambition was all-consuming, and he never truly stopped running for president after his 1852 convention defeat. His close working relationship with the Southern bosses and the trust of the Pierce administration made Douglas the only man who could effectively challenge Buchanan's lead. From the start of his campaign in the spring of 1855, Douglas enjoyed firm western support, but he knew he needed help in the slave states. For that task, he looked to Breckinridge of Kentucky to build relationships and make deals. "He has more confidence in your sagacity, judgment & friendship, than that of any other man living," wrote a Douglas agent to Breckinridge. In October, Douglas headed east to speak at political events and strategize with wire-pullers. He met with the president and the Southern bosses in Washington, declined to speak in Boston (carefully avoiding any antislavery taint), rallied proslavery voters in St. Louis, and joined Breckinridge in Lexington for a Democratic barbeque.[57]

Douglas's primary task was not to get his name out to the public, since he already enjoyed national attention, but rather to heal party divisions in the Northern and western states. Buchanan held the South in his palm, but was deeply unpopular in the North; Douglas, on the other hand, had some Southern support but located his voting base among the remnants of the Northern Democracy. "Douglas is rending *heaven* and *earth* to get the nomination," reported a New Yorker to Buchanan, "and his strength is considerable at the west." If he hoped to challenge Buchanan for the nomination, he would have to unite the Northern organizations behind him, for every Northern state still voted at national conventions, regardless of the size and condition of the state party.[58]

With the faltering Northern Democracy in mind, Douglas urged Northern states to pass an unambiguous "Illinois Platform" (unveiled at Lexington with Breckinridge) that read anti-Nebraska Democrats out of the party and endorsed the Kansas-Nebraska Act. "No concessions to the enemy in any form," explained Douglas to Cobb. "We can and will crush all our enemies by a bold avowal of & strict adherence to our principles." To run his Northern campaign, he selected longtime friends former representative David Disney of Ohio and Illinois politico James Singleton, and for his Southern interests he looked to Soulé of Louisiana, Atchison of Missouri, and Andrew Johnson of Tennessee. Since he had agreed to give up Pennsylvania to Old Buck, Douglas turned his attention to the Empire State, specifically to Dickinson and the Hards. Perpetual party divisions, however, prevented Douglas from making any inroads. Dickinson seemed open to negotiate but was wary of Douglas's apparent alliance with the Pierce administration.[59]

Perhaps Douglas's biggest obstacle, though, was Bright of Indiana. Long-time rival for control of the old Northwest, Bright had come to loathe Douglas to an irrational degree. That hatred pushed Bright close to Buchanan, who shared Bright's suspicions of the Little Giant. To defeat his enemy, Bright employed patience and duplicity. Through a series of disingenuous letters and overtures made by friends, Douglas came to believe Bright would support him for the nomination. Even outsiders were convinced. "Douglas & Bright have made up all their differences & are now friends," reported Dan Sickles to Buchanan. To show his appreciation, Douglas invited Bright, along with Breckinridge, William Corcoran, and Robert Hunter, to participate in some land schemes in Wisconsin. (Expecting that the town would become a new commercial hub, they invested heavily in Superior City, on the western end of Lake Superior.) At the same time, however, Bright solidified his alliance with the Buchanan camp and made a deal with Slidell for complete control of northwestern patronage in a Buchanan administration. "We can rely on Bright," reported Slidell to Buchanan.[60]

Bright was in firm control of the Indiana Democracy, and Douglas's inability to control that key western state was a serious blow to his candidacy. Although most Hoosier Democrats supported the Little Giant, Bright packed Indiana county and district meetings with his minions to produce a pro-Buchanan state convention, which Bright personally attended. At the convention, he and his lieutenants strong-armed delegates, installed a Bright loyalist as chair, and "fixed" the resolutions committee in Buchanan's favor. "A majority of the delegates are his tools," remarked a disgusted Joseph Wright. Under Bright's control, the meeting proceeded to denounce the anti-Nebraska movement, instruct the delegation to the national convention to vote as a unit (a critical decision, since it would allow Bright to dictate the vote of the delegation), and endorse Bright for president. Nevertheless, in the months leading up to the June 1856 convention, the Little Giant was confident that he could rely on Bright to help beat Old Buck for the nomination. Douglas would not discover Bright's duplicity until it was too late.[61]

Bright, of course, was not a serious presidential contender, but the state endorsement signaled to Buchanan and Douglas that Indiana's vote was under his firm control. Bright, in fact, would play a decisive role at the 1856 national nominating convention in Cincinnati, Ohio. Not only would he direct the Hoosier vote, but his control of northwest patronage under a potential Buchanan administration gave him a powerful weapon. Moreover, his burning hatred for both Douglas and Pierce, and his devotion to slavery and the Slave Power, made him a powerful ally for the Buchanan camp. Bright and Slidell were exactly the ruthless political operators that Buchanan needed to finally gain the nomination after three failed attempts. Yet Douglas was not to be underestimated, and his support among Northern Democrats was considerable. Would the Little Giant be defeated by Old Buck, and, more important, would either be able to win in a general election against an antislavery candidate with solid Northern support? The crises of the Pierce administration—diplomatic embarrassments, patronage disputes, the Kansas-Nebraska Act, war in Kansas, violence in the halls of Congress—had eroded the Northern Democracy to a dramatic degree. Northern Democrats had been cut down at the polls, and Democratic policies were more unpopular than ever in the free states, giving rise to new, unpredictable anti-Democratic parties and coalitions. If Democrats were to win the presidency in 1856, they would have to heal internal divisions, sell their proslavery program to Northern voters, and put forth a candidate who could inspire confidence and moderation—three tasks easier said than done.

CHAPTER 6

"The Strongest Northern Man on Southern Principles"

James Buchanan and Southern Power

In February 1856, Jesse Bright of Indiana and John Slidell of Louisiana put into action their plans to make thrice-failed presidential candidate James Buchanan of Pennsylvania the next chief executive of the United States. Bright and Slidell first traveled to Philadelphia, where they met with Buchanan managers in that state, then held strategy meetings with Southern leaders in Washington, DC. By the time they had left the capital, the Buchanan cabal had been joined by Judah P. Benjamin of Louisiana, who would become the Confederate secretary of war, and Bright's longtime friend James Bayard of Delaware, a crafty and cultured manipulator. All four men were slave owners and masters of political machinery. While Bright and Slidell sought to punish Pierce for his patronage decisions, as well as elevate a true proslavery conservative, Benjamin and Bayard were eager to advance their personal careers.[1]

From Washington, the cabal rushed west in late May to the bustling river town of Cincinnati, where the 1856 Democratic national nominating convention would be held in June, and where the agents of Senator Stephen Douglas and President Franklin Pierce were already active. Bright, Slidell, Benjamin, and Bayard met at the Burnet House, the finest hotel in "the Queen City of the West." They secured a luxurious suit for meetings and deal-making, but established battle headquarters across the street, at the residence of S. M. Barlow. Other Buchanan men, such as financier William

Corcoran, editor John Forney, and diplomat Dan Sickles, arrived soon thereafter. The Buchaneers, as they had been known since the 1852 convention, hoped to use northwest factionalism, as well as the promise of patronage, to prevent united regional support for Douglas. Likewise, division would be encouraged in New York, and the Pennsylvania delegation was instructed to bring along hundreds of Buchanan supporters to influence the convention.[2]

Indiana, however, was the key state. Douglas desperately needed it in his column to gain the nomination, but Bright remained in control of the Hoosier Democracy. Nevertheless, most Indiana Democrats wanted Douglas, and pro-Douglas rallies back home pressured the Hoosier delegates in Cincinnati. Though Bright himself was not a delegate, he managed the delegation from Barlow's house, and his lieutenants, duly elected delegates William English and John Pettit, operated from within the convention. When the delegation met on the Saturday before the convention (May 31), Bright was able to twist enough arms to secure a unit vote for Buchanan. Indiana's decision to support Buchanan, in turn, convinced many Ohio and New York delegates to switch to the Sage of Wheatland. "Indiana is all gone—& wrong," cried William Richardson to Douglas, who was taken aback at Bright's treachery.[3]

Meanwhile, Pierce's interests were handled by the spectacled Harry Hibbard of New Hampshire, who had lost his seat in the U.S. House of Representatives because of his support of the Kansas-Nebraska Act, and the stout and balding Charles Peaslee, still serving in the House from the Granite State. Headquartered in rooms above the Custom House Retreat restaurant, they were in close communication with the Southern party leadership and were determined to woo New York Softs who owed their offices to Pierce. The Douglas clan, on the other hand, was represented by New York financier Edward West, Douglas's brother-in-law Julius Granger, and the ever-present, ever-loyal "Old Dick" Richardson. Richardson was the floor manager, while West and Granger made deals at the Burnet House. They were proud, patient, and persistent. Douglas, they believed, had earned the nomination with his compromise in 1850, the Fugitive Slave Law, and the Kansas-Nebraska Act—there would be no dark horse candidate this time.[4]

On the eve of the convention, as delegates, wire-pullers, political agents, and reporters poured into Cincinnati, little changed for Northern Democrats. They were still divided between Pierce, Buchanan, and Douglas, and the South was nearly united on Buchanan. The South will be "one unbroken column of fifteen states united for the preservation of their own rights," proclaimed Robert Toombs. Knowing that they could never elect a candidate of their own, Southerners would only support a diehard doughface, "the strongest northern man sound on Southern principles," as J. Glancy Jones phrased it. There was no doubt that the meeting would produce a proslavery nominee on an aggressively proslavery platform. Though Northern Democrats knew their subservient place and were willing to oblige the Southern bosses, they also knew that such a proslavery course would be enormously unpopular with their free state constituents.[5]

The 1856 Democratic National Convention

The Democratic convention gathered in Smith and Nixon's Hall on Monday, June 2, 1856. As in previous conventions, rival groups competed for choice committee assignments, but a fistfight erupted over the admission of an anti-Douglas delegation from Missouri. Richardson quickly had them ousted.[6] Day two saw the election of Buchanan ally John Ward of Georgia as permanent chair of the convention. Ward proceeded to place Buchanan protégé Glancy Jones on the crucial Committee on Resolutions and broke with precedent to permit Buchanan agents to circulate freely, negotiating with delegations during convention proceedings. Simultaneously, Bayard on the Committee on Credentials kept the divided Empire State delegation inert by delaying a decision on their status. Finally, the two-thirds rule was adopted to maintain Southern control of the convention. "The indications are so strong for Buchanan that it is difficult to see how men can resist," confided Ward to Howell Cobb.[7]

In light of Buchanan's momentum, the Illinois delegation went into a long caucus on the night of June 3 to discuss how to withdraw the Little Giant without damaging his reputation. Richardson also sought the counsel of Breckinridge, a Douglas and Bright intimate. That same night, Richardson received a telegram from his chief instructing him to withdraw his name if the convention became deadlocked—Douglas did not want to be responsible for another dark horse disaster. The next day, the third of the convention, the platform was read and voted on. Unsurprisingly, the document included a complete denial of congressional authority over slavery, an endorsement of the Fugitive Slave Law and the Kansas-Nebraska Act, and a call for a more aggressive foreign policy. More important, it did away with the ambiguity of popular sovereignty and specified that territorial voting on slavery could occur only at statehood, long after slavery had been established. Though this section of the platform went unnoticed in the interest of party harmony, it would soon cause a dramatic rift within the Democracy.[8]

On the fourth day, June 5, Bayard deftly neutralized the threat of an anti-Buchanan New York delegation by calling for both of the rival factions to be seated (thus canceling each other out, since the Hards, led by Sam Beardsley,

wanted Buchanan, and the Softs, headed by Horatio Seymour, wanted either Pierce or Douglas). With platform and credentials settled, the convention turned to nominations and voting. Virginia put forth Buchanan, New
Hampshire endorsed her native son, and Richardson nominated Douglas.
Old Buck led on the first ballot with 135, Handsome Frank came in a close
second with 122, and the Little Giant trailed with 33. The next several ballots
saw gains for Buchanan and losses for his competitors. By the end of the day,
fourteen ballots had been cast with no winner. Bright had kept Indiana out
of the Douglas column, Buchanan held the commanding lead, and Pierce's
candidacy appeared comatose.[9]

That evening, colossal efforts were made by the candidates' managers to
sway delegations to switch votes. Claiming that the president had no chance
and that Douglas had been the administration's greatest champion, Richardson was able to convince Pierce supporters to swing to Douglas. Old Dick
also received another telegram from his boss, once again authorizing him to
withdraw his name. Richardson, however, was not yet ready to give up the
fight, while Hibbard recognized the futility of Pierce's candidacy. The next
morning, Hibbard gained the floor and withdrew the president's name.

With the president out, the balloting resumed in earnest. Two more
rounds of voting, the fifteenth and sixteenth ballots, increased Buchanan's
lead but still did not produce the two-thirds necessary to gain the nomination. Finally, William Preston of Kentucky, a key Douglas advocate, took
the floor, announced that it was clear the convention wanted Buchanan, and
called on Douglas men to end the struggle. Through shouts of "No! No!,"
Preston yielded the floor to Richardson, who made the surrender official. "I
am satisfied that I cannot advance his [Douglas's] interests or the interests of
the common cause, or the principles of the Democratic party, by continuing him in this contest," intoned Richardson. "I will, therefore, state that I
have a dispatch from Judge Douglas, which I desire, may be permitted to
be read, and I shall then withdraw his name from before the Convention."
He then read Douglas's June 3 letter aloud and urged party harmony. "If
the withdrawal of my name will contribute to the harmony of our Party or
the success of the cause," Douglas had telegrammed, "I hope you will not
hesitate to take the step."[10]

The final vote was largely a formality, as delegates rushed to the Buchanan banner, making the nomination unanimous. As a nod to the defeated
president and senator, the convention adopted another resolution praising
the Kansas-Nebraska Act and the Pierce administration. In the afternoon
session, the Illinois delegation put forth filibuster John Quitman of Mississippi for vice president, and Louisiana nominated the young and handsome

Breckinridge, a favorite among doughfaces. Though Quitman led on the first ballot (displaying Democratic exuberance for filibustering), Breckinridge prevailed on the second. Bright, who had overseen the Kentuckian's rise for years, had finally managed to place him in a national administration. Not only would Bright control patronage in the Old Northwest, but both Buchanan and Breckinridge would owe their nominations to him.[11]

The 1856 Elections

The nomination of "Buck and Breck" was not only a tremendous personal victory for Bright but also a resounding triumph for the South. The general election, however, was far from secure. The elderly Buchanan faced a three-way race with former president Millard Fillmore of New York, nominated by the nativist Know-Nothings, and the dashing adventurer John Frémont, put forth by the antislavery Republicans. To complicate matters, the American Party (the political vehicle of the Know-Nothings) split in early 1856 over slavery. "North Americans," as the Northern wing was called, opposed the expansion of slavery and rejected Fillmore, while the "South Americans" were proslavery and supported him. This unusual partisan situation made for an exciting political environment, with voter enthusiasm unmatched since the hard-cider and log cabin campaigns of 1840. "The canvass had no parallel in the history of American politics," recalled politician and lawyer George Julian.[12]

Mass meetings, huge rallies, and religious-like partisan zeal were the order of the day, and the Northern Democrats did all they could to make their conservative, proslavery agenda appealing to free state voters. Since the antislavery movement had swept most of Ohio and New England, Democrats focused on Iowa, Illinois, Indiana, New York, and Pennsylvania, where there was substantial Southern sympathy and where Northern Democrats still operated effective political machines. Fillmore could not match Frémont in the free states or Buchanan in the South, especially after the split in the American Party, so his only hope was to throw the election to the House of Representatives. Southerners, for their part, saw little difference between Fillmore and Frémont. Buchanan, on the other hand, enjoyed solid Southern support and aimed to court conservative Whigs in the North. "You have nothing to fear from the South," Cobb assured him.[13]

Regardless of electoral strategy, the central issue of the campaign was slavery and Southern power. Against the backdrop of perpetual war in the Kansas Territory, Northern Democrats advertised their proslavery agenda as "non-intervention," while Republicans advocated the Wilmot Proviso and an immediate halt to the expansion of slavery. "The all engrossing subject every where is the slavery question," noted one traveler in the North. "Every where I hear one universal cry against the extension of slavery." Despite the antislavery tide, however, Northern Democrats had distinct advantages. Buck and Breck could run on firm proslavery credentials, both in domestic and foreign policy, and there was no doubt about their future course, but Republicans were untested and suffered from divisions in their ranks caused by nativists and abolitionists chafing at party discipline.[14]

Unlike Republicans, moreover, the Democrats had battle-tested party machinery and partisan fidelity spanning generations, not to mention the considerable power of an incumbent Democratic administration. Given Frémont's inexperience with governance and the newness of the party, Democrats easily painted the Republicans as abolitionist fanatics bent on disunion. To dissuade Northern nativists from supporting the Republican ticket, Democrats spread lies about Frémont's religion, claiming he was a closet Catholic, a false charge that "the Pathfinder" failed to refute. In the end, Frémont proved more a liability to the Republicans than an asset. Though he was hugely popular in the free states, he was an inept party leader. Nevertheless, Republicans enjoyed an enthusiasm advantage over the Democrats and used "Bleeding Kansas" and "Bleeding Sumner" to great effect.[15]

To counteract Republican enthusiasm and distract from their disastrous policy record, Northern Democrats employed a powerful weapon: fear. They claimed that Buchanan was the only candidate whose election would not result in disunion and race war. Fillmore's party had already divided over slavery, and the South would never accept a Republican president. To make real on the rhetoric, Southern leaders ratcheted up their perennial threats of secession and civil war. Buchanan, for his part, allowed his career to speak for him; he made no speeches and remained at Wheatland tending to mail and meetings. Through letters, though, Buchanan instructed Democrats on how the campaign should be run, knowing full well the power of fear. *"The union is in danger & the people every where begin to know it,"* he wrote to Glancy Jones. "This race ought to be run on the question of union or disunion." "Should Fremont be elected," he informed a Massachusetts Democrat, "the consequence will be *immediate* and inevitable." To pay for the massive effort at the national level, a special committee of eight was created in Washington to direct pamphlets, speaking tours, and letters. Bright, Slidell, Cobb, Corcoran, and Glancy Jones managed the effort, pulling wires, forcing state organizations into line, and raising money. Slidell and Cobb even took over management of the official party organ, the *Washington Union*.[16]

With their assets and experience, Democrats were certainly confident of victory, but they received a rude awakening when Maine went overwhelmingly Republican in the September state elections. "The news from Maine is alarming, showing the abolition tendency every where North," exclaimed one Georgian. Indeed, Democrats had no choice but to intensify their rhetoric and redouble their efforts if they wanted any Northern votes. In the South, Governor Henry Wise of Virginia, a Buchanan adviser, wrote to his fellow slave state governors calling for an emergency meeting in Raleigh, North Carolina, to discuss a united response to a possible Frémont victory. Simultaneously, Southern governors began to mobilize their militias and prepare for war. "If Fremont is elected," wrote Wise, "there will be a revolution." Such rumblings from the slave states only aided the Democratic fear machine.[17]

After the defeat in Maine, attention turned to the key state of Indiana, the domain of Senator Bright. Hoosier Democrats, who had wanted Douglas, were unhappy with Buchanan and furious with Bright. Moreover, most Indiana Democrats still identified with the Wright majority. Despite their unpopularity, however, Bright and Buchanan benefited from opposition infighting over temperance, nativism, and slavery. Indiana Democrats were relatively united, while the opposition was divided, thanks in no small part to the ability of Bright and Corcoran to bribe the American Party state manager Richard Thompson. To distract from the uproar over the Kansas-Nebraska Act and the Southern agenda, Indiana Democrats appealed to racial fears, calling Republicans "amalgamationists" and claiming that they wanted total racial equality. Democratic parades, according to the *Indianapolis Daily Sentinel*, often featured young white girls holding banners pleading, "Fathers, save us from nigger husbands!"[18]

As election day approached, Bright and the Democrats smelled victory. Though they were politically and personally unpopular, the opposition simply could not unite to produce an effective challenge. "I remain confident as to Buchanan's success in Indiana," Bright wrote on October 12. "He will be hard run at our State Election, but look to the vote on the members of Congress as affording the *test* of parties. The Fillmore party in Ind is rapidly being absorbed by the Fremont or Abolition party." And thirteen days later, he penned, "The work goes . . . on in this State. A few days more and all that will be left of the Republican Party in this State will be the Record they have made; and a most infamous one it is. . . . We have run the iron through their corrupt hearts, and on the 4th of next month, we will as certainly clinch it."[19]

Bright's confidence was well founded, and Democrats were generally successful in Indiana. Through racist rhetoric and fearmongering they were able in October to elect the governor, as well as their entire state ticket, gain four congressional seats, and retain two. One of the two retained was that held by Bright confidant William English, from the vehemently pro-Southern Second District. "I am as well pleased," he wrote, "over your triumphant election as I am at anything that has occurred in the political world, for years." The Democrats were also able to carry the state for Buchanan in November, further elevating Bright's importance to a would-be Buchanan administration. If Old Buck gained the presidency, Bright would control the patronage of the Northwest and would be free to reward his proslavery friends and punish his antislavery enemies.[20]

Democrats were far less united in the Empire State, where deep divisions between Hards and Softs persisted. As usual, the proslavery Hards, commanded by Daniel Dickinson and Sam Beardsley, were intractable and refused to compromise to achieve unity with the Softs, led by Governor Horatio Seymour and Secretary of State William Marcy. "In this state our party was weakened & demoralized by our past divisions & disputations," explained one New York Democrat to Breckinridge. Moreover, antislavery sentiment was fast sweeping the state, and Buchanan was disliked by most Yankees. "Buchanan has totally collapsed in this State," observed journalist Charles Dana. The state was mostly lost for Democrats, with the crucial exception of New York City, where major financial interests had important economic ties to the South. Many financiers and industrialists, however, were weary of the Democratic Party's traditional animosity toward banking and manufacturing. Nevertheless, Slidell, Sickles, and Augustus Schell were able to raise enormous sums of money by asserting that a Republican victory would result in disunion and thus a dramatic disruption of business and commerce. These fear tactics were lent credence by the actions and threats of Southern leaders. By the end of September, Democrats had raised over fifty thousand dollars, which would be put to use in other key battleground states such as Pennsylvania.[21]

The Keystone State was an absolute must-win for Buchanan. Democrats believed they could carry the solid South, but they still needed populous Pennsylvania. Plus, it was Old Buck's home state and it would be a huge embarrassment if he could not deliver it. All eyes turned to state elections in October to see how the state would go in November. "If we can carry Pa. for our state ticket every thing is safe—if we lose that election I fear that all is lost," wrote Cobb to Buchanan. "Too much importance cannot be attached to the result of your state elections," he added. Keystone Democrats faced a similar situation to Indiana: Democrats were unpopular, but the opposition was fragmented. Fusion among Know-Nothings and Republicans had gone poorly, and nativist sentiment continued to be a powerful force, distracting from the central issue of slavery. In addition, Democrat-turned-Republican Simon Cameron maintained his own political organization separate from Republicans, hampering fusion. While Buchanan sat at Wheatland spreading fears of the "imminent danger of disunion, should Fremont be elected," as he often phrased it, Glancy Jones took command of the state canvass, aided by newspaper editor John Forney in Philadelphia. As chairman of the Pennsylvania State Central Committee, Forney flooded the state with speakers and pamphlets and saw to the mobilization of the immigrant vote through hasty and sometimes fraudulent naturalization proceedings.[22]

Unlike New York, Pennsylvania Democrats were firmly united behind skilled, energetic leadership. Money, primarily from Wall Street, poured into the state, allowing Jones and Forney to counter the opposition at every move ("We spent a great deal of money," recalled Forney years later). Fear continued to be the best weapon, and newspapers and traveling orators filled the heads of Pennsylvanians with images of bloody disunion and gruesome race war. African Americans, claimed the *Pennsylvanian*, were so dangerous that they must be kept in bondage to protect whites. Cobb and Herschel Johnson of Georgia were brought in for a whirlwind proslavery speaking tour. "The state has been canvassed with extraordinary zeal & energy by the ablest Democrats of the party," assured William Preston to Breckinridge. Charges that Fremont was a Catholic were especially potent in Pennsylvania, and many conservative Whigs preferred the Democracy to the Republicans. These small advantages gave narrow victory to the Democrats, including the reelection of Glancy Jones to Congress in a hard-fought, bitter contest in the former Democratic stronghold of Berks County. "The glorious results of the elections of the 14th Inst in Pennsylvania, Indiana . . . have made the calling and election of B and B by the people next month 'a fixed fact!'" exclaimed Democrat W. Grandin to Senator Robert Hunter of Virginia.[23]

Results were more mixed in Illinois, where Democrats were frustrated with Douglas's convention defeat and were quickly losing ground to the Republicans. Douglas had been disappointed with his failure to obtain the nomination at Cincinnati but was pleased with the firm proslavery platform and the endorsements of the Kansas-Nebraska Act. He entered the fall canvass determined to attack all anti-Democratic parties and coalitions. "Make war upon the common enemy," he instructed editor James Sheahan. After the convention, the Little Giant spoke at rallies in Washington, New York, and Philadelphia, asserting that the Democracy was the only national party and that a vote for Republicans was a vote for disunion. He was a tireless campaigner and brilliant politician; he enlisted the help of William Corcoran to frighten the financial elites, wrote letters urging his supporters to embrace Buchanan, established a German-language newspaper to appeal to the immigrant community, and even sold some of his Chicago property to raise cash for the campaign.

But Douglas was in Washington until the adjournment of Congress at the end of August, and the day-to-day management of the Illinois Democracy fell to Richardson. At the Democratic state convention in May, Richardson ensured that antislavery men were kept out of the party, that the Kansas-Nebraska Act continued to be a test of party loyalty, and that he received the gubernatorial nomination (a decision dictated by Douglas months earlier). Any lingering antislavery Democrats—if any—were driven into opposition ranks, thus strengthening the Republicans. In the gubernatorial race, Richardson's challenger, William Bissell, was a Catholic, a fact that Democrats used to sow dissention among their competitors. Douglas and Richardson even encouraged the Fillmore campaign in Illinois, hoping it would take votes away from Republicans. They knew their only chance of success lay with a divided adversary.[24]

Douglas penned to Buchanan at the end of September, "We are in the midst of the most exciting contest ever known in this State. The opposition are making desperate efforts." After Congress adjourned, Douglas hurried west to take charge personally, stopping only in Indiana for campaign events with Bright, Breckinridge, and James Orr. Once in Illinois, he crisscrossed the state with impressive energy, giving rousing speeches and railing against Republicans. To give the Democrats a boost, outside orators, such as Seymour, Wise, Cobb, and Cass, were brought in to help paint Republicans as fanatics. As for Richardson's race, he had a particularly hard time. His drunkenness, proslavery course, and high-handed tactics proved a real liability, and the opposition press had a field day describing his doughface exploits. On election day in October, he was soundly defeated, and Democrats across the state failed at the polls. Though Buchanan would go on to win the state in November, the October defeats essentially ended a generation of Democratic rule in the Prairie State. "The power of Douglas & slavery is forever broken in Illinois," crowed one voter. Douglas was devastated, and he could not have failed to realize the implications for his own reelection in 1858.[25]

As a culmination of the tumultuous state campaigns, the November presidential election saw a remarkable voter turnout. Almost 83 percent of eligible Northern voters went to the polls, an increase of 7 percent from 1852. "It was one of the most severe political struggles through which we have ever passed," recalled Buchanan. Buck and Breck emerged victorious, carrying every Southern state except Maryland, which went for Fillmore.

In the free states, however, the Democrats carried only Pennsylvania, New Jersey, Illinois, Indiana, and California, all of which had significant Southern populations. "In this state we have done badly—It would take too long to tell all the causes," explained one New York Democrat to the vice president–elect. Frémont carried the rest of the North, but Fillmore had drawn away just enough old Whigs to prevent a Republican victory. Frémont ballots were available in only four Southern states (Delaware, Maryland, Virginia, and Kentucky), but Republicans were still able to rival Buchanan for the popular vote. The close election frightened many Democrats, who blamed the unpopularity of the Pierce administration. "It is true we have a glorious triumph in Indiana," wrote an angry Bright, "but we do not feel the least indebted to 'Franklin Pierce' for it. His administration was a mill stone around our neck."[26]

The Republicans, on the other hand, failed to elect Frémont but saw the election as a "victorious defeat" and an amazing triumph for an infant party. While the Democrats watched their command of state and national politics slip away, Republicans realized that if they added Pennsylvania and either Indiana or Illinois to their 1856 column, they would win in 1860. "I arrived here [Washington] Saturday night and find our Republican friends in great spirits for a defeated party," penned Senator Lyman Trumbull. "They are bold, confident and united, ready for another fight and feel that they will certainly win next time." And Buchanan was the first president since 1828 to win an election without carrying a majority of the free states. He would be a Southern-elected executive, with a Southern agenda and Southern principles.[27]

Regardless, Buchanan was in "extacies" when he learned of his election. He had finally achieved that for which he had strived since at least 1844. Also on the bright side, he would have three critical doughface advocates in the U.S. Senate, that supposedly sectionally balanced body where Southern control rested on the shoulders of Northern Democrats. Newly elected William Bigler of Pennsylvania would prove a valuable friend in the upper chamber, casting decisive votes and defending the Slave Power at every turn.

Born in January 1814 and raised in the hills of central Pennsylvania, Bigler was educated by his older brother after their father died. He dabbled in printing and lumber but soon entered the political arena, where he was elected to the state senate in 1841. Because of his dedication to his party, he quickly rose to statewide prominence and leadership in the legislature. Though many Keystone Democrats distrusted Bigler, rising star Glancy Jones saw promise in his colleague and arranged for his election as governor in 1851. Bigler's gubernatorial term, however, proved problematic, as he flip-flopped on issues, ignored Jones's counsel, and made unpopular appointments. Thrown out of office in the post-Kansas-Nebraska upheaval, Bigler continued to estrange himself from the Buchanan-Jones machine, which controlled the state party.[28]

FIGURE 8. Senator William Bigler, Pennsylvania (Library of Congress)

Yet Pennsylvania Democrats took the 1854 defeats hard and sympathized with Bigler's losing to "a coalition between the Wooly Heads, Know-
Nothings, and Bogus Democrats." Bent on vindication, and short on qualified candidates, Democrats put Bigler up for the Senate in the fall of 1855.
Three circumstances resulted in the election of this unpopular doughface.
First, Bigler reconciled with Buchanan, who was in London. Second, the
anti-Democratic opposition in the state legislature was fragmented, while
the Democrats were united. And third, Bigler ran an especially vigorous
campaign. "Bigler has and is making desperate efforts to be elected, begging
beseeching and I do not know but almost going down upon his knees to affect it," reported Daniel Jenks to a suspicious Buchanan. Remarkably, Bigler
was elected, and he entered the Senate on January 14, 1856.[29]

This Pennsylvanian may have been an inept governor and an unreliable
factional warrior, but he had an unquestionable doughface record and his
proslavery vote in the Senate would be dependable. He was a man of few
principles, dedicated entirely to the Democratic Party and his own advancement. He adhered to no ideology and was often described by his contemporaries as politically "timid," meaning unwilling to take stands on issues. Like
Cass, Bigler endeavored to avoid clarity in his politics and sought to make
friends in all factions. He also exhibited a deep sense of white supremacy,
believing all nonwhites, especially African Americans, were created by God
to be subjugated for servitude. Nonwhites, he maintained, were incapable
of intelligent thought and, left to themselves, were dangerous barbarians.
"The ideal liberty as it existed in Greece & Rome, among the European
nations generally, and in America ever since a European planted his foot on
this mighty Continent, was never dreamed of by the negro," he wrote in a
discussion of racial hierarchy. "The negro race have no history, no rise and
progress, no decline & fall." Needless to say, Bigler was an ardent advocate of
proslavery legislation.[30]

Trouble in Indiana

The two other key Northern Democrats in the U.S. Senate came from
Indiana. Though highly unpopular at home, Bright continued to control
the Hoosier Democracy through strong-arm tactics and force of will, and
the election of Buchanan and Breckinridge strengthened his position in the
national party. His control of northwestern patronage and the allegiance to
him of both the president and vice president made him the most powerful
Northern Democrat in Congress. His reelection, however, was far from certain. Hoosiers loathed him, and Democrats had long tired of his tyrannical,

vengeful rule. With the Indiana state legislature divided (Democrats controlling the house and Republicans the senate), Bright was sufficiently concerned to pursue a cabinet position in case his election bid failed. Equally concerning to Bright was the vacancy left since January 1855, when Democrats refused to go into joint session to elect a senator. Governor Wright's term expired in January 1857, and he made it clear he wanted the Senate seat. Wright and Bright were still implacable rivals, and there was no way Bright would tolerate Wright at his side in Washington. Instead, Bright pushed the candidacy of his proslavery friend Dr. Graham Fitch of Logansport.[31]

Fitch was a New York transplant, born outside Rochester in December 1809. He attended Middlebury Academy and received medical training from the New York College of Physicians and Surgeons. Thereafter, he moved to Logansport, Indiana, where he established his own practice. He was elected to the state legislature in 1836 and 1839, then became a professor of anatomy at the Rush Medical College in Chicago. In the late 1840s, he returned to Indiana politics and served in the U.S. House of Representatives from 1849 to 1853, developing a reputation as a two-faced politician, simultaneously running as a Free Soiler and condemning the Wilmot Proviso as a "wooly headed humbug." His vacillation, however, was short-lived, and he soon became "enlightened to the rewards of doughface politics," as one scholar has put it. Fitch was never popular, even in his own district, and Democrats certainly preferred Wright to Fitch for the vacant Senate seat. But Bright's machine was now more powerful than ever, and he was confident he could browbeat Democrats into accepting Fitch and himself. On January 15, 1857, three days before the Democratic nominating caucus, Bright wrote to his close friend Corcoran, "Give yourself no fear about my Reelection. If an election takes place I will receive the *unanimous* vote of my Party, and more than even that."[32]

Such arrogance was unfounded, however, for when the caucus met on January 18, Bright was forced to negotiate with his hated rival. Wright had the majority, but he recognized that Bright had the support of the South and the incoming administration. Shortly before the caucus convened, Wright man Representative John Davis approached Bright agent Representative James Hughes to discuss a deal. No agreement was cemented, but soon after Lieutenant Governor Abram Hammond negotiated an accord whereby Wright would allow Fitch the nomination in exchange for Bright's support for a cabinet post. The caucus meeting solidified the agreement, and attendees signed a pledge: "We the undersigned members of the Legislature, in signing a Recommendation in favor of Gov Wright's receiving a first class appointment, understood that if Mssrs. Bright and Fitch received the nomination for U.S. Senator, that Gov Wright was to receive the highest office given to the State of Indiana." Bright, though, had no intention of placing his nemesis in the cabinet, and he explained to Corcoran that a diplomatic assignment was the best Wright would get, especially since it would get him out of the country. "I write on the wing amid shouts & cheering over the result of our Caucus nomination" penned Bright. "Fitch & myself were nominated by acclamation, Wright declining *on the organization of the* Caucus. He has been recommended for a first class appointment, rather pro forma. This means a foreign appointment & we will all go for it to get rid of that loud demagogue."[33]

Bright's reelection troubles were not at an end, though. He may have forced Democrats to swallow Fitch and himself, but Republicans in the state legislature had other plans. Using tactics employed by the Democrats in 1844 and 1855, Republicans refused to go into joint session to elect senators. On February 4, 1857, Democrats, led by Bright, met with some Know-Nothings and elected Bright and Fitch without the Republican majority. The election was clearly illegitimate, and Republicans instantly cried foul. The state legislature launched an investigation and the press proclaimed a "sham election," but Bright, Fitch, and the Democrats proceeded regardless. "Oh! shame! shame! that Indiana has to be thus misrepresented," wailed one Hoosier. Bright, for his part, claimed he acted entirely within the law and that his seat in the Senate was secure. "Come what may," he assured Corcoran, "*you* may be assured *I* will do nothing that is not right just and proper." On February 9, Bright presented Fitch's credentials to the Senate, which sparked a debate over the irregular election. The matter, including Bright's own legitimacy, was referred to the Judiciary Committee, where Bright's fire-eating friend Robert Hunter of Virginia would see to a favorable hearing.[34]

The Judiciary Committee would not report on the Bright-Fitch matter until over a year later, when it eventually found in favor of the Hoosier Democrats. Republicans in Indiana and Washington protested vehemently and declared that the vote had been biased, since there were five Democrats on the committee and only two Republicans. On the floor of the Senate, Lyman Trumbull, William Seward, and John Hale led the attacks. Bright's ally Hunter was able to postpone the final vote on Bright and Fitch for another several months, until June 2, 1858, two days before adjournment. Predictably, voting occurred along party lines, thirty to twenty-three, sustaining the Democrats. It is important to note, however, that Douglas voted against his Democratic colleagues, further widening the breach between the Little Giant and Bright. "At long last Jesse D. Bright was secure in his third term," explains Bright's principal biographer. "But it was a Pyrrhic victory, for there is little doubt that when the question of expelling Bright came before the Senate three years later, many considered it as merely the final act of the contested election of 1857."[35]

President-Elect Buchanan

With Bigler, Bright, and Fitch in the Senate, President-elect Buchanan could focus his attention on forming a cabinet and preparing his administration. Buchanan realized that his support lay almost entirely in the South and that if the Northern Democracy eroded any further, Republicans would win in 1860. Thus, it fell to Old Buck to repair the factionalism among Northern Democrats and reenergize Democratic voters. Yet that task would prove extraordinarily difficult, not only because Buchanan was disliked in the free states, but also because the South demanded that he adhere to a strict pro-slavery, pro-Southern line in both policy and patronage—not a recipe for wooing Northern voters. "His cabinett [sic] must be composed of men thoroughly with us on the Kansas Nebraska issue—no dodging, no compromising it," insisted Senator Toombs of Georgia. After the troubles and perceived vacillating of the Pierce administration, the South would accept nothing less than pure proslavery conservatism from the new president.[36]

The first order of business was the cabinet. Political agents and would-be advisers flocked to Buchanan's luxurious estate in sleepy Lancaster, a three-hour train ride west from Philadelphia. Like his predecessor Pierce, Buchanan opted to stay mum on appointments, leaving partisans in limbo. To aid with the flood of visitors and mail, Buchanan summoned to his side Forney; his chief clerk in London, John Appleton; and trusted lieutenant Glancy Jones. Newly elected Senator Bigler was also often at Wheatland, along with top advisers Bright, Slidell, and Wise.

Bright, in particular, expected a cabinet spot, since his Senate seat was potentially insecure. Indiana had gone for Buchanan in the election, and most Democrats expected the state to receive a lucrative post, such as secretary of the interior, which managed land sales, territorial matters, and Indian affairs. Though Bright had made the deal with Wright to advocate him for the cabinet, Bright had no intention of honoring the pledge. Moreover, Bright maneuvered to block Douglas in the patronage scramble. "I cannot shut my eyes to the fact that [Douglas] is both jealous of, and hostile to me," Bright confessed to Corcoran, "but for the present, I intend not to seem to notice it. 'His star has set in the West.'" Buchanan, though, was wary of giving Bright a cabinet appointment. Bright had proved enormously useful in the convention and campaign, but his poor relationship with Hoosier voters was a problem and his famous physical aggression and anger were not appropriate for high counsels. Buchanan and his managers would have to find a compromise for the cabinet, someone who would placate Bright, please Douglas, and not cause trouble.[37]

In general, Buchanan sought to learn from Pierce's mistakes and appoint only respected conservatives. Since antislavery sentiment had effectively been banished from the party, there was no need to woo Softs or Barnburners as there had been in 1852. Prominent Southern Democrat and former Speaker of the House Cobb was an obvious choice for the State Department, but Cobb was perceived as a moderate and Southern fire-eaters insisted on one of their own, namely Hunter. Buchanan agreed to set Cobb aside for the moment but would not accept Hunter, since Hunter's rival in Virginia politics was Buchanan's close friend Henry Wise. "The great difficulty will be in the selection of a Secretary of State," Buchanan confided to Jones. To explore his options, the president-elect met with Slidell in Philadelphia. Leading cabinet candidates, Slidell explained, included former Virginia governor John Floyd; former Tennessee governor Aaron Brown; Mississippi planter and rabid Southern nationalist Jacob Thompson; and Judah Benjamin of Louisiana, who had been part of the convention "cabal." Buchanan had to be equally careful with Northern candidates. Dickinson was the leading Hard, but Empire State divisions and quarrels made a New York choice impossible; plus Buchanan had not won the state. "At present they are a perfect chaos," Buchanan wrote to Wise concerning New York politics.[38]

In the West, the Bright-Douglas feud spelled trouble. Bright had been key to Buchanan's nomination and victory, but Douglas had formidable support in both the North and South that could not be ignored. The Little Giant pushed Richardson, recently defeated for Illinois governor, for the cabinet, and Bright was angling for himself. As a compromise, Bright suggested Cass. If Buchanan took Cass, who was about to be ousted from office by Michigan Republicans, for the top spot, it would avoid a fatal clash between Bright and Douglas. The only problem was that Buchanan did not care for Cass, and Cass was senile and irrationally Anglophobic, the latter an especially dangerous trait for a secretary of state. At the same time he considered Cass for State, Buchanan toyed with Cobb at Treasury, which further upset the Hunter faction. To address the matter personally, Buchanan traveled from Lancaster through a heavy blizzard to Washington in January 1857. There, he inquired of Cass's health (a real concern), and met with Cobb, Wise, Slidell, Douglas, and Pierce. The conference with Douglas was critical. Buchanan did not like Douglas and did not want his advice, but Buchanan had to discuss the choice of Cass and explain that Illinois would not receive a cabinet post. Douglas, recalling the same treatment by Pierce, became flippant and insistent, demanding his share of the patronage and condemning Bright's perfidy. Buchanan was unimpressed, and Douglas left the interview seething with rage and resentment.[39]

In February, it was Bright's turn to press his claims on Old Buck. Meeting at Wheatland, the Hoosier boss defended himself against Douglas's charges, urged Cass for State, and convinced Buchanan to give Wright a foreign assignment, brazenly breaking his pledge to Indiana Democrats. Instead of the promised cabinet appointment, Wright would be offered the mission to Prussia, at Berlin, safely removed from Hoosier politics. "I consider [Bright] corrupt and faithless as Hell," wrote an enraged Indiana legislator to Representative Davis. "A more damnable act of ingratitude was never perpetrated than this of betraying his solemn pledges made in this Hall, to destroy and thwart our wishes & desires. Joe Wright may fall at Washington, but the people the bone & sinew of Indiana will yet come to his rescue and hurl from power those who intend and desire to ride over their expressed will." By agreeing to banish Wright and accept Cass, Buchanan was paying his dues to Bright and ensuring political peace for his incoming administration. The selection of the lethargic Cass, in particular, was a deft move. Not only would it prevent a Bright-Douglas war, it would allow Buchanan, the experienced diplomat and self-assured statesman, to run his own State Department.[40]

To ensure that Cass would not try to assert himself as chief diplomat, however, Buchanan forced on him three humiliating conditions. First, Cass could not appoint as his assistant his son-in-law, on whom he depended physically and intellectually; that post would be reserved for Buchanan aid John Appleton. Second, he would have to accept that Appleton, who would report directly to the president, would act as supervisor rather than assistant. And third, he would have to moderate his fierce Anglophobia, especially since Buchanan had spent the past four years building relationships in London. Though essentially agreeing to be nothing more than an aid to the president, Cass eagerly accepted. He had been defeated for president in 1848, had been denied the nomination in 1852, and had just been thrown out of office—Cass would take any offer he could get.[41]

With the west placated with Cass, Buchanan could return to Southern demands. In the end, he followed Slidell's advice and appointed Southerners Cobb to Treasury, Floyd to War, Brown to the patronage-rich postmaster generalship, and Thompson to Interior. Buchanan had intended to make his protégé Jones attorney general, especially after his critical roles in the House and in the campaign, but Jones's Pennsylvania rivals, led by a jealous Forney, forced Buchanan to find a substitute. Eventually, he settled on his humorless friend Jeremiah Black. And finally, for Navy, Buchanan acquiesced to the pleas of Pierce men and appointed Isaac Toucey of Connecticut, who had voted for the Kansas-Nebraska Act.

The finished product was strikingly proslavery, with four slave owners and three doughfaces. Conspicuously absent were any Douglas men or Democrats of the Young America stripe, who were interested in internal improvements and were suspicious of the traditional party leadership. All the cabinet members, including the new president, were old, intractable Democrats from the era of General Jackson, fearful of change and immovably conservative. "I am an outsider," lamented Douglas. "My advice is not coveted nor will my wishes probably be regarded." Overall, the constitution of the cabinet was dramatically different from that of the outgoing administration. While Pierce had surrounded himself with leading men who would advise him, Buchanan chose weak, unremarkable men who would not challenge; Buchanan sought subordinates, not counselors. The three Northern Democrats, in particular, were nearly nonentities. While Pierce had allowed Marcy a free hand at State, Cass would be reduced to signing forms and dealing with correspondence; while Pierce had rejoiced in Cushing's expansion of federal power in the name of slave hunting, Buchanan would issue instructions to his Pennsylvania subordinate Black; and while Pierce had deferred to Davis in almost all matters, Buchanan would ignore Floyd, recognizing that he was virtually incompetent.[42]

Cabinet concerns may have taken a priority in the winter of 1856–1857, but the president-elect also contemplated policy and his inaugural address. He had come to the conclusion long ago that the slavery issue had to be removed from the halls of Congress, that the debate had to be stifled decisively, and that an expansive ruling from the Supreme Court would do just that. Luckily for Buchanan, there was a case presently before the court that dealt ostensibly with Southern rights and slavery in the territories—*Dred Scott v. Sanford*.[43]

The case began as a small legal question in Missouri concerning a slave, Dred Scott, suing his owner, John Sanford, for his freedom, arguing that time spent in free Illinois and the free territory of Wisconsin meant that he was a free man being held against his will. The case had snaked its way through the state judicial system, where it acquired quite a bit of political baggage, and finally ended up before the U.S. Supreme Court. Opening arguments began on February 11, 1856, but the case received scant attention. In May, the suit was postponed to the next term, possibly a move by the Southern-controlled court to avoid a proslavery ruling before the fall presidential election. Issuing a decision on slavery in the territories would have undermined the "popular sovereignty" platform of Buchanan and the Democrats. Furthermore, it is important to note that all the Supreme Court justices were politically active and well connected; they were closely attuned to congressional activity, the national debate over slavery, and the Democratic agenda. Chief Justice Roger Taney, for instance, vacationed with President Pierce at Fauquier White Sulphur Springs, Virginia, in December 1855.[44]

Buchanan, too, was in close contact with the justices and worked with Stephens to influence the *Scott* ruling. On his January 1857 trip to Washington, the president-elect had met with Justice John Catron of Tennessee specifically to discuss the matter. On his return home, Buchanan penned a letter to Catron about their conversation, a letter that was intended to be shown to the other justices. When Buchanan questioned Catron about a decision date, Catron replied that nothing had been set but that he would continue to supply Buchanan with information. In turn, Buchanan made it clear that only a broad proslavery ruling, particularly on the constitutionality of the 1820 Compromise Line, would be acceptable. He was so insistent, in fact, that he wrote Catron again on February 10 asking if a ruling would be made in time for his inaugural address on March 4. Finally, Catron revealed that the case would be settled on February 14, but without a general ruling on slavery in the territories. That was not what Old Buck wanted to hear.[45]

The subsequent exchange of letters between Buchanan and Catron reveal a strange turn of events that resulted in the now-famous ruling. As expected, the Supreme Court had taken up the case and ruled against Scott, but the majority agreed to dispose of the matter with a simple statement that the court would not assume jurisdiction, thus leaving Scott in slavery. Taney, Stephens, and an assortment of other Democratic grandees, however, pressured Justice James Wayne of Georgia to urge the court to issue a broad ruling to be composed by Taney. Five of the seven justices favored the proposal, but a five-man majority was considered too weak by the party leaders to settle the slavery issue once and for all. Hence, Catron suggested that Buchanan pressure one of the Northern doughface judges who opposed an expansive ruling, namely, Justice Robert Grier of Pennsylvania. "Will you drop Grier a line," wrote Catron, "saying how necessary it is—and how good the opportunity is, to settle the agitation by an affirmative decision of the Supreme Court, the one way or the other?" The spectacled, whiskey-drinking Grier, it so happened, owed his place on the bench to Buchanan, who had declined the appointment from President Polk. The Pennsylvanian, not surprisingly, was amenable to Buchanan's overtures and agreed to concur with the Southern majority on a broad ruling. Old Buck had finally achieved the dramatic proslavery ruling he had desired, and he fully intended to make use of it in his inaugural address. He hoped that it would usher in an era of peace at the start of his administration, and Democrats in general were eager for a proslavery ruling that would end the debate and raise the Slave Power above challenge.[46]

A New Administration

The president-elect departed for the nation's capital on March 2, 1857, in a special rail car built for the occasion, amid all the pomp and circumstance little Lancaster could muster. Six feet tall with a crown of white coiffed hair and a bulging belly, Buchanan was a formidable figure. He often dressed in stiff white collar and neck cloth, looking more clerical than presidential, and exhibited an air of cold distance and formality; even his niece, perhaps the person closest to the bachelor, called him Mr. Buchanan. His most remarkable physical trait were his different-colored eyes, one blue, one hazel. In addition, he had poor vision in one eye, which caused Old Buck to cock his head to one side in an off-putting manner. Though generally considered, even by his friends, to possess a mediocre intellect at best, he was supremely confident in his own abilities, believing that a lifetime of public and partisan service made him most qualified to captain the ship of state.[47]

March 4, Inauguration Day, dawned bright and springlike. Crowds thronged the steps of the Capitol, and Democrats and Republicans alike were eager to hear what the new president would announce in his address.[48] After the installation of Vice President Breckinridge in the Senate chamber, Buchanan appeared on the east portico. Dressed in black and fortified with brandy, he stepped forward to take the oath of office from Chief Justice Taney. Before he did, however, the crowd noticed that he had a brief whispered conversation with Taney, the substance of which is unknown, but possibly could have concerned the impending *Dred Scott* decision.

Regardless, Buchanan proceeded to deliver a lengthy address that was devoid of oratorical flourish. "He was notably deficient in both ingenuity and in rhetorical brilliancy," recalled Senator Henry Foote. The new president began by declaring an electoral mandate that did not exist and undercut his own authority by announcing he would not seek a second term. He then proceeded to praise the Kansas-Nebraska Act and dismiss the debate over slavery in the territories as "a matter of but little practical importance." Next, with illicit knowledge about the *Scott* decision, he declared that slavery in the territories was "a judicial question, which legitimately belongs to the Supreme Court." There was even a case now before the court, he continued, that would settle the slavery question forever. And "to their decision," he proclaimed with false humility and innocence, "I shall cheerfully submit, whatever it may be." But Buchanan did not stop there. He added his own opinion that a territory could not vote on slavery until it was ready for statehood (effectively ensuring the spread of slavery) and that the federal government had no authority over slavery anywhere. The address was less explicitly proslavery than Pierce's but more activist in its content, paving the way for *Dred Scott* and announcing the unlimited spread of slavery. It was "pre-eminently moderate and conservative," remarked one pleased Southern observer.[49]

Once installed in office, the new president turned his attention to patronage and political awards. Democrats, they did not fail to realize, were in a rather unusual situation: this was the first Democratic administration to follow a Democratic administration since Van Buren succeeded Jackson in 1837. Democrats were already in patronage positions in 1857, and Buchanan had to be careful choosing whom to replace and why. In the end, the new president decided to purge the government of all but the most dedicated doughfaces and proslavery politicos. "Pierce men are hunted down like beasts," cried one correspondent to Marcy.[50]

Buchanan used his "rotatory rule" selectively. To reduce disruption to government business, for instance, he allowed more capable Pierce appointees, such as minister to France John Y. Mason of Virginia, to complete their diplomatic assignments before being replaced. There was also a distinct sectional bias in his application of the rule—it was applied only in the free states. Buchanan allowed the Southern bosses to make their own decisions and did not interfere with their plans. "Southern men very generally denounced it [rotation] and claimed—nay more—demanded—that their section of the country should be exempt from its operation," wrote Marcy with disgust. "This demand has been complied with." Such patronage decisions, politically motivated and sectionally charged, produced the desired discipline but resulted in staggering corruption. Ideological purity was valued above all else, and party hacks were chosen above qualified professionals; the good of the party was placed above the good of the community.

In addition, Buchanan's doughface appointees in the free states were highly unpopular with voters, who depended on them for public services. "The offices were made the sport of shear personal caprice," groaned Marcy. Within just two years, Buchanan's patronage decisions had produced unprecedented levels of corruption at the local level (when wielded by machines such as Tammany Hall in New York), as well as in the federal government (such as Secretary Floyd's pilfering of the War Department through an astounding series of complex, illegal land-selling schemes and no-bid contracts). "You have systematized corruption," complained a correspondent of Cobb in June

1858, and an acquaintance of James Henry Hammond complained of the "branded, corrupt few of the worst desperados in policies, [who] trade off for pay and promises by wholesale the Peoples' Highest Office to some of the vilest of mankind." Congressional inquiries and investigations later revealed the depths of corruption, everything from secret slush funds to buy votes in Congress to exorbitant printing contracts to cronies. The Buchaneers, indeed, were ruthless political pirates.[51]

Northerners may have been angered by Buchanan's patronage policy and cronyism, but they were appalled by the *Dred Scott* decision, delivered at 11:00 a.m. on March 6, 1857, just days after Buchanan deferred to the court in his inaugural address. In the windowless and musty Supreme Court chamber deep within the Capitol Building, the eighty-year-old chief justice announced the 7–2 decision and read his much-anticipated majority opinion on slavery in the territories. Taney, for his part, was a true voice from the past. Appointed to the bench by Jackson, he was an angry partisan from Maryland with tobacco-stained teeth and a prominent hunch; "he sat in his black gown like a skeleton in a shroud," recalled Forney. In a voice that was almost inaudible, Taney explained that blacks were not citizens of the United States and thus had no right to sue, that Congress had no power to regulate slavery in the federal territories, and that since Congress had no authority and that since slaves were property protected by the Constitution, the 1820 Line had been unconstitutional. In essence, the Supreme Court ruled that slavery could spread anywhere prior to statehood and that the government was powerless to stop it—ultimate vindication of the Slave Power. "The Court decides that the Constitution of the United States recognizes property in man, and that under it, and by force of it, human slavery is nationalized, and must be protected and defended in its spread and perpetuation," reported the *New York Tribune*. In addition, the ruling virtually outlawed the Republican Party, which was organized on the principle that Congress could stop the spread of slavery.[52]

Though constitutionally sound, the court's ruling was decried as "a political harangue in defense of slavery," as contemporary politico George Julian phrased it. Indeed, it was the crowning achievement of the Slave Power, and Republicans immediately seized on the issue as proof of a nefarious plot among Northern Democrats and Southern leaders to spread slavery and increase Southern power. Already irate, Northern voters were enraged at the Slave Power's bravado, even before the collusion between Buchanan, Stephens, Taney, Grier, and Catron had been revealed. "The barbarous doctrine that white men were not bound to respect the *right of black men to live*," wrote Republican Joshua Giddings, "awakened among the people an intense abhorrence not merely of the principle but of the men who enunciated a doctrine so revolting to Christianity."

Douglas Democrats, too, had reason to be upset. The decision, in declaring that government of any kind was powerless to stop the spread of slavery, eviscerated the concept of popular sovereignty—no amount of voting in the territories could stop Southerners from bringing along their human chattel. This, of course, placed Douglas, who had built a career on popular sovereignty, in a precarious political position. By the spring of 1857, he found himself not only shut out of patronage and the administration but also advocating a policy that was apparently no longer an option.[53]

Adding to Northern woes was the financial crisis that struck late in the summer of 1857, and which was barely noticed by the Southern planters. The panic, caused by the collapse of several large banks and railroads, as well as the opening of western territory to slavery thanks to the *Dred Scott* ruling, soon metamorphosed into a long-term economic downturn. Unemployment soared, and Secretary of the Treasury Cobb feared the worst. "I am preparing for the storm if it comes and lasts," he wrote in early October. "The country has experienced mighty changes indeed a revolution," added New York businessman John Bigelow. Even the president was forced to recognize the crisis, and he devoted to it a sizeable chuck of his first annual message to Congress. The address, however, was pure conservatism: no reform, no relief. He acknowledged the "suffering and distress prevailing among the people" but asserted that government had no power to act (an ominous foreshadowing of the secession crisis).

Instead, Buchanan defended economic cycles and claimed that depressions were a natural market correction; to have great prosperity, we must take great risks and be willing to accept economic downturns. "Deplorable, however, as may be our present financial condition," he lectured the nation, "we may yet indulge in bright hopes for the future. . . . The buoyancy of youth, the energies of our population, and the spirit which never quails before difficulties will enable us soon to recover from our present financial embarrassments, and may even occasion us speedily to forget the lesson which they have taught." These tired platitudes were of little comfort to unemployed Americans who had lost their savings and investments and were angry with an unregulated financial system. Since the crisis was largely limited to the Northern states, Southern planters became all the more convinced of the superiority of their slave economy. Moreover, the panic and depression were a boon to Republicans, who objected to Democratic laissez-faire policies and advocated government action and financial reforms.[54]

Foreign Policy

Since Buchanan felt no need to act on the financial crisis, and the Supreme Court had seemingly settled the slavery issue, he turned his attention to foreign policy and territorial acquisition. In his inaugural, he coyly stated that "no nation will have a right to interfere or to complain if in the progress of events we shall still further extend our possessions," essentially warning other countries to stay out of the way of American expansion. Buchanan had every intention of escalating Pierce's attempts at territorial acquisition and succeeding where his predecessor had failed. He sought to finally acquire Cuba, achieve U.S. dominance over the Caribbean, wrest more land from northern Mexico, extract trade and transit agreements from Central American nations, and curb British attacks on slave ships flying the Stars and Stripes. It was a bold agenda, and Buchanan personally saw to its implementation. With Secretary Cass inert and in full agreement, the president assumed direct management of the State Department, even going so far as to maintain his own office in the building. Together with John Appleton, Buchanan would deliver on the proslavery promises made to the Southern party bosses back in 1852.[55]

Central to Buchanan's foreign policy agenda was Latin America. In grandiose style, Old Buck used his first annual message to declare the United States protector of the "weak and feeble states" south of Mexico. He then listed various American claims against Latin American nations, vowed to maintain control of an isthmian transit route, and requested authorization to use the military to protect U.S. interests in Panama. He also admitted to strained relations with Great Britain and "numerous claims" against Spain, hoping to provide rationale for the seizure of Cuba. Finally, he bowed to the demands of slave state leaders gathered at the Southern Commercial Convention (held in Knoxville in August 1857) by denouncing the Clayton-Bulwer Treaty, which limited British and American imperialism in Central America. Buchanan's message made it clear that he had a two-step program to achieve his foreign policy goals: first, sweep European influence out of Latin America and, second, establish U.S. control through force, purchase, or treaty.[56]

A key component of the Buchanan program was the filibusters. Like his predecessor, President Buchanan only paid lip service to international agreements and neutrality laws and either aided or turned a blind eye to illegal filibustering expeditions against foreign nations. In March 1857, Henry Crabb and his "Arizona Colonization Company" invaded northern Mexico; Texan William Henry flaunted his plans to invade Mexico from the Lone Star State;

Governor Sam Houston of Texas announced to the War Department that he planned to recruit ten thousand men for an invasion; and the Knights of the Golden Circle, a fraternal organization dedicated to filibustering and the spread of slavery, operated openly and paraded in American cities.

Buchanan even allowed that Grey-Eyed Man of Destiny, William Walker, to launch another invasion of Nicaragua. Forced out of that country by nationalists in May 1857, Walker traveled to the United States, where he received an enthusiastic welcome from Democrats and immediately declared his intention to launch another expedition. "Our sympathies are all with the filibusters," wrote Stephens in early 1858. In June 1857, Walker actually met with President Buchanan, who, if he did not directly encourage the young filibuster, allowed him to continue his preparations for another invasion. "It is well understood that the Genl's expedition was countenanced in every practicable way by the administration," recorded one observer.[57]

Walker recruited openly in New Orleans, New York, and Mobile before embarking once again for Nicaragua in November 1857, confident that he had the support of the president, the South, and the Democratic Party. Buchanan's support was so firm, in fact, that he reprimanded, then dismissed, U.S. commodore Hiram Paulding for trying to apprehend the filibusters. The disciplining of Paulding caused an uproar in the free states, where voters condemned Buchanan's countenance of illegality. When Paulding secured Walker in custody, Buchanan released him to complete his mission. Within two years, however, Buchanan would turn away from Walker, allowing the Grey-Eyed Man of Destiny to be executed by a Honduran firing squad.[58]

Buchanan's disregard for international treaties and state sovereignty was so flagrant that the leaders of Nicaragua and Costa Rica issued the Rivas Manifesto, denouncing Buchanan's proslavery, profilibustering policies. Buchanan, in turn, was incensed and launched a plan to reorganize Latin America in the likeness of the United States. Meanwhile, he worked to extract as many concessions as possible from the United States' neighbors. He forced Nicaragua to grant transit rights across the isthmus, he bullied Mexico into accepting U.S. occupation during times of civil disturbance, and he sent nineteen warships with two hundred guns to Paraguay to force acceptance of U.S. economic interests. Old Buck was particularly interested in acquiring more land from Mexico, through either force or purchase. In his Second Annual Message, Buchanan claimed Mexico was in "a state of constant revolution" with "lawless violence," and it was a matter of national security for the United States to step in and take more land. "Abundant cause now undoubtedly exists for a resort to hostilities against the Government," he insisted.[59]

Buchanan was equally persistent with Cuban annexation. He hoped to make its acquisition the crowning achievement of his administration, the culmination of a long diplomatic career. While Pierce and Marcy had vacillated, Buchanan made it clear he would obtain Cuba *"by any means and at all costs,"* as one Spanish paper phrased it. He authorized Secretary Cass and the minister to Spain to reopen negotiations with the Spanish government, and he used his Annual Messages to denounce Spanish despotism. The island must be annexed, he reasoned, in order to end Spanish outrages, protect the Mississippi River, and improve British-American relations. "The truth," he concluded, "is that Cuba, in its existing colonial condition, is a constant source of injury and annoyance to the American people." When negotiations with Spain proved fruitless, Buchanan's top adviser, Slidell, introduced into the Senate on January 1, 1859, a bill authorizing thirty million dollars for the purchase of "the Pearl of the Antilles." The bill, not surprisingly, inflamed the sectional debate, and Republicans succeeded in killing it. Congress, by then controlled by Republicans, was determined to thwart Buchanan's proslavery agenda and refused to grant appropriations for his military operations.[60]

Connected to the Cuban issue was the illegal slave trade. Though the United States had outlawed the trade in 1808, it continued to flourish and new slaves arrived in Southern ports regularly. As Cuban annexation became more and more unlikely, Southern leaders moved to protect the slave trade, with some even advocating its legalization (if they could not have Cuba as a slave state, Southerners at least wanted its slaves). Standing in the way of that agenda was Great Britain and its zealous prosecution of slave ships. The Webster-Ashburton Treaty of 1842, negotiated by Whig Daniel Webster and despised by Democrats, not only prevented U.S. expansion in Latin America but also bound the United States to provide ships to an antislavery naval squadron in the Atlantic. Needless to say, the United States, under the control of Southern slave owners, rarely fulfilled its responsibility and repeatedly pressed Great Britain to modify the treaty.

Also at stake were U.S. neutrality and maritime rights, since the antislavery squadron stopped suspected slavers. The U.S. government thus cloaked its proslavery motives in patriotism, claiming that no ship flying the Stars and Stripes could be stopped for any reason. With this knowledge, slavers often flew the American flag to avoid search and seizure. As an agent of the Slave Power, Old Buck had no intention of honoring U.S. treaty obligations regarding the search of slavers. When the British ignored Buchanan's warnings and continued to stop slavers flying the Stars and Stripes, Southerners, as in 1811–1812, cried foul and demanded immediate action. Tensions heightened in 1858, when Great Britain expanded the squadron's scope and sent cruisers into Cuban waters. Buchanan, in return, strenuously objected and ordered every available naval vessel to the Gulf of Mexico to protect "U.S." ships. The "crisis of 1858" lasted only a few weeks but almost resulted in war with Great Britain, again.[61]

Great Britain eventually backed down and agreed to leave alone "U.S." ships, which allowed the illicit slave trade to blossom, even more than under Pierce, whose secretary of state, William Marcy, had not been so quick to dismiss treaty obligations. Under Buchanan's watch, the slave trade with Cuba rose to its highest levels since the 1830s. In sum, the Southern grandees could not help but be pleased. Old Buck had run an effective national campaign that played on Northern fears of secession and had delivered key free states, despite the growing Northern antislavery majority; he had orchestrated the monumental *Dred Scott* decision, which negated congressional authority in the territories and nullified that annoyingly ambiguous policy of popular sovereignty; he had purged the government of Softs; he had prevented federal action during an economic crisis; he had initiated a new era of aggressive foreign policy; and he had defied the British to ensure the survival of the illegal slave trade. He had fulfilled the hopes of Democrats and succeeded in purging the party's Northern wing of its last antislavery vestiges. All that was left for Buchanan to do to satisfy the South was to produce a new slave state from the war-torn Kansas Territory and a national slave code.

CHAPTER 7

"Let Us Stand by Our Colors"

Lecompton and Minority Rule

President James Buchanan was nominated and elected by the South with the implicit understanding that he would produce a Democratic slave state out of the Kansas Territory. He was not to interfere with the proslavery minority in the territory and its use of violence, fraud, and terrorism to force slavery on an unwilling free state majority. Buchanan's predecessor, Franklin Pierce, had failed to quash the free state Topeka government that arose to challenge the proslavery legislature recognized by the federal government. By the time of Old Buck's election, Kansas had degenerated into civil war and had become the most pressing domestic issue. The Sack of Lawrence and the Pottawatomie Massacre in the spring of 1856 had inaugurated a new, far more brutal phase of guerrilla war in the territory.[1]

In his last months in office, Pierce had labored to aid the proslavery faction and achieve some kind of peace. When his agents threw the popularly elected free state governor Charles Robinson in jail for treason in May 1856, the free state majority mobilized and took up arms to defend itself, in turn allowing Pierce to more easily label them violent insurrectionaries. As the situation worsened, Pierce-appointed Governor Wilson Shannon turned to the use of federal troops. In July 1856, on orders from Pierce and Shannon, Colonel Edwin Sumner successfully dispersed the Topeka government through threat of force, leading to increased Northern outcry against the administration's course in Kansas. Moreover, Missourians, led by Senator David

Atchison, continued to wreak havoc in the territory, attacking antislavery settlers and illegally voting in territorial elections. By the fall of 1856, Pierce had replaced the inept Shannon with John Geary, a physically imposing veteran of the Mexican War and former mayor of Gold Rush San Francisco.[2]

Geary was determined to achieve peace by staying neutral in the fight over slavery—he would treat both sides fairly, punishing all acts of terrorism, and bring order to the territory through force of will. His watchword was *impartiality*, and the new governor made it clear he did not care which side emerged victorious. His only concern was that Kansas would enter the Union as a Democratic state, regardless of slavery. Though he was able to achieve a tenuous peace, he was unable to control the Missourians and proslavery faction, who maintained management of Kansas's courts and civil services.

Since they desired the extermination of the Topeka government rather than peace, the proslavery faction was unhappy with Geary and his failure to aid their cause. The proslavery legislature, still recognized as the legitimate authority in the territory, decided to undermine Geary's power by overriding all his vetoes and instructing judges to ignore the governor's directives. Furthermore, the legislature proceeded to pass a series of extraordinary proslavery laws (such as making it a felony to deny the legality of slavery in Kansas and making "rebellion" a capital crime) that made a mockery of Geary's program and outraged Northerners. Furthermore, Geary came to realize that the Democratic Party in Kansas *was* the proslavery party, and a Democratic state meant a slave state. "This virulent spirit of dogged determination to *force* slavery into this territory, has overshot its mark, and raised a storm," Geary reported to Pierce. Unwilling to choose between his impartiality and the Democratic state he hoped to achieve, the governor resigned in March 1857, at the end of Pierce's term.[3]

The new president could thus start with a blank slate of sorts and selected the diminutive but influential Robert Walker of Mississippi to be the new territorial governor. Walker was a close associate of Buchanan's, a former member of the Polk cabinet, and a major power within the Democratic Party. Walker, Buchanan hoped, would lend legitimacy to the party's Kansas policy, as well as bring to bear his considerable political experience to the territorial quagmire. Walker, for his part, was wisely reluctant to accept the mission. Kansas had already seen a slew of failed executives, and the Mississippian was not interested in ruining his reputation. Moreover, Pierce had proved an inconsistent and vacillating boss, and Walker wanted assurances that Buchanan would stand by him as he wrestled with proslavery militants and suspicious free state activists. To placate Walker, Buchanan made a fateful decision—he promised him not only that he would enjoy full administration support and confidence but also that the forthcoming state constitution would be submitted to a popular vote of legal residents.[4]

Governor Walker arrived in Kansas in May 1857, too late to shape the summer elections for a constitutional convention. Earlier in the year, on February 19, the proslavery territorial legislature had called for a constitutional convention to be held on September 7, at the town of Lecompton. The legislature planned to ignore the free state majority and craft a proslavery, minority rule document that would preserve slavery and enthrone the Democratic Party. Despite Buchanan's guarantees to Walker and Walker's very public announcement in his inaugural address that under no circumstances would Kansas be admitted to the Union without a popular ratification of the constitution, the legislature had no intention of submitting the final product to a vote. To make matters worse, the election of convention delegates, scheduled for June, would be based on an old, unrepresentative proslavery census conducted by proslavery commissioners. The free state majority, rightly outraged, boycotted the June election, thereby guaranteeing that the September convention would be unrepresentative; roughly 10 percent of the territorial population, mainly from proslavery areas, elected the sixty total delegates. The resulting document—the Lecompton Constitution—was both boldly proslavery and blatantly unrepresentative.[5]

Northern voters were appalled at the Lecompton Constitution, calling it a "swindle" and "grand fraud," and pressured Buchanan to keep his pledge to Walker and submit the document to a popular vote. Southerners, on the other hand, were delighted and made support for Lecompton a test of the president's loyalty to the party and the Slave Power. Simultaneously, Southern leaders revived their threats of disunion if Kansas was not delivered as a slave state. The legislatures of Alabama, Georgia, and Texas considered secession, and Senator Robert Hunter of Virginia published a letter calling Lecompton "the test by which I shall judge his administration." The renewed Southern militancy made Buchanan regret his promises to Walker, especially when Southerners demanded Walker's immediate dismissal after the governor's inaugural address. "I have just read Walker's inaugural in Kansas and if the document I have seen is genuine it is clear Buchanan had turned traitor," wrote one correspondent of Alexander Stephens. But while Buchanan wavered, Walker remained steadfast. "I was then very bitterly denounced," he recalled, "at which I felt profoundly indifferent, because I thought that any man who would approve or endorse such forgeries was a base and dishonest man."[6]

To calm the storm, Buchanan claimed to Southerners, both publicly and privately, that his instructions to Walker required only a plebiscite on slavery, not a vote on the whole constitution. To aid his friend the president, Secretary of the Treasury Howell Cobb operated as intermediary between Buchanan and agitated Southerners. Nevertheless, Walker continued to inflame the sectional crisis by giving speeches guaranteeing a vote on Lecompton. If the constitutional convention did not submit its product to a popular vote, he told Kansans, "I will join you, fellow citizens, in lawful opposition to their course." Southerners, positive of Buchanan's fidelity, saw Walker as the traitor, labeling him a rogue Free Soiler in Democratic clothing. Old Buck, however, privately reassured Walker of his support, writing, "On the question of submitting the Constitution to the bona fide residents of Kansas, I am willing to stand or fall." Despite such assurances, Walker read the writing on the wall and came to understand that Buchanan was the tool of the slave states and that there was a concerted effort on the part of the administration to force slavery on Kansas.[7]

Determined to confront the president, Walker traveled to Washington and met with him on November 26, 1857. He pressed Buchanan to reject the fraudulent constitution and call for a new convention that would represent the territorial majority. Buchanan would have none of it, and Walker left the White House convinced he had been betrayed. The next day, Buchanan met with his cabinet and announced that he would embrace Lecompton and oppose popular ratification. Cobb even encouraged the president to publicly repudiate Walker. The news traveled quickly, and when Stephen Douglas intercepted the embattled governor in New York City, he informed him of the president's decision. Walker was less than surprised but decided to wait for the president's Annual Message to decide his course.[8] Douglas, too, had a fateful decision to make. He could continue to support the administration's policy in Kansas, stay loyal to the Southern agenda, and set himself up for the 1860 Democratic nomination at the cost of his Northern base. Or he could defy the party, oppose Lecompton, and rally his base at the cost of Southern support. Such a choice had to be weighed carefully, and the Illinois senator did not immediately make known his course. "There is great anxiety here to know Douglas['s] exact position," wrote Representative Thomas Harris to Illinois editor Charles Lanphier.[9]

On December 3, Douglas met with the president to explain his reservations about Lecompton. The Little Giant became furious when Buchanan remained unmoved, even after Douglas made it clear that supporting Lecompton would most likely kill the Northern Democracy and endanger his own reelection in October 1858. Fifty-five of fifty-six Illinois newspapers, Douglas explained, had already denounced Lecompton as a swindle and a farce. Buchanan, unimpressed, warned Douglas against opposing the party, threatening to destroy him if he did so. Knowing his strength among Northern Democrats and better appreciating the depth of anti-Lecompton sentiment in the free states, Douglas stormed out of the meeting determined to defy the administration. That same evening, Douglas ally Representative Thomas Harris was able to declare to Lanphier, "Douglas will make the greatest effort of his life in opposition to this juggle." "The Battle will soon begin," proclaimed Douglas two days later. "We will nail our colors to the mast and defend the right of the people to govern themselves against all assaults and all quarters."[10]

The Battle in the Senate

As Walker and Douglas expected, Buchanan announced his endorsement of the Lecompton Constitution in his annual message to Congress on December 8, 1857. The message, introduced into the Senate by Jesse Bright, laid down the proslavery party policy. After acknowledging the "alarming condition in Kansas" and the "excited state of public feeling," Buchanan dismissed the hubbub over slavery in the territories as a nonissue. The Supreme Court had ruled in the *Dred Scott* case, he reminded the nation, that slaves were property and Congress did not have the authority to prevent Southerners from taking their human property into the territories. The best course of action, he concluded, was to admit Kansas immediately under the Lecompton Constitution and speak no more of fraudulent elections, squatter sovereignty, or border ruffians. "The message of the President showed . . . clearly that support of this slave-holding constitution was to be the test of democratic orthodoxy," explained Republican leader Joshua Giddings. "The whole power of the Administration, acting as the hired man of slavery," added Indiana representative George Julian, "was ruthlessly employed for the purpose of spreading the curse over Kansas, and establishing it there as an irreversible fact." Indeed, the message was surprising in its simplicity and impressive in its disregard for the illegality and violence that had produced the Lecompton Constitution.[11]

Immediately after the Senate reading of Buchanan's message, Douglas jumped to his feet to declare his opposition. In a speech the following day, Douglas reaffirmed his disapproval of Lecompton but attempted to prevent a direct break with the administration. "I rejoice, on a careful perusal of the message, to find so much less to dissent from than I was under the impression there was," he said sheepishly, weighing his own political future. But Lecompton, he reiterated, was unrepresentative, and forcing it on the people of Kansas was a violation of the doctrine of popular sovereignty. The proposed constitution was "a system of trickery and jugglery to defeat the fair expression of the will of the people." Do you intend "to force a constitution on the people against their will, in opposition to their protest, with a knowledge of the fact?" he asked the Democratic scions sitting around him in the chamber. "Am I to be called upon to forfeit my faith and my honor in order to enable a small minority of the people of Kansas to defraud the majority of that people out of their elective franchise?" Realizing the answers to both of these questions would be a resounding yes, the Little Giant concluded with a courageous statement of defiance. "If this constitution is to be forced down our throats, in violation of the fundamental principles of free government, under a mode of submission that is mockery and insult, I will resist it to the last." His booming voice filled the marble hall, and Republicans and anti-Lecompton Northern Democrats cheered his declaration.[12]

Like Walker and Douglas, most Northerners were outraged by Buchanan's support of Lecompton and his plan to impose the constitution on an unwilling free state majority. "We rec'd last night Douglas's Speech," penned one Hoosier; "it is the true position, and meets the views of all here. The President made a woeful mistake." Even Democratic officeholders who had supported the Southern agenda throughout their careers announced their opposition. Norman Eddy, who had served in the U.S. House of Representatives from Indiana and had voted for the Kansas-Nebraska Act, wrote to

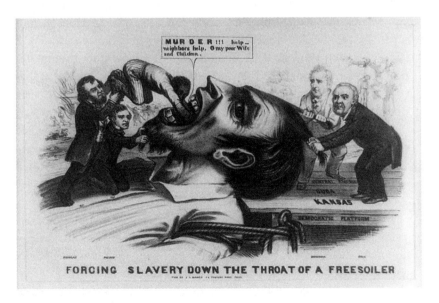

FIGURE 9. "Forcing Slavery down the Throat of a Freesoiler" (Library of Congress)

John Davis, "I cannot and will not support the administration in its policy of forcing the Lecompton Constitution upon the people of Kansas. On the contrary I sustain and endorse fully the speech of Judge Douglas." Northern Democrats had supported the expansion of slavery and Southern power, but they could not countenance the blatant violation of majority rule.[13]

On December 13, Douglas met with Republican leaders in Washington to discuss opposition to Lecompton, and two days later, Walker resigned as governor of the Kansas Territory. To accompany his resignation, Walker published a "manifesto," drafted by Douglas, charging Buchanan with treachery and reminding Americans that the Lecompton Constitution represented only 10 percent of the territorial population.[14]

Back in the Senate, Douglas continued his opposition, employing a variety of legal and moral arguments against Lecompton. On December 16, he avoided the issue of voter fraud and insisted that the convention that had produced the constitution had been "irregular," lacking a proper enabling act from Congress that would have granted authority to craft a constitution. Because the convention did not have the permission of Congress, and because the free state majority had boycotted the elections, he reasoned, the constitution must be submitted for popular ratification. "I said before, and I say now, that the constitution must be the act and deed of the people of Kansas. . . . No constitution should be received by Congress, and none can fairly be considered republican which does not embody the will of the people." "When the broad fact stands admitted before the world that this constitution is the act of a minority, and not of the majority," Douglas continued, "the injustice becomes the more manifest and the more monstrous."[15]

Five days later, Pennsylvania's William Bigler took the floor to speak for the administration and defend the Slave Power. Douglas was reckless, Bigler asserted, and his arguments rested "on a very unsound and insufficient foundation." The president's motives were above suspicion, and there was nothing nefarious about Lecompton. "The idea that he [Buchanan] would seek to oppress any class of people of Kansas, or desire to impose upon them an odious Government," explained Bigler, "should not be, and I trust is not, entertained in any quarter." Lecompton was a party measure, concluded the Pennsylvanian, and all Democrats were expected to support it. Though Douglas proceeded to vigorously defend his opposition to Lecompton, Bigler had made the party line clear and cemented Douglas's status as party traitor. "All the bluster of reading Doug. out of the party," observed Harris, "exacts contempt in every man of honor."[16]

Yet the more Douglas defended himself, the more he came under attack. Newly elected Northern Democrats, in particular, lined up to condemn

the Little Giant and oust him from his leadership position. Bigler spoke for
Buchanan, who had long distrusted and disliked the young upstart, and Graham Fitch of Indiana did the bidding of Bright, whose hatred of Douglas
had been smoldering for years. On December 22, Fitch took his turn, labeling Douglas a dangerous rogue seeking to exploit the crisis in Kansas for
his own political benefit. "But if there, unfortunately, be men, high in the
Democratic party, who desire to avail themselves of the present phase of this
question to take a position outside the party, with the hope—by throwing
fire-brands into its midst, or by directing their artillery against it—to destroy
it, in return for some past grievance, real or fancied, I would commend to
such the lessons fairly deducible from the result of every such attempt, from
Burr's to Van Buren's," declared the Hoosier doctor, referencing Aaron Burr's
near election as president in 1800 and Martin Van Buren's Free Soil heresy in
1848. The Democratic Party, he persisted, was the last bisectional coalition,
and opposing its policies meant opposing the Union itself. "The Democratic
is the great conservative party of the country—the only national party. It is
the only mere political link in the chain which now binds the States in one
common country." Dumfounded at the personal affront, Douglas struggled
to defend his course and explain once again his objections to Lecompton.
He felt persecuted, he confessed to his colleagues, as though he was the only
Democrat not permitted to dissent on any grounds.[17]

   Though under siege in Congress, Douglas and anti-Lecompton Demo-
crats won a major victory in January 1858 when a new round of elections in
Kansas produced a free state legislature and a decisive rejection of Lecompton. "That the Lecompton constitution is not the act of the people of
Kansas . . . is now conclusively and undeniably established by a vote of the
people, taken at a fair election, held on the 4th of January, 1858," beamed
Douglas to Forney. Fortified by the election results and the knowledge of
Northern Democrats' flocking to his banner, the Little Giant was emboldened in his battle with the administration. He promptly submitted a resolution calling on the president to deliver to Congress all papers concerning his
Kansas policy, the first step in an official investigation. But the investigation
was quashed, and, as punishment for his treachery, Senate Democrats delivered a severe rebuke by removing Douglas from the chairmanship of his
beloved Committee on Territories. This was the final straw for the proud
Illinoisan, and instead of being cowed into submission, he declared war. "Let
the enemy, threaten, proscribe & do their best or worst," Douglas wrote to his
troops. "Let us stand by our colors, & make no compromise."[18]

   With Douglas and anti-Lecompton Democrats in obstinate rebellion, little
changed in the Senate. The Little Giant stood his ground, and administration

Democrats made threats, condemned his selfishness, and proclaimed that nothing could prevent the spread of slavery. "Slaves are now in that Territory; slaves can go there and be held there. Congress cannot prevent it. The people, or the majority, cannot prevent it," declared Bigler on March 15, 1858.[19] The stalemate even inspired Senator Bright, who almost never gave speeches, to take the floor. Summarizing the administration argument for the final time, Bright noted with calmness, "The properly constituted and legally authorized civil power of Kansas, after full proclamation of its purposes, adopted this constitution in the way in which other constitutions have been adopted, and in the way approved by the philosophy and genius of our Government." Then aiming to woo his reluctant Northern colleagues, Bright reframed Lecompton as the natural product of popular sovereignty. "Popular sovereignty," he explained, meant "non-intervention," and "non-intervention" meant Congress had no business interfering in Kansas affairs. Thus, Lecompton should be accepted as is. Rejecting Lecompton meant rejecting popular sovereignty, the avowed principle of the Northern Democracy and the centerpiece of Douglas's career.[20]

Two days later, on March 22, the Little Giant, now exhausted from months of battle, offered his closing remarks to packed galleries. Starting at 7:00 a.m., Douglas orated for three hours but failed to present any new arguments. Of more import was Douglas's direct attack on the administration, which he charged with corruption and "despotism." "I do not recognize the right of the president or his Cabinet, no matter what my respect may be for them, to tell me my duty in the Senate Chamber," he declared with defiance. "Is it seriously intended to brand every Democrat in the United States as a traitor who is opposed to the Lecompton constitution?" pleaded Douglas. "We are traitors if we vote against Lecompton; our constituents are traitors if they do not think Lecompton is right; and yet you expect those whom you call traitors to vote with and sustain you." Despite Douglas's impassioned protestations, however, the bill to admit Kansas to statehood under the Lecompton constitution passed the Senate the following day, March 23, 1858, thirty-five to twenty-five. The administration offensive had been successful, and Douglas was the only Northern Democrat to vote against the measure.[21]

Machinations in the House

Buchanan and the Democrats may have won the battle in the Senate, but the war for Lecompton and Kansas was not yet over—a separate struggle awaited in the House of Representatives, where opposition to Lecompton was more pronounced and better organized. Unlike their long-winded colleagues in the upper chamber, House members were elected by popular vote every two years and were thus more sensitive to the demands of their constituents. Northern Democrats in the House knew that supporting Lecompton would mean immediate political suicide. Moreover, while Democrats ruled in the Senate, the House was far more fractious, with ninety-two Republicans, fourteen nativist "Americans," one hundred regular Democrats, and twenty-one anti-Lecompton Democrats. Because the exact number of the anti-Lecompton Democrats changed on a daily basis, the fate of Lecompton was perpetually in doubt. "I never had so much work—hard work—to do before. I am at it night and day. . . . I am wearing out," confessed an exasperated Alexander Stephens, the administration's point man in the House. Nevertheless, the president remained optimistic. "The Kansas question, from appearances, will not be one of much difficulty. . . . Kansas must be brought into the Union at the present session, or many of the Democratic members who now hesitate will be certain to lose their seats at the next election. Their safety consists in their firmness & fidelity," he explained to a correspondent in language reminiscent of 1850.[22]

Indicative of the challenge faced by Democrats in the House was the stand taken by Representative Samuel Cox of Ohio, who first opposed Lecompton then later cast a crucial vote for it. Cox was a dynamic fellow, with diverse interests and an intellectual streak that set him apart from many of his Democratic cohorts. Born in September 1824 in Zanesville, Ohio, Cox was the second of thirteen children in a family of loyal Democrats. His father was a local officeholder, and young Cox imbibed Democratic rhetoric from the start. He proved a popular youth who excelled at school and earned a reputation as a prankster. In 1842, he enrolled at the Ohio University at Athens, where he rose to the top of his class and developed a talent for writing, politics, and public speaking. Seeking more challenge, he transferred to Brown University in Rhode Island in the spring of 1844. He gained notoriety as a gifted orator and a rabid antiabolitionist, railing against those who questioned Southern power and human bondage.[23]

After graduation, the twenty-two-year-old returned to Ohio to work with his father and study law in Cincinnati. Soon thereafter, he married and left for an extended tour of Europe, from October 1849 to September 1852. Fascinated by European society, he composed an account of his travels, published in 1852 as *A Buckeye Abroad*, a delightful read that earned him national attention. On his return to the United States, Cox commenced his law practice (opening a firm with future U.S. senator George Pugh) and purchased a controlling interest in the *Ohio Statesman*, the Democratic organ

at the state capital. As editor and now recognized diarist, Cox rose to prominence in the state party, gaining him the attention of the embattled Pierce
administration. In May 1853, Cox authored an article describing, in impressive detail, a sunset, which led to his lifelong nickname, "Sunset" Cox. Over
the following months and years, Cox rose to the chair of the Democratic
State Committee, became a leading figure in Ohio politics, and orchestrated
the election of Democratic governor William Medill.[24]

In the national arena, young Cox was an ardent advocate of the Kansas-
Nebraska Act and a defender of Douglas. "I have kept up the fight for
you," Cox reported to the Illinois senator. "You have made cords of friends
here. . . . We can today whip the Whigs and Abolitionists clean out." As
reward for his fidelity, President Pierce offered Cox the post of secretary of
legation at the Court of St. James, in London. The adventurous Buckeye
was uninspired and suggested exotic Peru instead, to which Pierce agreed.
The South American mission was not meant to be, however, as Cox fell ill
on the voyage and was forced to turn back and resign. Nevertheless, he was
elected to the U.S. House of Representatives in October 1856. The thirty-
two-year-old editor had won on a plurality in a bitter three-way contest; the
anti-Democratic opposition had been fierce, but divided.[25]

Entering Congress on March 4, 1857, Cox made his maiden speech on
December 16, a fateful oration personally approved by Douglas. In no uncertain terms, Sunset Cox laid out his objections to Lecompton and announced
his opposition to the administration. "I claim the right now to place myself
and my constituency unequivocally in the position of protestants against any
doctrine which would seem to approve of the conduct of the constitutional
convention in Kansas," he stated with bravado. Comparing himself to Martin
Luther, the Buckeye nailed his "theses" to the castle door for all to see. He did
not oppose slavery, he explained, but the "fraud" and "treachery" of Lecompton were too much to swallow. Warming to the topic and gaining confidence
in his stand, he began employing the rhetorical flourishes for which he had
a well-earned reputation. "Any attempt to abridge or take away this popular
sovereignty is a fraud of so hideous a character, that language has no term of
reproach, nor the mind any idea of detestation, adequate to express or con-
ceive its iniquity." It is *not* interference or intervention, Cox concluded, for
Congress to protect the right of the people to choose their own constitutions
and institutions. "Let Congress, when it guarantees self-government, see to it
that it is not a mockery, or a phantom, but a real, living, glowing reality—an
opportunity for public volition, informed by conscience, and irradiate with
intelligence—to decide for themselves, under the constitution, as to the laws
under which they are to live."[26]

Cox's speech was not only the first address delivered in the new House chamber in the newly constructed south wing, but it was also the first House defiance of the administration on Lecompton. Cox carefully, albeit grandiosely, laid out Northern Democratic objections to that constitution. Congress should not interfere in territorial matters (popular sovereignty), unless there was a blatant violation of the majority will, such as the Lecompton Constitution. Forcing Lecompton upon the people of Kansas was truly "tyrannical" and "monstrous." In Cox's eye, Congress should be the guarantor of rights and democracy—a view that did not sit well with most Democrats. Indeed, administration devotees were enraged by the audacity of this freshman representative.

Buchanan's unwavering support for the Lecompton "swindle," as well as Cox's courageous stand, energized House anti-Lecompton Democrats. With his lieutenants William Richardson and John McClernand having been ousted from office, Douglas turned to Thomas Harris of Illinois and Cox to mobilize and organize an anti-Lecompton coalition. Harris was made chairman of the anti-Lecompton caucus, and John Haskin of New York served as secretary. "The Administration have drawn the sword, & the Pres says Lecompton shall go through in 20 days. We are to have war to the knife— that is certain," wrote Harris to Charles Lanphier on January 21. "Harris seems to be the boldest man here among the Anti-Lecompton Democrats against the Administration and the pro-slavery party," observed Republican Lyman Trumbull. Leading the "Douglas defection" in the House, Harris, Cox, and Haskin conferred regularly with the Little Giant and received counsel from Robert Walker.[27]

At the end of January, after elections in Kansas had proved the unrepresentative nature of Lecompton, anti-Lecompton Democrats caucused and created a committee to confront the president and plead with him to reject the constitution. At the White House, they explained that supporting Lecompton would kill the remnants of the Northern Democracy and that the president lacked the votes to push the measure through the House. Buchanan was unmoved, however, and dismissed them, adding that he would force Lecompton through Congress regardless. Even if anti-Lecompton Democrats bolted the party, Buchanan could still rely on the solid South to carry the day. Plus, Old Buck believed he could suppress dissent and enforce discipline through patronage, social pressure, bribery, and all manner of personal threats. The power of the presidency would be brought to bear as never before, and recalcitrant Democrats would be severely punished.[28]

On Tuesday, February 2, 1858, Buchanan's special message endorsing Lecompton arrived in the House. In it, he ignored the January elections and reaffirmed his decision to force the constitution on the territory. Personally approved by Stephens, it was a "bold and able document, and has the true ring of the Jackson metal," according to Edmund Burke. "It is bold, fearless, and defiant, and fully establishes the firmness and courage of the President." But while most Democrats cheered Buchanan's determination, Republicans and anti-Lecompton dissenters were appalled. Surely the president could appreciate the import of the territorial elections and see the inherent injustice in supporting Lecompton. "The Presidents message meets with universal Condemnation," recorded one angry Hoosier. Immediately after its reading, a fight erupted in the House over how to treat the message. Instead of sending it to the Committee on Territories, as was the custom, anti-Lecomptonites labored to create a new committee armed with investigatory powers. Buchanan and the regular Democracy certainly did not want a congressional probe and had the matter tabled for the moment. While the administration readied for battle, anti-Lecompton men bided their time.[29]

A fight, indeed, occurred on the House floor two days later. Described as a "battle royal" by Stephens, the brawl involved thirty representatives resorting to fisticuffs to settle their differences. Waiting until evening, when regular Democrats were away at social gatherings hosted by the administration, Harris moved the previous question on his resolution to create an investigatory committee. Stephens, still on the floor as Democratic House leader, frantically tried to stall a vote by repeatedly calling for time-consuming roll calls on successive motions to adjourn. At the same time, he ordered the sergeant at arms to fetch Democrats from their soirees. Tensions increased as Stephens's roll call votes dragged on late into the night. At 2:00 a.m., a fight erupted between Pennsylvania Republican Galusha Grow and South Carolina Democrat Laurence Keitt when Grow wandered onto the Democratic side of the House while addressing the chamber. Keitt, who was already in a foul mood, assaulted Grow, grabbing his neck and making threats. A tremendous melee ensued, as House members took sides and jumped into the fray. Keitt, who had assisted Preston Brooks when that young South Carolinian had nearly killed Charles Sumner in May 1856, was not easily subdued, and the fight persisted until one member's wig was knocked off and the assemblage burst into laughter.[30]

Regardless, the parliamentary sparring continued until 6:25 a.m., when an agreement was reached to adjourn until Monday. Buchanan and the Democrats were determined to use the weekend reprieve to punish dissenters and enforce party discipline. With this in mind, the president and his cabinet hosted special events, extending personal invitations to anti-Lecompton Democrats. Once in his clutches, the president made promises, issued threats, and used the psychological power of his office (not to mention his imposing six-foot-tall height and off-putting glare) to cow wayward House members. When the chamber reassembled on Monday morning, Secretaries Cobb and Toucey were in attendance, twisting arms and making final offers. But all the cajolery and coercions were to no avail—the administration could not overcome the intense Northern opposition to their Kansas policy. Harris's motion carried 114 to 111, a huge defeat for the Democracy. Their one consolation, though, was that Speaker James Orr of South Carolina packed the committee with party loyalists, including Stephens. When the committee eventually met, Stephens assumed command and saw to it that no investigation occurred.[31]

Such administration setbacks greatly concerned regular Democrats and led Southerners to move closer toward secession. "If Kansas is rejected," wrote Governor Joseph Brown of Georgia to Stephens, "I think self respect will compel the Southern members of Congress and especially the members from Georgia to vacate their seats and return to their constituents to assist them in drawing around themselves new safeguards for the protection of their rights in future." "There is a bad state of feeling here," noted Harris of Illinois. "Worse than in 1850. The southern members most of them are much hurt at the turn things have taken." Under mounting Southern pressure, the administration became more intractable, determined to force slavery on Kansas at all costs—it would be a fight to the death. Democrats labeled all who opposed the president as "Black Republicans," disunionists, and abolitionists, and inaugurated what one partisan called a "*reign of Terror.*" "Douglas and his followers are to be excommunicated from the Dem. party. There is no mistake about it," observed Republican Schuyler Colfax.[32]

Buchanan's biggest weapon was executive patronage. The president had at his command thousands of appointive offices across the country, and he could remove, retain, and appoint at whim. Loyalists would be rewarded, and opponents would be "decapitated," as one Democrat phrased it. In particular, Buchanan aimed to destroy Douglas. Prominent Douglas men were removed from offices in Chicago, Cleveland, and Columbus, and the president began making overtures, through John Slidell, to Illinois Republicans hoping to further erode Douglas's position. In addition, anti-Douglas newspapers were aided or established, and lucrative government printing contracts were denied to pro-Douglas presses. "I despise the president for everything he has done," cried an aggrieved Douglas supporter. "Everything proved him to be a decayed superannuated old imbecile as senseless as a hindoo idol. . . . It is awful to think of the destruction of the democratic party, but I fear it will come."[33]

Buchanan also used cold hard cash. Secret slush funds were created to bribe House members, establish proadministration presses, and finance proadministration candidates. Administration lobbyist and printer Cornelius Wendell spent up to forty thousand dollars, remarking later, "I disguised them [cash bribes] as much as I could." "It has become apparent," complained Douglas, "that the administration is more anxious for my destruction than they are for the harmony & unity of the Democratic Party." To woo the emotional Forney, Attorney General Jeremiah Black offered him a ten-thousand-dollar cash bribe, then a plum foreign appointment, then an eighty-thousand-dollar post office printing contract. "He [Black] was very desirous, indeed, that Col. Forney should give some pledge in his newspaper that he meant to remain with the Democratic party," reported Black's agent, Mr. Webster. Remarkably, Forney declined and grew resentful, vowing anew to fight Lecompton. "Col. Forney indignantly refused to comply with Judge Black's wishes, and was very emphatic in expressing his refusal," Webster added. Soon thereafter, Forney's paper, the *Philadelphia Press*, grew in popularity to become the top-selling journal in Philadelphia, and second in the state. For his treachery, Forney was expelled from the party. "I was proscribed and hunted down, simply because I would not sanction a proceeding far more despotic and unjust," he recorded years later.[34]

In the Midwest, where Bright and Fitch were especially eager to destroy Douglas, the witch hunt was impressively thorough. Though most Indiana Democrats followed Douglas and three-fourths of the state's Democratic papers condemned the "Lecompton fraud," Bright maintained control of the party apparatus. Postmasters lost their jobs, a U.S. district attorney was dismissed, and, in the Senate, Fitch held up lucrative contracts. In Illinois, the Chicago postmaster was fired, mail agents were replaced, and newspapers lost their contracts. Of particular attention was Sunset Cox in Ohio, whose maiden speech had made a mockery of the president's agenda. When young Cox resisted initial administration pressure, Buchanan removed Cox's close friend Thomas Miller from the postmastership of Columbus (to be replaced by loyalist Samuel Medary). Such removals and reprisals made dissident Democrats frantic, as the fall elections were fast approaching.[35]

Democratic disciplinary efforts extended into the House of Representatives as well. To steady nerves, regulate the ranks, and reap the benefits of administration pressure, Stephens created a special partisan committee. With himself as chair, the group reiterated patronage offers, mobilized members for votes, and kept drunkards off the floor. "If the South would but have the right sort of men here, there would not be the least difficulty," Stephens wrote to his brother. "We should carry the Lecompton Constitution, and achieve the greatest triumph in our history." The Democratic machine was never so well organized, but it was not enough to suppress the impassioned anti-Lecompton movement. "The time has now arrived," Douglas told his supporters in the Empire State, "when the Democracy of the whole country should hold meetings in the cities, towns, and counties, and proclaim . . . their determined and unyielding hostility to the consummation of a scheme so monstrous as to force a constitution at the point of the bayonet down the throats of an unwilling people."[36]

One of the members of Stephens's disciplinary committee was Bright protégé William English of Indiana. Even more than Cox, English would come to play a decisive role in Lecompton's eventual victory. Born in August 1822 to Democratic faithfuls from Kentucky, English attended Hanover College in southern Indiana but did not graduate. Instead, he received a teaching certificate, began a study of law, and dove into local politics. In November 1842, twenty-year-old English, seeking the minor elected position of enrolling clerk for the Indiana statehouse, reached out to thirty-year-old Jefferson County Democratic boss Jesse Bright. It was the beginning of a close personal and professional relationship. Though English was defeated, he was not deterred and soon won election as principal clerk for the legislature. In 1844, he worked for the failed presidential candidacy of Kentucky slave owner Richard Johnson, but then received an appointment from President Polk as clerk in the Treasury Office of the Second Auditor. While in the nation's capital, English roomed with Andrew Johnson of Tennessee and romanced Virginia belle Emma "Mardy" Jackson, whom he married in November 1847. Over the next several years, as his political career matured, English amassed an impressive fortune from railroad investments and real estate ventures.[37]

With Bright as his guide, English rose quickly in Democratic ranks, and the two were able to deliver Indiana to Cass in 1848. In March 1850, English was selected as clerk of the Senate Claims Committee, a position that made him many friends and increased his political connections. Moreover, the post allowed him to witness the debates and crises of that year firsthand, from which he no doubt learned a great deal. Back in Indiana, English earned the attention of Bright's brother Michael, also a political chief of note, and influential editor Phineas Kent. The latter became English's campaign manager, and with his help English was elected state representative from Scott County in August 1851. In the statehouse, English proved a popular member and was soon elected Speaker and grew closer to the Bright brothers. He served as Jesse's loyal lieutenant in the battles with Joseph Wright and became Jesse's closest political confidant. You are the only one of my friends who shares

FIGURE 10.   Representative William English, Indiana (Library of Congress)

my views on everything, he wrote English in 1852, you are "always right *instinctively.*" Nevertheless, signs of strain between them emerged that year, when English preferred Douglas for president over Cass.[38]

Yet English remained loyal to Bright, and with his support in 1852 gained the U.S. House nomination for the notoriously pro-Southern Second

District. In October, twenty-nine-year-old English achieved election because of a divided opposition and the popularity of Wright, who won the
governorship. In December the following year, English was only one of two
Indiana representatives to help elect Linn Boyd of Kentucky Speaker, for
which English was rewarded with a coveted seat on the Committee on Territories. When Bright broke with the Pierce administration, English did his
best to protect his own career and remain out of the fray, much to his mentor's consternation. "I am about as much interested in your political position
& future success as yourself," Bright wrote to English in January 1854. In the
coming months, as debate raged over Douglas's Kansas–Nebraska bill, English
continued to chart a moderate Democratic course, fully supporting the bill
and the Southern bosses while avoiding political confrontations. His conservatism and loyalty to the South were once again rewarded when Speaker
Boyd appointed him chair of the Committee of the Whole (composed of all
House members, and which considers legislation of extraordinary import).[39]

In October 1854, after the passage of the Kansas–Nebraska Act and when
most Northern Democrats were being booted out of office, English narrowly held his seat by running an extremely pro-Southern campaign to attract the significant Southern population of his district. Also, opposition to
him was again divided, while English enjoyed full Democratic support. His
surprising reelection and his fidelity to the Southern agenda made English
the new darling of the party leadership, and on his return to Washington
he found himself in a position of power and influence. "The fact that he
[English] was one of the most active members in securing the passage of the
Nebraska Act, is justly appreciated by the National Democracy," observed
one Washington journalist. In the coming battles over Kansas and Southern
power, English stood firmly with Pierce and the party. When he had to
choose sides in the 1856 contest between Douglas and Buchanan, he set
aside his sympathy for the Little Giant and supported Old Buck. English's
reelection had not strengthened Bright's position with the incoming administration but made English all the more important to the party. He was now
one of the few remaining Northern Democrats whose doughface credentials
were unquestionable.[40]

As his prominence in the party grew, so did English's belief that he
must defend Northern Democrats from Southern charges of Free-Soilism.
Northern Democrats were as loyal to the party as any Southerner, he reasoned, and the growing antislavery sentiment in the North should in no
way affect the Northern Democracy. In December 1856, he gave a rousing
speech in the House in defense of Northern conservatism, praising Democrats for standing up for the South's "constitutional rights." Southerners had

nothing to fear, he explained, since Northern Democrats had successfully purged their ranks of Free-Soilism. His bid for party harmony backfired, though, as Southerners remained unconvinced of the reliability of Northern Democrats. When the Lecompton debates threatened to destroy the party, English was torn. He supported the Southern agenda and the expansion of slavery but opposed forcing the constitution on an unwilling territorial majority; he was loyal to Bright, Buchanan, and the party leadership but believed Lecompton was bad policy. Instead of making a decision, as Douglas and Cox had done, English chose to stay on the fence, caucusing with both regular Democrats and anti-Lecomptonites.[41]

Few knew what English would do, least of all his Hoosier neighbors. If English "sustains the Lecompton fraud," wrote an Indiana voter to John Davis, his constituents will "cast him aside." English finally took the floor on March 9, 1858, well after all the arguments for and against Lecompton had been put forward. Instead of clarifying his position, he offered another defense of Northern Democrats. In emotional terms, English explained the misery of the Northern Democracy, as they faced antislavery constituents at home and proslavery party bosses in Washington. Our "southern brethren" have scarce appreciated the "fierce and vindictive character" of the anti-Democratic movement in the free states. "We were denounced as dough-faces and traitors; our names were paraded in the papers of the day, in large type, encircled with black lines, and headed, 'The roll of infamy;' we were hung in effigy, and every indignity that the ingenuity and malignity of fanaticism could devise was heaped upon us . . . [while] you, gentlemen of the South, were at home at your ease, because *you* had not run counter to the sympathies and popular sentiments of *your* people." Save the Northern Democracy, he pleaded to Southerners, by not making Lecompton a party measure. You depend on us, he reminded them, and destroying the Northern Democracy would only prevent the South from advancing its goals. "Look to it, ye men of the South, that you do not, for a mere shadow, strike down or drive from you your only effective support outside the limits of your own States!" We want to help the South, we do not oppose the expansion of slavery, English explained, but if you make Lecompton the "*chief test* of party fidelity," we will be cut down at the polls.[42]

English's oration won praise from anti-Lecomptonites but condemnation from regular Democrats. "Your Anti-Lecompton speech in the House is highly spoken of by all your constituents here whom I have heard express any opinions," gushed one Hoosier supporter. "I esteem it a truly able, well-tempered and *telling* speech." Bright was particularly disappointed in his protégé, writing to English the day of the speech, "It is to be regretted that *you & I* could not have harmonized on this question. I hope, *sincerely hope,* we yet will be able to do so." But while anti-Lecomptonites were cautiously optimistic about English's future course, Buchanan and Stephens saw an opportunity. Here was a young man eager to redeem himself and the Northern Democracy in the eyes of the party bosses yet willing to express views attractive to the dissidents.[43]

English would prove a useful tool, indeed. Shortly after English's March 9 oration, Stephens met with the young representative and convinced him to take part in a "compromise" effort. If English was willing to follow the script provided by Stephens, Cobb, and Buchanan, he could save Lecompton and redeem the Northern Democracy from the heresy of Douglas. On March 27, the House Democratic caucus met to discuss the compromise. Most of the anti-Lecomptonites were in attendance, and Stephens expressed his desire for harmony and cooperation. On cue, English took the floor, warned against the "calamity" of division, and offered a resolution to create a committee that would address the concerns of the dissidents. The motion passed, and, as the resolution's sponsor, English was named chair of the twenty-man team. Anti-Lecompton Democrats were thoroughly fooled, and, with English's speech fresh in their minds and ignorant of his secret deal with Buchanan, Cobb, and Stephens, they believed English to be one of the ten anti-Lecompton men on the committee; they agreed to the move because English supposedly opposed Lecompton and the administration's policy. Stephens served on the committee as well, and English knew to follow his lead.[44]

From this point forth, Stephens and English worked as a pair to push Lecompton through the House. The compromise committee was essentially designed to fail, and it only met once, on March 29. As expected, the Southern members of the committee refused to discuss any changes to the Lecompton bill (S. 161), and though Chairman English maintained his anti-Lecompton facade, the committee yielded nothing. The following day, the full House Democratic caucus reassembled to hear English's abortive report. When it became clear that the caucus remained under Southern control and would endorse the president's policies, the anti-Lecomptonites bolted. The departure of dissident Democrats allowed the rump caucus to announce its support of Buchanan, slavery, and Lecompton. Meanwhile, Buchanan and Stephens labored to keep English's Janus-faced role *"perfectly confidential"*; English's credentials as a possible anti-Lecompton man were critical to success. "W. English's name must not be used or communicated to any one," Buchanan instructed Cobb on March 31.[45]

The very next day, the House voted on Lecompton. With galleries packed with anxious observers, and the House floor crowded with agitated members,

Stephens brought the bill to the floor. Immediately, sparring erupted over
the addition of amendments, which would weigh the bill down and delay a
vote. An anti-Lecompton coalition of Republicans and Douglas Democrats
successfully replaced the Senate version (S. 161) with a House version; if they
could not kill Lecompton, at least they could drag out its passage. The new
bill passed 120 to 112 and was sent to the Senate.

Throughout, Cox and English voted with the administration. Cox had
been an ardent anti-Lecompton man, in daily communication with Douglas,
but when Buchanan removed his friend from the Columbus postmastership,
Cox cracked. To sweeten the deal, Buchanan promised to reappoint Miller
as soon as Cox cast his critical votes. "Differing with Buchanan, I was con-
strained afterwards to differ with Judge Douglas," Cox noted coldly in his
memoirs. English, for his part, had followed the script assigned him, allowing
his votes to finally reveal his true colors. Anti-Lecomptonites were shocked
and dismayed, leading to cries of "traitor" and "Judas." Overall, however,
anti-Lecompton Democrats celebrated. They had prevented the passage of
the Senate bill, which would necessitate a conference committee and a new
round of maneuverings. "The Anti Lecompton Democrats of the House
have achieved a glorious triumph to day," wrote Representative Samuel Marshall of Illinois. "Few in number, yet by indomitable courage they have held
this powerful and proscriptive administration in check."[46]

Twelve days later, the Senate rejected the House bill and called for a conference committee. To convince the fractious House to go along, Buchanan
renewed his patronage offensive. The secretaries of the Treasury and Interior
stalked the House floor offering favors; Ohio congressmen were promised a
series of military commissions in the army's drive into Utah; New Yorkers
were offered various federal appointments; California lands were tendered
to New York and Ohio Representatives; and Iowa patronage requests were
fast-tracked to reward the loyalty of Senator George Jones. An Ohio editor
was given twenty thousand dollars, and Owen Jones of Pennsylvania was offered five thousand dollars outright, apparently the going rate for Northern
Democratic votes, since Ohio representatives were bought for the same sum.
Not only did Buchanan purchase votes, but the reshuffling of patronage at
the local level caused chaos and confusion in anti-Lecompton ranks. The
administration's efforts paid off when, on April 14, the House agreed to
participate in the conference committee in one of the most dramatic roll
call votes in congressional history; Speaker Orr of South Carolina cast the
deciding vote to break the 108–108 tie.[47]

Not surprisingly, Stephens was named chair by Orr, and English was appointed as an anti-Lecompton member, though it was obvious to all that he

was a puppet of the party bosses. Anti-Lecompton men fumed, but there was little they could do—Orr, Stephens, Buchanan, and English were in league. "It looks now as though English would strand our ship," Owen Loveyjoy penned to journalist James Pike. The committee had a pro-Lecompton majority of Senators James Green of Missouri and Robert Hunter of Virginia and Representatives Stephens and English; and the anti-Lecompton minority consisted of Senator William Seward of New York and Representative William Howard of Michigan. English was the only Northern Democrat on the committee, and his vote would be decisive. He received counsel from all quarters but continued to take instructions from Buchanan, Bright, and Stephens.[48]

On Sunday, April 18, the Democratic committee members convened at the residence of Stephens, who was recovering from an illness. After much discussion, they agreed on a plan of action: offer an exorbitant land grant to the people of Kansas to purchase their support of the Lecompton constitution. In previous instances, territories had been given large tracts of land to accompany their entry to the Union. Chaotic Kansas, however, had demanded an unusually massive grant, and Stephens and English saw they could use this to their advantage. The Stephens-English plan was simply a terrific bribe. If Kansans accepted Lecompton, they would receive even more land than they requested; if they rejected the deal, admission to the Union would be delayed until their population warranted reconsideration by Congress. "The suggestion of Mr. English to which you referred last night meets with a good deal of favor among our friends," Robert Toombs wrote to Buchanan. "And if it meets your approbation I think it will pass." The plan certainly pleased Southerners, and its simplicity was irresistible.[49]

When English submitted the report to the full conference committee on Tuesday, April 20, it was a bombshell. Stephens, English, Hunter, and Green were united in its defense, while Seward and Howard were dumbfounded. Howard tried to replace the plan with one that would allow Kansans to vote on a free state constitution, but it was quickly rejected. Seward was more circumspect and called for a two-hour adjournment to meet with his Republican colleagues. When Seward and Howard returned at 2:00 p.m., the Democrats were nowhere to be found. Eventually, they located Green, who informed the two Republicans that negotiation was futile. When news of the stonewalling spread, anti-Lecomptonites cried foul. The Stephens-English plan was "a most audacious cheat," fumed Norman Eddy, and another Hoosier called it "an open bold faced bribe by a few million [acre] grant of public [land], given as a magnificent grant to the people of Kansas to seduce them to swallow Lecompton, slavery, and all." Nevertheless, the conference committee adopted the plan, and English prepared to introduce it into the House.[50]

As scheduled, at 1:00 p.m. on April 23, English presented the conference bill to the House floor. To sell his plan, he discoursed on patriotism, duty, and the need for expediency. "The amendment agreed upon may not be perfect; but, if this fail [*sic*], it is fair to presume that all available parliamentary expedients for reconciliation will be exhausted, and that the question will be left open to still further excite sectional prejudices, and endanger the peace and prosperity of the country," English explained. "If the substitute is passed, the Kansas question departs at once from the Halls of Congress, perhaps never to return." It was not a new argument, but one that nonetheless appealed to worn and weary congressmen.[51]

At the end of the speech, English acted to prevent debate by moving to postpone consideration of the bill until 1:00 p.m. the next day. When Howard rose in protest, Speaker Orr swiftly silenced him. Over the coming days, Stephens and English worked alongside Secretary Cobb, who no longer bothered going to the Treasury Department and spent all his time in the House. "The tide of battle every day ebbs and flows like that of the sea," recorded Stephens. Rumors swirled about how much money English had received to betray his anti-Lecompton cohorts; some claimed that Bright and English had accepted generous land titles, and New York representative Francis Spinner called for an investigation. "The English scheme is a miserable one," grumbled Thomas Harris. "No one likes it . . . but it may pass."[52]

On the day before the final vote, Cox took the floor to defend his course and urge Northern Democrats to embrace Lecompton. He was the first in the House to stand in opposition, he reminded the chamber, but now he came "forward, in the spirit . . . of honorable concession." "That I opposed the admission of Kansas under the Lecompton constitution all know," he continued. "But now, sir, after the most careful reflection upon the subject, after the most careful consideration of it in every relation . . . I have come to a deliberate conclusion this morning to vote for the conference bill." Amazingly, Cox reasoned that the best way to oppose Lecompton was to support it, to grant congressional endorsement and then allow the people to reject it. What he failed to consider was the centrality of slavery—congressional acceptance of Lecompton would legitimate the fraudulent actions of the Slave Power and deny Kansans any vote on the spread of slavery into their territory. Yes, they could reject it (eventually), but only after slavery had been legitimized and institutionalized. As for the Stephens-English land bribe that was now at the heart of the bill, Cox accepted it unquestioningly, claiming that Kansas would receive a grant regardless.

In the end, however, Cox made it clear he was more concerned about his reputation as a Northern Democrat than with the issues of majority rule, slavery, and executive corruption. "I owe to the Democracy all I am and all I hope to be," he declared. "And I owe that party my fealty, and I am ready to show it in this matter when I can see that I am acting for the best." When anti-Lecomptonites attacked him for flip-flopping and kowtowing to the Slave Power, Cox lied about administration pressure and concluded that Lecompton "is the best, under the circumstances, for the country and the party."[53]

With all the posturing, orating, lying, and scheming completed, the day of the final vote—April 30—had arrived. After some parliamentary wrangling and last-minute attacks on Cox, the bill passed, 112–103. News of Lecompton's success in the House reached the Senate via Bigler, who was only too glad to interrupt an antislavery address by Seward. With little fanfare, it soon passed the Senate thirty-one to twenty-two, with Douglas again the only Northern Democrat dissenting. In all, forty-one Northern Democrats voted for Lecompton, and nine Northern Democrats in the House made last-minute switches, thanks to patronage promises and threats ("The object was accomplished, and the money was paid," recalled administration agent Cornelius Wendell). The administration has "bought men like hogs in the market," fumed Harris. "*It is universally condemned*, and English will now enjoy the most unenviable reputation of any public man in the State," exclaimed Ezra Read.[54]

Years later, Cox would admit that Lecompton had been "a stupendous fraud" and a major cause of the Civil War, but even then, with the tempering of time past, he still denied culpability and blamed Douglas for the fragmentation of the party. English, on the other hand, was proud of his accomplishment, and Buchanan made it clear that the young Hoosier had been key. "I omit no opportunity of expressing my opinion of how much the country owes you for the English amendment," wrote the president to the hero of the hour. "The Kansas question has placed your name in the front of all other names belonging to the Democratic party," agreed a Kentuckian. "I think from present indications that your course & bill will meet with a very hearty approval in the south & I cannot see why it should not meet with the same throughout the union—I have heard but one opinion expressed & that is that the English bill is better for the south than the original bill."[55]

The Antidemocratic Doctrine

More than their votes, however, Northern Democrats had given voice to a virulent strain of antidemocratic, minority rule theory that has heretofore been ignored by scholars. The first, and most prominent, argument in favor of minority rule was that the crisis in Kansas had created a national calamity that needed to be brought to a swift end. A conclusion to the crisis, Northern Democrats asserted, could only be achieved through a speedy acceptance of the flawed Lecompton Constitution, regardless of the will of the territorial majority. A second argument reasoned that it made no difference whatsoever that Lecompton violated the will of the majority, only that the process of its creation *appeared* to be legal. Others fashioned an alternative view of history in order to rationalize forcing Lecompton onto Kansas, emphasizing the dangers of the mob and claiming that the federal government had been designed by the Founding Fathers to *prevent* majority rule. Still others justified their actions in the service of the Slave Power by claiming that congressmen, once elected, were free follow their own judgment, regardless of the wishes of their constituents. And finally, a fifth rationale maintained that the public could not always be trusted to vote on legislation and constitutions, and therefore the sentiments of majorities—either in Kansas or the nation as a whole—were sometimes irrelevant. These themes, though distinct, often operated simultaneously in the reasoning of Northern Democrats as they struggled to defend their service to the South.

From President Buchanan's message on the first day of the first session of the Thirty-Fifth Congress, to closing remarks and final votes in April 1858, determined doughfaced Democrats labored to convince their colleagues and the nation that proslavery, minority rule in Kansas was both desirable and necessary. The first argument, that of expediency, was the most common. Following the lead of President Buchanan, doughfaced senators and representatives asserted that Bleeding Kansas and the crisis over slavery in the territories could only be brought to a conclusion through a speedy, unceremonious acceptance of Lecompton. It mattered not, they argued, that Lecompton was unrepresentative, fraudulent, and enormously unpopular. Rather, it was the only bill before Congress that would bring the territory into the Union immediately; Lecompton and Kansas were just waiting for admission, and all Congress had to do was vote aye.

The expediency rationale was first put forth in December 1857 by Bigler. Claiming that he represented "a spirit of concession and compromise," he labeled the Kansas free state majority criminals and asserted that the Lecompton convention had good reason to act as it did, since the free-staters had no intention of obeying the law and were hell-bent on defying federal authority. Admission of Kansas under the Lecompton Constitution, he announced, was the only way to end the crisis, and therefore Congress *must* accept it; the fact that it did not represent the will of the majority was not grounds for rejection. "It was always my understanding that the convention would have a right to make a constitution, and send it here, without submitting it to the people," Bigler insisted, adding that, since Kansas was in chaos, Congress should simply take what it could get. This view would be repeated dozens of times in the Senate and found its way into the House, where English became its leading proponent.[56]

Like the plea for expediency, the second rationale—the veneer of legality (provided by administration recognition) was enough to accept Lecompton, despite its many flaws—appeared in the arguments of several Democrats. President Buchanan's message to Congress on December 8, 1857, provides an example of this line of thought. Downplaying election frauds in Kansas, Buchanan declared that since the elections that produced the constitutional conventional in Lecompton appeared legal, the results must be binding, regardless of the will of the majority. The free state majority that boycotted the elections, he reasoned, had been given every opportunity to exercise their voting rights and chose not to do so, thus forfeiting its right to oppose the outcome. "A large portion of the citizens of Kansas," he explained, "did not think proper to register their names and to vote at the election for delegates; but an opportunity to do this having been fairly afforded, their refusal to avail themselves of their right could in no manner affect the legality of the convention." Or, as Senator Fitch of Indiana later stated, "That many, and perhaps a majority of the citizens of Kansas did not vote either at the election of representatives to the Territorial Legislature, or delegates to the convention, may be true. Where is your remedy? You cannot compel men to vote. They can only be permitted and invited to do so." This rationale stunned Northern voters who saw clearly that the Kansas free state majority had boycotted the elections because of widespread electoral fraud and violence. Buchanan concluded his message by implying that the entire discussion of majority will in Kansas was pointless, since the U.S. Supreme Court had recently ruled in the *Dred Scott* decision that slaves were property protected by the U.S. Constitution. With such coolness, Buchanan (and others) revealed his disregard for the will of the territorial majority or the legitimacy of the Lecompton Constitution.[57]

The third argument against majority will—that majorities are dangerous—can be seen in Senator Fitch's attacks on Douglas in late December. The Hoosier senator argued that citizens should not have control over their own constitutions and that popular approval of constitutions was undesirable. "The recognition of popular sovereignty by the repeal of the Missouri line," he claimed, "consisted in the fact that it placed the question of slavery where all others previously were. It did not provide, nor did it contemplate, nor did its supporters imagine, nor did its author intimate, that it contemplated the submission of every bank proposition, every internal improvement *project*, every school system, every election qualification in a new constitution, to the people, before the people by and for whom it was formed should be admitted to the Union." Fitch then launched an attack on majority rule in general. "Our Government is one of checks and balances; and some of its checks apply even to the people themselves. Among the objects of our government, one is to protect the legal rights of the minority against an illegal assumption or a denial of those rights by a majority. . . . If a majority resolve itself into a mob, and will neither vote nor observe law or order, the minority who are law-abiding, who form and obey government, cannot be deprived of the benefits and protection of that government by such majority. Is mobocracy to be substituted for democracy?" By equating majority rule with "mobocracy," Fitch dismissed any opposition to Lecompton as catering to the ignorant masses and violating the intent of the Founding Fathers. "The Democratic is the great conservative party," he insisted, and it was up to the Democrats to beat back the tide of popular sentiment.[58]

In addition to Fitch's surprising attack on majority rule, still another argument was raised in defense of the Slave Power and the minority. Senator Bright took the floor in March 1858 to make a last stand against opponents of Buchanan and Lecompton. His lecture on republican government presents a fourth theme in the fight for Lecompton and minority rule. He argued that congressmen, once elected, were no longer bound to follow the wishes of their constituents. Their election, he maintained, constituted a moral and political blank check, regardless of the manner of election. "Nothing . . . can be clearer to my mind than the proposition that the act of delegates legally elected, and acting within the scope of the powers conferred upon them, is the act of the people themselves. According to the genius and theory of American constitutions, it is entirely immaterial by what majority such delegates are elected, or what number of voters appeared at the polls." It did not matter, reasoned Bright, if the election was fraudulent or unrepresentative, only that it occurred; the will of the majority was irrelevant.

Furthermore, Bright asserted that the public could exercise its will only through an election. "No matter how unanimous public sentiment may be," he orated, "no matter how strongly a conviction may have fastened itself upon the people, they are utterly and entirely powerless for all the purposes of legislation except through the medium of representation." And that election, in turn, vested the elected official with absolute authority. "The representative opinion may be in conflict with the popular voice; an overwhelming majority may raise an indignant protest against the expressed legislative will;

yet it stands as the controlling law until set aside in accordance with legal forms. He who supposes that the opinions of a majority, even when clearly expressed, necessarily make the laws, has mistaken the whole theory of our Government. That majority, before it can make itself effectual, must fix upon its representative and clothe him with the authority to speak in its behalf at the proper time and place. . . . The acts of the representatives of the people," he concluded, "should be deemed the acts of the people themselves." Truly, this unusual theory of representative government was a rationale for congressmen to disregard their constituents.[59]

Bright's lecture led him to a fifth argument in favor of ignoring the will of the majority—that the American people could not be trusted to make decisions. The practice of submitting constitutions to a popular vote, or subjecting legislation to the majority will, he asserted, was both against the wishes of the Founding Fathers and destructive to American government. "So strong . . . is my conviction of the viciousness of the principle of submitting to a direct vote of the people the propriety of the enactment or rejection of laws, that for one I am prepared to extend the same objection to the submission of entire constitutions to the same tribunal." The people, either the majority in Kansas or the nation as a whole, should have no voice in government, except at elections, and then only as long as the will of the people did not run counter to the interests of the Slave Power. This was, to say the least, a remarkable theory to enunciate on the floor of the Senate. Though Bright explained it best, many other Northern Democrats used this rationale to defend their own actions in the service of slavery. These five arguments in favor of minority rule rationalized their disregard for their constituents and their support for a highly unpopular and blatantly undemocratic policy in Kansas.[60]

The success of Lecompton was a tremendous victory for the Buchanan administration, the Democratic Party, and the South (though Kansans subsequently rejected the constitution and Kansas did not enter the Union until January 1861). Democrats celebrated openly in the streets of Washington, and bands serenaded leading Democrats at their residences. The evening following Lecompton's passage, Democratic revelers gathered outside the White House to congratulate their chief and hear victory speeches from Buchanan, Toombs, English, and others who were in attendance. In his brief remarks, English blamed the crisis on "bad men" with "evil purposes," specifically "Black Republicans." Three days later, Buchanan signed the bill, and the South was exultant. "Let us all rejoice," proclaimed Toombs at a White House soiree. "I cannot forbear to express to you my great gratification at the success of the Kansas bill," wrote Governor Brown of Georgia.[61]

Northerners, however, were despondent. Forcing slavery and minority rule on Kansas was a blatant violation of basic American principles. Anti-Lecompton Democrats, in particular, were fearful of the future. "Can the *democratic party continue without reorganization?*" wrote one Hoosier Democrat to John Davis. "My great objections to the English Kansas bill are that it incorporates anti-democratic doctrines and establishes the So. Carolina heresy as the democratic creed." Indeed, the future of the Northern Democracy seemed bleak. Southern control of the party and the federal government appeared as impregnable as ever, and Southern determination to spread slavery and minority rule at all costs was frightening. Dissident Democrats had been expelled from their party, and now they faced angry voters at the polls. Even the Little Giant doubted his reelection, especially against the capable and persistent Abraham Lincoln. Of even larger import was the looming Democratic National Convention of 1860 in Charleston, South Carolina, where the crippled Northern Democracy would confront the unyielding, solid South.[62]

CHAPTER 8

"We Regarded You as Brothers"

Defeat and Division

While battle raged in Congress over the co-
lossally controversial Lecompton Constitution and the virtues of slavery
and minority rule, Northern Democrats struggled to hold on to their state
political machines. In the torrent of free state outrage over the expansion
of slavery and Southern power, Northern Democrats fared poorly. After
the adjournment of Congress in June 1858, Northern Democrats returned
home to fight not only for their own survival but also for the survival of
the Northern wing of the party. Moreover, at stake in the state elections of
1858 was not just the future of Northern Democratic officeholders but also
the outcome of the 1860 presidential election. The division between the
Douglas dissidents, who were virtually "excommunicated" from the party,
and administration regulars spelled disaster for the party both nationally and
locally. While Republicans entered the fall 1858 races energized, organized,
and joyful over the influx of free state voters into their ranks, Northern
Democrats faced the contests disillusioned, divided, and dejected.[1]

Hoosier Woes

In Indiana, Northern Democratic chieftains Jesse Bright and William
English had to cope with a tsunami of anti-Democratic, antislavery sentiment
triggered by Lecompton. Considered an "audacious cheat" even by some

Democrats, Lecompton was enormously unpopular in the free states, and Indiana voters refused to kowtow to the Southern grandees. "Will Kansas with the Lecompton Constitution be forced into the Union against the expressed and well-known wishes of her people?" gasped one exasperated Hoosier. "Shall we tamely submit to so grave a wrong—such a violation of principle and such a flagrant and infamous betrayal of the confidence of the people, and thus permit the Democratic party to be beaten in every Northern state." "No man," declared a correspondent of Representative John Davis, "now in Congress from the state of Indiana who advocates the Lecompton swindle and sustains the administration will be returned."[2]

It was clear to even the most jaded observer that the overwhelming majority of Indiana residents opposed Buchanan's Kansas policy. Special anger was reserved for Senators Bright and Graham Fitch, who were leading congressional advocates for the Southern agenda. They were considered "corrupt vampires" who operated through "rascality and trickery." "They misrepresent the Democracy of Indiana in going for and sustaining the *Lecompton fraud*," fumed one Democrat, while another noted with a touch of sarcasm, "I presume Mssrs Bright & Fitch are both anxious to retire into private life, as their course has been without regard to the opinions of their constituency."[3]

On January 8, 1858, as Lecompton snaked its way through Congress, Indiana Democrats met for a state convention, where Bright's opponents expected to dethrone him once and for all. The opposition, however, was unable to overcome Bright's well-oiled machine, supported in full by the Buchanan administration. Through patronage bribes, threats of removal, and sheer force of will, the regular Democrats were able to beat down pro-Douglas resolutions and platform planks. In the end, Bright maintained control and dictated a pro-administration platform, as well as resolutions praising Buchanan, Fitch, and Bright. Disgusted, the Douglas dissidents bolted and convened their own meeting on February 22, wherein they made their break from the party official and proceeded to endorse popular sovereignty and condemn Lecompton. "Senator Douglas can now bid defiance to the admin. He now stands high in the affections of the people. And is recognized as their Champion," exclaimed one Douglas Democrat to Representative Davis. "Bright & Fitch can not control all the Democrats in this part of the State," added another, "there is men they are not rich enough to buy." Indeed, succeeding district conventions saw rival Democratic slates, each claiming legitimacy. In the eyes of the party bosses, though, there was no confusion: Bright and Fitch represented the authentic Democracy, while Douglas men were heretics and pseudo-Republicans.[4]

For his critical role in the "English Compromise," Representative English was labeled a "*political* traitor . . . a Judas." The English bill "*is universally condemned*," wrote Ezra Read to Davis, "and English will now enjoy the most unenviable reputation of any public man in the State." Unlike Senators Bright and Fitch, who enjoyed six-year terms, English had to face the voters in the fall. Aware of the symbolic significance of the sudden retirement of the author of the compromise, English reneged on his pledges to constituents and family to not run for another term. On June 15, he departed Washington for his home state to defend his role in Lecompton. Armed with letters of praise from President Buchanan, English waged a bitter battle against challengers both inside and outside the party. When October came, English was narrowly reelected, thanks to the large community of Southern-born voters in his district. Outside that district, however, Democrats went down to resounding defeat. Republicans captured eight of eleven House seats, as well as control of the Indiana legislature, and Representative Davis, frustrated with Southern rule, was on his way into Republican ranks. In a dramatic political realignment, Republicans had replaced Democrats as the dominant party in the Hoosier state.[5]

Keystone Catastrophe

In Pennsylvania, dissident Democrats faced a decidedly less-organized opposition. The regular party, run by J. Glancy Jones and Robert Tyler, and monitored by the president himself, was reeling from factionalism and bankruptcy. In addition, editor John Forney had been read out of the party and his considerable skill and energy was put to work for Douglas. Nevertheless, Democrats did their best to paint anti-Lecomptonites as heretics and outcasts. "You must act with the President or be denounced," wrote Davis to Pennsylvanian Lewis Coryell. Desperate for cash, party managers turned to pilfering state funds, abusing government printing contracts, and demanding contributions from officeholders. Administration agent Cornelius Wendell, who had played an instrumental role in getting congressmen to switch their votes on Lecompton, transitioned from bribing politicians to raising money. To make matters worse, in district and state elections, Douglas Democrats often ran third-party candidates against regular Democratic nominees. In Philadelphia, in July, Republicans, Douglas men, old Whigs, and Know-Nothings united in a "People's Party," which Democratic regulars dubbed the "Mulatto Party."[6]

Hoping to split this new anti-Democratic, antislavery challenge, Democrats employed bribery and patronage, but to no avail. The Democratic state ticket was defeated, and eleven of fifteen Democratic congressmen lost their seats. In Philadelphia, the Democratic vote fell from 53 percent in 1857 to 45 percent. "We have met the enemy in Pennsylvania & we are theirs," acknowledged Buchanan to his niece. Of particular concern to the president was the downfall of his protégé and the chair of the House Committee on Ways and Means, Glancy Jones. Jones's Eighth District, centered in Berks County, had been considered the "Gibraltar of Democracy," and its loss garnered national attention. In the campaign, Republicans made easy use of Jones's proslavery and antitariff record, while he avoided all issues, asserting that "there are no questions that are agitating the country now. . . . We are now in the midst of peace and prosperity." Jones's defeat was also a personal rebuke to Buchanan, who was determined to reward his loyal lieutenant. "With the blessing of Providence I shall endeavor to raise him up & place him in some position where they cannot reach him," pledged the president. To save his friend the humiliation of returning to Congress a defeated man, Buchanan appointed Jones minister to Austria.[7]

Empire Crumbling

Like that of neighboring Pennsylvania, the Empire State Democracy found its strength limited primarily to urban areas. "No part of the State is Democratic, except a few cities, & the Counties immediately around New York," penned one voter. Though the state party headquarters remained in Albany, the largest Democratic organization—Tammany Hall—was in New York City. Even that machine, however, was crippled by corruption, personal feuds, and mounting unpopularity. Fiery Fernando Wood had been defeated for mayor in 1857, sparking a war over the control of Tammany, with various factions vying for administration support. To win the attention of the Southern party bosses, Wood remade himself as the New York champion of Southern slavery. "Wood was the South's most reliable friend in New York City, and defended its institutions with all the fire of his personality and the ingenuity of his political skills," notes biographer Jerome Mushkat. Indeed, Wood swung his support behind Lecompton, Buchanan, and the regular party leadership, aiming for the vice residential spot on the 1860 national ticket.[8]

Despite his impressive efforts, however, Wood was unable to wrest control of Tammany and decided to create his own rival Democratic machine, Mozart Hall. This dramatic split, characteristic of divisions throughout the Northern Democracy, was especially worrisome in New York—a must-win state in 1860. With an eye toward that year, Wood aimed to manipulate supporters of Daniel Dickinson and Stephen Douglas in order to produce a deadlock at the national convention. A deadlocked meeting, he hoped, might turn to a Southern candidate with himself in the second position.

Since his open opposition to the regular Democratic machine was distasteful to most Democrats, Wood increased his efforts to woo Southern and administration support. Simultaneously, Tammany, under the management of Dan Sickles and Dean Richmond, labored to prevent recognition of the Mozart Hall upstarts. "Never was New York politics more of a puzzle than now," lamented J. W. Byrdsall to Senator James Hammond of South Carolina. Given this squabbling, New York Democrats entered the fall elections deeply divided and unable to combat the popularity of their Republican competitors. Seven Democratic congressmen were defeated in 1858, anti-Lecompton Democrats like John Haskin bolted to the Republicans, anti-Democratic candidates swept the New York City elections, and Democrats, who had won the state canvass in 1857, went down to defeat in those contests in 1858.[9]

The New York reversal was a severe blow to the Northern Democracy, making subsequent setbacks in other states all the more unbearable. In Iowa, expansionist and former minister to Spain Augustus Dodge led the Democratic ticket in a near hopeless contest against a determined Republican majority. Claiming that slavery was a positive good, Dodge was easily beaten for the gubernatorial chair, and the Democratic ticket failed miserably at the polls. Even when Democrats were able to pull off victories, it was often at the expense of the administration. In Ohio, for instance, Representative Samuel "Sunset" Cox, whose last-minute support for Lecompton had proved decisive, was able to survive by claiming to his constituents (perhaps disingenuously) that he was a true popular sovereignty man and loyal Douglas supporter. His reelection can in no way be perceived as a victory for the regular Democratic Party given this stand against the administration.[10]

Titanic Struggle in Illinois

Perhaps the most important contest of 1858, however, was Senator Douglas's fight for reelection. Read out of the party, hunted by the administration, and denounced by Southerners as a monstrous traitor, Douglas faced a challenge from both Democrats and Republicans. "No patriot either in the North or the South should ever again place confidence in S.A. Douglas," fumed Senator George Jones of Iowa. Because state legislatures selected U.S. senators, Douglas's survival depended on local elections. "It is *all important* that we should carry the representative from your county and the senator from your district," he penned to a supporter in August. Yet Douglas was stuck in Washington until the adjournment of Congress in June, so the management of his campaign fell to his trusted associate William "Old Dick" Richardson, who had been swept out of office following the Kansas-Nebraska debacle.[11]

As in other free states, it was unclear in Illinois if Democrats would rally to the regular party banner or follow Douglas into uncharted, third-party waters. Buchanan continued to punish all Douglas dissidents, with Secretary of the Treasury Howell Cobb leading the hunt. "The knife is to be used freely," wrote Representative Thomas Harris with disgust. Aside from patronage punishments, Buchanan and Cobb made alliances with Douglas's opponents, including Republicans. Nevertheless, Douglas men were able to gain control of the state convention in April 1858 and push through a series of pro-Douglas resolutions. Unwilling to give up the fight, regular Democrats, labeled "Danites" by Douglas men, after a despised sect of Mormonism, reorganized the state machine and held their own convention in June. Led by Isaac Cook in the Chicago Post Office and motivated more by patronage, personal grudges, and political score-settling than principle, the Danite alliance put forward former U.S. senator (and fierce Douglas rival) Sidney Breese to challenge Douglas for the Senate seat. We need to get rid of "luke warmers," Cook instructed Breese.[12]

Once organized, and with full administration support, Danites waged an unrelenting war against the Little Giant. They denounced him as an abolitionist and vowed to crush any sympathizer. Yet by midsummer, Buchanan began doubting the efficacy of fighting Douglas in Illinois and curtailed his witch hunt in hopes of reconciliation. Many observers who witnessed this sudden change of policy posited that if Douglas made a public apology, he would be welcomed back into the party. Douglas, on the other hand, perceived that a rapprochement with Buchanan would do more damage to his candidacy than good; it would restore his standing within the party and set up Southern support for his 1860 presidential run, but it would decimate his Northern base. Angry and bitter over the administration's attacks on him, and confident of victory, Douglas chose to reject Buchanan's olive branch. This hardly altered the political situation in Illinois, however, as most voters, especially Republicans, saw little difference between Douglas outcasts and Democratic regulars. "He is at war with Mr. Buchanan personally and that is the extent of his opposition," observed Senator Lyman Trumbull.[13]

As soon as Congress adjourned, Douglas departed the Capitol for Illinois, stopping along the way to meet with key supporters. Needing cash, he sold some of his Chicago property and received loans from New Yorkers August Belmont and Fernando Wood, the latter looking to hedge his political bets.

Meanwhile, with the reconciliation a bust, Buchanan renewed his offensive and moved toward a formal alliance with Republicans, who were happy to keep Democrats divided. Though the operation was supposed to be covert, almost everyone knew that the administration was "giving direct support to Mr. Lincoln and the Republican Party," as an Illinoisan reported to Henry Wise of Virginia.[14]

Of more pressing concern to Douglas, though, was the June 16 nomination for U.S. Senate of former Whig Abraham Lincoln, a formidable opponent and highly regarded attorney. In his acclaimed "House Divided" acceptance speech, Lincoln bravely connected the dots between the various Northern henchmen of the Slave Power, illustrating in detail Douglas's leading role. This significantly hindered Douglas's attempt to distance himself from the administration, and Lincoln's address made clear the ideological divide between Democrats and Republicans. Douglas's supposed middle ground disappeared when Lincoln took charge of the Republican assault.[15]

After Lincoln's opening shots, Douglas had no choice but to risk his plans for 1860 by further separating himself from Democratic regulars. Buchanan's enormous unpopularity was an asset for both Lincoln and Douglas, and Douglas did his best to use administration hostility as proof of his independence. On July 9, the Little Giant delivered a rousing speech in Chicago reaffirming his opposition to Lecompton and commitment to popular sovereignty. Not surprisingly, when news of the oration reached the administration in Washington, its leaders were furious. Buchanan "decapitated every friend of Judge Douglass," reported politico Henry Dean, and Douglas exclaimed to a friend that "the hell-hounds are on my track." John Slidell, who, according to Cox, "combined the fox with the tiger," raced to Illinois with cash to use against Douglas, and Buchanan agent John Dougherty met several times with Lincoln to discuss anti-Douglas strategy.[16]

Simultaneously, Slidell, Bright, Glancy Jones, and Attorney General Jeremiah Black launched a letter-writing campaign, reminding voters of either Douglas's ownership of slaves or his sympathy for abolition, depending on the audience. "If Judge Douglas has done as he promised he would do on his return to Illinois—that is, acquiesce in the action of his party in the passage of the English bill—and ceased his war upon the Administration then you would be right and all of us ought to have sustained him," wrote Cobb to Stephens. "Such has not been his course. *Publicly* he attacks the administration and the Democratic party as having attempted to perpetuate a fraud, and is doing today more than any other man in the country to arouse and organize opposition to the only feature in the English bill which made it acceptable to the South." In short, Democratic leaders would stop at nothing to destroy Douglas.[17]

Douglas's reelection campaign became a national battle between the Little Giant and Old Buck. "This is a deeper and more important question than the election of Douglas," Cobb confessed to Stephens. "In my judgment it is a question of maintaining the Democratic party upon its true principles." Though his challenger on the stump was Lincoln, Douglas, in many ways, was debating with Buchanan and the Southern leadership. Over the coming months, Douglas would appear in sixty Illinois communities and give countless speeches, but his seven debates with Lincoln received the most attention.

In the famed Lincoln-Douglas Debates, from August 21 to October 15, 1858, Lincoln labored to show how Democratic policy, embodied by the *Dred Scott* decision, negated Douglas's vaunted popular sovereignty doctrine. By doing so, Lincoln forced Douglas to argue against the administration and his own party. When, on August 27 in Freeport, the tall and lanky Lincoln asked the short and squat Douglas, "Can the people of a United States Territory, in any lawful way, against the wish of any citizen of the United States, exclude slavery from its limits prior to the formation of a State Constitution?" Democrats were more anxious for the reply than Republicans, who knew what the Little Giant would say. Realizing the trap, Douglas tried to avoid a definitive answer by sustaining *Dred Scott* but claiming that slavery required "appropriate police regulations." Ignoring the realities of Kansas, he asserted that "slavery cannot exist a day in the midst of an unfriendly people with unfriendly laws." Northerners, Lincoln knew, would object to Douglas's endorsement of *Dred Scott*, and Southerners would not accept Douglas's assertion that *Dred Scott* did not nullify popular sovereignty.[18]

Lincoln asked the same question in subsequent debates, hammering Douglas on his proslavery record and forcing him to take uncomfortable stands that pleased neither North nor South. Douglas's answers were not new, but his inability to effectively deal with a Republican antislavery challenge eroded his national standing. When Douglas defended Democratic proslavery policy, he lost Northern votes; when he distanced himself from the administration and defended ambiguous popular sovereignty, it only confirmed Southern suspicions of his unreliability. Thus, the real import of the Lincoln-Douglas Debates was to make plain Douglas's impossible position between the Northern antislavery majority and the solid proslavery South. Nevertheless, Douglas, like English in Indiana, was able to eke out a victory. Though Republicans did remarkably well, winning a majority of Illinois voters and carrying the state races, enough Douglas sympathizers remained in the state legislature to return the Little Giant to the Senate. "The great Battle is over & Stephen A. Douglas has triumphed against the allied Powers of the two extremes the Southern Administration and Northern abolition," rejoiced a Hoosier supporter. "The success of Douglas is *the political event* of the 19th century," added another.[19]

The Waning Thirty-Fifth Congress

Douglas's success may have been bittersweet, but the Northern Democratic harvest of 1858 bore mostly sour grapes. There were fifty-three Northern Democrats in the Thirty-Fifth Congress, but there would only be thirty-four in the Thirty-Sixth. Only seven regular, pro-Lecompton Democrats were reelected, while most of the Douglas dissidents saw victory. Of the nine anti-Lecompton Democrats who switched to support the English bill, only three survived; and of the thirteen who opposed it, eight were reelected. Northern voters had rebuked the Democracy and the House of Representatives was given over to the Republicans, who would enjoy a three-to-one advantage in the new Congress. Such losses meant that the Northern Democracy had been nearly reduced to a patronage machine, with administration officeholders and newly arrived immigrants constituting the only regular Democratic organization. "What are we to look for in the North?" queried one disappointed Southerner. Though Southern Democrats may have rejoiced in the Lecompton victory, they quickly realized that it cost them the Northern wing of their party.[20]

Northern Democrats returned to the Thirty-Fifth Congress in December 1858 severely weakened and decisively repudiated. They were reeling from losses and ready to strike out against Douglas for his treachery. Moreover, the national party was on the verge of bankruptcy, and the Buchanan administration had expended all its patronage, power, and influence on the war against Douglas. Even the social scene was "palpably perfunctory," according to the wife of Alabama senator Clement Clay. "The present session is promising to be a hard and laborious one," noted John Davis. Luckily for Davis and others dreading the remnants of the Thirty-Fifth Congress, it would be a short session, though one focused primarily on settling old scores and positioning for 1860. The Senate Democratic caucus, under the guidance of Slidell, Bright, and Jefferson Davis, met on December 9, ousted Douglas from the chairmanship of the Committee on Territories and reaffirmed the expulsion of anti-Lecomptonites from the party. Douglas supporters, not surprisingly, were apoplectic with anger. "The actors in this piece of low flung meanness and malevolence have raised a storm that they will find it difficult to allay," grumbled an Illinoisan. "Farewell to all hope of harmony, and all hopes of the Success of the Charleston nominee in 1860." In the coming months, Southern Democrats, led by Davis and reacting to Douglas's

"Freeport Doctrine," made it clear that the party's focus would be a federal slave code for the territories, guaranteeing federal protection of slavery and Southern power, what Senator Henry Foote termed "the positive *intervention* of Congress in the vacant Territories of the Union in favor of slavery."[21]

Positioning for 1860

When Northern Democratic congressmen returned home in March 1859, they sought to rebuild their battered machines and prepare for upcoming state conventions. Buchanan and the Southern bosses, of course, were determined to prevent any pro-Douglas resolutions or pro-Douglas delegations to the 1860 national meeting. "Already the Judges enemies are calculating the chances of defeating him in the Charleston convention by virtue of the 'two third rule,'" penned an angry J. C. Allen to Charles Lanphier. "What a commentary on the strength of this august Administration!"[22] When Postmaster General Aaron Brown died in March, Buchanan used the opportunity to turn that patronage-rich position over to an anti-Douglas activist, Joseph Holt of Kentucky, who proceeded to crack down on the disbursement of "incendiary" pamphlets from Douglas. But the administration itself was crippled by its own corruption, finally succumbing to years of robbing the Treasury, granting extravagant printing contracts to cronies, and exhausting slush funds on bribery. "Never has the party been so weak, never so divided never so prostituted by any one man for purposes so venal, so malignant so suicidal," recorded Henry Dean of Illinois.[23]

Meanwhile, division continued in the Empire State as Fernando Wood maneuvered for advantage. When the administration refused to endorse Mozart Hall, despite its bold championing of Southern rights, Wood began to court Douglas, believing that a strengthened Douglas movement in New York would ensure a deadlocked national convention. In response, Buchanan cut Wood off from patronage and solidified his alliance with Tammany. Next, Wood sought allies in the old Hards, who were receptive, imagining a presidential lightning strike for their man Dickinson.

Throughout the summer of 1859, Wood caused untold confusion by simultaneously supporting the presidential aspirations of Douglas, Dickinson, and Henry Wise of Virginia. Such perpetual divisions in New York were especially worrisome to Douglas, who needed united Northern support in 1860 to obtain the nomination. If the Empire State collapsed into infighting, as it had done in conventions past, his chances would decline precipitously. On the bright side, leading New York Democrat Dean Richmond favored Douglas, and his band of Softs were leaning in his direction, despite their alliance with Buchanan. Of more immediate concern to the Softs, however, were the machinations of Wood.[24] At the September 1859 state convention at Syracuse, factions vied for control, knowing that the outcome would shape events in 1860. Wood proved the most daring, and his Mozart brawlers gained command through fisticuffs. Nevertheless, the Tammany regulars proceeded to elect a state slate excluding Mozart, enduring along the way an oration from Dickinson in which he pleaded for a presidential nomination. In the end, Douglas men would control the New York delegation to the national convention, and Wood would present his own rival assemblage, guaranteeing that the Empire State family feud would wreak havoc in Charleston.[25]

Douglas, for his part, launched his presidential campaign almost as soon as he was reelected. Throughout 1859, he announced that he would abide by the nomination decision of the 1860 convention, but made it clear he would only accept a popular sovereignty platform. His speeches were circulated, his defiance of the Slave Power celebrated, and a new lithograph portrait printed and distributed. In Illinois, Danites continued their war against him, wielding patronage like a club. "I cannot retain in an important position any man who preaches rebellion against a decision of the Supreme Court of the United States," Buchanan informed one Ohio Democrat. And James Singleton warned Douglas against "men, who under the guise of *disinterested friendship* would barter your chances for the succession for the smallest crum [*sic*] of executive favor."[26] Aside from a hostile administration, Douglas's biggest problems were money and scant Southern support. Late in the year, he toured the slave states, reestablishing old ties and making new connections. His chief Southern allies were John Forsyth of Alabama, proprietor of the *Mobile Register* and former minister to Mexico who harbored a personal hatred of Buchanan, and Pierre Soulé, that flamboyant, unstable Louisianan who caused diplomatic headaches for the Pierce administration.[27]

Douglas's Southern supporters believed that popular sovereignty was still an effective proslavery vehicle and saw no need to alienate the remnants of the Northern Democracy. They were able to set aside their policy differences with Douglas, knowing that his stand against Lecompton made him the only Democrat able to win Northern votes. "Douglas is the only man that has any show for the presidency in 1860, for he can carry more free states than any Democrat that I know of," wrote a Louisiana voter to John Davis. Unfortunately for the Little Giant, few Southerners cared that the free states would never accept a Southern candidate on a federal slave code platform. Douglas, though, was undaunted, and he remained determined to capture the nomination. In a reassuring letter to Singleton, he wrote, "I do not intend to make peace with my enemies, nor to make a concession of one iota of principle, believing that I am right in the position I have taken, and that neither can the Union be preserved or the Democratic party maintained upon any other basis."[28]

Confident of victory, Douglas took every opportunity to affirm his commitment to popular sovereignty. In a public letter to the editor of the *Dubuque Daily Express and Herald* in June 1859, he declared that he would not accept the nomination if the national convention produced a federal slave code platform. To shore up his New York support, Douglas penned optimistic letters to factional leaders, making it seem as though his nomination was a foregone conclusion.[29] With Dickinson, he used flattery, calling him "the leader of a united Democracy in the Empire State," and to Peter Cagger, a powerful Albany attorney, Douglas reported, "Our friends are in the best of spirits here and have implicit confidence in the entire good faith of our friends in New York." In September, he inaugurated a war of words with the administration when he published an article in *Harper's Magazine* on the *Dred Scott* decision. Though not much more than a recapitulation of his well-known positions, Democratic regulars inaccurately considered it the death knell of his candidacy.[30]

Little could Democratic scions have guessed that a political bombshell would explode in October, when a small band of abolitionists, led by John Brown of Kansas fame, launched a daring assault on a federal arsenal in western Virginia in the hopes of sparking a massive slave uprising. The abortive mission was over within twenty-four hours, and Brown was tried, arraigned, and hanged with remarkable speed. The Harpers Ferry raid and the subsequent trial and execution of Brown galvanized American public opinion. Many in the free states were horrified by Brown's tactics but sympathized with his antislavery goals. "It is my honest opinion that a majority of the people of [New York] sympathize with John Brown and honor his memory," explained former governor Horatio Seymour. Southerners, on the other hand, were unanimously appalled, reinforcing their commitment to a federal slave code and strengthening their belief in the evil of the Republican Party. "All the indications seem to me to point to a dissolution of the Union, and that at an early day. There must be a speedy and a radical change in Northern sentiment, or we cannot remain a united people," wrote the governor-elect of Virginia. All Northerners, they came to believe, were enemies.[31]

Regardless, the Harpers Ferry raid was political gold for Northern Democrats. They gleefully drew nonexistent connections between Brown and the Republican Party, smearing Republicans as lawless, murderous abolitionists bent on race war and disunion, while painting themselves as defenders of the Constitution. Moreover, Northern Democrats used the opportunity to prove their fidelity to the Slave Power by denouncing Brown as the Devil incarnate and condemning all Northerners who did not loudly agree.

Seasoned doughfaces like Dickinson and English moved ever closer to the Southern leadership, hoping to benefit from slave state outrage. In early December, Dickinson gave a speech in his home state "in a manner which would have satisfied the most ultra Southern man," according to one attendee. Days later, he wrote to administration insider Samuel Barlow, "[Brown] has been canonized by the blasphemous orgies of those who demand an anti-slavery Bible and an antislavery God, as a second St. John in the wilderness of Harper's Ferry, who was to prepare the way for their grim deity by rapine, arson, and murder. . . . The safety of the Southern people," Dickinson continued, "depends upon the peace of the existing relations between the races, and they cannot be expected to submit tamely to that officious and offensive interference which destroys and degrades them." Nevertheless, the fall 1859 elections saw further Republican gains—free state voters clearly had little stomach for doughface diatribes and fearmongering.[32]

A New Congress in Crisis

Three days after Brown's execution, the new Thirty-Sixth Congress convened on December 5, and Democrats were in an ugly mood. They were furious about Brown's raid, frustrated by Douglas's stubborn independence, and dejected over electoral defeats. In addition, Democrats were now in a minority, and their new Republican colleagues, elected in the wake of the Lecompton debacle, were ready for a fight. Democrats had three goals in the coming session: unite on a nominee and platform principles for 1860, produce legislation that would woo back Northern voters, and not do anything that would give Republicans more ammunition. The second two fell by the wayside as Democratic congressmen anxiously eyed the 1860 convention. In the Senate, for instance, at least ten Democrats were presidential hopefuls, while the rest imagined themselves kingmakers. Republicans, too, were focused on 1860, and hoped to score easy political points against the divided Democrats. "The old fogies in the Senate are all candidates for the presidency from highest to lowest, and are as silent, sanctimonious and demure as a wh—e at a christening," wrote a disgusted Robert Toombs. As soon as the chamber convened, Senators fell to sparring and attacks that produced nothing but ill will.[33]

With the Senate kings and kingmakers distracted, national attention turned to the House of Representatives, where a monumental fight over the Speakership was brewing. There were 88 regular Democrats, 13 ousted anti-Lecomptonite Democrats, 109 Republicans, and 27 old Whigs and nativist "Americans." Election of a Speaker required 119 votes, which put Republicans ten short. With this in mind, Republicans moved swiftly to ally with anti-Lecomptonite outcasts and the Whig/Americans, a combination Democrats were frantic to prevent. The outcome was especially worrisome to the Buchanan administration, which knew that a Republican-controlled House would launch destructive investigations into executive corruption. On December 3, the Saturday before opening session, the House Democratic caucus met and, under the supervision of the administration, selected Thomas Bocock of Virginia for the Speakership. Republicans, in turn, put forth moderate John Sherman of Ohio.[34]

Balloting began on December 5. Bocock led on the first vote, but only three Douglas dissidents voted for him. On the second ballot, Sherman jumped to the lead, a position he maintained in succeeding ballots. Sherman's position proved so secure, in fact, that the House found itself in a stalemate for weeks. Aiming to erode Sherman's Northern support, Democrats exposed his endorsement of Hinton Helper's 1857 controversial work on class and slavery in the South, *The Impending Crisis of the South: How to Meet It*. Helper, who President Buchanan considered "of doubtful personal character," was a white antislavery Republican from North Carolina. A rare combination of proud Southerner and fierce abolitionist, Helper aimed to unite non-slave-owning whites and slaves in an attempt to overthrow the tyranny of the planter elite. With impressive, yet faulty, statistics, he argued that slavery was thwarting Southern progress and that slave states were falling fast into economic decline. In addition, he asserted that slavery equally oppressed poor whites, a claim that enraged the wealthy planting grandees who depended on racial solidarity to maintain their stranglehold on Southern life. Ironically, Southern bluster over *The Impending Crisis* only fueled public interest in the book, leading to wider circulation. "In this way," gloated the *New York Tribune*, "the work is penetrating the whole South in a manner that no hunter for incendiary pamphlets would suppose or can possibly arrest."[35]

Democratic inability to crack Sherman's lead resulted in renewed threats of secession from the South, as well as a spate of alternative Democratic candidates. While Democrats flailed, Republicans waited patiently, the federal government sat idle (waiting for appropriations), and the nation watched. "We are all at sea here; no organization of the House. . . . The Black Republicans are stern, confident and defiant. They manage their side of the house with ten times the skill of ours," Toombs recorded. In a weak attempt to break the impasse, Buchanan delivered his annual message on December 17. It was pure proslavery propaganda and Democratic partisanship. There was, he announced, "an open war by the North to abolish slavery in the South," and Republican principles were "subversive of the Constitution." More important than its tired content were the reactions among Democrats. Toombs considered the message "satisfactory to the South on the slavery question," but Illinois editor Charles Lanphier labeled it *"rank treason to democracy."* "The Message, in its slavery and territorial views, is damnable," added John McClernand.[36]

With each passing week, the divide between Democratic regulars and Douglas dissidents became more pronounced. Regulars, like English, labored to keep Southern trust, while Douglas courted Northern voters. On January 3, English delivered an oration in defense of Lecompton and Northern Democratic fidelity, reminding the party leadership of the crucial role played by their Northern brethren. Southerners must not forsake the Northern Democracy, he pleaded. "We regarded you as brothers, and determined not only to stand by you in all your constitutional rights, but to join you in a war of political extermination against your foes." Admitting that Northern Democrats had grown "weak" and "feeble in numbers," he remained optimistic. "I am the only member, save two, left on this floor, from the free States, of all the men who voted for the Kansas-Nebraska bill; but yet I am not discouraged." United, Democrats could reclaim the North, defeat Republicanism, and ensure the survival of the Slave Power. English failed to perceive that many Southerners preferred secession and did not desire to have the House organized.[37]

Despite English's emotional pleas and Buchanan's proslavery platitudes, the stalemate became so intractable that balloting was suspended on January 11. "The long delay in organizing will make the session a long and unpleasant one," reported John Davis to his daughter. Balloting resumed fourteen days later, with Sherman still safely in the lead. On January 30, however, Sherman withdrew in favor of colorless William Pennington of New Jersey. A deal had been struck between Republicans and Douglas Democrats: Pennington for Speaker, and John Forney, an anti-administration partisan, for Senate printer. The accord was made official on February 1, when Pennington won 117 votes and secured the Speakership. It had been the longest stalemate in congressional history, but Republicans had finally emerged victorious and could now, for the first time, control parliamentary procedure and committee assignments—the grip of the Slave Power had been loosed.[38]

With the House organized, attention returned to the Senate, where the party titans positioned and postured. Of most pressing concern to Democrats was the 1860 platform, which would determine the fate of both Douglas and the party. As expected, Democratic regulars pushed for a federal slave code, which Douglas dissidents opposed. Douglas and Jefferson Davis sparred over everything from the Constitution to the territories. On February 2, Davis, acting with administration approval, presented six resolutions designed to be a blueprint for the 1860 platform. "Neither Congress, nor a Territorial Legislature," read the key passage, "whether by direct legislation or legislation of an indirect and unfriendly nature, possess the power to annul or impair the constitutional right of any citizen of the United States to take his slave property into the common Territories; but it is the duty of the Federal Government there to afford for that, as for other species of property, the needful protection." It was a direct reply to Douglas's 1858 campaign assertion that slavery could not survive under "unfriendly laws." The resolutions were also a version of the popular "Alabama Platform" championed by the fire-eater William Yancey.[39]

Eight days later, the Democratic caucus adopted Davis's resolutions as official party policy, further alienating Douglas dissidents. The resolutions were submitted to the Senate again, in slightly modified form, on March 1. These were concerted attempts to decide the 1860 platform *before* the national convention, where Northern delegations, despite the exodus of free state voters, would be in the majority. "Look out for ultra measures in Congress," warned Iowa representative William Holman. Because the stakes were so high, congressional tempers flared and patience wore thin. As in the crises of 1850, members came armed with revolvers and knives. Southerners were the more physically aggressive, threatening to kill their colleagues in cold blood if they dared to indulge in antislavery diatribes. Some Southerners even advocated immediate secession, showing little interest in the Thirty-Sixth Congress or the 1860 convention. "Every sentence uttered in Senate or House was full of hot feeling born of many wrongs and long-sustained struggle," observed Virginia Clay. "The Presidential struggle is growing more and more vehement," McClernand penned to Lanphier. "The fight is hand to hand."[40]

Republicans certainly enjoyed watching Democrats squirm, and they gloried in their newfound power. With command of the Speakership came control of committees, and in March 1860, Republicans launched a mammoth investigation into executive corruption. Chaired by John Covode of Pennsylvania, the committee dissected the Buchanan administration and delivered a sensational report in June. Dismissed by Democrats as a partisan witch hunt, the Covode Committee actually uncovered unprecedented illegality and illuminated the inner workings of the administration. Former Kansas governor Walker explained how there was a concerted effort to thwart majority rule in the territory, and hosts of political agents and intermediaries, including point man Cornelius Wendell, testified to delivering cash payments to buy votes for Lecompton. "The object was accomplished, and the money was paid," Wendell stated with impressive bluntness.

Of course, Buchanan and the Democrats did what they could to cover up the findings and explain away their actions, but the evidence was overwhelming. "[Mr. Buchanan]," the committee reported, "attempted to drag Kansas as a State into the Union with a slave Constitution, against the consent of its people, employing military force, fraud, and corruption." The evidence was so damning and the public outrage so severe that Buchanan even feared impeachment. To preempt any congressional action against him, Buchanan declared in special messages in March and June that the entire investigation was a violation of the separation of powers.[41]

At the same time that the Buchanan administration was enduring investigations, the Douglas camp celebrated a much-needed victory. In Indiana, pro-Douglas men were finally able to wrest control of the state party from Bright. Bright and Buchanan had used patronage and cash to hold on to the Hoosier Democracy, but by the January 1860 state convention the popular movement against Democrats in general and the administration in particular could no longer be contained. In the weeks before the January meeting, county conventions passed anti-administration resolutions, praised popular sovereignty, and denounced Bright and Buchanan. Even Bright's own Jefferson County came out for Douglas, resulting in the "complete overthrow of the Bright faction," according to one politico.[42]

To combat the trend, Bright arrived in Indianapolis for the state convention on January 9 with U.S. Treasury official Findley Bigger and eight thousand dollars in cash, but to no avail. Three days later, the convention saw a triumph for Douglas and popular sovereignty. Regular Democrats, led by Bright and Fitch, were easily overwhelmed by the pro-Douglas majority, managed by Thomas Hendricks and former representative Norman Eddy. "Bright & Fitch received a rebuke that was richly merited and the incorruptibility of the masses of the democrats was forcibly demonstrated," gloated a correspondent of John Davis. "We have defeated the slave code party in that convention." Indeed, Bright's overthrow and Douglas's command of Indiana would have important consequences at the upcoming national convention in Charleston. Douglas's inability to carry Indiana in 1856, it should be recalled, was largely the result of the machinations of his nemesis Bright, and it cost Douglas the nomination in that year.[43]

The Little Giant was determined to make sure that did not happen again in 1860. The Charleston convention, set for April 23, was earlier than usual, which meant less time for preparation and a longer presidential campaign. With Buchanan committed to a single term, Douglas, despite all the drama and division, was still the front-runner. If he was to triumph, though, he needed superior organization and the firm support of the free states. He certainly enjoyed the former, but did not have the latter.

Learning from his 1852 and 1856 losses, Douglas entered the 1860 fray with the best organization of any candidate. His campaign managers were William Richardson, Virginia editor A. D. Banks, emotional George Sanders, and New York financier August Belmont. Pro-Douglas newspapers, such as the *Chicago Times*, were put into overdrive, his Washington Senate staff was expanded, and a campaign biography authored by his friend James Sheahan was put into production. In addition, Douglas maintained close correspondence with key politicos in nearly every state, and he did his best to build relationships with moderate Southerners. To accomplish the latter, Douglas emphasized his reliability on slavery and insisted that his quarrel with the Democracy was over Lecompton, not principle. "I maintain Slave property stands on an equal footing with all other property," he explained to a Democrat in late March. "I endorse the decision of the Court in the Dred Scott case." Many were convinced, although the majority of Democrats remained hostile. "He is as good a friend as we are likely to find in the Northern states," admitted a Southerner to Senator Hammond of South Carolina. "In any event, we should use him for our own aggrandizement."[44]

As for the state delegations, Douglas had a mixed bag. He was undoubtedly the most popular Democrat in the free states, but the Buchanan administration saw to it that Douglas delegations would be contested by rival, regular delegations. Moreover, the key state of Pennsylvania was not in his column and remained in the hands of Buchanan and Senator Bigler. There was a vocal Douglas contingent, however, and it was unclear what the Keystone State would do at the convention. To improve his relationship with Southerners, Douglas floated the idea of Stephens of Georgia as his vice presidential running mate. Though he failed to make inroads in slave state delegations, Douglas benefited from the fact that Southerners could not unite behind any one candidate, instead putting forward an array of favorite sons. "No one of the Southern aspirants have the ascendancy," a South Carolinian told Douglas on the eve of the meeting.[45]

The Charleston Convention

Delegates to the 1860 Democratic National Convention began congregating in Charleston, South Carolina, on Wednesday, April 18. The city was a hotbed of secessionism and a stronghold of the Slave Power, the lion's den for Northern Democrats. Combined with the damnable, sweltering Lowcountry heat, Northern attendees found Charleston a decidedly unwelcoming venue. Doors were wide open for Southerners, but Northerners were treated with suspicion, if not outright hostility. In almost every way, it was a foreboding, foreign land for free state visitors. "Charleston is an old . . . city," attendee John Davis wrote to his wife. "The few are rich, the many are poor, and the rich own and grow the poor. The slave population greatly outnumbers the white. Every private dwelling is a fort, that is surrounded by high brick walls, or iron fences, and iron gates, which are barred and bolted every night." Moreover, Charleston hotel operators charged Northerners exorbitant prices for subpar room and board—an act that had both social and political ramifications, as it was designed to discourage Northerners from lingering long. "The Charleston people are acting with extraordinary meanness," complained Lanphier. "Is there not some trick in this—either on the part of Douglas' enemies to keep away northern outsiders, or on the part of the republicans to the effect?" Perhaps so, as Northern Democrats saw the success of Douglas and the defeat of the federal slave code as their last hope and were determined to fight to the death in Charleston.[46]

Led by the battle-hardened "Old Dick" Richardson, the optimistic, well-organized Douglas clan rented Hibernia Hall, just a few steps away from the convention venue, and converted its spacious second floor into a makeshift dormitory with rows of cots and stacks of Sheahan's biography of Douglas. Other delegations set up at the Mills House, which boasted a capacity of fifteen hundred, with five or more to a room, while the luxurious Charleston House attracted Southern delegates. In the days leading up to the meeting, there was the usual carousing, caucusing, and cajoling as Douglas men hunted for support and Democratic regulars solidified plans to sink him. "There are great portly fellows with protuberant stomachs and puffy cheeks, red foreheads, thin and grizzly hair, dressed in glossy black and fine linen, with the latest style of stove-pipe hats and ponderous gold-headed canes—perspiring and smoking, and engaged in mysterious conversations concerning caucus stratagems of intense interest to themselves," observed Cincinnati reporter Murat Halstead. To liven the mood, the Pennsylvania, New York, and New England delegations, which had arrived by barge, produced barrels of booze, which made for a great deal of drunkenness.[47]

But while the Northerners drank, Southerners schemed. The senatorial "Clique" of Bright, John Slidell, and James Bayard, which had been so effective in 1856, was back in full force in 1860. They represented the administration and aimed to control the convention, produce an unambiguously proslavery platform, nominate a reliable Southerner or doughface, and defeat Douglas. The senators expected that Robert Hunter of Virginia was the man to beat Douglas, but Jefferson Davis, Daniel Dickinson, and Vice President John Breckinridge were equally acceptable. "I heard Slidell Bayard Benjamin Toombs & many others avow, that with *you*, we could carry every Southern State, and with your nomination they would be entirely satisfied," Bright penned to an eager Dickinson. The important thing, however, was to stall Douglas's momentum and quash his candidacy. "Mr. Bright's hatred of Douglas is, perhaps just now, the strongest passion of his soul," recorded Halstead, who studied events in Charleston carefully. If Dickinson could keep New York split, the Clique would have a shot.[48]

In particular, the Clique aimed to work through the key committees of credentials, organization, and resolutions. In the committees, each state had one vote. Fifteen slave states gave fifteen votes on each committee, but the doughfaces from Oregon and California had pledged their fidelity to the Southern bosses in advance. Thus, at least seventeen of the thirty-three members of each committee were willing to follow the dictates of the Clique. Once the committees were set, Bright, Slidell, Bayard, and Bigler planned to achieve adoption of the Alabama Platform before candidate nominations, knowing that Douglas would never stand on a federal slave code platform.

To accomplish this feat, the Clique let it be known among the delegates that the Gulf states would bolt the convention if the Alabama Platform was rejected. If the convention ended up splitting and producing two candidates, Bright, Slidell, Bayard, and Bigler reasoned that the national election would be thrown to the House of Representatives, where members were too fragmented to agree on a candidate. Power would shift to the Senate (still controlled by the South) which would choose a vice president who would act as chief magistrate while the House languished in chaos. It was a daring plan, but not impossible, given the electoral outcomes in 1800 and 1824. Their efforts were buttressed by public declarations from Georgia, Alabama, Mississippi, Louisiana, Florida, Arkansas, and Texas that they would leave the convention if the federal slave code was rejected. Delegate William Yancey was especially eager to break up the national party. Though he was not in league with the administration Clique, his efforts aided their plans.[49]

The Douglas clan were certainly aware of the Clique's strategy but were unconcerned; they believed that if a few Southern states bolted the convention, it would make Douglas's nomination all the easier. "If our friends stand to their post and refuse to alter the platform the delegates from Alabama are bound to withdraw. Of course two or three states will follow," explained Orlando Ficklin to McClernand. Some scholars have come to see the Charleston Convention as an epic personal battle between Douglas and Yancey, but there was far more at work than the egos and personal aspirations of these two Democrats. The convention witnessed a contest with roots deep in the party's history. Since its inception, the Democracy had been controlled by Southerners and designed to perpetuate slavery and Southern power. The coalition had remained bisectional through potent Jeffersonian/Jacksonian rhetoric and because many Northern politicians in the 1830s and 1840s either supported slavery or had no qualms about using the Slave Power to advance their careers. By 1860, though, the Northern Democracy had withered as free state voters came to recognize the lie of Democratic rhetoric and the antidemocratic, proslavery agenda of the South.

The Northern Democrats who arrived in Charleston to craft a platform and nominate a candidate were deeply divided between those, like Bright, Fitch, and Bigler, who remained devoted to the Southern bosses and were willing to risk the survival of the Northern Democracy to ensure the spread of slavery, and those, like Douglas, Richardson, and John Davis, who had grown weary of Southern supremacy and perceived that a federal slave code would kill the party in the free states. This battle for command of the party went beyond Douglas, Yancey, or even Buchanan—it was about slavery, Southern power, and the ability of Southern slaveholders to thwart the will of an American antislavery majority.[50]

CHAPTER 9

"Though the Heavens Fall"
1860 and Beyond

With the future of the party and nation heavy on their minds, 303 Democrats assembled in Institute Hall, on the grand thoroughfare of Meeting Street on April 23, 1860, Stephen Douglas's forty-seventh birthday. It was a large venue, with old wooden chairs, gaudy ornamentation, and terrible acoustics. Delegates, hungover from late-night drinking, staggered in around noon and the meeting was called to order. The heavy and tall Thompson Flournoy of Arkansas, one of the few Douglas supporters from the South, was elected temporary chair with no opposition. It was a small victory, one quickly overshadowed by the ensuing fight over the admission of dual delegations. If regular Democratic delegations, particularly Isaac Cook's Danite group from Illinois and Fernando Wood's Mozart Hall clan, were seated instead of the pro-Douglas delegations, it would kill Douglas's candidacy before the first ballot could be even be cast. The matter was sent to the Committee on Credentials, which would not report for several days.[1]

Regular Democrats scored a victory on day two with the election as permanent chairman of Caleb Cushing of Massachusetts, President Pierce's attorney general who had won the hearts of Southerners with his vigorous enforcement of the Fugitive Slave Law. Cushing was a virulent white supremacist and a staunch anti-Douglas man, and his selection by the Southern-controlled Committee on Credentials was no surprise. Like

Daniel Dickinson, Cushing hoped for a presidential lightning strike at the convention; he was a dutiful doughface who was untainted by the Kansas/Lecompton imbroglio. Cushing even imagined a Jefferson Davis–Cushing ticket once Douglas failed. But while Douglas men lost on the selection of chairman, they enjoyed a significant victory when they convinced the Committee on Organization to pass a rule that freed convention delegates from states that had not been instructed to vote as a unit to instead vote individually. This rule suddenly made the pro-Douglas minorities in state delegations a powerful voting bloc and prevented the senatorial clique of Jesse Bright, James Bayard, William Bigler, and John Slidell from imposing a unit rule on the convention. By the end of the day, however, the Douglas dissidents had made a terrible error: they agreed to vote on a platform before choosing a nominee. Since Douglas had pledged not to accept the nomination on a federal slave code platform, this fateful decision could spell his doom. We can never know for sure what their motivations were in accepting this order of business, but, given the Douglas clan's confidence and optimism, it seems probable that they expected to shape the platform and prevent a federal slave code plank. Regardless, the Committee on Resolutions assembled and began its deliberations.[2]

Day three, Wednesday, April 25, saw a major triumph for the Douglas group. The anti-Douglas Cook and Wood delegations, from Illinois and New York, respectively, were officially excluded. The session, nevertheless, was cut short when the chair of the Vermont delegation died suddenly. The meeting adjourned, and the delegates congregated for strategy meetings while the Committee on Resolutions debated the platform late into the night. Douglas's victories had befuddled Democratic regulars, and Southerners were especially frustrated. The latter met that evening to discuss their options, including secession. Some argued that bolting the convention would hand Douglas the nomination, while others, led by Yancey and the fire-eaters, had no interest in a harmonious, productive convention. "If Southern States remain in convention Douglas nomination impossible. If they go out he is certain," Thomas Bocock telegraphed to Robert Hunter. No decision was made, and day four dawned with uncertainty. Regulars waited anxiously for the platform report, while Douglas men were confident yet cautious, unwilling to trigger a walkout just yet. When it became clear that the committee was not ready to present, the meeting again adjourned.[3]

After much deliberation and debate, the Committee on Resolutions presented its platform recommendations on day five, April 27. But instead of one report, the committee produced a confusing three, unable to come to any agreement. The majority report was drafted by Bayard and was essentially the Alabama Platform (federal protection of slavery in the territories); the minority report was endorsed by the Douglas men and embraced popular sovereignty; and the third, put forward by Ben Butler of Massachusetts, was a restatement of the 1856 platform. Despite the seeming gulf between the majority and minority reports, it is important to note that delegates agreed on the lack of congressional authority in the territories; for all the blustering, there was little difference between the Douglas dissidents and the Democratic regulars on the spread of slavery. The differences arose over the *method* of slavery expansion, be it federal protection or territorial voting. Regardless, debates ensued and orations were offered. The most notable speech of the day was given by Yancey, who claimed that Southerners were always victims and Northerners always aggressors, that Northern Democrats had betrayed their party by failing to quash the antislavery movement, and that Southern delegations were ready to walk out if the Alabama Platform was not accepted. When Chairman Cushing refused to allow Northerners to rebut, the hall erupted in chaos.[4]

That night, telegraph wires hummed with news of the dramatic events: three rival platforms, Yancey's threats, and hours of bedlam. In addition, delegates wired to agents and associates in Washington for instructions. Senators James Hammond and Robert Toombs advised the Georgia and South Carolina delegations to follow Alabama's lead in a walkout, while Jefferson Davis disagreed, believing slavery better protected within the Democracy than without. Meanwhile, Douglas's manager, William Richardson, was meeting with delegations, urging courage and faith; he was "full of hope, giving every assurance of success," reported one delegate.

When the sixth day began, both sides expected the fight to continue. The convention was now the longest in memory; delegation budgets had been sucked dry by Charleston prices, drinking, and gambling; and money, alcohol, and patience were in thin supply, making for frayed nerves at a crucial moment. Bigler, acting on behalf of the administration, worked to postpone a blowup by moving to have all three reports resubmitted to the Committee on Resolutions. When the committee returned several hours later, no changes had been made—the three reports remained intact and the committee remained deadlocked. When the meeting proceeded to take up debate and votes on the platforms, the Southern bosses, who desired to have Sunday for strategy meetings, instructed Cushing to postpone the vote until Monday. He did what he was told, and the session adjourned.[5]

Sunday saw feverish negotiations—a far cry from a day of rest. Leading the administration forces, the clique fought a patronage duel with Douglas men, each side promising a wealth of offices and contracts. The president watched carefully, weighing his options. George Sanders urged him to relent and support Douglas as Douglas had done in 1856 (giving the nomination to Old Buck), but Buchanan was adamant: the Little Giant must be punished. All the while, Southern leaders conferenced on strategy. Both fire-eaters and Douglasites were open about their willingness to see some slave states secede, causing many Southerners to be all the more determined to stand firm and not give Douglas the satisfaction of a walkout.[6]

By the time the convention reconvened on Monday morning, many of the Northern observers had departed, their money and alcohol consumed too freely. Now the galleries would be filled with hostile Charlestonians who hissed, booed, and spat tobacco down upon the Northern delegates. Nevertheless, the Douglas men were disciplined and presented a united front. With little fanfare, they were able to substitute the minority pro-Douglas report for the majority Alabama Platform. When Southerners raised their voices in protest and renewed their threats of violence, Richardson offered an olive branch. Douglas men would be willing to accept a reiteration of the 1856 platform if Democratic regulars abandoned their commitment to a federal slave code. Regulars had already passed the philosophical point of no return, however, and ambiguous popular sovereignty was no longer accept-able. With the Northern Democracy in shambles, Southern Democrats were convinced that only an explicit federal slave code would protect their way of life. Negotiation was now futile. And when the Douglas delegates proceeded to adopt a popular sovereignty platform, the slave states bolted. With Yancey "smiling like a bridegroom," Leroy Walker of Alabama announced his state's refusal to participate. Alabama, followed closely by the "Gulf squadron" of Mississippi, Louisiana, South Carolina, Florida, and Texas, left the hall.[7]

The seceders marched to St. Andrew's Hall, just around the corner on Broad Street. Bayard went with them to represent the administration and guide them in reconstituting the Democracy. They were soon joined by delegates from Arkansas, Missouri, Georgia, Virginia, and Delaware. Call-ing themselves the Constitutional Democratic Party, the new convention consisted of 118 delegates, including 41 from New York under the manage-ment of Wood. With little fuss, the assemblage selected Bayard as chairman, adopted a federal slave code platform, and decided to wait for nominations until the Institute Hall meeting acted. Down the street, Douglas men were pleased; they expected to easily command two-thirds of the remaining del-egates and achieve a Douglas nomination. Still, the Little Giant, observ-ing from Washington, took the news hard. He was seen outside the Senate chamber drunk and ranting after learning of the day's events. Douglas was not naive, and he knew that a nomination would be meaningless without the support of the administration and the regular Democracy. Regardless, Douglas men and fire-eaters celebrated alike that night in Charleston, albeit for very different reasons. The former celebrated the imminent nomination of their idol, while the latter rejoiced in the first step toward disunion.[8]

Day eight, Tuesday, May 1, of the Institute Hall convention was decidedly more somber. The remaining delegates continued as if they were the regular Democracy, although the overwhelming majority were Douglas dissidents who had been read out of the party. The morning saw the departure of more Southern delegates, as well as some pleas for unity by moderates. Cushing still sat as chairman, however, and he had one card left to play. Doing the bidding of the Southern bosses, Cushing ruled that a legitimate presidential nomination required a two-thirds vote of the *entire* original convention, not just two-thirds of the remaining members.

Possibly motivated by his own ambition and visions of himself as a dark horse compromise, Cushing well knew that his ruling made Douglas's nomination in Charleston impossible. And if the Douglas men hoped to portray themselves as the true Democracy, they had to abide by it. Thus, balloting over the next two days produced nothing; no candidate, not even the Little Giant, was able to garner the two-thirds votes necessary. Northern notables, such as William English, took the floor to urge unity against the Republican onslaught, celebrate slavery, assert the inherent inferiority of the black race, and remind the assembly that Republican victory would result in race war and social chaos, but these were familiar themes that failed to alter the electoral situation. On the tenth day, with barely a quorum, the Douglas managers decided upon a new plan: recess the convention for six weeks and reconvene at Baltimore on June 18. During the break, they could capitalize on fears of secession and disunion to rally public support for Douglas. They could also appeal to moderate, Union-loving Southerners and replace the original Charleston delegations with new pro-Douglas ones.[9]

Rival Camps in the Recess

Though they failed to achieve Douglas's nomination, Douglas dissidents remained confident of ultimate success. They had adopted a popular sovereignty platform that could be sold to Northern voters, and they had defied the Slave Power. "I have been much rejoiced to see that the Northern Democracy stood firm to the very last [at Charleston], and contended manfully and to a great extent successfully for the great principles of Popular Sovereignty," wrote an Indiana voter to John Davis. "If southern states want to withdraw from their best friends because we wont stultify ourselves, and back square down from the great cardinal principles of the Democratic party, I say for one let them go. I will not go with them." The bolters, for their part, were taken aback by the boldness of the Douglas clan. They had not expected the lengthy recess and now had to go home to fight for control of their delegations. They quickly wrapped up business at St. Andrew's Hall and agreed to meet again in Richmond on June 11. In Washington, the administration was displeased—the clique was supposed to destroy Douglas, not rend the party. "The country is in a bad state," observed Alexander Stephens. "This may be the beginning of the end." Indeed, few could see how the party could be reunited. The recess would only serve to harden the position of each side, and as the November elections approached anxiety would turn to panic.[10]

While Douglas declined into alcoholism, his managers scrambled to make Southern alliances and arrange for more friendly delegations to Baltimore. "Be indulgent to the Northern Democracy *at this crisis*," pleaded William Wick of Indiana to Senator Hunter, "and we can come through. The time for a Southern Candidate, and for the presentation of Southern views is not now, but will come with future Territorial Acquisition if not precede the same." The Douglas camp did have some friends in the slave states, and there were opportunities for success in Louisiana, Alabama, Georgia, and Arkansas, where Douglas had ties to local powerbrokers like Stephens and Pierre Soulé. Douglas agents also allied with the rivals of fire-eaters, such as John Forsyth, who challenged Yancey in Alabama. As further inducement, Douglas dangled the vice presidency to leading Southerners. Although he was unable to secure the commitment of entire delegations, Douglas's efforts did yield powerful minorities to the Baltimore meeting.[11]

In many ways, the South had more to fear than Northerners. A true Democratic split would permit a Republican presidential victory and the overthrow of the Slave Power. They had to find a way to eliminate Douglas and popular sovereignty without destroying the remnants of the Northern Democracy. Somehow, they had to advance their own interests with a federal slave code and simultaneously placate the free states. "I wish Douglas defeated," Toombs confessed to Stephens, "but I do not want him and his friends crippled or driven off. Where are we to get as many or as good men in the North to supply their places?" Governor John Letcher of Virginia, however, was not so optimistic. "I do not see how the divisions and dissensions in our party are to be adjusted," he wrote to Hunter. "The complications and embarrassments seem to me rather to increase than diminish. . . . It really looks to me, as if the Democratic party, was going to pieces." The only option appeared to be Douglas on a federal slave code platform, which was highly unlikely. To assist regular Democrats, the administration renewed its patronage war against the Little Giant. If the Douglas outcasts were made to suffer anew, perhaps they would come to their senses and accept a compromise candidate. The 1860 census was imminent, and Buchanan had a plethora of federal offices to distribute.[12]

The most crucial state for both sides was New York, and Empire State Democrats saw themselves as kingmakers. In addition, Dickinson was angling for the nomination, which would require a Douglas meltdown. Administration forces focused on getting New Yorkers to sever their ties to Douglas, suggesting Governor Horatio Seymour as an alternative. Secretary Cobb sent Treasury agent Junius Hillyer to make deals, and Bright continued to reach out directly to Dickinson. "In a conversation to day between the President Mr. Slidell & myself," Bright penned to him in late June, "I heard the former express himself as anxious to know *your* views as to what removals and appointments ought to take place in New York." Seymour, however, was unresponsive, and New Yorkers knew better than to get in bed with Buchanan. "As there is not one man in the State who holds office upon my recommendation I feel no responsibility to the Administration," wrote Seymour to Samuel Barlow.[13]

Douglas forces, too, were active in New York. Richardson met with key politicos, such as August Belmont and Dean Richmond, to make it clear the bolters must be kept out of the Baltimore meeting. But the Douglas clan endured a setback when New York City postmaster and Douglas supporter Isaac Fowler was removed from office on May 10 after auditors discovered he had been funneling public funds into partisan pockets. His subsequent flight to Cuba was hardly an indication of innocence. Richardson personally handled damage control, and a mass Douglas rally at the Cooper Institute in New York City on May 22 improved spirits. "The N.Y. delegation have given us every assurance that they will stand firm at Baltimore," reported John Logan to John McClernand, "if they do we will nominate our man." Buchanan, on the other hand, observed, "The information from New York is not very encouraging."[14]

Much to Douglas's dismay, all the seceding delegations from Charleston, except South Carolina and Florida, agreed to join the dissidents at Baltimore. But attendance did not guarantee recognition and admission. As in Charleston, there would be a fight over credentials—would new pro-Douglas delegations be seated, or would it be the original regular delegations? If the former, Douglas would receive the nomination; if the latter, the split would be permanent. Along with the original delegations, the senatorial clique resumed its activities, now joined by Cobb and Jacob Thompson from Buchanan's cabinet. Unlike Charleston, though, Douglas men were in firm control of the Baltimore convention from the start. Despite the plethora of brass bands, wire-pullers, gawkers, and reporters, the mood was anxious; the fate of the party hung in the balance, and neither side appeared willing to accommodate the other. "I have no idea what will be done in Baltimore," lamented Stephens; "my conjecture is that they will blow up in a row. The seceders intended from the beginning to rule or ruin; and when they find that they cannot rule, they will then ruin."[15]

Baltimore in June

The meeting convened on Monday, June 18 in the Front Street Theater. Cushing resumed his duties as chairman, and the battle began as soon as his gavel brought the convention to order. Douglas wanted the new pro-Douglas delegations from the South seated, instead of the bolters; Southerners were adamant that the original delegations had the right to reclaim their seats. To prevent a breakup before any business could be conducted, Douglas agents offered a compromise: they would accept the original delegations from Mississippi, Texas, Arkansas, and Georgia, but wanted the new delegations from Alabama and Louisiana, led by Douglas men Forsyth and Soulé, respectively. The credentials fight continued over the next several days. Southerners threatened another walkout, rival factions gave dueling orations, and at night crowds enjoyed endless balcony bluster as each side painted the other as villains. On day four, the credentials committee finally produced a report, but just as the report was about to be read to the hall, the stage collapsed and panic ensued. There were no injuries, however, and the scaffold was quickly repaired. The much-awaited report turned out to be two reports, a popular sovereignty majority and a slave code minority.[16]

As in Charleston, the conflicting reports sparked impassioned debates and all manner of threats. Day five dawned with the near unanimous expectation that the party would "fall to pieces," as Virginian James Mason believed. Douglas managers moved to implement their compromise offer, where each delegation would be voted on individually, with the expectation that the Forsyth and Soulé groups would be admitted, but before voting could occur, the matter had to be debated. It was in the South's interest to delay the votes as long as possible, in the hope of extracting concessions from the Douglas men. In particular, slave state leaders warned New Yorkers not to support the admission of the Forsyth and Soulé delegations. Unsure how to proceed, New York chief Dean Richmond kept debate open. Richmond had only a tenuous hold on the Empire State delegation, and old divisions between Softs (who supported Seymour) and Hards (who were loyal to Dickinson) threatened to destroy the state organization. If he came out for Douglas at the convention, the Hards would revolt and the New York Democracy would be in shambles; if he rejected Douglas for an alternative candidate, he would keep the state party intact, but the national party would be destroyed.[17]

Douglas was well aware of Richmond's impossible choice, and he wired both Richardson and Richmond to withdraw his name if the convention deadlock persisted. In a way, Richardson saved Richmond by refusing to withdraw his boss's name, knowing that as long as the northwest stood firm for the Little Giant, no one else could be nominated. In the evening, Richmond and New York agreed to accept the Douglas credential plan, ending debate on that topic. The voting proceeded as expected, and the Yancey and Slidell delegations were replaced by Forsyth and Soulé. With that accomplished, the meeting could finally turn to a presidential nomination. When Douglas men moved to start the balloting, Virginia walked out, followed by North Carolina, Tennessee, half of Maryland, California, and Oregon. Kentucky and Missouri left as well, but only to discuss their options. "I understand that the action of this Convention upon the various questions arising out of the reports from the Committee on Credentials has become final, complete and irrevocable," declared Virginia's Charles Russell. "And it has become my duty now, by direction of a large majority of the delegation from Virginia, respectfully to inform this body that it is inconsistent with their convictions of duty to participate longer in its deliberations."[18]

Nevertheless, several Southerners remained in the hall and urged moderation. They announced in no uncertain terms that the Democratic Party remained the safeguard of slavery and that Northern Democrats could be trusted to further Southern interests. W. B. Gaulden of Georgia declared, "I am an advocate for maintaining the integrity of the National Democratic party; I belong to the extreme South; I am a pro-slavery man in every sense of the word, aye, and an African slave trade man. This institution of slavery, as I have said elsewhere, has done more to advance the prosperity and intelligence of the white race, and of the human race, than all else together." "I am an out-and-out pro-slavery man," added S. H. Moffat of Virginia. "I believe in the institution all the time. I believe it is right morally, socially and politically. . . . I ask you who are true to us in the North, not to desert us, but to stand by and defend us henceforth as you have done in times past." And the next day, Flournoy of Arkansas asserted, "I am a Southern man, born and reared amid the institution of slavery. . . . Everything I own on earth is the result of slave labor. The bread that feeds my wife and little ones is produced by the labor of slaves. . . . If I could see that there is anything intended in our platform unfriendly to the institution of slavery—if I could see that we did not get every constitutional right we are entitled to, I would be the last on earth to submit to this Union. . . . But I feel that in the doctrine of non-intervention and popular sovereignty are enough to protect the interests of the South." There was no doubt among these Southerners that Northern Democrats were devoted to slavery and could be entrusted to continue their work for the Slave Power. It was hotheads and fire-eaters like Yancey, they believed, who falsely claimed that the Democracy and the Union were no longer safe for slavery.[19]

On day six, things unraveled quickly. Flournoy's comments were in reaction to the departure of more Southern delegates, mostly from Kentucky, Missouri, and Arkansas. Seeing no future for the Northern Democracy and hoping for a Supreme Court appointment from Buchanan, Cushing stepped down as chair and was replaced by Douglas supporter David Tod of Ohio. Cushing's resignation triggered the departure of the Massachusetts delegation, under the direction of Ben Butler. Soon, only 192 1/2 votes of the original 303 remained. With regular Democrats absent, the convention voted to nominate a candidate with two-thirds of the *present* delegates rather than two-thirds of the entire convention. This cleared the path for Douglas, who was nominated on the second ballot. The Little Giant had urged Stephens for vice president, but the Georgian's close ties to the administration, frail health, and opposition to the Mexican War (which Democrats planned to use against the Republican nominee Abraham Lincoln) worried many. Instead, the assembly turned to Yancey rival Senator Benjamin Fitzpatrick of Alabama. It did not matter to the delegates that Fitzpatrick did not support Douglas and had endorsed Jefferson Davis's federal slave code platform.[20]

Not far away, in Baltimore's Maryland Institute Hall, where the 1852 Democratic presidential nominating convention had been held, the Southern states, joined by Oregon, California, eleven delegates from Pennsylvania, two from New York, and one from Minnesota assembled, styling themselves as the regular Democratic Party. Indeed, their 240 delegates gave truth to their claim, especially when compared with the 192 at the Front Street Theater. They were all smiles and good humor—the Democracy had finally been shorn of the popular sovereignty "luke warmers," as Isaac Cook had called them two years earlier.

Convention organization was swift, and Cushing assumed his role as chairman, further lending the meeting Democratic credentials. The gathering quickly adopted the federal slave code and proceeded to nominations. Dickinson was in line as a dependable doughface, but Southerners were in no mood for a Northerner, no matter how loyal. Rather, charming Vice President John Breckinridge of Kentucky was the choice of the assembly. "He was a man of a high order of talents, of most fascinating manners, and of great popularity," recalled Stephens. "Very few contributed more than he did in the House, to the Kansas-Nebraska legislation of 1854." The vice presidency went to Senator Joseph Lane, as a nod to Oregon and the far West. Cobb considered Lane "true as steel," and the party hoped he would garner some Northern votes. Before adjourning, however, the convention turned to Yancey, who had done so much to make the purge possible. In a brief address, the Alabama fire-eater celebrated slavery and the South and labeled Douglas "that arch-enemy of true democracy."[21]

The Elections of 1860

The great war of 1860 had begun. Democrats would be fighting not only against Lincoln and the Republicans but against each other. The prospect of two Democratic campaigns brought tears of joy to Republicans. "And thus ended the Democratic party!" exclaimed the *New York Tribune* on the last night of the Baltimore convention. The 1860 presidential election would be the most confusing and critical in U.S. history. In the free states, Douglas would fight not only Lincoln and regular Democrats but also a fourth-party challenge from the newly formed Constitutional Union Party led by Tennessee slave owner John Bell and Massachusetts Whig doughface Edward Everett and composed of old Whigs, nativists, and Southerners unhappy with the Breckinridge-Lane ticket. It was a status quo platform that would leave the Slave Power in command of the federal government but stopped short of a national slave code.

Douglas was left very little room to maneuver as he fundamentally agreed with both Breckinridge and Bell on the sanctity of slavery. Douglas was still essentially a Democrat; his disagreement with the administration and Democratic regulars was not over the perpetuation of slavery but over the *means*. Popular sovereignty, he maintained, was an effective proslavery vehicle that used the basic American principle of self-government. If slavery were to survive and flourish, as the South demanded, Northerners would have to acquiesce, and the only way to achieve that was by allowing settlers to vote. Southerners, on the other hand, wanted to guarantee the safety of slavery in the territories through a national slave code.[22]

Even more daunting to the Douglas campaign was the fact that Northern voters had decisively rejected popular sovereignty in the 1854, 1856, and 1858 congressional elections. They saw little difference between Douglas and Democratic proslavery regulars. Similarly, regular Northern Democratic ranks had been decimated so thoroughly that there was virtually no chance of Breckinridge winning any free states. Republican victory in the North was nearly a foregone conclusion, especially when Lincoln made it clear that Republicans had no intention of disturbing the "peculiar institution" where it already existed. Nevertheless, Douglas dissidents and Democratic regulars entered the race eager for the fight. The future of the nation was at stake. The last bonds of Union—the bisectional Democratic Party—had been severed.

In several ways, Douglas had the most difficult task of the four presidential competitors. Obvious Republican momentum, enthusiasm, and popularity meant that no free states would rally to Breckinridge; thus regular Northern Democrats could focus their attention on destroying Douglas. The Little Giant's base, however, was located in Northern states sure to vote for Lincoln. In addition, votes for Bell would come out of the moderate proslavery Douglas column rather than Breckinridge or Lincoln's.[23]

Though read out of the party, Douglas Democrats proceeded as though they were the regular Democracy. A National Democratic Executive Committee was established in Washington, composed of one representative from each state, and Douglas's personal headquarters, run by Miles Taylor of Louisiana, was established at the National Hotel. New York financier August Belmont was made chair with the aim of frightening financial markets into raising money for Douglas; the Illinois senator, they asserted, was the only candidate who could prevent a disruptive civil war. Before they could gain national traction, however, Douglas Democrats faced an immediate embarrassing situation: their vice presidential candidate, Senator Fitzpatrick of Alabama, declined the nomination. Not only did Fitzpatrick oppose Douglas and support a federal slave code, but administration agents pressured Fitzpatrick to reject the nomination. Even the wives of prominent Southerners were involved, convincing the young Mrs. Fitzpatrick that her husband's career and reputation would be ruined if he joined with Douglas. To replace Fitzpatrick, Douglas turned to Hershel Johnson of Georgia—a reliable proslavery Democrat with no ghosts in the closet. Johnson was one of the few Southern Democrats who maintained ties to the Douglas outcasts and believed that the South and slavery were perfectly safe with Douglas at the helm.[24]

To increase his scant support in the South, Douglas aligned with the rivals of party bosses Toombs, Slidell, and Cobb. He also labored to convince Democrats that he, not Breckinridge, was the regular, legitimate Democratic standard-bearer. His difference with the administration was over Lecompton, he emphasized, not principles. Furthermore, Douglas speeches were widely circulated, as were testimonials from respected Democrats such as Senator George Pugh of Ohio and Representative Albert Rust of Arkansas.

Special attention was paid to Catholic voters, calling attention to Douglas's championing of religious freedom and his wife's Catholicism. Despite the obstacles, the Little Giant remained optimistic of victory. Southern voters, he believed, would recognize his outstanding proslavery credentials and his ultimate reliability on the Southern agenda, while Northern voters would correctly perceive that a vote for Lincoln would lead to disunion, a vote for Bell would perpetuate an untenable status quo, and a vote for Breckinridge would strengthen the Slave Power.[25]

Most Douglas Democrats were not nearly so optimistic. They realized that defeat was likely and began planning for 1862, hoping to preserve their state machines and weather the political storm. Nevertheless, bands of Little Giants organized to compete with Republican "Wide-Awakes." Marches and rallies were held, and a vigorous pro-Douglas press offensive was launched. The two vital states of New York and Pennsylvania, however, remained uncertain. Keystone Democrats were controlled by Buchanan, Bigler, and former representative J. Glancy Jones. The Empire State, as always, was divided. Dickinson and the Hards aimed to please the Southern bosses, Richmond and the Softs did what they could for Douglas, and Wood positioned for his own advancement. The national administration, of course, remained firmly behind Breckinridge and the regular Democratic organization. To shore up his Northern base, Douglas traveled to New York, while Richardson toured New England and New Jersey. Douglas instructed his agents that no compromise or alliance was to be made with regular Democrats, but that cooperation with Bell men was a possibility. "We should treat the Bell & Everett men friendly and cultivate good relations with them. . . . *We can have no partnership with the Bolters*," Douglas advised Illinois newspaper man Charles Lanphier.[26]

The Little Giant had little institutional support in the slave states. Hence, his supporters had to build makeshift organizations, hoping that personal feuds and rivalries would create local divisions. The same went for Breckinridge Democrats in the free states—they had to assemble hasty coalitions and resuscitate ailing machines without much local support other than Buchanan appointees and newly arrived immigrants. Cushing and Bright took the lead in disciplining Northern Democrats, and Bright managed the national committee in Washington.

Though they lacked popularity and a firm voter base, Democrats enjoyed the full support of the administration, with all its patronage and influence. Secretaries Cobb and Thompson used their offices to reward loyalty and punish dissention, and the bribery practices established during the Lecompton battles were revived. Edmund Burke operated in New England, eager for revenge against the Pierce Softs, and Bigler was sent to New York to counter the activities of Belmont. Aided by banker William Corcoran and collector of the Port of New York Augustus Schell, Bigler focused on Manhattan merchants with close financial ties to Southern slavery. Bright and Graham Fitch ran the show in the West, and Stephens led the Southern campaign, despite his near selection as Douglas's running mate. Across the board, the message was that Douglas was an unprincipled, unreliable heretic and that Breckinridge represented true, conservative Democratic principles.[27]

Added to Democratic woes in the North was the lingering economic downturn brought about by the Panic of 1857. Buchanan's conservative, do-nothing policy was opposed by free state business, commerce, and craftsmen, who were eager for recovery and federally sponsored projects. Republicans saw the opportunity, and catered to disgruntled Northerners with a protective tariff and a variety of probusiness planks. Knowing that they could not win the free states, regular Democrats focused on keeping New York, Pennsylvania, and New Jersey out of Republican hands. The Douglas clan, on the other hand, sought combinations that would bring victory at the polls. Efforts at fusion between Douglas dissidents and regulars were fruitless, however, as neither side would agree to yield to the other. Regular Democrats' only hope, then, was to carry the solid South and pray for Northern divisions. "Our friends now confidently expect to carry every State south of the Potomac," observed Buchanan in September.[28]

Douglas Democrats were not yet ready to give up the North. Though severely weakened by illness and alcoholism (he would be dead within a year), Douglas launched an unprecedented campaign tour. From July through October, the Little Giant unabashedly stumped for the presidency as no candidate had ever dared. The old rhetoric of disinterred republicanism was shoved aside in these months of anxiety. He traveled first to New England, then the South, then the mid-Atlantic, then the west, and then back South, spending several weeks in each region. As the weeks passed, though, he became increasingly aware of his inability to win and began to shift his attention to gaining control of the Northern Democracy. If he could not beat Lincoln, he reasoned, at least he could emerge from the election the undisputed monarch of Northern Democrats. With this in mind, he came to the aid of Northern Democrats of all stripes, even those who had voted for Lecompton. On September 20, in Columbus, Ohio, for instance, Douglas publicly endorsed for reelection Samuel "Sunset" Cox, a Douglas man who had succumbed to administration pressure to support Lecompton. Cox's vote for Lecompton, Douglas declared, should in no way mar an otherwise outstanding career. In addition, Douglas tried to minimize differences between

Democrats and recast the Lecompton debate as an amiable discussion among friends. No opportunity was wasted to strengthen his standing with regular Democrats, though he still objected to official fusion with Breckinridge men.[29]

As the campaign progressed, what little regular Democratic support existed in the free states evaporated. The tide was turning even in reliable Pennsylvania, the president's own domain. "There are but seven or eight professed democrats in Guelis township," penned one Pennsylvanian to Bigler, "and I know that one half of these are inclined to vote the Republican ticket." Hard hit by economic depression, Keystone voters were attracted to the Republican tariff and disgusted with Buchanan's conservatism. In addition, Buchanan's June 1860 veto of the Homestead bill, opening western lands to settlement, was especially unpopular. The state party chairman, Robert Tyler, was a Buchanan intimate who worked tirelessly for the Breckinridge ticket and a federal slave code. The rest of the state's Democrats, however, feared defeat and sought temporary combinations against the Republicans. When Keystone Democrats approached the Douglas men, managed by John Forney, they were rebuffed; Douglas supporters would vote only for Douglas candidates.

On June 26, Douglas Democrats held a state convention in Harrisburg, where they ratified the state ticket but called for the election of new, pro-Douglas presidential electors. Next, they adopted a pro-tariff platform to woo fence-sitters, and Douglas gave a rousing pro-tariff speech in Reading. We need to "rally our forces" and "speak plainly," advised Richard Vaux to Douglas. Not surprisingly, regular Democrats were appalled by the Douglas clan's refusal to unite and their rejection of traditional Democratic antitariff principles. The president himself instructed the collector of the Port of Philadelphia to secure from every federal appointee a pledge to support the regular Democracy and ignore the Douglas upstarts. Nevertheless, Pennsylvania Republicans, in the form of a "People's Party," carried the October elections, including governor, by a large majority. The overall Democratic vote in Pennsylvania fell from 49 percent in 1856 to 47 percent. It was a crushing defeat and a harbinger of November.[30]

Setbacks continued in Indiana, where Bright vehemently refused to unite with the pro-Douglas majority. There would be no compromise. Bright rightly perceived that a divided northwest Democracy hurt Douglas more than Breckinridge, since supporters of the latter were few and far between. "I am for Breckinridge & Lane, and intend to make that Ticket beat the 'Squatter Sovereignty' in Indiana," Bright reported to Dickinson. Uncharacteristically, Bright, aided by Fitch, took to the stump to rail against the

Douglas dissenters and rally the regulars. On July 17, he launched the publication of a triweekly newspaper in Indianapolis, the *Old Line Guard*, which, according to one Hoosier historian, was "more strongly anti-Douglas than anti-Lincoln." That same month, Bright called a "Friends of Breckinridge" rally in Indianapolis, which proceeded to endorse the Southern platform, select electors, and applaud Bright, Buchanan, and Fitch.[31]

To combat Republican popularity, Indiana Democrats played the race card, capitalizing on white fears of racial equality. "At the suggestion of the National Democratic Central Committee, I am preparing a document for general circulation at the approaching Presidential canvass," wrote English to N. Caper. "The object of which is to show that the Republican party are in favor of establishing equality between negroes and white people." Despite the rallies and rhetoric, however, Hoosier Democrats were "discouraged, disorganized and demoralized," as one observer put it. The October elections saw impressive Republican victories, as the party won all the state offices, clear majorities in the state legislature, and all eleven congressional seats (including English's Second District). In addition, Republican Henry Lane was elected governor with a commanding majority. The reign of Bright and the Democrats had ended in 1858, but the 1860 elections ensured it would not return for many years.[32]

The final scene of the drama played out in the Empire State, where Democrats continued to suffer from chronic confusion and discord. "The great difficulty in New York is the *old quarrels* among the leaders of factions," admitted one correspondent of Sam Tilden. For once, however, the chaos yielded opportunity, as there was sufficient room for negotiation among the rival Democratic factions. Dickinson was upstate avidly for Breckinridge, Tammany was tenuously behind Douglas, and Mozart Hall was open for trading, though Wood favored Breckinridge and offered his services to the administration for a price. When Buchanan rejected him, the New York City mayor turned to the Douglas clan, which was receptive. Surprisingly, a cautious alliance was forged between Mozart and Tammany, and an August state convention produced a somewhat united ticket.

Simultaneously, Douglas men accepted fusion offers from Bell supporters, realizing that New York was the last chance "to save the federal Union from the calamities which would become the inevitable consequences of the election of Lincoln and [Hannibal] Hamlin," according to Belmont. While Dickinson and the Democrats remained in isolated opposition, the Douglas-Bell-Mozart alliance proceeded with a massive campaign against Lincoln and the Republicans. The fear machine was put in high gear trying to convince financial elites that a vote for Lincoln was a vote for disunion and the disruption of business. Republicans, they claimed, were abolitionist socialists who aimed to steal wealth, destroy private property, and free the slaves.[33]

Meanwhile, Democratic regulars in New York, directed by Cobb, extolled the virtues of human bondage and the benevolence of the Slave Power. Yancey even appeared in several New York cities to orate on the blessings of slavery. In September, they held their own convention and nominated their own ticket. "I highly approve of our present political position, for we have now gained a place secure from sale," wrote Dickinson to a friend. Despite the defeats in Indiana and Pennsylvania in October, and the clear portents of doom in November, Empire State Democrats refused to unite with the Douglas-Tammany-Mozart majority. To make matters worse, fund-raising was going poorly for both sides, since bankers and businessmen remained unconvinced that the Republicans could be beaten.[34]

Efforts at fusion in the free states proved too little too late; plus electoral returns from August, September, and October showed serious defections to the Republicans. In the South, Douglas's whirlwind tour and the publicity of Hinton Helper's *Impending Crisis* had done much to crack Democratic unity, though divisions aided Bell more than Douglas. While Douglas barnstormed, Breckinridge sat quietly at home in Lexington, Kentucky. Moreover, Southerners were distracted by rumors of slave insurrection and accusations of Republican plots to murder Southerners, á la John Brown. "As the day of election approached . . . apprehensions as to the result became serious, and many of the leading men and presses supporting the ticket headed by Mr. Breckinridge . . . declared openly for Secession," recalled Stephens. Indeed, for the first time since Jefferson's rise to the presidency in 1800, the Slave Power was in danger of being overthrown. Southern leaders pleaded with Douglas to step aside, but he refused—he was the only man, he maintained, who could beat Lincoln.[35]

On election day in November, Lincoln easily captured a majority of the electoral votes. It was, one Democrat lamented, a "disaster." He carried all the free states except New Jersey, which gave him four of its seven electoral votes, with the other three going to Douglas. The latter won only Missouri (by a narrow plurality), but 29 percent of the national popular vote. The Little Giant may have lost the election, but he achieved his final wish of emerging as the undisputed leader of the Northern Democracy. Also, he was consoled by his victory over Breckinridge and the regular Democrats in the Northwest; his enemies Bright, Fitch, Buchanan, and Cook had been decisively repudiated at the polls.

Ironically, the chief beneficiary of Douglas's last-minute fusion campaign was Bell, who polled 14 percent. Breckinridge carried the Deep South, Bell the Upper South, and Lincoln the free states. But even if Bell, Breckinridge, and Douglas had united, Lincoln still would have won the election. "Actually," observes historian Don Fehrenbacher, "the Democrats divided were in some ways more formidable than if they had been united, because a Douglas untainted with the support of the slaveholders probably had a better chance of winning enough electoral votes in the North to prevent Lincoln's election." Regardless, the message was clear: Northern voters wanted no more of a Southern-dominated Democratic Party. The national Democracy had been shattered. The free states had finally united against the Slave Power.[36]

As tempting as it is to see the election of 1860 as a contest of personalities, particularly between Douglas and the Democratic leadership of Bright, Buchanan, Breckinridge, Slidell, Toombs, Cobb, and Yancey, it is important to remember that the party's divisions were born of policy and methods. Yes, Democrats, especially Southerners, had come to loathe the Douglas dissidents because of their stand against the party's Lecompton policy, but the debates in Congress and the breakup at Charleston and Baltimore reveal that it was not Douglas but resistance to the Slave Power that Southern Democrats could not tolerate. Antislavery sentiment had spread throughout the North so thoroughly that the Northern Democracy was reduced to a rump of doughfaces. Southerners valued slavery more than the Union, and when the Democratic Party ceased to be an effective vehicle for Southern power and the expansion of slavery, they discarded it.[37]

Northern Democrats and the Crises of the 1850s

From the moment the Thirty-First Congress assembled in December 1849 up through the tumultuous election of 1860, Northern Democrats played the key role in events that caused sectional crises, inflamed passions, and triggered Southern secession. The national Whig Party, never sturdy to begin with, collapsed by 1853, and the Republican coalition, an entirely Northern entity, did not mature until 1856, leaving the Democratic Party the only bisectional partisan organization throughout the 1850s. The Democracy, in turn, was dependent on an acquiescent Northern wing, despite its dedication to slavery and Southern power. When Northern Democrats were cut down at the polls in 1854, 1856, and 1858 (because of fast-increasing free state frustration with Southern domination and the expansion of slavery), and when the party split in 1858 between pro-Lecompton regulars and anti-Lecompton dissidents, it spelled disaster for the Union. By the end of the decade, the Northern wing had been decimated and Southerners were no longer interested in sectional compromise or negotiation.

At every step of the way, Northern Democrats sought to please the Southern party bosses, purge their ranks of antislavery sentiment, and convince free state voters of the benevolence of the Slave Power; they helped create a national political environment where proslavery and pro-Southern was "moderate" and "Unionist," while any challenge to slavery and Southern supremacy was denounced as "radical," "socialist," "abolitionist," and "disunionist." At the state level, they built up political machines that weathered the winds of change and remained in power long after the voters had tired of their policies. They repeatedly and willfully violated the wishes of their free state constituents and the instructions of their state legislatures when they consistently aided proslavery legislation and endorsed proslavery policies. In Congress, they gave the crucial votes on bills, resolutions, parliamentary procedure, and the election of officers and leadership, giving victory to the South on every occasion.

In 1850, Northern Democrats provided the precious Northern votes and leadership in Congress to elect a Southern Speaker; kill antislavery legislation; and pass a series of pro-Southern bills, including the heinous Fugitive Slave Law, that constituted a so-called compromise package. It was the Democratic Little Giant of Illinois, Stephen Douglas, not the Whig Great Pacificator of Kentucky, Henry Clay, who forged the Compromise of 1850. In addition, the compromise itself, which was in sum proslavery, was an instance of Southern aggression and Northern compliance rather than sectional negotiation and mutual benefit. In the wake of their legislative achievement, Northern Democrats labored to implement the new Fugitive Slave Law with vigor, purge their state organizations of antislavery men, and fortify themselves for the elections of 1852 in the face of mounting antislavery sentiment. To achieve victory in that year's presidential election, Free Soil Democrats (who had bolted the party in 1848) were wooed back with promises of patronage and policy changes, but they were never truly readmitted into Northern Democratic ranks. Free state party leaders such as Buchanan, Dickinson, and Bright made sure that reunion with the Free Soilers was brief and that they were expunged from the party as soon as the election had been won.

Knowing that a Southerner could not be elected president in 1852 because of the growing population of the free states, and seeking to reward Northern Democrats for their fidelity in the "compromise" of 1850, the Southern party bosses turned to a Northerner for that year's nomination—reliable Franklin Pierce of New Hampshire. Pierce's New England roots plus party unity and a divided adversary, not the popularity of Democratic policy, produced a Democratic victory in 1852.

The Pierce administration, in turn, proceeded to implement a bold proslavery agenda, both in domestic and foreign affairs. His administration oversaw the energetic prosecution of the Fugitive Slave Law; several abortive attempts to acquire Cuba as a slave state; a variety of illegal proslavery filibustering expeditions; and the passage of the Kansas-Nebraska Act, which permitted the spread of slavery into the western territories. Northern Democrats, including "Handsome Frank," made possible all these policy initiatives. In particular, Douglas and his lieutenants drafted the Kansas-Nebraska Act and orchestrated its passage, mobilizing just enough Northern Democratic votes to achieve success despite fierce free state opposition. Along the way, Northern Democrats—first Dickinson, then Cass, then Douglas—developed the doctrine of popular sovereignty, wherein territorial settlers could vote on slavery. The policy manifested in the Kansas-Nebraska Act and was uniquely suited to serve the needs of Northern Democrats, who could claim to their constituents that it extended democracy, while at the same time reassure Southerners that it would allow the expansion of slavery, since the policy allowed slave owners to bring their human chattel into a territory.

In 1856, the Southern party bosses again turned to a dutiful Northern Democrat, Buchanan of Pennsylvania. "Old Buck" continued Pierce's aggressive foreign policy initiatives and increased efforts to spread slavery into the territories. More important, Buchanan personally manipulated Supreme Court justices to produce the infamous *Dred Scott* decision that declared congressional authority void in the territories and denied the humanity of African Americans. When Southern militants attempted to force slavery on an unwilling antislavery majority in the Kansas Territory, both the Pierce and Buchanan administrations mobilized behind the proslavery faction. When that same faction produced a fraudulent, unrepresentative, proslavery state constitution (the Lecompton Constitution), Buchanan declared his support and successfully pushed it through Congress, against the will of both the Kansas majority and the Northern antislavery public.

Aiding Buchanan and the Southern bosses were Northern Democrats who provided the congressional votes and patronage bribes needed to achieve passage. Not surprisingly, this violation of majority will in Kansas was difficult to stomach for many Northern Democrats, even for tried-and-true partisans like Douglas. Claiming that such a course violated cherished American principles of self-government and majority rule, Douglas led a significant segment of Northern Democrats in opposition to Lecompton. The resistance of Douglas and the anti-Lecomptonites caused a fatal split within the national Democratic Party, one that eventually led to two Democratic presidential candidates in 1860. That split, in turn, made Republican victory that year all the easier and the secession of Southern slave states a foregone conclusion.

But Northern Democrats offered more than votes for proslavery policies and legislation—they carried the antidemocratic, minority rule crusade of the Southern grandees to the free states. When Northern sentiment slowly turned away from proslavery Democratic principles starting in the late 1840s, Northern Democrats began to craft an antidemocratic ideology that blossomed in full view during the Lecompton debates of 1857–1858. When former senator Dickinson was asked in 1853 why he had repeatedly turned a deaf ear to both his constituents and the instructions of the New York State legislature, he struck a cavalier attitude: "I should best discharge my duty to the constitution and the Union by disregarding such instructions altogether; and although they were often afterwards repeated, and popular indignities threatened, I disregarded them accordingly." By 1857, these attitudes had evolved into a dynamic party doctrine, which stipulated that majorities were dangerous, minority rule was enshrined in the Constitution, and elected officials were free to act in any manner they pleased, regardless of their constituents. Though enormously unpopular with free state voters, this ideology was designed to rationalize forcing slavery and minority rule on an unwilling Kansas Territory and to prove the fidelity of Northern Democrats, who had come under Southern scrutiny after Douglas's defiant stand.[38]

In 1860, the two Democratic candidates, Breckinridge and Douglas, were defeated and Abraham Lincoln and the young Republican Party assumed command of the federal government. The mere election of a Republican, despite the fact that he was dedicated to protecting slavery where it already existed, was too much for Southern militants, and the winter of 1860–1861 saw the secession of seven slave states. In April 1861, South Carolina attacked the U.S. garrison at Fort Sumter, triggering civil war—Northerners finally confronted the Slave Power that had dominated the nation since 1801.

Beyond 1860

Though the antebellum era had come to an end and they had been thoroughly repudiated at the polls, Northern Democrats lingered in national and state politics, sometimes playing important roles in the war effort or in the reformation of their beloved party. Before his expulsion from the Senate, Bright served as a leading critic of the Lincoln administration. When his letter to Jefferson Davis surfaced, both the U.S. Congress and the Indiana state legislature began the process of his removal. Following his ouster, he officially relocated his residence to his Carroll County, Kentucky, plantation, joined the Knights of the Golden Circle (a fraternal organization devoted to filibustering and the expansion of slavery), and, in 1864, was elected to the Kentucky state legislature. Throughout, he continued to pen angry letters about emancipation and Republicans. To better manage his business investments, Bright moved to Baltimore in 1874, where he died in May 1875.[39]

"Old Dick" Richardson, Democratic manager in the House of Representatives, was able to pull off a narrow victory in his Illinois Fifth District in 1860. He opposed secession and worked for compromise in Congress, but when President Lincoln embraced emancipation, Richardson announced his firm opposition. He continued to harbor deep white supremacist beliefs, and he reverted to his prewar position of fierce pro-Southern Democratic partisan. In January 1863, he accepted the nomination of Illinois Democrats for the U.S. Senate, and, thanks to the striking rebel victory at Fredericksburg in December 1862, was elected. On entering the Senate, Richardson launched an all-out attack on the Lincoln administration's handling of the war, calling for an immediate end to combat and a revocation of the Emancipation Proclamation. In debates over reconstruction, he maintained his opposition to racial equality and any assistance to newly freed slaves. Richardson was not a candidate for reelection in 1864, though he applauded President Andrew Johnson's pro-Southern "moderation" and maintained his fight against black suffrage. He died in Quincy, Illinois, on December 27, 1875.[40]

Other Democratic notables were not nearly so active after the 1850s. Buchanan, following his disastrous final months in office, spent the war years in angry isolation on his luxurious Lancaster estate, Wheatland. "I have carefully reviewed all my public conduct since the day of Mr. Lincoln's election until I left office, & I would not change it, if I could, in any important particular," he wrote to a friend in October 1861. In 1866, he published a poison-pen memoir titled *Mr. Buchanan's Administration on the Eve of Rebellion*, where he blamed Republicans for the nation's woes and painted his own policies as moderate and patriotic. Suffering from what he described as "Rheumatic gout," he died only two years later, on June 1, 1868.[41]

Buchanan's protégé, J. Glancy Jones, served as minister to Austria after his electoral defeat in 1858 and returned to his law practice and a war-torn nation in December 1861 (removed by President Lincoln). A good Democrat, he sympathized with the Southern rebellion, condemned Lincoln as a "despot," defended clients who were active in the antiwar movement, and vigorously opposed civil rights for African Americans. He died an angry partisan on March 24, 1878.[42] Likewise, Bright's close friend English was defeated in 1860 and would never hold elective office again. Out of office at only thirty-eight years old, he began a second career in banking, using his political connections to help establish the First National Bank of Indianapolis, of which he served as president until 1877. Yet all the while he maintained his Democratic principles and vigorously defended slavery, opposed emancipation, and railed against rights for freedmen and women. His partisan fidelity made him an attractive candidate once again, and in 1880 he was nominated for the U.S. vice presidency on an abortive pro-Southern ticket with Winfield Scott Hancock. Despite defeat, his financial endeavors had allowed him to add to his already impressive fortune, and when he died in February 1896 he was one of the wealthiest men in Indiana.[43]

Pierce, too, returned to private life after his controversial administration. Out of office, he toured Europe with his wife and kept abreast of political events through his numerous correspondents. In the election of 1860, the former president supported the proslavery Breckinridge ticket, and during the secession winter he quietly sympathized with his Southern friends. When war erupted, Pierce joined the majority of his Democratic cohorts in condemning the Lincoln administration, especially the Emancipation Proclamation. As the years progressed, Handsome Frank became increasingly depressed and despondent as he lost family, friends, and influence—what his principal biographer has termed "the dissolution of a personality." He died alone in the predawn hours of October 8, 1869.[44]

Yet there were also instances of Northern Democrats shedding their proslavery records in defense of the Constitution. Quite unlike his partisan brothers, Dickinson embraced the Union cause when the war came. Though he supported Breckinridge in 1860 and had spent a career serving the Slave Power, Dickinson rallied to the flag when South Carolina launched its attack on the U.S. government. Addressing Union meetings across New York, Dickinson urged national unity in the face of the Southern aggressor and vowed to defend the Constitution and the United States. Once peace had failed, he reasoned, war must be prosecuted vigorously (though he still blamed abolitionists for the crisis). Throughout the conflict, he denounced antiwar "Copperheadism" and urged President Lincoln to be more aggressive against the Southern traitors. In September 1861, he was nominated by New York Democrats to serve as state attorney general, which he did for two years. He declined a gubernatorial nomination in 1864, and was a serious contender for the vice presidency that same year. Dickinson accepted Lincoln's offer to serve as district attorney for the Southern District of New York in 1865 but died of "strangulated hernia" in New York City shortly thereafter, in April 1866.[45]

Similarly, Douglas rose to defend the U.S. government against slave state aggressions. Following his electoral defeat in 1860, he returned to Congress and urged resistance to secession. As the crisis deepened, he moved slowly toward the Republican position, announcing that secession was treasonous and unconstitutional, though he preferred conciliation to coercion. He played a leading role in congressional compromise initiatives during the secession winter of 1860–1861, but campaign fatigue, exhaustion from his years of unending legislative labor, and alcoholism had finally taken their toll. In April 1861, he departed Washington for his home in the Prairie State, stopping along the way to give speeches and address public gatherings. He died in Chicago on the morning of June 3, issuing final instructions to his absent sons to obey the laws and support the Constitution.[46]

Despite their postbellum careers, however, Northern Democrats in the 1850s had voted like Southerners, defended slavery like Southerners, attacked free-soilism like Southerners, and played on racial fears like Southerners, and even some, like Bright and Douglas, were themselves slave owners. Their personal motives and political paths may have differed dramatically, but the repercussions of their actions were the same: their proslavery legislation and rhetoric tore the nation apart and led to civil war. "It will not much longer be tolerated for a public man to cry out in favor of the Union & yet pursue such a course of policy as is calculated to destroy it. Men must show their faith by their works," observed Buchanan in 1850, showing no sense of his own irony.[47]

Indeed, it was the "works" of Northern Democrats—from the Fugitive Slave Law, to the pro-Southern "Compromise" of 1850, to the Kansas-Nebraska Act, to the *Dred Scott* ruling, to the Lecompton debacle, as well as years of illegal proslavery filibustering and Bleeding Kansas—that tore asunder both the party and the nation. These men were so wedded to the status quo of a Southern-dominated Democracy and Union, both politically and philosophically, that they were willing to openly defy their constituencies, actively pursue proslavery policies, and rend their own party as they vied with each other for Southern support. As the sole remaining bisectional party, the fracturing and split of the Democratic Party in 1860 paved the way for Republican ascension and Southern secession. One is reminded of the timeless Roman maxim: "Let justice be done, though the heavens fall."

Abbreviations

ADDM—Augustus Dodge Papers, Iowa State Library, Des Moines
ADIC—Augustus Dodge Papers, Iowa State Library, Iowa City
BaDM—Gideon Bailey Papers, Iowa State Library, Des Moines
BFLC—Breckinridge Family Papers, Library of Congress
BiHSP—William Bigler Papers, Historical Society of Pennsylvania
BiNYPL—John Bigelow Papers, New York Public Library
BJLC—Buchanan and Johnston Papers, Library of Congress
BeNYPL—August Belmont Papers, New York Public Library
BrCHS—Jesse Bright Papers, Chicago Historical Society
BrISL—Jesse Bright Papers, Indiana State Library
BuHSP—James Buchanan Papers, Historical Society of Pennsylvania
BuLC—James Buchanan Papers, Library of Congress
BuLPL—James Buchanan Letters, Abraham Lincoln Presidential Library
BuNYHS—James Buchanan Collection, New-York Historical Society
CG—Congressional Globe
CHS—Chicago Historical Society
CoHSP—Lewis Coryell Papers, Historical Society of Pennsylvania
CoLC—William Corcoran Papers, Library of Congress
CuMHS—Cushing Family Papers, Massachusetts Historical Society
DaIHS—John Davis Papers, Indiana Historical Society
DeCHS—Henry Dean Papers, Chicago Historical Society
DeDM—Henry Dean Papers, Iowa State Library, Des Moines
DiNew—Daniel Dickinson Papers, Newberry Library
DoIC—Augustus Dodge Letters, University of Iowa Library, Iowa City
DoLPL—Stephen Douglas Papers, Abraham Lincoln Presidential Library
DoNYHS—Stephen Douglas Papers, New-York Historical Society
EBLC—Edmund Burke Papers, Library of Congress
EnCHS—William English Papers, Chicago Historical Society
EnIHS—William English Papers, Indiana Historical Society
EnISL—William English Papers, Indiana State Library
FCNYHS—Fairchild Collection, New-York Historical Society
GoNYSL—William Gorham Papers, New York State Library
GrISL—John Graham Letters, Indiana State Library
HaLC—James Henry Hammond Papers, Library of Congress
HGUVA—Hunter-Garnett Papers, University of Virginia

HOBIHS—Holman-O'Brien Papers, Indiana Historical Society
IHS—Indiana Historical Society
ISL—Indiana State Library
JBHP—*John P. Branch Historical Papers of Randolph-Macon College* 4, no. 1 (1913)
(Richmond, VA: Richmond Press).
JoNYHS—Cave Johnson Papers, New-York Historical Society
KeIHS—John Ketchum Papers, Indiana Historical Society
LaIHS—Charles Lanman Collection, Indiana Historical Society
LaL PL—Charles Lanphier Papers, Abraham Lincoln Presidential Library
LOC—Library of Congress
MaLC—William Marcy Papers, Library of Congress
MaNYSL—William Marcy Papers, New York State Library
McCL PL—John McClernand Collection, Abraham Lincoln Presidential Library
MiLC—George Fort Milton Papers, Library of Congress
MWNYHS—Mike Walsh Papers, New-York Historical Society
NYHS—New-York Historical Society
PiLC—Franklin Pierce Papers, Library of Congress
PiNYHS—Franklin Pierce Letters, New-York Historical Society
ReCHS—Logan Reavis Papers, Chicago Historical Society
RiCHS—William Richardson Letters, Chicago Historical Society
RiL PL—William Richardson Letters, Abraham Lincoln Presidential Library
SBL PL—Sidney Breese Papers, Abraham Lincoln Presidential Library
SCISL—Schuyler Colfax Letters, Indiana State Library
SCLL—Schuyler Colfax Papers, Lilly Library, Indiana University
SDL—Stephen Douglas, *The Letters of Stephen A. Douglas*, edited by Robert Jo-
hannsen (Urbana: University of Illinois Press, 1961).
SeNYHS—Horatio Semour Papers, New-York Historical Society
SeNYSL—Horatio Seymour Papers, New York State Library
SiL PL—James Singleton Papers, Abraham Lincoln Presidential Library
SmLC—Caleb Blood Smith Papers, Library of Congress
ThISL—Richard Thompson Letters, Indiana State Library
TiNY PL—Samuel Tilden Papers, New York Public Library
TrNY PL—Albert Tracy Papers, New York Public Library
TSC—Robert Toombs, Alexander Stephens, and Howell Cobb, *The Correspondence
of Robert Toombs, Alexander H. Stephens, and Howell Cobb,* edited by Ulrich
Bonnell Phillips, Annual Report of the American Historical Association for
the Year 1911, vol. 2 (Washington, DC, 1913).
TwNYHS—William Tweed Papers, New-York Historical Society
WaNYHS—Robert Walker Papers, New-York Historical Society
WoNYHS—Fernando Wood Papers, New-York Historical Society

NOTES

Introduction

1. Francis Pollard to siblings, Feb. 6, 1862, IHS; *CG*, 37C-2S, 89; "The Proceedings of Congress," *New York Times,* Dec. 16, 1861; Thornbrough, *Indiana in the Civil War*, 115; Van Der Weele, "Jesse David Bright," 272, 274, 277–280; Murphy, *Political Career of Bright*, 138.

2. In what must have been a final insult to the Democratic titan, Bright's replacement in the Senate was his arch nemesis in Indiana, former governor Joseph Wright ("Gov. Morton," *Daily Cleveland Herald*, Feb. 25, 1862); Francis Pollard to siblings, Feb. 6, 1862 (quoted), IHS; *CG*, 37C-2S, 651–655; "Jesse D. Bright," *Daily Cleveland Herald*, Jan. 24, 1862; "Important from Washington," *New York Times*, Feb. 6, 1862; "The Expulsion of Bright," *New York Times,* Feb. 6, 1862 (quoted); Woollen, *Sketches of Early Indiana*, 229; Van Der Weele, "Jesse David Bright," 266, 286–288; Thornbrough, *Indiana in the Civil War*, 115; "Jesse D. Bright," *Lowell Daily Citizen and News*, Feb. 6, 1862 (quoted).

3. Marcy to unknown Southern Democrat, Nov. 28, 1849 (quoted), MaLC.

4. Richards, *Slave Power*, 60–61, 114–116, 144–145.

5. Richards, *Slave Power*, 60–63, 113–116; Duff Green to Lewis Coryell, Nov. 21, 1850 (quoted), Richard Brodhead to Lewis Coryell, Sept. 28, 1851 (quoted), CoHSP.

6. *Pittsburgh Statesman*, Apr. 26, 1820, found in Moore, *Missouri Controversy*, 103–104; Richards, *Slave Power*, 85–86; Wood, "John Randolph," 106–143. For alternative meanings of "doughface," see Summers, *Plundering Generation*, 225.

7. See Cooper, *Politics of Slavery*.

8. Cooper, *Liberty and Slavery*, 50 (quoted). For a superior explanation of the Three-Fifths Clause and slavery in the Constitution, see Finkelman, *Slavery and the Founders*, 3–33.

Chapter 1

1. Charles Coffin to Smith, Mar. 24, 1849, Thomas Stevenson to Smith, Jan. 17, 1849 (quoted), SmLC; John Barbour to Ritchie, Aug. 17, 1847, in *JBHP*, 398–400; Hopkins Holsey to Cobb, Feb. 13, 1849, Henry Benning to Cobb, July 1, 1849, in TSC, 148–152, 168–172; Stegmaier, *Texas*, 44.

2. John Calhoun continues to confound scholars today, exhibiting energetic nationalism as a young "War Hawk" in the 1810s and as President Monroe's secretary of war in the 1820s, then making a dramatic switch to nullifier, secessionist, and states' rights champion in the 1830s–1840s. Many have concluded that Calhoun, twice relegated to the vice presidency, in 1824 and 1828, decided that his only path to the

White House lay with unified Southern support. Thus, in 1828, he authored the South Carolina *Exposition and Protest* that made him a hero to Southern fire-eaters and disunionists. Benton, *Thirty Years' View*, 733; Toombs to John Crittenden, Jan. 3, 1849, in TSC, 139–140; Stegmaier, *Texas*, 86.

3. For an in-depth study of the Nashville Convention of 1850, see Jennings, *Nashville Convention*. Sinha, *Counterrevolution*, 96–98; Walther, *William Lowndes Yancey*, 119, 122–123; Barnwell, *Love of Order*, 86–88, 95–97, 101–102; Buchanan to Henry Foote, Nov. 14, 1849 (quoted), BuHSP; John Forsyth to Cobb, Nov. 10, 1848 (quoted), James Cooper to Cobb, Nov. 11, 1848, in TSC, 136, 137.

4. William Lewis to Ritchie, June 18, 1850 (quoted), Marcy to Ritchie, July 18, 1849, in *JBHP*, 402–405; Julian, *Political Recollections*, 50–51 (quoted), 67–68; Dickinson to Dougherty et al., Jan. 20, 1851, in Dickinson and Dickinson, *Speeches, Correspondence Etc.*, 459–464; W. C. Daniell to Cobb, July 1, 1848, in TSC, 113–114; Stephens to brother, Mar. 1848, in Johnston and Browne, *Life of Stephens*, 226–227, 236–237; "Report of the New York Delegates to the National Democratic Convention of 1848 . . .," in Tilden, *Writings and Speeches*, 234–247.

5. Dickinson to Dougherty et al., Jan. 20, 1851, in Dickinson and Dickinson, *Speeches, Correspondence, Etc.*, 459–464; William Marcy to Ritchie, July 18, 1849 (quoted), William Lewis to Ritchie, June 18, 1850, in *JBHP*, 402–405, 408–414; Julian, *Political Recollections*, 50–51, 67–68; Stephens to brother, Mar. 1848, in Johnston and Browne, *Life of Stephens*, 226–227, 236–237; "Report of the New York Delegates," in Tilden, *Writings and Speeches*, vol. 1, 234–247; Holt, *Rise and Fall*, 368–381.

6. Hokins Holsey to Cobb, Feb. 13, 1849, in TSC, 148–152; Marcy to Ritchie, July 18, 1849 (quoted), in *JBHP*, 402–405; James MacLanahan to Buchanan, Dec. 2, 1849, Forney to Buchanan, Dec. 13, 1849 (quoted), BuHSP; Buchanan to Marcy, Nov. 12, 1849, MaLC; Dickinson to Manco Dickinson, Dec. 8, 1849, Dickinson to Lydia Dickinson, Dec. 22, 1849, in Dickinson and Dickinson, *Speeches, Correspondence, Etc.*, 417–418; Hamilton, *Prologue to Conflict*, 43–44; Stephens, Dec. 2, 1849, Dec. 3, 1849, in Johnston and Browne, *Life of Stephens*, 237–238; Julian, *Political Recollections*, 77.

7. Cobb to wife, Nov. 27, Dec. 2, 1849, in TSC, 176–177; George Plitt to Buchanan, Dec. 2, 1849, BJLC; *CG*, 31C-1S, 2–3; John McClernand to Charles Lanphier, Dec. 9, 1848, MiLC.

8. *CG*, 31C-1S, 4–9; McClernand to Lanphier, Dec. 9, 1849, MiLC; Thomas Harris to Lanphier, Jan. 12, 1850 (quoted), LaLPL.

9. Frederick Stanton to Buchanan, Dec. 24, 1849, BuHSP; Cobb to wife, Dec. 4, Dec. 20, 1849, in TSC, 177–179; Stephens, Apr. 1849, Dec. 3, 1849, in Johnston and Browne, *Life of Stephens*, 219–220, 238; Marcy to Ritchie, Nov. 29, 1849, in *JBHP*, 405–408; Harris to Lanphier, Jan. 12, 1850 (quoted), LaLPL; Preston King to Tilden, Dec. 15, 1849, TiNYPL; Julian, *Political Recollections*, 77.

10. Stephens, Dec. 10, 1849, in Johnston and Browne, *Life of Stephens*, 239; Stephens, *Constitutional View*, 2:217 (quoted); Barnwell, *Love of Order*, 88–89.

11. Forney to Buchanan, Dec. 13, 1849, BuHSP; *CG*, 31C-1S, 27–28 (quoted); Stephens, Dec. 10, 1849, in Johnston and Browne, *Life of Stephens*, 239; Forney, *Anecdotes of Public Men*, 2:165.

12. James Shields to Buchanan, Dec. 8, 1849 (quoted), BuHSP; John Wool to Dickinson, Jan. 30, 1850, DiNew; Stephens to Linton Stephens, Jan. 21, 1850 (quoted), in Johnston and Browne, *Life of Stephens*, 243–245.

13. Hamilton, *Prologue to Conflict*, 44; Johannsen, *Stephen A. Douglas*, 265; John Sullivan to Buchanan, Dec. 8, 1849, Richard Brodhead to Buchanan, Jan. 6, 1850, BuHSP.

14. Frederick Stanton to Buchanan, Dec. 24, 1849, BuHSP; Buchanan to Cobb, Dec. 29, 1849, in TSC, 180–181.

15. Forney to Buchanan, Dec. 23, 1849, Frederick Stanton to Buchanan, Dec. 24, 1849, BuHSP; Cobb to wife, Dec. 22, 1849, in TSC, 179–180; Harris to Lanphier, Jan. 12, 1850, LaLPL; E. G. Spaulding to Tracy, Dec. 22, 1849, TrNYPL; Ch. S. Benton to Bigelow, Dec. 26, 1849, BiNYPL; Julian, *Political Recollections*, 77; Johannsen, *Stephen A. Douglas*, 265; Benton, *Thirty Years View*, 740.

16. For a concise legal history of the Fugitive Slave Law, see Baker, *Rescue of Joshua Glover*, 26–57. Hamilton, *Prologue to Conflict*, 45–46; Johannsen, *Stephen A. Douglas*, 267–268; Campbell, *Slave Catchers*, 8–9, 15; *CG*, 31C-1S, 41, 99, 136–137; Douglas to the editors of the *Chicago Tribune*, Jan. 29, 1850, in SDL, 184–186; Stegmaier, *Texas*, 95; Finkelman, *Millard Fillmore*, 16, 60–63; Morris, *Free Men All*, 131.

17. Richardson to D. Berry, Dec. 16, 1849, RiCHS.

18. *CG*, 31C-1S, 195 (quoted); Stephens to Linton Stephens, Jan. 21, 1850, in Johnston and Browne, *Life of Stephens*, 243–244; Stegmaier, *Texas*, 95–97; Julian, *Political Recollections*, 79; Bauer, *Zachary Taylor*, 300.

19. Benton, *Thirty Years View*, 741; William Lewis to Ritchie, June 18, 1850, in *JBHP*, 408–414; Stephens to Linton Stephens, Jan. 21, 1850, in Johnston and Browne, *Life of Stephens*, 243–244; Stegmaier, *Texas*, 45; Hamilton, *Prologue to Conflict*, 47–48; Bauer, *Zachary Taylor*, 300.

20. Davis, *Rhett*, 267; John Lamar to Cobb, Feb. 7, 1850, in TSC, 182–183; *CG*, 31C-1S, 183–184 ("peril" quote); Julian, *Political Recollections*, 80; Barnwell, *Love of Order*, 89–90; *Appendix to the CG*, 31C-1S, 58–74 ("sentiments" quote).

21. *CG*, 31C-1S, 182; Julian, *Political Recollections*, 92.

22. *CG*, 31C-1S, 87; Douglas to James Woodworth, Mar. 5, 1850, in SDL, 187–189; Stegmaier, *Texas*, 95; Johannsen, *Stephen A. Douglas*, 629.

23. *CG*, 31C-1S, 244–247; Douglas to Lanphier and George Walker, Aug. 3, 1850, in SDL, 191–193; Stegmaier, *Texas*, 87–88, 89, 97–98; Hamilton, *Prologue to Conflict*, 53–54; Stephens, *Constitutional View*, 2:198–200; Julian, *Political Recollections*, 81; Cobb to wife, Feb. 9, 1850, in TSC, 183–184; Finkelman, *Millard Fillmore*, 64–65.

24. Finkelman, *Millard Fillmore*, 64–69; Fehrenbacher, *Slaveholding Republic*, 227; Benton, *Thirty Years View*, 742; Stephens, *Constitutional View*, 2:200; Stephens to James Thomas, Feb. 13, 1850, in TSC, 184; Barnwell, *Love of Order*, 90–91, 112; Davis, *Rhett*, 275–278; Stephens to Linton Stephens, Jan. 15, 1850 (quoted), in Johnston and Browne, *Life of Stephens*, 243–244.

25. *CG*, 31C-1S, 356, 365–369; Foote, *Casket of Reminiscences*, 25–26; Stegmaier, *Texas*, 103; Hamilton, *Prologue to Conflict*, 61–62; Julian, *Political Recollections*, 85.

26. *CG*, 31C-1S, 375–385; Stephens, *Constitutional View*, 2:201; Johannsen, *Stephen A. Douglas*, 272.

27. Stephens, *Constitutional View*, 2:202–204; Johannsen, *Stephen A. Douglas*, 272–273; Stegmaier, *Texas*, 104–105; Hamilton, *Prologue to Conflict*, 67; Thavenet, "William Alexander Richardson," 99–100; Phillips, *Life of Robert Toombs*, 74–75.

28. Harris to Lanphier, Feb. 21, 1850, MiLC; John Quitman to Walker, Feb. 13, 1850, WaNYHS; Richardson to unknown, Feb. 19, 1850 (quoted), RiCHS; Stephens, *Constitutional View*, 2:200–202; Stegmaier, *Texas*, 104.

29. John Catron to Buchanan, Feb. 23, 1850, David Sturgeon to Buchanan, Mar. 9, 1850 (quoted), BuHSP; Marcy to George Newell, Mar. 24, 1850, MaLC; Stephens, *Constitutional View*, 2:205–206, 211; Benton, *Thirty Years View*, 744; Hamilton, *Prologue to Conflict*, 71–78, 84–85; Stegmaier, *Texas*, 1–2.

30. *Appendix to the CG*, 31C-1S, 364–375; Stephens, *Constitutional View*, 2:211; Hamilton, *Prologue to Conflict*, 86–87.

31. *Appendix to the CG*, 31C-1S, 423–425; Thavenet, "William Alexander Richardson," 102–104.

32. For a superior study of Southern politics and unity on slavery, see Cooper, *Politics of Slavery*; Douglas to Lanphier and Walker, Aug. 3, 1850, in SDL, 191–193; Foote, *Casket of Reminiscences*, 8; Hamilton, *Prologue to Conflict*, 92.

33. Foote, *Casket of Reminiscences*, 338–339; Stephens to brother, Apr. 17, 1850, in Johnston and Browne, *Life of Stephens*, 253–254; Stegmaier, *Texas*, 113–114; Hamilton, *Prologue to Conflict*, 93; Johannsen, *Stephen A. Douglas*, 285; Julian, *Political Recollections*, 90–92.

34. *CG*, 31C-1S, 763–764, 769–774, 779–782; Douglas to Lanphier and Walker, Aug. 3, 1850, in SDL, 191–193; Stephens, *Constitutional View*, 2:211–212; Benton, *Thirty Years View*, 742; Foote, *Casket of Reminiscences*, 26; Johannsen, *Stephen A. Douglas*, 285; Hamilton, *Prologue to Conflict*, 94.

35. Thornbrough, *Indiana in the Civil War*, 42–43; Woollen, *Sketches of Early Indiana*, 228–229; Bright to Corcoran, July 10, 1848, May 5, 1857 (quoted), CoLC.

36. Ketchum to Father, Dec. 17, 1845, KeIHS; Bright to sister, July 22, 1850, BrISL; J. A. Bayard to Corcoran, July 10, 1848, Bright to Corcoran, May 5, 1857, Bright to Corcoran, May 24, 1857, CoLC; Thornbrough, *Indiana in the Civil War*, 42–43; Woollen, *Sketches of Early Indiana*, 223, 228–229, 232.

37. Bright to Lanman, May 18, 1858, LaIHS; Woollen, *Sketches of Early Indiana*, 223–225; Weele, "Jesse David Bright," 4–5, 8, 11–25; Schimmel, "William H. English," 22.

38. Ketchum to father, Dec. 17, 1845, KeIHS; Weele, "Jesse David Bright," 27–46.

39. Weele, "Jesse David Bright," 47–54, 47 (quoted); Johannsen, *Stephen A. Douglas*, 222.

40. Collins to Smith, Dec. 14, 1848, Smith Papers, LOC; Weele, "Jesse David Bright," 47–56; Johannsen, *Stephen A. Douglas*, 222–223.

41. Bright to Samuel Covington, July 4, 1848, Harlow Lindley Collection, IHS; Weele, "Jesse David Bright," 61–63, 67–68, 88–93; Schimmel, "William H. English," 114.

42. *CG*, 31C-1S, 944–948, 956; William King to Buchanan, May 8, 1850, BuHSP; Lewis Cass to Cobb, May 5, 1850, in TSC, 190; Stephens, *Constitutional View*, 2:212; Hamilton, *Prologue to Conflict*, 95; Stegmaier, *Texas*, 135–139; Weele, "Jesse David

Bright," 68–70, 79; Stephens to brother, May 10, 1850, in Johnston and Browne, *Life of Stephens*, 254–255.

43. For the best study of the Texas–New Mexico crisis, see Stegmaier, *Texas*. J. M. Folty to Buchanan, May 20, 1850, BuHSP; Stephens, *Constitutional View*, 2:214–217; Stegmaier, *Texas*, 137, 148–150, 154–156; Hamilton, *Prologue to Conflict*, 98–101; Barnwell, *Love of Order*, 115–116.

44. Hunter to Mrs. Hunter, July 1, 1850, HGUVA; William Lewis to Ritchie, June 18, 1850, in *JBHP*, 408–414; *CG*, 31C-1S, 1114–1116; Stegmaier, *Texas*, 154–157; Johannsen, *Stephen A. Douglas*, 287–288; Barnwell, *Love of Order*, 103–106.

45. Finkelman, *Millard Fillmore*, 1–2, 9, 57–58, 64, 71, 80; Bauer, *Zachary Taylor*, 314–316; Stephens, *Constitutional View*, 2:220–221; Stegmaier, *Texas*, 158–165, 169; Hamilton, *Prologue to Conflict*, 107–108; Harlan to Pratt, July 16, 1850, Daniel Pratt Papers, Indiana State Library; Thompson to Scott, July 14, 1850 (quoted), Richard Thompson Papers, ISL; Richardson to "My Friend," July 12, 1850 (quoted), RiLPL; William Duval to Hunter, Aug. 13, 1850, in Hunter, *Correspondence*, 115; John Lumpkin to Cobb, July 21, 1850, in TSC, 206–208; Benton, *Thirty Years View*, 765–767; Julian, *Political Recollections*, 93.

46. Harris to Lanphier, June 9, 1850, July 19, 1850, LaLPL; Hamilton, *Prologue to Conflict*, 108–109.

47. McClernand to Lanphier, July 31, 1850, LaLPL; Marcy to Arch Campbell, Aug. 2, 1850, MaLC; Douglas to Lanphier and Walker, Aug. 3, 1850, in SDL, 191–193; William Duval to Hunter, Aug. 13, 1850, in Hunter, *Correspondence*, 115; King to Buchanan, Apr. 4, 1850, BuHSP; Stephens, *Constitutional View*, 2:221; Hamilton, *Prologue to Conflict*, 109–111; Stegmaier, *Texas*, 172–200, 202.

48. Hamilton, *Prologue to Conflict*, 113–114; Hinman, *Daniel Dickinson*, 85.

49. Proctor, *Lives*, 537, 539–540, 550, 552–553, 560–561; Hinman, *Daniel Dickinson*, 3–6, 10–11, 25–28; Dickinson to Edwin Croswell, Sept. 4, 1842, William Bouck to Dickinson, Sept. 10, 1842, Cash to Dickinson, Sept. 17, 1842, John V. L. Pruyn to Dickinson, Sept. 21, 1842, Clark to Dickinson, Feb. 8, 1843, Dickinson to Strahan, Dec. 17, 1845, Mitchell to Dickinson, Jan. 23, 1845, in Dickinson and Dickinson, *Speeches, Correspondence, Etc.*, 353–358, 374, 378–379; Ferree, "New York Democracy," 21; Dix, *Memoirs*, 1:194.

50. James Polk to Dickinson, June 10, 1846, DiNew; *CG*, 30C-1S, 157–159; Hinman, *Daniel Dickinson*, 32–33, 39–41, 50–52; Ferree, "New York Democracy," 58; Forney, *Anecdotes of Public Men*, 1:324.

51. Cass to Dickinson, Mar. 4, 1847 (quoted), Clinton to Dickinson, Apr. 14, 1847, in Dickinson and Dickinson, *Speeches, Correspondence, Etc.*, 404, 405; *Appendix to the CG*, 29C-2S, 444–445; Hinman, *Daniel Dickinson*, 53–56; Ferree, "New York Democracy," 27–28.

52. Dickinson to Mrs. Dickinson, Apr. 2, 1850, Apr. 23, 1850, Dickinson to Lydia Dickinson, Apr. 23, 1850, in Dickinson and Dickinson, *Speeches, Correspondence, Etc.*, 428–430; Klunder, *Lewis Cass*, 180; Hinman, *Daniel Dickinson*, 69–70, 85; Ferree, "New York Democracy," 36–50, 172–178; Tilden, *Writings and Speeches*, 237–242; Walther, *William Lowndes Yancey*, 108–109; Stephens to Cobb, Nov. 26, 1851 (quoted), in TSC; Peterson, *Great Triumverate*, 467–468.

53. Hamilton, *Prologue to Conflict*, 135; Stegmaier, *Texas*, 201, 205.

54. Thomas Stevenson to Smith, Dec. 12, 1848, Smith Papers, LOC; Douglas to Asa Whitney, Oct. 15, 1845, Douglas to Augustus French, Dec. 27, 1849, Douglas to Lanphier and Walker, Jan. 7, Aug. 3 (quoted), 1850, Douglas to James Woodworth, Mar. 5, 1850, Douglas to George Crawford, Mar. 8, 1850, in SDL, 127–133, 178–181, 182–183, 187–189, 191–193; Johannsen, *Stephen A. Douglas*, 235–272.

55. Douglas to Lanphier and Walker, Aug. 3, 1850, in SDL, 191–193; Johannsen, *Stephen A. Douglas*, 268; Stegmaier, *Texas*, 203.

56. Marcy to P. M. Witmore, Aug. 8, 1850 (quoted), MaLC; CG, 31C-1S, 99, 103, 554–556, 1659–1660; *Appendix to the CG*, 31C-1S, 79–83; Cobb to wife, Aug. 10, 1850, William Woods to Cobb, Sept. 15, 1850, in TSC, 210; Stegmaier, *Texas*, 118–119, 152, 203, 204–220, 261, 300–304; Finkelman, *Millard Fillmore*, 83; Campbell, *Slave Catchers*, 8–9, 15–18, 20–23; Johannsen, *Stephen A. Douglas*, 294–296; Hamilton, *Prologue to Conflict*, 138–141.

57. Douglas to Lanphier and Walker, Sept. 5, 1850, in SDL, 194; Bright to English, Sept. 2, 1850, EnIHS; Harris to Lanphier, Aug. 23, Sept. 6, 1850, LaLPL; J. M. Folty to Buchanan, Sept. 8, 1850, Alfred Gilmore to Buchanan, Sept. 9, 1850, BuHSP; Foote, *Casket of Reminiscences*, 28; Johannsen, *Stephen A. Douglas*, 297; Stegmaier, *Texas*, 268–269, 289–295.

58. Buchanan to Robert Tyler, Dec. 30, 1850, BuNYHS; CG, 31C-1S, 1806–1807, 1829; Campbell, *Slave Catchers*, 23; Morris, *Free Men All*, 145; Stegmaier, *Texas*, 262, 266–267, 298–299; Finkelman, *Millard Fillmore*, 85; Hamilton, *Prologue to Conflict*, 141, 161; Fehrenbacher, *Slaveholding Republic*, 230.

59. CG, 31C-1S, 1647, 1659–1660; *Appendix to the CG*, 31C-1S, 1123; Hamilton, *Prologue to Conflict*, 142–143, 161; Pelzer, *Augustus Caesar Dodge*, 146–147; Streeter, *Political Parties in Michigan*, 120; Barnwell, *Love of Order*, 112, 119–123.

60. More recent scholars have given Douglas his due in the crises of 1850, but their scholarship has not permeated public memory; the "Compromise of 1850" is still most often associated with "the Great Compromiser" Henry Clay. See Huston, *Douglas and Dilemmas*; Johannsen, *Stephen A. Douglas*; Stegmaier, *Texas*. CG, 31C-1S, 554–556; Hamilton, *Prologue to Conflict*, 148–149; Stegmaier, *Texas*, 217–218, 220; Douglas to Lanphier and Walker, Aug. 3, 1850, in SDL, 191–193.

61. Dickinson to John Breckinridge, Feb. 3, 1852 (quoted), BFLC; Thavenet, "William Alexander Richardson," 123; Klunder, *Lewis Cass*, 253–257; William Morton to Cobb, July 10, 1850, in TSC, 194–195.

62. Harris to Cobb, Feb. 2, 1852, in TSC, 277–278; Buchanan to Dickinson, Sept. 9, 1850 (quoted), in Dickinson and Dickinson, *Speeches, Correspondence, Etc.*, 448; Daniel Webster to Dickinson, Sept. 27, 1850, Webster Papers, NYHS.

63. Cass to Dickinson, July 14, 1851, in Dickinson and Dickinson, *Speeches, Correspondence, Etc.*, 465–466; CG, 31C-1S, 1829.

64. B. Bates to Buchanan, Oct. 21, 1850, Marcy to Buchanan, Nov. 10, 1850, BuHSP; William Bouck to Horatio Seymour, June 4, 1851, FCNYHS; Ferree, "New York Democracy," 301, 315–319, 321–322.

65. Dougherty et al. to Dickinson, Dec. 5, 1850, Dickinson to Dougherty et al., Jan. 20, 1851, in Dickinson and Dickinson, *Speeches, Correspondence, Etc.*, 457–459, 459–464; Marcy to Buchanan, Nov. 10, 1850, BuHSP; Buchanan to Marcy, Nov. 21, 1850, MaLC; Ferree, "New York Democracy," 352–356.

66. Seymour to Dickinson, Dec. 30, 1850, DiNew; William Flinn to Buchanan, Dec. 7, 1850, BuHSP; Campbell, *Slave Catchers*, 8–14; Streeter, *Political Parties in Michigan*, 123–124; Baker, *Rescue of Joshua Glover*, 26–57.

67. For the best summary of the Fugitive Slave Law of 1850, see Finkelman, *Millard Fillmore*, 86–89; Cave Johnson to Buchanan, Nov. 10, 1850, BuHSP; Campbell, *Slave Catchers*, 24; Julian, *Political Recollections*, 95–96; Morris, *Free Men All*, 133–134, 145–146.

68. George Plitt to Buchanan, Oct. 7, 1850, BJLC; Buchanan to Marcy, Nov. 21, 1850, MaLC; H. H. to Burke, Oct. 25, 1850, EBLC; Douglas to Thomas Settle, Jan. 16, 1851, in SDL; Streeter, *Political Parties in Michigan*, 130–131.

69. Finkelman, *Millard Fillmore*, 102–107; Campbell, *Slave Catchers*, 50–55; Baker, *Rescue of Joshua Glover*, 52–53; Weele, "Jesse David Bright," 145; Thornbrough, *Indiana in the Civil War*, 47–49; Schimmel, "William H. English," 82–83, 202–204; Julian, *Political Recollections*, 102; Thavenet, "William Alexander Richardson," 115–117; John Ketcham to Cobb, Aug. 9, 1853, in TSC, 331–334; Streeter, *Political Parties in Michigan*, 123–125, 131–132 (quoted).

70. Bigler to Buchanan, Mar. 29, 1851, BiHSP; Thomas Dorr to Burke, Apr. 9, 1851 (quoted), EBLC; Bigler to Committee of Invitation, June 26, 1851 (quoted), Bigler Collection, Pennsylvania Historical Commission; Campbell, *Slave Catchers*, 54–58, 107 (quoted).

71. For a clear assessment of the Compromise's proslavery nature, see Finkelman and Kennon, "Appeasement of 1850," in *Congress and the Crisis*, 36–79.

Chapter 2

1. Douglas to Thomas Settle, Jan. 16, 1851 (quoted), in SDL, 206–208; Thomas Dorr to Burke, Apr. 9, 1851, EBLC; Buchanan to Robert Tyler, Dec. 30, 1850, Bu-NYHS; Thomas Campbell to Lanphier, Dec. 2, 1851 (quoted), LaLPL.

2. Julian, *Political Recollections*, 115 (quoted); Johannsen, *Stephen A. Douglas*, 340–341; Thomas Smith to Cobb, June 27, 1848, in TSC, 111–113.

3. Woollen, *Sketches of Early Indiana*, 223 (quoted); Van Der Weele, "Jesse David Bright," 133.

4. Van Der Weele, "Jesse David Bright," 90–93, 99–107, 110–114; Woollen, *Sketches of Early Indiana*, 226–227; Robert Dale Owen journal entry found in Van Der Weele, "Jesse David Bright," 117.

5. Van Der Weele, "Jesse David Bright," 96, 97, 105, 117; Thornbrough, *Indiana in the Civil War*, 41–45; Woollen, *Sketches of Early Indiana*, 101, 224–225; Schimmel, "William H. English," 114–117.

6. Van Der Weele, "Jesse David Bright," 97–98, 119–120; Thornbrough, *Indiana in the Civil War*, 41; Schimmel, "William H. English," 116, 169–172; Bright to English, Dec. 16, 1851, Nov. 21 (quoted), Dec. 5, 1852, Graham Fitch to English, Nov. 22, Dec. 31, 1852, Bright to English, Jan. 25, 1853 (quoted), EnIHS; Woollen, *Sketches of Early Indiana*, 96–97, 101.

7. Ferree, "New York Democracy," 237–252; Levi Woodbury to Burke, May 13, 1848, EBLC; John Tamblin to Marcy, May 28, July 6, 1849, Marcy to P. M. Witmore, May 31, 1849, MaLC. Marcy's description of New York divisions is also

useful: "*The hunkers* are the section of the party which supported Genl. Cass in '48, and the *barnburners* those who voted for Van Buren. There are also two classes of *hunkers*—one composed of some rather influential leaders who opposed the policy of uniting the party in '49—a measure which I favored—the other—the mass of the *hunker* section that highly opposed of the Union measure. The former section are called *ultra hunkers* and have continued to cherish a bitter hostility to the *barnburners*. Dickinson may be considered at the head of them." William Marcy to James Berret, Dec. 14, 1851, MaLC.

8. Marcy to Witmore, June 29, 1849 (quoted), MaLC; Marcy to Buchanan, Mar. 10, 1850, BuHSP; Marcy to Ritchie, July 18, 1849, in *JBHP*, 402–405; Marcy to Seymour, July 28, 1851 (quoted), William Bouck to Seymour, July 30, 1851, FCNYHS.

9. Spencer, *Victor and the Spoils*, 2–30, 17 (quoted); Proctor, *Lives of Lawyers and Statesmen*, 401–403.

10. Spencer, *Victor and the Spoils*, 18–23, 27–30, 34–36, 54–63, 73, 76–81, 103–105, 126–136, 181–182; Proctor, *Lives of Lawyers and Statesmen*, 401–406, 411–416, 418.

11. Spencer, *Victor and the Spoils*, 181–186; Proctor, *Lives of Lawyers and Statesmen*, 401–418; Marcy to Van Buren, Jan. 29, 1828, William Marcy Papers, New York State Library; Marcy to Dickinson, Jan. 27, 1850, in Dickinson and Dickinson, *Speeches, Correspondence, Etc.*, 420–421; Marcy to Witmore, Apr. 24, July 23, 1849, May 20, 1850 (quoted), Marcy to unknown Southern Democrat, Nov. 28, 1849, Marcy to Arch Campbell, Aug. 2, 1850 (quoted), draft of speech or letter on sectional extremism (quoted), draft of message to Tammany Society, marked "Very Important," May 13, 1850 (quoted), MaLC.

12. Duff Green to Marcy, Apr. 17, 1852 (quoted), Marcy to Witmore, May 11, 1849 (quoted), Seymour to Marcy, Aug. 7, 1851, S. B. Jerrett to Marcy, Aug. 11, 1851, Marcy to Campbell, Feb. 3, 1850, Mar. 25, 1852, Marcy to T. A. Osborne, Aug. 27, 1852, Dickinson to Marcy, Jan. 29, 1850, MaLC; Seymour to Josiah Miller, Aug. 14, 1850, SeNYHS; Hinman, *Daniel Dickinson*, 71–77; Dickinson to Randall, Mar. 27, 1850, in Dickinson and Dickinson, *Speeches, Correspondence, Etc.*, 425–426; Marcy to Seymour, July 28, 1851, FCNYHS.

13. C. Eames to Marcy, Sept. 14, 1851, MaLC; Marcy to Buchanan, Dec. 10, 1849 (quoted), BuLC; Andrew Donelson to Buchanan, Nov. 2, 1851, BuHSP; Donelson to Cobb, Oct. 22, 1851, in TSC, 262–263.

14. Marcy, "Sketch of a letter, afterwards changed & turned into the one published in the Argus, Aug 31, 1849," Aug 27, 1849, MaLC; Marcy to Buchanan, Mar. 10, 1850 (quoted), BuHSP; Ferree, "New York Democracy," 329–330; Seymour to Josiah Miller, Aug. 14, 1850, William Bouck to Seymour, July 30, 1851 (quoted), SeNYHS.

15. Marcy to Ritchie, Nov. 29, 1850, in *JBHP*, 405–409; Spencer, *Victor and the Spoils*, 191; Ferree, "New York Democracy," 337–346; Marcy to Buchanan, Sept. 20, 1850 (quoted), BuHSP.

16. For other issues in the Barnburner-Hunker feud, see Summers, *Plundering Generation*, 125–137; Spencer, *Victor and the Spoils*, 196–197; Marcy to Seymour, July 28, 1851, William Bouck to Seymour, July 31, 1851 (quoted), FCNYHS; Marcy to Witmore, Sept. 9, 1851, Sanford Church to Marcy, Sept. 17, 1851 (quoted), Campbell to Marcy, Sept. 5, 1851, MaLC; Ferree, "New York Democracy," 392–399.

17. Nichols, *Democratic Machine*, 59; Henry Walsh to Buchanan, Dec. 28, 1850, William Bigler to Buchanan, Mar. 29, 1851, James Campbell to Buchanan, May 11, 1851, Alfred Gilmore to Buchanan, Sept. 26, 1851, BuHSP; Buchanan to J. S. York, Mar. 6, 1851, BuNYHS; J. Glancy Jones to Bigler, June 24, Aug. 21, 1850, George Sanderson to Bigler, Aug. 20, 1850, BiHSP; Buchanan to J. Glancy Jones, June 1, June 12, 1851, George Plitt to Buchanan, June 13, 1851, BJLC; Savage, *Our Living Representative Men*, 93–94; Simon Cameron to Burke, June 15, 1849 (quoted), EBLC.

18. Coleman, *Disruption of Pennsylvania Democracy*, 42; Bigler to Committee of Invitation, June 26, 1851, Bigler Collection, Pennsylvania Historical Commission; Nichols, *Democratic Machine*, 59–60; Henry Walsh to Buchanan, Aug. 25, 1850, BuLC; Buchanan to Marcy, Nov. 21, 1850, MaLC.

19. Plitt to Buchanan, Oct. 27, 1851, BJLC; Richard Brodhead to John Forney, Jan. 20, 1851, G. H. Goundie to Forney, Jan. 22, 1851, Brodhead to Buchanan, Jan. 27, 1851, A. H. Reeder to Buchanan, Sept. 10, 1851, J. Glancy Jones to Buchanan, Sept. 12, 1851, BuHSP; Brodhead to Coryell, Sept. 28, 1851, CoHSP; E. A. Penniman to Bigler, Jan. 11, 1851, BiHSP; Marcy to James Berret, Dec. 14, 1851, W. W. Snow to Marcy, Dec. 27, 1851, MaLC; Coleman, *Disruption of Pennsylvania Democracy*, 41–42.

20. Alfred Gilmore to Buchanan, Sept. 9, Nov. 3 (quoted), Dec. 24, 1850, Henry Walsh to Buchanan, Aug. 25, Dec. 28, 1850, Charles Brown to Buchanan, Feb. 14, 1851, BuHSP; George Sanderson to Bigler, Aug. 20, 1850, J. Glancy Jones to Bigler, Aug. 21, 1850, Forney to Bigler, Aug. 23, 1850, BiHSP; Eames to Marcy, Sept. 14, 1851, MaLC; Buchanan to York, Mar. 6, 1851 (quoted), BuNYHS; Coleman, *Disruption of Pennsylvania Democracy*, 51.

21. Coleman, *Disruption of Pennsylvania Democracy*, 41–41, 51–52; Buchanan to Glancy Jones, Sept. 10, 1851, BJLC; Buchanan to York, Mar. 6, Aug. 30, 1851, BuNYHS; Buchanan to Bigler, Mar. 24, 1851, BiHSP; Bigler to Buchanan, Mar. 29, 1851, Reeder to Buchanan, Sept. 10, 1851 (quoted), Glancy Jones to Buchanan, Sept. 12, 1851, BuHSP.

22. Coleman, *Disruption of Pennsylvania Democracy*, 42; Morris, *Free Men All*, 154–156; Seth Salisbury to Bigler, July 14, 1851, Buchanan to Bigler, Oct. 18, 1851, Glancy Jones to Bigler, Oct. 18, Oct. 31, 1851, A. Beaumont to Bigler, Oct. 24, 1851, T. M. Pettit to Bigler, Oct. 22, 1851, Bigler to Buchanan, Oct. 28, 1851, BiHSP; H. K. Smith to Marcy, Nov. 5, 1851, MaLC; D. B. Taylor to Buchanan, July 25, 1851, John Houston to Buchanan, Sept. 4, 1851, Cave Johnson to Buchanan, Sept. 15, 1851, William King to Buchanan, Oct. 14, 1851, J. D. Hoover to Buchanan, Oct. 17, 1851, John Parker to Buchanan, Oct. 31, 1851, Isaac Toucey to Buchanan, Nov. 13, 1851 (quoted), BuHSP.

23. Alfred Gilmore to Buchanan, Dec. 24, 1850 (quoted), BuHSP.

24. Toombs to Cobb, Jan. 2, 1851, Donelson to Cobb, Oct. 26, 1851, in TSC, 218–220, 264.

25. For the most recent study of the Young America movement, see Eyal, *Young America Movement*. Marcy to James Berret, Nov. 21, 1851 (quoted), MaLC; George Sanders to R. M. T. Hunter, Mar. 21, 1851, Henry Wise to Hunter, Jan. 15, 1853, HGUVA; Marcy to Buchanan, Dec. 19, 1850, Gilmore to Buchanan, Dec. 24, 1850, Wise to Buchanan, Feb. 20, 1851, King to Buchanan, Mar. 6, Mar. 24, 1852 (quoted), BuHSP; Welles to Burke, Nov. 3, 1851 (quoted), EBLC. For Douglas's ownership of slaves and a

plantation, see the correspondence between Douglas and Ja. S. Strickland and Brander Williams & Co., New Orleans, in DoL PL. Johannsen, *Stephen A. Douglas*, 207–209, 211, 232, 299–300, 337–338; Douglas to Lanphier, Aug. 3, 1850, Douglas to James Sheahan, Mar. 10, 1855, Douglas to editor of the Washington *States*, Jan. 7, 1859, Douglas to James McHatton, April 4, 1861 in SDL, 189–191, 335, 433–434, 508–509.

26. Douglas to Cass, Aug. 13, 1851, Douglas to Richard Arnold, Aug. 30, 1851, Douglas to George Roberts, Sept. 8, 1851, Douglas to George Sanders, Sept. 22, 1851, in SDL, 230–232; Johannsen, *Stephen A. Douglas*, 347; Sanders to Hunter, Aug. 4, 1851, HGUVA; Wise to Buchanan, Apr. 20, 1851 (quoted), BuHS P; Hunter to Sanders, May 9, 1851 (quoted), in Hunter, *Correspondence*, 127–128.

27. Johannsen, *Stephen A. Douglas*, 339–352; E. Peck to Lanphier, Feb. 13, 1852, LaL PL; Welles to Burke, Nov. 3, 1851 (quoted), EBLC; Douglas to English, Dec. 29, 1851, DoL PL; Douglas to E. Peck, Feb. 1852, in SDL, 236; John Parker to Buchanan, Mar. 11, 1852, BuHS P.

28. Thomas Campbell to Lanphier, Apr. 4, 1852 (quoted), LaL PL; David Porter to Buchanan, May 24, 1852, King to Buchanan, Mar. 6, May 24, 1852 (quoted), Cave Johnson to Buchanan, May 6, 1852 (quoted), BuHS P; Welles to Burke, Nov. 3, 1851, EBLC.

29. Slidell to Buchanan, May 9, 1851 (quoted), Belmont to Buchanan, Feb. 28, 1852, BuHS P; Donelson to Marcy, Apr. 16, 1851, J. White to Marcy, Feb. 5, 1851, Slidell to Marcy, Oct. 10, 1851, Buchanan to Marcy, Sept. 30, Nov. 10 (quoted), 1851, Marcy to Campbell, Nov. 10, 1851, MaLC; Welles to Burke, Nov. 3, 1851, EBLC; Nichols, *Democratic Machine*, 66–67.

30. Marcy to Witmore, Feb. 17, Sept. 28 (quoted), 1851, Marcy to S. M. Shaw, Oct. 28, 1852, D. Wager to Marcy, Dec. 17, 1851, Marcy to Stryker, Sept. 20, 1851, Marcy to Campbell, Dec. 6, 1851 (quoted), Beardsley to Marcy, Dec. 15, 1851, MaLC; Spencer, *Victor and the Spoils*, 195–196; Woodbury to Breckinridge, Apr. 13, 1852, BFLC; Nichols, *Democratic Machine*, 92–95.

31. Ferree, "New York Democracy," 392–399; Spencer, *Victor and the Spoils*, 198–201; J. Addison Thomas to Marcy, Apr. 1, May 28, 1852, Marcy to James Berret, Nov. 21, Dec. 14, 1851, Marcy to Witmore, Nov. 26, 1851, S. B. Jerret to Marcy, Nov. 26, 1851, Marcy to Campbell, Dec. 6, 1851, D. Wager to Marcy, Dec. 17, 1851, Eames to Marcy, Nov. 11, 1851, MaLC; Marcy to Buchanan, Oct. 6, 1851, BuHS P.

32. Marcy to Beardsley, Dec. 17, 1851 (quoted), Marcy to Campbell, Feb. 8, Mar. 25 (quoted), 1852, MaLC; Ferree, "New York Democracy," 424–430.

33. Ferree, "New York Democracy," 424–430; Nichols, *Democratic Machine*, 98–99, 103–104; Marcy to C. T. Chamberlain, Feb. 2, 1852, J. Addison Thomas to Marcy, Feb. 14, 1852, S. M. Shaw to Marcy, Feb. 18, 1852, H. K. Smith to Marcy, Feb. 18, 1852, B. F. Angel to Marcy, Mar. 11, 1852, Marcy to James Berret, Jan. 2, Jan. 12, 1852, MaLC; Spencer, *Victor and the Spoils*, 203–204.

34. Byrdsall to Buchanan, May 23, 1852 (quoted), BuHS P; Marcy to Seymour, May 29, 1852 (quoted), FCNYHS; Marcy to James Berret, Apr. 17, 1852, Seymour to Marcy, Apr. 26, 1852, Marcy to Campbell, May 28, 1851 (quoted), MaLC; Marcy to Tilden, Apr. 2, 1852, TiNY PL.

35. Woodbury to Breckinridge, Apr. 13, 1852, BFLC; Ferree, "New York Democracy," 406–407, 436–437; Marcy to Seymour, Apr. 3, 1852, FCNYHS; Marcy to Witmore, Nov. 29, 1851, Seymour to Marcy, Dec. 9, 1851, Beardsley to Marcy,

Dec. 9, Dec. 16, 1851, Marcy to Beardsley, Dec. 10, 1851, J. A. Corey to Marcy, Dec. 10, 1851, W. W. Snow to Marcy, Dec. 13, 1851, Marcy to James Berret, Dec. 14, 1851, Marcy to E. W. Lewis, Dec. 30, 1851, E. D. Smith to Marcy, Dec. 3, 1851, Marcy to Campbell, Dec. 6, 1851, MaLC; Hinman, *Daniel Dickinson*, 116; Proctor, *Lives of Lawyers and Statesmen*, 566; Dickinson to Rodgers, May 22, 1852 (quoted), in Dickinson and Dickinson, *Speeches, Correspondence, Etc.*, 469; Marcy to Seymour, Dec. 6, 1851, SeNYHS; Forney, *Anecdotes of Public Men*, vol. 1, 324.

36. Klunder, *Lewis Cass*, 1–17; Forney, *Anecdotes of Public Men*, vol. 2, 168–169; Hickman, *Life of General Lewis Cass*, 7–14.

37. Klunder, *Lewis Cass*, 18–90; Forney, *Anecdotes of Public Men*, vol. 2, 168–169; Hickman, *Life of General Lewis Cass*, 14–22.

38. Klunder, *Lewis Cass*, 92–144; Streeter, *Political Parties in Michigan*, 71–74, 84, 88–96; Hickman, *Life of General Lewis Cass*, 22–47.

39. Klunder, *Lewis Cass*, 144–237; Cobb to wife, Apr. 3, 1846, in TSC, 75; Cave Johnson to Buchanan, Jan. 20, 1850, L. Harper to Buchanan, Apr. 5, 1851 (quoted), King to Buchanan, Aug. 26, 1850, BuHSP; *Appendix to the CG*, 31C-1S, 74; Welles to Burke, Nov. 3, 1851, EBLC; Streeter, *Political Parties in Michigan*, 84, 88–96; Hickman, *Life of General Lewis Cass*, 47–72.

40. Klunder, *Lewis Cass*, 173–237; Julian, *Political Recollections*, 51 (quoted); Luther Glenn to Cobb, Feb. 12, 1848, Thomas Cobb to Cobb, May 31, 1848, Thomas Thomas to Cobb, June 5, 1848, James Dobbin to Cobb, June 15, 1848, in TSC, 95–96, 106–109; Marcy to Ritchie, Nov. 29, 1849 (quoted), in *JBHP*; Streeter, *Political Parties in Michigan*, 103–107.

41. J. M. Folty to Buchanan, May 20, 1850, Toucey to Buchanan, July 5, 1850, Alfred Gilmore to Buchanan, Nov. 3, Dec. 24, 1850, BuHSP; Nichols, *Democratic Machine*, 44–46; Snow to Marcy, Mar. 25, 1852 (quoted), MaLC; Marcy to Seymour, Dec. 26, 1851 (quoted), Apr. 28, 1852, FCNYHS.

42. Henry Orr to Dickinson, Dec. 21, 1851 (quoted), DiNew.

43. Marcy to Seymour, Apr. 3, 1852, FCNYHS; John Striker to Marcy, Jan. 11, 1851, S. M. Shaw to Marcy, Mar. 19, 1851, Marcy to James Berret, Feb. 4, Apr. 11 (quoted), 1852, MaLC; Byrdsall to Buchanan, May 23, 1852, King to Buchanan, May 26, 1852, BuHSP; Cass to Dickinson, May 27, 1852 (quoted), in Dickinson and Dickinson, *Speeches, Correspondence, Etc.*, 469.

44. Welles to Burke, Nov. 3, 1851, B. F. Hallett to Burke, Aug. 28, 1852, Gideon Pillow to Burke, Sept. 4, 1852, EBLC; Marcy to Seymour, May 4, 1852, FCNYHS; Sanders to Hunter, Mar. 21, 1851, HGUVA; John Peters to Marcy, Oct. 6, 1851, W. C. Walson to Marcy, Oct. 7, 1851, Buchanan to Marcy, Oct. 8, 1851, Stryker to Marcy, Dec. 3, 1851, Eames to Marcy, Jan. 4, 1852, Snow to Marcy, Mar. 25, 1852, Caleb Lyons to Marcy, Feb. 6, 1852, MaLC; Toucey to Buchanan, July 5, 1850, L. Harper to Capt. Richard Philips, Mar. 4, 1851, Wise to Buchanan, July 8, 1851, Alfred Gilmore to Buchanan, Apr. 15, 1852, King to Buchanan, May 24, May 26, 1852, BuHSP; Buchanan to York, June 16, 1851, BuNYHS; Welles to Tilden, Sept. 24, 1851, TiNYPL; Burke to Pierce, Apr. 9, 1852, PiLC; Buchanan to Bigler, Mar. 24, Apr. 10, 1851, Robert Tyler to Bigler, Apr. 13, 1851, David Lynch to Bigler, May 20, 1852 (quoted), BiHSP.

45. Buchanan to C. L. Ward, July 17, 1845, BuNYHS; Owen Connolly to Buchanan, Nov. 5, 1849, Bigler to Buchanan, Nov. 16, 1849, Slidell to Buchanan,

Dec. 7, 1849, Buchanan to Henry Foote, Nov. 14, 1849 (quoted), John Sullivan to Buchanan, Dec. 8, 1849, BuHSP; Buchanan to Marcy, Nov. 12, 1849, Jan. 1, Nov. 21, 1850, MaLC; Hopkins Holsey to Cobb, Dec. 31, 1847, Joseph Lumpkin to Cobb, Jan. 21, 1848, Toombs to Cobb, Jan. 2, 1851, in TSC, 91–93, 94–95, 218–220; Buchanan to Glancy Jones, May 21, 1842, Jan. 2, 1844, Mar. 8, 1850 (quoted, "the greatest evil of all political calamities"), BJLC; Binder, *Empire*, 54–55, 130; Forney, *Anecdotes of Public Men*, vol. 1, 67, 327.

46. Slidell to Buchanan, Dec. 7, 1849, May 9, 1851, King to Buchanan, Jan. 13 (quoted), Aug. 26 (quoted), 1850, Cave Johnson to Buchanan, Jan. 20, Aug. 10, 1850, John Hodges to Buchanan, Feb. 1850 (quoted), Gilmore to Buchanan, Nov. 3, 1850, A. H. Chappell to Buchanan, Mar. 26, 1851, James Ramsey to Buchanan, Apr. 30, 1852, Toucey to Buchanan, Nov. 13, 1851, BuHSP; Donelson to Cobb, Oct. 26, 1851, Stephens to Cobb, Nov. 26, 1851, in TSC, 264, 265–267; Buchanan to Glancy Jones, Nov. 11, 1851, BJLC; James Berret to Marcy, Feb. 7, 1852, MaLC; Douglas to William Brown, June 21, 1851, in SDL, 226–227.

47. Slidell to Buchanan, Oct. 14, Dec. 7, 1849, Feb. 5, July 13, Sept. 11, Oct. 9, Oct. 15, Oct. 18, Dec. 16, 1850, May 9, July 9, 1851, John Sullivan to Buchanan, Oct. 20, 1849, Henry Foote to Buchanan, Nov. 2, Nov. 7, Nov. 15, 1849, Mar. 25, Mar. 31, Apr. 14, May 13, 1850, Buchanan to Foote, Nov. 14, 1849, May 15, 1850, Cave Johnson to Buchanan, Jan. 20, Apr. 14, June 5, Aug. 10, Nov. 10, Dec. 13, 1850, BuHSP; Slidell to Marcy, Oct. 10, 1851, MaLC.

48. King to Buchanan, Jan. 6, Jan. 13, Mar. 11, Mar. 20 (quoted), May 8, June 8, June 11, June 19, Aug. 4, 1850, Jan. 12, 1851, BuHSP.

49. Marcy to Buchanan, Mar. 10, 1850, Jefferson Davis to Buchanan, Mar. 15, 1850, Foote to Buchanan, May 13, 1850, Buchanan to Foote, May 15, 1850, King to Buchanan, Mar. 11 (quoted), June 8, June 11, June 19, 1850, Cave Johnson to Buchanan, Aug. 10, 1850 (quoted), J. M. Folty to Buchanan, May 20, 1850, BuHSP; William Lewis to Ritchie, June 18, 1850, in *JBHP*; Hopkins Holsey to Cobb, Dec. 31, 1847, John Lumpkin to Cobb, July 21, 1850, Toombs to Cobb, Jan. 2, 1851, in TSC, 91–93, 206–208, 218–220.

50. Benjamin Brewster to Burke, Sept. 3, 1852 (quoted), EBLC; Marcy to James Berret, Dec. 14, 1851 (quoted), MaLC; Marcy to Buchanan, Mar. 10, 1850 (quoted), Buchanan to William Dack, July 12, 1851 (quoted), King to Buchanan, May 24, 1852, BuHSP; Buchanan to Bigler, Apr. 10, 1851 (quoted), BiHSP.

51. Marcy to Campbell, May 28 (quoted), Nov. 10, 1851, Buchanan to Marcy, Dec. 3, 1851, James Berret to Marcy, Dec. 5, 1851, Snow to Marcy, Dec. 5, 1851 (quoted), Campbell to Marcy, Apr. 26, 1851, MaLC; Slidell to Buchanan, Oct. 10, Nov. 17, 1851, Marcy to Buchanan, Nov. 16, Nov. 24, 1851, BuHSP.

52. Nichols, *Democratic Machine*, 68–69; John Parker to Buchanan, Jan. 16, Feb. 9, Apr. 18, July 1, 1851, Wise to Buchanan, Feb. 20, 1851 (quoted), BuHSP; Willis Bocock to Hunter, Feb. 13, 1851, in Hunter, *Correspondence*, 124–126; Buchanan to Wise, Apr. 13, 1852, BJLC.

53. Buchanan to Wise, Feb. 20, June 8, July 8, 1851, Apr. 13, 1852 (quoted), BJLC.

54. Plitt to Buchanan, Mar. 4, May 14, 1852, Buchanan to Glancy Jones, May 14, June 1, June 12 (quoted), Sept. 10, Oct. 18, Nov. 11, Nov. 17, 1851, Apr. 3, 1852, BJLC; Wise to Buchanan, Mar. 11, Apr. 3, 1851, D. H. London to Buchanan, Apr. 14, 1851, George Bowman to Buchanan, Mar. 15, 1851, John Parker to

Buchanan, July 1, 1851, Gilmore to Buchanan, Apr. 5, 1852, King to Buchanan, Mar. 6, 1852 (quoted), Belmont to Buchanan, Mar. 11, 1852, BuHSP; D. M. Brodhead to Dickinson, June 14, 1853, DiNew; Buchanan to C. L. Ward, Jan. 6, 1852, BuNYHS.

55. Buchanan to Ward, Mar. 29, 1852, BuNYHS; Campbell to Marcy, May 3, 1852, MaLC; King to Buchanan, Mar. 24, Mar. 31, 1852, David Porter to Buchanan, Mar. 24, 1852, D. H. Long to Buchanan, Mar. 26, 1852, David Lynch to Buchanan, Mar. 26, 1852, John Mason to Buchanan, Mar. 30, 1852, BuHSP; Nichols, *Democratic Machine*, 74–75; Unknown to Buchanan, Mar. 29, 1852, Plitt to Buchanan, Apr. 4, 1852 (quoted), BJLC; David Lynch to Bigler, Mar. 29, May 20, 1852, BiHSP; Burke to Pierce, Apr. 9, 1852, PiLC.

56. Nichols, *Franklin Pierce*, 9–98, for undisciplined youth and trickery, see 14–27, for election to the U.S. House, see 58.

57. Nichols, *Franklin Pierce*, 130–196; Sewell, *John P. Hale*, 54–60, 66; Pierce to Burke, Feb. 13, Feb. 15, Feb. 22, Mar. 1, Mar. 2, Mar. 4, May 22, June 30, 1847, EBLC; Pierce et al., Democratic State Central Committee to Levi Woodbury, Feb. 6, 1843, Hale to Pierce, Dec. 3, 1844, Jan. 18, 1845, C. G. Atherton to Pierce, Jan. 13, 1845, Charles Lane to Pierce, Jan. 17, 1845, Pierce to Hale, Jan. 24, 1845, Marcy to Pierce, Feb. 18, Mar. 22, 1847, Adjutant General to Pierce, Mar. 6, 1847, Pierce to Unknown, Feb. 2, 1851, Pierce to brother, Feb. 10, 1851, PiLC.

58. Nichols, *Democratic Machine*, 121; Klunder, *Lewis Cass*, 196; Thomas Harris to Lanphier, June 9, 1850, LaLPL; Nichols, *Franklin Pierce*, 128; Sewell, *John P. Hale*, 45, 54–55; James Polk to Burke, Apr. 16, 1845, Burke to Buchanan, May 6, 1845, Richard Johnson to Burke, May 1845, Cass to Burke, Mar. 3, 1846, Mar. 27, 1850, dinner invitations from Buchanan, Oct. 20, 1845, Jan. 19, 1847, Jan. 2, 1849, dinner invitations from Polk, Apr. 2, 1846, Mar. 13, 1848, G. M. Dallas to Burke, June 21, 1847, Dorr to Burke, Apr. 9, 1851, Pierce to Burke, Nov. 18, 1846, Feb. 13, Feb. 15, Feb. 22, Mar. 1, Mar. 2, Mar. 4, Mar. 10, May 22, June 30, 1847, Feb. 1, Nov. 17, 1848, EBLC.

59. Nichols, *Democratic Machine*, 121–128; Burke to Pierce, Apr. 9, 1852, PiLC; Barnes to Breckinridge, Jan. 19, 1852, BFLC; Pierce to Burke, Apr. 13, May 10, 1852, B. F. Hallett to Burke, Aug. 28, 1852, Bedford Broms to Burke, Sept. 1, 1852, B. B. French to Burke, Sept. 17, 1852, James Barbour to Burke, Oct. 8, 1852 (quoted), EBLC; Eames to Marcy, Nov. 11, 1851, James Berret to Marcy, Dec. 5, 1851, MaLC; Gilmore to Buchanan, Jan. 25, 1852, BuHSP; Nichols, *Franklin Pierce*, 195–202.

Chapter 3

1. Johannsen, *Stephen A. Douglas*, 365; Thomas Harris to Cobb, May 28, 1852, in TSC, 298–299; Nichols, *Democratic Machine*, 31; Hincks and Smith, *Proceedings*, 4; James Seddon to Hunter, Jan. 18, Feb. 7, 1852, in Hunter, *Correspondence*, 136–139; W. W. Snow to Marcy, Mar 16, 1852, MaLC; Thomas Campbell to Lanphier, Apr. 4, 1852, LaLPL; Jesse Bright to English, Feb. 16, 1852, EnIHS; Klein, *President James Buchanan*, 219.

2. Klein, *President James Buchanan*, 219; Bright to English, Feb. 16, May 15, 1852, "Meeting of the Democracy of Indiana, on the Subject of Nominating a Candidate for President of the United States," certificate of appointment as delegate for the 1852 Democratic national convention, English Papers, IHS; Nichols, *Democratic*

Machine, 129–130; Klunder, *Lewis Cass*, 260–261; Schimmel, "William H. English," 119–121, 124.

3. F. Byrdsall to Buchanan, May 18, 1852, John Cadwalader to Buchanan, May 20, 1852 (quoted), BuHSP; Henry Orr to Dickinson, Dec. 21, 1851 (quoted), DiNew; A. J. Donelson to Cobb, Apr. 15, 1852, Stephens to Cobb, Nov. 26, 1852 (quoted), in TSC, 293–294, 265–267; Ferree, "New York Democracy," 444–445; Klunder, *Lewis Cass*, 260–261; John Mason to Marcy, Apr. 22, 1852, Horatio Seymour to Marcy, Apr. 26, 1852, MaLC; Marcy to Seymour, Apr. 3, 1852, FCNYHS.

4. William King to Buchanan, Dec. 12, 1851 (quoted), John Slidell to Buchanan, Mar. 19, 1852, John Catron to Buchanan, Jan. 24, 1852 (quoted), BuHSP; Thavenet, "William Alexander Richardson," 126; Douglas to David Yulee, June 1 (quoted), June 2, June 3, June 4, June 5, 1852, Douglas to William Richardson, June 5, 1852, in SDL, 250–252; Johannsen, *Stephen A. Douglas*, 366, 380; James Seddon to Hunter, Feb. 7, 1852, in Hunter, *Correspondence*, 136–139.

5. Belohlavek, *Broken Glass*, 234; Franklin Pierce to Burke, Apr. 13, May 10, 1852, W. B. Lawrence to Burke, Aug. 11, 1852, B. B. French to Burke, Sept. 17, 1852, EBLC; Burke to Pierce, Apr. 9 (quoted), June 14, 1852, PiLC.

6. Klunder, *Lewis Cass*, 257, 261; P. R. George to John Breckinridge, Apr. 2, 1852, BFLC; Slidell to Buchanan, Oct. 14, 1849, Feb. 26, 1852 (quoted), Hendrick Wright to Buchanan, Dec. 17, 1851, Alfred Gilmore to Buchanan, Apr. 15, 1852, John Cadwalader to Buchanan, May 20, 1852, BuHSP; Harris to Cobb, Apr. 7, May 28, 1852, George Jones to Cobb, Apr. 14, 1852, Cass to Cobb, Apr. 15, 1852, A. J. Donelson to Cobb, Apr. 25, May 10, 1852, Toombs to Cobb, May 27, 1852, in TSC, 289, 290, 291, 293–294, 294–295, 297–298, 298–299; James Shields to Lanphier, Feb. 16, 1852, MiLC; William Lewis to Ritchie, June 18, 1850, *JBHP*, 408–414; Sam Beardsley to Marcy, Dec. 9, 1851, J. A. Corey to Marcy, Dec. 10, 1851, MaLC; James Seddon to Hunter, Feb. 7, 1852, Edmund Hubard to Hunter, May 8, 1852 (quoted), in Hunter, *Correspondence*, 136–39, 140–42.

7. J. A. Thomas to Marcy, May 29, 1852, MaLC; Gideon Welles to Samuel Tilden, Sept. 24, 1851 (quoted), TiNYPL; Slidell to Buchanan, May 9, 1851 (quoted), Hendrick Wright to Buchanan, May 7, 1852, William Mathiot to Buchanan, May 28, 1852, King to Buchanan, Dec. 12, 1851, May 24, 1852, James Gadsden to Buchanan, Apr. 14, May 13, 1852 (quoted), Isaac Toucey to Buchanan, May 15, 1852, David Porter to Buchanan, May 26, 1852, BuHSP; Edmund Hubard to Hunter, May 8, 1852, in Hunter, *Correspondence*, 140–142; Buchanan to C. L. Ward, Mar. 29, 1852, May 1852, BuNYHS.

8. Stewart to Dickinson, Oct. 27, 1851 (quoted), Dickinson to Mrs. Dickinson, June 2, 1852, in Dickinson and Dickinson, *Speeches, Correspondence, Etc.*, 467–468, 469–470; Eames to Marcy, Sept 17, 1851, MaLC; F. Byrdsall to Buchanan, May 18, 1852 (quoted), Gadsden to Buchanan, May 13, 1852, Cave Johnson to Buchanan, Dec. 11, 1851, BuHSP.

9. J. A. Thomas to Marcy, May 28, May 31, 1852, James Berret to Marcy, Feb. 7, 1852, Mason to Marcy, Apr. 22, 1852, Eames to Marcy, Sept 17, 1851, Marcy to Snow, Apr. 1852, Marcy to Mason, May 21, May 25, 1852, Marcy to Robert Scott, May 25, 1852, Mason to Marcy, May 27, 1852, James Benett to Marcy, Mar. 22, 1852, Marcy to Campbell, May 10, 1852 (quoted), Campbell to Marcy, May 14, 1852, Marcy to James Berret, May 15, May 30 (quoted), 1852, John V. L. Pruyn to Marcy,

May 31, 1852, MaLC; Marcy to Seymour, Apr. 3, May 29, 1852, June 1852, Marcy to Seymour, Skinner, Corning, May 24, 1852, FCNYHS; Spencer, *Victor and the Spoils*, 208; Ferree, "New York Democracy," 404, 449, 453; Klunder, *Lewis Cass*, 260–261; F. Byrdsall to Buchanan, May 18, 1852, Gadsden to Buchanan, May 13, 1852, Cave Johnson to Buchanan, Dec. 11, 1851, BuHSP.

10. Pruyn to Marcy, May 31, 1852, Thomas to Marcy, May 31, 1852, MaLC; Porter to Buchanan, May 28, 1852, Gilmore to Buchanan, May 29, 1852, BuHSP; Hincks and Smith, *Proceedings*, 3, 5–9; Ferree, "New York Democracy," 449, 451; Douglas to Yulee, May 1852, June 1, June 2, June 3, June 4, 1852, in SDL, 249–251; Klein, *President James Buchanan*, 219; http://www.mica.edu/About_MICA/Facts_ and_History/Historical_Timeline/1847–1878_Renewal_and_Expansion_in_the_ Industrial_Age.html.

11. Hincks and Smith, *Proceedings*, 9–18, 27–28; Ferree, "New York Democracy," 452, 454; Douglas to Yulee, June 3, 1852, in SDL, 250–251; Pruyn to Marcy, June 2, 1852, Stryker to Marcy, June 2, 1852, Thomas to Marcy, June 2, 1852 (quoted), Witmore to Marcy, Nov. 23, 1852, MaLC; Klein, *President James Buchanan*, 219.

12. Hincks and Smith, *Proceedings*, 27–38; Pruyn to Marcy, June 3, 1852, MaLC; Johannsen, *Stephen A. Douglas*, 367; Van Der Weele, "Jesse David Bright," 121–124; Schimmel, "William H. English," 124–126; Ferree, "New York Democracy," 456.

13. Johannsen, *Stephen A. Douglas*, 367; Hincks and Smith, *Proceedings*, 38–47; Thomas to Marcy, June 7, 1852, MaLC; Klein, *President James Buchanan*, 219–220; Ferree, "New York Democracy," 455; Van Der Weele, "Jesse David Bright," 122–124; Schimmel, "William H. English," 126; Douglas to Yulee, June 4, 1852 (quoted), in SDL, 251–252; Henry Wise to Pierce, June 22, 1852, Wise, *Recollections of Thirteen Presidents*, 35–39.

14. Hincks and Smith, *Proceedings*, 47–51; Spencer, *Victor and the Spoils*, 206; Hinman, *Daniel Dickinson*, 117–119; Paine to Dickinson, July 2, 1852, Dickinson to Brown, Dec. 1, 1852, in Dickinson and Dickinson, *Speeches, Correspondence, Etc.*, 470, 471–472; H. K. Smith to Marcy, June 5, 1852 (quoted), Witmore to Marcy, Nov. 23, 1852, MaLC; Harris to Burke, Aug. 16, 1852, EBLC; Henry Wise to Pierce, June 22, 1852, in Wise, *Recollections of Thirteen Presidents*, 35–39.

15. Hincks and Smith, *Proceedings*, 50–67; Witmore to Marcy, Nov. 23, 1852, Thomas to Marcy, June 7, 1852 (quoted), MaLC; Spencer, *Victor and the Spoils*, 210–211; Johnson to Buchanan, June 8, 1852, Gilmore to Buchanan, June 6, 1852, BuHSP; Harris to Burke, Aug. 16, 1852, B. F. Hallett to Burke, Aug. 28, 1852, L. Harper to Burke, Feb. 1, 1853, EBLC; Burke to Pierce, Apr. 9, 1852, PiLC; Nichols, *Franklin Pierce*, 207; John Lumpkin to Cobb, June 6, 1852, in TSC, 299–300; Van Der Weele, "Jesse David Bright," 122–124.

16. Harper to Burke, Feb. 1, 1853 (quoted), EBLC; Burke to Pierce, June 6, 1852, PiLC; Hincks and Smith, *Proceedings*, 66–69; Klein, *President James Buchanan*, 111, 220; Julian, *Political Recollections*, 120; Klunder, *Lewis Cass*, 260–261; Ferree, "New York Democracy," 453; Johannsen, *Stephen A. Douglas*, 368–369; Lumpkin to Cobb, June 6, 1852, James Jackson to Cobb, June 8, 1852, G. W. Jones to Cobb, June 13, 1852, in TSC, 299–300, 300–301, 301–302; Marcy to Campbell, June 5, 1852 (quoted), MaLC; Nichols, *Franklin Pierce*, 203; Gilmore to Buchanan, June 6, 1852, H. W. Pickens to Buchanan, June 16, 1853, Pierce to Buchanan, June 15, 1852 ("few events" quote), BuHSP.

17. Lumpkin to Cobb, June 6, 1852 (quoted), in TSC, 299–300; Gilmore to Buchanan, June 6, 1852 (quoted), Johnson to Buchanan, June 8, 1852, King to Buchanan, June 12, 1852 (quoted), J. G. Jones to Buchanan, June 16, July 23 (quoted), 1852, Slidell to Buchanan, June 23, 1852, James C. Van Dyke to Buchanan, July 10, 1852, BuHSP; S. Pleasanton to Buchanan, July 10, 1852 (quoted), BJLC.

18. R. J. Scott to Marcy, June 7, 1852, James Berret to Marcy, June 7, 1852 (quoted), Witmore to Marcy, June 7, June 17, 1852, Marcy to Witmore, June 8, 1852 (quoted), Buchanan to Marcy, June 10, 1852, H. Sutton to Marcy, June 10, 1852, Snow to Marcy, June 11, 1852, Marcy to Thomas Osborne, June 12, 1852, Peter Chivvis to Marcy, June 10, 1852, Campbell to Marcy, June 16, 1852 (quoted), Thomas to Marcy, June 16, 1852, John Tracy to Marcy, June 24, 1852, Marcy to Buchanan, June 6, 1852, MaLC; Ferree, "New York Democracy," 451–457.

19. Sutton to Marcy, June 10, 1852, J. F. Lee to Marcy, June 7, 1852, Marcy to Witmore, June 8, 1852, Thomas to Marcy, June 7, 1852, MaLC; Col. Paine to Dickinson, July 2, 1852, Dickinson to Brown, Dec. 1, 1852 (quoted), in Dickinson and Dickinson, *Speeches, Correspondence, Etc.*, 470, 471–472; Byrdsall to Buchanan, Nov. 15, 1852, BuHSP; Cass to Dickinson, June 10, 1852, DiNew.

20. Charles Woodbury to Breckinridge, June 13, 1852, BFLC; Ferree, "New York Democracy," 459–469; Marcy to Buchanan, June 6, 1852, BuHSP; David Briar to Thompson, June 9, 1852 (quoted), ThISL; Isaac G. M. to Burke, June 8, 1852, EBLC; W. A. Bissell to Breese, June 10, 1852, SBLPL; Sutton to Marcy, June 10, 1852, Marcy to Witmore, June 8, 1852, John Tracy to Marcy, June 24, 1852 (quoted), MaLC; J. G. Jones to Bigler, June 16, 1852, BiHSP; Dickinson to Walsh, Nov 15, 1852, MWNYHS; John Lumpkin to Cobb, June 6, 1852, in TSC, 299–300; Buchanan to Johnson, June 24, 1852, Buchanan to Alexander McKeever, July 26, 1852, in Curtis, *Life of James Buchanan*, 40, 42–43.

21. Hunter to Richard Rowzee, Aug. 9, 1852 (quoted), George Booker to Hunter, Nov. 5, 1852, Herschel Johnson to Hunter, Nov. 8, 1852, in Hunter, *Correspondence*, 146–147, 149–150, 151; Charles Heiniteh to Buchanan, Sept. 11, 1852, John to Buchanan, June 23, 1852, King to Buchanan, June 12, 1852 (quoted), BuHSP; Charles Winfield to Marcy, June 16, 1852, MaLC; Gideon Pillow to Tracy, Aug. 10, 1852, TrNYPL; Walther, *William Lowndes Yancey*, 142; Wise, *Recollections of Thirteen Presidents*, 43.

22. Johannsen, *Stephen A. Douglas*, 370; Holt, *American Whig Party*, 726–727, 732, 739–742–745, 758–760; Julian, *Political Recollections*, 119–120, 124–125.

23. Nichols, *Franklin Pierce*, 206–209; Pierce to J. F. H. Claiborn, June 17, 1852, PiLC; Foote, *Casket of Reminiscences*, 88; Holt, *American Whig Party*, 731, 736, 742 (quoted); James Buchanan Speech, Greensburgh, PA, Oct. 7, 1852, in Curtis, *Life of James Buchanan*, 43–67; Coleman, *Disruption of Pennsylvania Democracy*, 54–55.

24. Thornbrough, *Indiana in the Civil War*, 50–54; Van Der Weele, "Jesse David Bright," 125–127; Bright to English, Jan. 26, Feb. 10, Feb. 16, May 15, Aug. 22, Nov. 21, Dec. 5, 1852, Certificate of Election, State of Indiana, Oct. 12, 1852, EnIHS; Schimmel, "William H. English," 150–167.

25. W. H. Herndon to Richard Yates, July 23, 1852, ReCHS; Johannsen, *Stephen A. Douglas*, 370, 372; Thavenet, "William Alexander Richardson," 127–134; Holt, "Political Career of Richardson," 234.

26. Slidell to Buchanan, Sept. 15, Sept. 27, 1852, BuHSP; J. S. France to Bigler, Mar. 27, 1852, Joseph Thompson to Bigler, Mar. 29, 1852, David Tucker to Bigler, Sept. 2, 1852, BiHSP; Buchanan to Johnson, June 24, 1852, in Curtis, *Life of James Buchanan*, 40; Klein, *President James Buchanan*, 221–222

27. Lynde Eliot to Bigler, Sept. 20, 1852, J. G. Jones to Bigler, Sept. 28, 1852, Kerry Welsh to Bigler, Sept. 28, 1852, BiHSP; Klein, *President James Buchanan*, 221–222; Benjamin Brewster to Burke, Sept. 3, 1852, EBLC; Buchanan speech, Greensburgh, PA, Oct. 7, 1852, in Curtis, *Life of James Buchanan*, 43–67; Francis Grund to Cobb, Oct. 29, 1852 (quoted), in TSC, 321; Simon Cameron to Coryell, Oct. 7, 1852, John Forney to Coryell, Oct. 20, 1852, CoHSP; Coleman, *Disruption of Pennsylvania Democracy*, 54–57; Van Dyke to Buchanan, July 10, 1852, Gilmore to Buchanan, Aug. 22, 1852, Byrdsall to Buchanan, Oct. 21, 1852, Andrew Miller to Buchanan, Oct. 29, 1852 (quoted), Pierce to Buchanan, Nov. 1, 1852, August Belmont to Buchanan, Nov. 5, 1852, BuHSP.

28. Campbell to Marcy, Sept. 9 ("arbiter" quote), Marcy to Campbell, July 30 ("toadies" quote), Sept. 21 ("mortification" quote), 1852, Snow to Marcy, Nov. 5, 1852 ("wisdom" quote), A. G. Jewett to Marcy, Sept. 4, 1852, J. G. Cooley to Marcy, Sept. 4, 1852, Timothy Jenkins to Marcy, June 29, 1852, George Guinness to Marcy, July 8, 1852, Thomas to Marcy, July 29, Oct. 20, Oct. 21, Oct. 22, Oct. 23, 1852, W. Russell to Marcy, Aug. 2, 1852, Charles Winfield to Marcy, Aug. 18, 1852, Seymour to Marcy, Aug. 20, 1852, Osborne to Marcy, Aug. 24, 1852, Marcy to Osborne, Aug. 27, 1852, Sept. 8, Oct. 9, 1852, Marcy to James Berret, Oct. 10, Oct. 22, Oct. 27, 1852, H. K. Smith to Marcy, Sept. 14, 1852, John George to Marcy, Oct. 14, 1852, Harry Hibbard to Marcy, Oct. 20, Oct. 27, 1852, James Nye to Marcy, Nov. 4, 1852, E. Roggen to Marcy, Nov. 4, 1852, MaLC; Marcy to Seymour, July 7, Aug. 10, Aug. 15, Aug. 22, Sept. 22, Oct. 5, Oct. 18, Oct. 27, Oct. 31, 1852, FCNYHS; N. Seymour Webb to Tracy, Apr. 19, 1852, TrNYPL; Nichols, *Franklin Pierce*, 209–210, 219; S. B. Garvin to Seymour, Apr. 21, 1853, John Themenz to Seymour, Nov. 6, 1852, SeNYSL.

29. Nichols, *Franklin Pierce*, 216; Forney, *Anecdotes of Public Men*, vol. 2, 420; Belmont to Buchanan, Nov. 5, 1852 (quoted), Johnson to Buchanan, Nov. 18, 1852 (quoted), BuHSP; E. J. Wry to Thompson, Nov. 13, 1852 (quoted), ThISL; Caleb Cushing to Burke, Nov. 1852, EBLC; Kerry Welsh to Bigler, Sept. 28, 1852, BiHSP; Campbell to Marcy, Sept. 9, 1852, MaLC; Dickinson to Walsh, Nov. 15, 1852, MWNYHS; Breese to George Sanders, Nov. 19, 1852, SBLPL; Julian, *Political Recollections*, 129.

30. King to Buchanan, Dec. 13, 1852 (quoted), BuHSP; Forney, *Anecdotes of Public Men*, 2:237.

31. Norman Eddy to Graham, Dec. 4, 1853 (quoted), GrISL; W. A. Bissell to Breese, June 10, 1852, SBLPL; George Plitt to Buchanan, Dec. 30, 1852, BJLC; Andrew Reeder to Buchanan, Nov. 11, 1852 (quoted), BuHSP; George Hastings to John Van Buren, Jan. 14, 1853, TiNYPL; Summers, *Plundering Generation*, 24–27; Schimmel, "William H. English," 186; Johannsen, *Stephen A. Douglas*, 375–376; Grund to Cobb, Oct. 29, 1852, in TSC, 321.

32. Pierce to Jefferson Davis, Dec. 7, 1852, PiLC; Thomas to Marcy, Oct. 28, Nov. 27, 1852, MaLC; Van Dyke to Buchanan, Nov. 26, Dec. 19, 1852, Byrdsall to Buchanan, Nov. 15, Nov. 24, 1852, Nathan Clifford to Buchanan, Nov. 23, 1852,

J. G. Jones to Buchanan, Nov. 30, Dec. 3, Dec. 22, 1852, Jan. 15, Jan. 20, 1853, Daniel Jenks to Buchanan, Feb. 25, 1853 (quoted), Belmont to Buchanan, Jan. 28, 1853, Wise to Buchanan, Nov. 20, 1852 (quoted), Pierce to Buchanan, Dec. 14, 1852, BuHSP; Nichols, *Franklin Pierce*, 217–218; Sewell, *John P. Hale*, 143–147; Coleman, *Disruption of Pennsylvania Democracy*, 59; Buchanan to J. G. Jones, Nov. 15 (quoted), Dec. 21, 1852, Feb. 21, 1853, BJLC; Marcy to Seymour, Feb. 22, 1853, Cushing to Seymour, Feb. 19, 1853, FCNYHS; Cass to Cobb, Dec. 18, 1852 (quoted), G. W. Jones to Cobb, Feb. 11, 1853, Harris to Cobb, Feb. 15, 1853, Stephens to Thomas, Nov. 16, 1852, in TSC, 322–323, 323–324, 325, 325–326; Buchanan to Ward, Nov. 16, 1852, BuNYHS; Michael Bright to English, Jan. 31, 1853, EnIHS; W. H. Tracy to Tracy, Feb. 10, 1853, TrNYPL.

33. Schimmel, "William H. English," 186; Johannsen, *Stephen A. Douglas*, 376–377; Dix, *Memoirs,* 1:269; W. H. Tracy to Tracy, Feb. 10, 1853 (quoted), TrNYPL; Belmont to Buchanan, Nov. 30, 1852, Lewis Clover to Buchanan, Dec. 6, 1852, Johnson to Buchanan, Nov. 18, 1852 (quoted), BuHSP; Thomas to Marcy, Dec. 20, 1852, Eames to Marcy, Nov. 4, Nov. 22, Nov. 26, 1852, John Stryker to Marcy, Nov. 7, 1852, Seymour to Marcy, Dec. 1, 1852, James Berret to Marcy, Dec. 18, 1852, Jewett to Marcy, Oct. 19, 1852, Marcy to Campbell, Nov. 17, 1852, J. M. Hatch to Marcy, Nov. 16, 1852, MaLC; Spencer, *Victor and the Spoils*, 215; Hinman, *Daniel Dickinson*, 120–121; Marcy to Seymour, Sept. 22, 1852, FCNYHS; George Hastings to John Van Buren, Jan. 14, 1853, Tilden to Charles Peaslee, Jan. 15, 1853, TiNYPL; Henry Wise to P. R. George, Dec. 11, 1852, in Wise, *Recollections of Thirteen Presidents*, 39–41.

34. Jenkins to Marcy, June 29, 1852, W. Russell to Marcy, Aug. 2, 1852, Charles Winfield to Marcy, Aug. 18, 1852, Seymour to Marcy, Aug. 20, 1852, Osborne to Marcy, Aug. 24, 1852, Marcy to Campbell, July 30, Nov. 17, 1852, Duff Green to Marcy, Nov. 18, 1852, Campbell to Marcy, Dec. 10, 1852 (quoted), Pierce to Marcy, Nov. 9, 1852 (quoted), MaLC; Spencer, *Victor and the Spoils*, 216–218.

35. Pierce to Marcy, Nov. 9, 1852, Marcy to Witmore, Nov. 16, 1852 (quoted), John Dix to Marcy, Oct. 21, 1852, Pruyn to Marcy, Jan. 25, Jan. 27, Feb. 4, 1853, Thomas to Marcy, Jan. 27, 1853, MaLC; Byrdsall to Buchanan, Nov. 24, 1852, Belmont to Buchanan, Nov. 20, 1852, J. G. Jones to Buchanan, Jan. 20, 1853, BuHSP; Schimmel, "William H. English," 186; Spencer, *Victor and the Spoils*, 216–218; Dix, *Memoirs,* 1:270–271; Tilden to Peaslee, Jan. 15, 1853 (quoted), TiNYPL.

36. Nichols, *Democratic Machine*, 174; David Wagener to Buchanan, Nov. 6, 1852, J. G. Jones to Buchanan, Nov. 22, 1852, BuHSP; Plitt to Buchanan, Aug. 30, 1852, Buchanan to J. G. Jones, Dec. 7, Dec. 13, 1852, BJLC.

37. Buchanan to J. G. Jones, Nov. 15, Nov. 19, 1852, Jan. 31, Mar. 4, 1853, BJLC; Klein, *President James Buchanan*, 222; Buchanan to Pierce, Dec. 11, 1852, in Curtis, *Life of James Buchanan*, 69–74; Coleman, *Disruption of Pennsylvania Democracy*, 58–59; J. G. Jones to Buchanan, Nov. 30, 1852, Jan. 29, Feb. 11, Feb. 25, 1853 ("Cameron Clique" quote), Pierce to Buchanan, Dec. 7, 1852, Daniel Jenks to Buchanan, Dec. 23, 1852, Feb. 25, 1853, Gilmore to Buchanan, Jan. 13, Jan. 14, Jan. 27, Feb. 28, 1853, Campbell to Buchanan, Feb. 13, Feb. 25, 1853, Van Dyke to Buchanan, Feb. 26, 1853, BuHSP.

38. Pierce to Davis, Dec. 7, 1852, PiLC; Foote, *Casket of Reminiscences*, 89–90; Slidell to Buchanan, Dec. 31, 1852, J. G. Jones to Buchanan, Jan. 15, 1853, BuHSP; Hunter to Sanders, June 20, 1851, in Hunter, *Correspondence*, 128.

39. Michael Bright to English, Jan. 31, 1853, EnIHS; Dix, *Memoirs*, 2:204–207, 223–226, 262, 271; J. W. Powell to Breckinridge, Feb. 4, 1853 (quoted), BFLC; Eames to Marcy, Nov. 22 (quoted), Nov. 25, 1852, Snow to Marcy, Dec. 13, 1852, Jan. 22, 1853, Thomas to Marcy, Dec. 20, 1852, Jan. 15, Jan. 16, Jan. 18, Jan. 22, 1853, Berret to Marcy, Jan. 14, 1853, Jenkins to Marcy, Jan. 22, 1853, MaLC; J. G. Jones to Buchanan, Jan. 15, 1853, Belmont to Buchanan, June 18, 1853, Gilmore to Buchanan, Jan. 13, 1853, BuHSP; G. W. Jones to Cobb, Feb. 11, 1853, in TSC, 323–324; Dix to I. P. Garvin, Aug. 31, 1853, in Dix, *Memoirs*, 2:328–329; Ferree, "New York Democracy," 122, 124, 129, 158, 192, 195; Daniel Draper to Burke, Jan. 16, 1852, EBLC; Nichols, *Franklin Pierce*, 227.

40. Eames to Marcy, Nov. 25, Nov. 26, 1852, Campbell to Marcy, Dec. 10, 1852, Pruyn to Marcy, Nov. 27, 1852, Jan. 21, 1853, Thomas to Marcy, Jan. 18, Jan. 22, 1853, Seymour to Marcy, Jan. 24, 1853, MaLOC; Spencer, *Victor and the Spoils*, 218–221; Nichols, *Franklin Pierce*, 228–229; Proctor, *Lives of Lawyers and Statesmen*, 419; Dix, *Memoirs*, 1:273–276; Garvin to Dix, Aug. 26, 1853 (quoted), in Dix, *Memoirs*, 2:328; Marcy to Seymour, June 15, 1853, FCNYHS.

41. Pierce to Robert McClelland, Feb. 5, 1853, PiLC; Gilmore to Buchanan, Feb. 28, 1853, Belmont to Buchanan, Mar. 5, 1853, BuHSP; Summers, *Plundering Generation*, 28; Nichols, *Franklin Pierce*, 228–230, 240–241, 248–249; Klein, *President James Buchanan*, 222–223; Wise to Hunter, Apr. 16, 1853, in Hunter, *Correspondence*, 156–157; Foote, *Casket of Reminiscences*, 90; Johannsen, *Stephen A. Douglas*, 376–377; Belohlavek, *Broken Glass*, 258; Spencer, *Victor and the Spoils*, 218; Clay-Clopton, *Belle of the Fifties*, 65, 70–71.

42. Coleman, *Disruption of Pennsylvania Democracy*, 59–60; George Bancroft to Pierce, Jan. 7, 1853, Pierce to Davis, Jan. 12, 1853, PiLC; Marcy to Seymour, Feb. 22, 1853, FCNYHS; Van Dyke to Buchanan, Feb. 17, 1853, BuHSP; Johannsen, *Stephen A. Douglas*, 374; Nichols, *Franklin Pierce*, 224–225, 230, 234–235; Belohlavek, *Broken Glass*, 243; Hunt, *Inaugural Addresses*, 163–172; Foote, *Casket of Reminiscences*, 91; Fehrenbacher, *Slaveholding Republic*, 235–236.

43. Nichols, *Franklin Pierce*, 251–253; Isaac Fowler to Pierce, Aug. 15, 1853, TiNYPL; George Jones to Cobb, May 19, 1853, in TSC, 327–329; Toucey to Buchanan, Apr. 4, 1853, BuHSP; Schuyler Colfax to Graham, Nov. 29, 1852, GrISL; Clay-Clopton, *Belle of the Fifties*, 75.

44. Stryker to Seymour, Jan. 1853, Garvin to Seymour, Mar. 29, Mar. 30, Mar. 31, 1853, SeNYSL; Nichols, *Franklin Pierce*, 254–255; Hinman, *Daniel Dickinson*, 121; Proctor, *Lives of Lawyers and Statesmen*, 568; Gilmore to Buchanan, Feb. 28, 1853 (quoted), J. G. Jones to Buchanan, Mar. 6, Mar. 9, Mar. 14, Mar. 28, 1853, Belmont to Buchanan, Mar. 14, 1853, Wise to Buchanan, Mar. 19, 1853, Hendrick Wright to Buchanan, Mar. 21, 1853, Jenks to Buchanan, Jan. 5, 1854, BuHSP; Buchanan to J. G. Jones, Feb. 21, 1853 ("astonished" quote), BJLC; Marcy to Tilden, Apr. 4, 1853, TiNYPL; Buchanan to Harriet Lane, Mar. 15, Mar. 19, 1853, in Curtis, *Life of James Buchanan*, 95–97; Coleman, *Disruption of Pennsylvania Democracy*, 60.

45. Schimmel, "William H. English," 186–187; Johannsen, *Stephen A. Douglas*, 378–382; Douglas to Lanphier, Nov. 11, 1853, Douglas to Pierce, July 22, 1855, in SDL, 267–268, 339–340; Bright to Buchanan, Apr. 20, 1853, BuHSP.

46. Belohlavek, *Broken Glass*, 258; Sanders to Breckinridge, May 2, 1853, BFLC; D. L. Gregg to Lanphier, Sept. 20, 1853, MiLC; Klein, *President James Buchanan*, 223, 235; Nichols, *Franklin Pierce*, 256, 287; Belmont to Buchanan, Mar. 26, Apr. 15,

June 18, June 25, 1853, Slidell to Buchanan, Mar. 30, 1853, Van Dyke to Buchanan, Mar. 24, Mar. 31, 1853, Pierce to Buchanan, Mar. 30, June 26, 1853, Bancroft to Buchanan, Apr. 12, 1853, Nahum Capen to Buchanan, Apr. 14, 1853, Wise to Buchanan, Apr. 16, 1853, King to Buchanan, July 15, 1853, BuHSP; Dix, *Memoirs*, 1:277; Buchanan to J. G. Jones, Mar. 12, Mar. 15 (quoted), 1853, Buchanan to Campbell, Apr. 3, 1853, Buchanan to Harriet Johnston, Apr. 7, 1853, BJLC; Binder, *James Buchanan*, 167–168; Coleman, *Disruption of Pennsylvania Democracy*, 60; Spencer, *Victor and the Spoils*, 221; Curtis, *Life of James Buchanan*, 76.

47. Grund to Burke, Aug. 17, 1853 (quoted), EBLC; Peter Wager to Bigler, June 17, 1853, BiHSP; Marcy to Berret, Jan. 1, 1853 (quoted), MaLC; George Coott to unknown leading Democrat, July 10, 1853 (quoted), PiNYHS; Belmont to Buchanan, Nov. 18, 1853 (quoted), BuHSP.

48. Campbell to Marcy, Dec. 10, 1852 (quoted), MaLC; Marcy to Seymour, Nov. 4, 1853, FCNYHS; Dickinson to Burke, Sept. 25, Dec. 3, 1853, Jan. 22, 1854, EBLC; Hinman, *Daniel Dickinson*, 120–126.

49. Hinman, *Daniel Dickinson*, 120–126; Seymour to Marcy, Jan. 7, 1853, MaLC; George Coott to Pierce, July 10, 1853, PiNYHS; Dickinson to Henry Orr, Sept. 13, 1853, in Dickinson and Dickinson, *Speeches, Correspondence, Etc.*, 475–481; Nichols, *Franklin Pierce*, 287–288; Marcy to Seymour, Apr. 10, May 18 ("embarrassment" quote), 1853, FCNYHS; Forney to Buchanan, Sept. 16, 1853 ("explosion" quote), J. G. Jones to Buchanan, Oct. 3, 1853, Ward to Buchanan, Oct. 22, 1853, BuHSP; James Maurice to Burke, Sept. 15, 1853, EBLC; Charles Wigely to Davis, Jan. 13, 1854, DaIHS; W. H. Tracy to Tracy, Oct. 30, 1853 ("broken up" quote), TrNYPL; Marcy to Tilden, Aug. 1853, Oct. 8, Oct. 16, 1853, Tilden to Marcy, Sept. 10, Oct. 12, 1853, TiNYPL.

50. Dickinson to Burke, Sept. 25, Dec. 3, 1853, Jan. 22, 1854, EBLC; Ward to Buchanan, Oct. 22, 1853, Forney to Buchanan, Jan. 10, 1854, Jenks to Buchanan, Jan. 5, 1854, BuHSP; Nichols, *Franklin Pierce*, 287–288; Marcy to Seymour, Nov. 4 ("zealously" quote), Dec. 4, 1853, FCNYHS; Dickinson to Burke, Dec. 3, 1853, Jan. 22, 1854, EBLC; Hinman, *Daniel Dickinson*, 120–126; Spencer, *Victor and the Spoils*, 274–275.

51. Marcy to Tilden, Oct. 8, 1853 (quoted), TiNYPL; Marcy to Seymour, Nov. 4 (quoted), Dec. 4, 1853, H. J. Redfield to Marcy, Apr. 11, 1852, FCNYHS; Jenks to Buchanan, Jan. 5, 1854, Ward to Buchanan, Oct. 22, 1853, Forney to Buchanan, Nov. 21, 1853, Slidell to Buchanan, Jan. 14, 1854 (quoted), Plitt to Buchanan, Dec. 15, 1853, J. G. Jones to Buchanan, Nov. 12, 1853, Johnson to Buchanan, Nov. 20, 1853 (quoted), BuHSP; Nichols, *Franklin Pierce*, 289, 292; Johannsen, *Stephen A. Douglas*, 387, 389; Hinman, *Daniel Dickinson*, 125–127; Colin Ingersoll to Cobb, Jan. 20, 1854, in TSC, 339–340; Dickinson to Burke, Dec. 3, 1853, Jan. 22, Mar. 13, Mar. 23, 1854, EBLC; Foote, *Casket of Reminiscences*, 91.

52. Nichols, *Franklin Pierce*, 278, 290; Burke to Pierce, June 8, 1852, PiLC; Andrew Ward to Burke, July 7, 1853 (quoted), James Maurice to Burke, Aug. 19, 1853, Burke to Sidney Webster, Nov. 18, 1853, Dickinson to Burke, Sept. 25 (quoted), Dec. 3, 1853, Jan. 22, Mar. 13, Mar. 23, 1854, Mar. 25, 1855, Grund to Burke, Aug. 17, 1853, EBLC; Burke to A. O. P. Nicholson, Nov. 27, 1854, Burke Letter, NYHS.

53. Buchanan to Ward, Dec. 6, 1853, BuNYHS; Grund to Burke, Aug. 17, 1853, EBLC; Jenks to Buchanan, Dec. 16, 1853, Jan. 5, 1854, Van Dyke to Buchanan, Nov. 26, 1852, Forney to Buchanan, Nov. 21, 1853, Jan. 10, 1854 (quoted), BuHSP;

Summers, *Plundering Generation*, 48; J. G. Jones to Bigler, July 19, 1853, C. Black to Bigler, July 20, 1853, Forney to Bigler, Aug. 11, 1853, "Extract of letter of Mr. Strong under date of Aug 23rd 1853," H. A. Muhlenberg to Bigler, Aug. 24, 1853, Wager to Bigler, June 17, 1853, BiHSP; M. Dimmick to Coryell, Mar. 15, 1853, CoHSP; Tilden to Pierce, Feb. 23, 1853, TiNYPL; Anbinder, *Nativism and Slavery*, 30–31.

54. Van Der Weele, "Jesse David Bright," 135–139, 141; Schimmel, "William H. English," 167–168, 187–188; Bright to English, Nov. 21, 1852, EnIHS; Bright to Corcoran, Aug. 7, 1853, CoLC; Forney to Buchanan, Nov. 21, 1853, Plitt to Buchanan, Dec. 15, 1853, BuHSP; Bright to T. C. Day, Jan. 9, 1854 (quoted), BrCHS; Dan Farley to Davis, Jan. 21, 1854, DaIHS; Summers, *Plundering Generation*, 45; Nichols, *Franklin Pierce*, 315–317; Bright to Breckinridge, June 5, 1853 (quoted), BFLC.

55. Certification of Election, Commonwealth of Kentucky, John Leathers to John Breckinridge, Aug. 25, 1851, Enos Lawrence to Breckinridge, Nov. 12, 1851, Cushing to Breckinridge, July 29, 1852, Bright to Breckinridge, Sept. 4, Sept. 23, Sept. 28, 1852, June 5, Aug. 7, 1853, Richardson to Breckinridge, July 1, 1853 (quoted), George Jones to Breckinridge, May 21, 1852, W. V. McKean to Breckinridge, June 17, 1853, R. H. Stanton to Breckinridge, Sept. 7, Sept. 12, 1853, E. B. Hart to Breckinridge, Aug. 4, 1853, Charles Woodbury to Breckinridge, Aug. 5, 1853, BFLC; *Biographical Directory of the United States Congress*, http://bioguide.congress.gov/scripts/biodisplay.pl?index=B000789; Savage, *Our Living Representative Men*, 67–75; Van Der Weele, "Jesse David Bright," 139–140; Bright to Breckinridge, May 10, 1853 (quoted), Breckinridge to Corcoran, May 23, 1853, Bright to Corcoran, Aug. 7, 1853, CoLC; D. L. Gregg to Lanphier, Sept. 20, 1853 (quoted), MiLC.

56. Foote, *Casket of Reminiscences*, 92; J. G. Jones to Buchanan, Oct. 3, 1853 (quoted), Slidell to Buchanan, Jan. 14, 1854, BuHSP.

Chapter 4

1. Hunt, *Inaugural Addresses*, 166; May, *Manifest Destiny's Underworld*, 117–121; J. R. Young to Lanphier, Oct. 22, 1853, LaLPL; Daniel Jenks to Buchanan, Jan. 5, 1854, John Slidell to Buchanan, Jan. 14, 1854, BuHSP.

2. May, *Manifest Destiny's Underworld*, 117–121; Joshiah Randall to Buchanan, Feb. 3, 1854, James Gadsden to Buchanan, Oct. 3, 1853, J. D. Andrews to Buchanan, Mar. 28, 1854, George Plitt to Buchanan, Apr. 8, 1854, John Forney to Buchanan, May 25, 1854, BuHSP; Nichols, *Franklin Pierce*, 266, 325, 330; Spencer, *Victor and the Spoils*, 256, 284–288; "The Gadsden Treaty," *Daily Scioto Gazette* (Chillicothe, OH), Mar. 23, 1854; "The Gadsden Treaty," *Daily Cleveland Herald* (Cleveland, OH), Jan. 26, 1854.

3. Pierce, First Annual Message, Dec. 5, 1853 (quoted), http://www.presidency.ucsb.edu/ws/index.php?pid=29494; Potter, *Impeding Crisis*, 183–184 (quoted); Klein, *President James Buchanan*, 234–235; "The Mission to Spain" *Weekly Herald* (New York, NY), Apr. 9, 1853; "Pierre Soulé," *Daily Register* (Raleigh, NC), Apr. 13, 1853; "Cuba and the Administration," *Frederick Douglass's Paper* (Rochester, NY), May 26, 1854; "The American Minister to Spain," *Daily National Intelligencer* (Washington, DC), Sept. 30, 1854; August Belmont to Buchanan, May 12, 1853, J. Mason to Buchanan, Mar. 5, 1854, Slidell to Buchanan, June 17, 1854, BuHSP; Buchanan to Pierce, Dec. 11, 1852, in Curtis, *Life of James Buchanan*, 69–74; Spencer, *Victor and the Spoils*, 318; Forney, *Anecdotes of Public Men*, vol. 1, 57.

4. May, *Manifest Destiny's Underworld*, xi, 3, 6–7, 9, 25–27, 33–34; Scroggs, *Filibusters and Financiers*, 3–4; Nichols, *Franklin Pierce*, 267, 340–341; Foote, *Casket of Reminiscences*, 344–356; "Gen. John A. Quitman," Apr. 7, 1849, "To the People of Mississippi," Feb. 8, 1851, *Mississippi Free Trader and Natchez Gazette* (Natchez, MS); "Gen. John A. Quitman . . .," *Arkansas State Democrat* (Little Rock, AR), Feb. 1. 1850; Forney to Buchanan, May 25, 1854 (quoted), Sept. 25, 1854, BuHSP.

5. May, *Manifest Destiny's Underworld*, 33–34, 120–121; Nichols, *Franklin Pierce*, 267, 328–329, 340–343; "Emancipation in Cuba," *Frederick Douglass's Paper*, Apr. 22, 1853; "Cuba, the United States, and England," Oct. 22, 1853, "Anticipated Rupture with Spain," May 13, 1854, "Shall Cuba Be African or American?," May 20, 1854, *Weekly Herald* (New York, NY); John Quitman to Mike Walsh, Mar. 14, Oct. 10, 1854, MWNYHS; Spencer, *Victor and the Spoils*, 321–323, 340; Alexander Stephens, May 9, 1854, in Johnston and Browne, *Life of Stephens*, 276–277; Belmont to Buchanan, Apr. 1, 1854 (quoted), John Y. Mason to Buchanan, Apr. 19, 1854, Edward Everett to Buchanan, May 8, 1854, Forney to Buchanan, May 25, 1854, Sept. 25, 1854, William Marcy to Buchanan, May 26, 1854, George Sanderson to Buchanan, May 2, 1855, BuHSP.

6. Nichols, *Franklin Pierce*, 340–343; Spencer, *Victor and the Spoils*, 323, 340; Klein, *President James Buchanan*, 236; "The President's Proclamation Concerning Cuba," June 2, 1854, *Boston Daily Atlas* (Boston, MA); "Cuba," June 9, 1854, *Mississippian and State Gazette* (Jackson, MS); Stephens, June 15, 1854 (quoted), in Johnston and Browne, *Life of Stephens*, 278; George Newell to Samuel Tilden, Apr. 14, 1855, TiNYPL; May, *Manifest Destiny's Underworld*, 34–35, 121, 123, 136; Slidell to Buchanan, June 17, 1854, BuHSP; "The United States and Cuba," May 11, 1854, *Daily Morning News* (Savannah, GA); "Anglo-French Intermeddling with Cuba," May 12, 1854, *Mississippian and State Gazette* (Jackson, MS).

7. Nichols, *Franklin Pierce*, 343, 357–359; Klein, *President James Buchanan*, 234–236; Buchanan to J. G. Jones, May 4, 1855, BJLC; Spencer, *Victor and the Spoils*, 325; "August Belmont," Nov. 5, 1853, *Daily Scioto Gazette* (Chillicothe, OH); Belmont to Buchanan, Jan. 28, Mar. 5, Mar. 7, Mar. 14, Mar. 16, May 12, 1853, Apr. 1, 1854, Slidell to Buchanan, June 17, Aug. 6, 1854, BuHSP; Marcy to Belmont, May 28, 1853, BeNYPL; Buchanan to Pierce, Dec. 11, 1852, in Curtis, *Life of James Buchanan*, 69–74.

8. Nichols, *Franklin Pierce*, 358–359, 366–367, 369–370; Binder, *James Buchanan*, 172–173, 200; Klein, *President James Buchanan*, 236–240; Forney to Buchanan, July 28, 1853, Aug. 18, 1854, Pierce to Buchanan, July 31, 1853, Aug. 12, 1854, Dan Sickles to Buchanan, Aug. 15, Sept. 23, 1854 (quoted), Pierre Soulé to Buchanan, Sept. 23, Sept. 29, 1854, James Mason to Buchanan, Sept. 24, Sept. 29, 1854, Belmont to Buchanan, Sept. 25, 1854, Slidell to Buchanan, Oct. 18, 1854, Apr. 1855, BuHSP; Forney, *Anecdotes of Public Men*, vol. 1, 318; Belohlavek, *Broken Glass*, 262; Buchanan to J. G. Jones, May 4, 1855, BJLC; Curtis, *Life of James Buchanan*, 139–140.

9. Nichols, *Franklin Pierce*, 367–369, 393. 396; "The Ostend Conference," Dec. 2, 1854, "The Ostend Conference," Dec. 9, 1854, *Weekly Herald* (New York, NY); "The Meeting at Ostend," *North American and United States Gazette* (Philadelphia, PA), Dec. 7, 1854; "History of the Ostend Conference," *Boston Daily Advertiser* (Boston, MA), Mar. 6, 1855; Marcy to Buchanan, Oct. 19, 1854 (quoted), Feb. 20,

1855, Slidell to Buchanan, Mar. 5, 1855, BuHSP; Curtis, *Life of James Buchanan*, 139–140 (quoted).

10. Nichols, *Franklin Pierce*, 367–369, 393. 396; Klein, *President James Buchanan*, 239–241; Spencer, *Victor and the Spoils*, 336; "Augustus Caesar Dodge's Appointment," *New York Daily Times* (New York, NY), Feb. 13, 1855; C. C. Gangh to John Breckinridge, Jan. 16, 1855, William Birney to Breckinridge, Jan. 16, 1855, W. C. Wagley to Breckinridge, Jan. 24, 1855, B. Magoffin to Breckinridge, Feb. 12, 1855, P. Rankins to Breckinridge, Feb. 13, 1855, BFLC; Pelzer, *Augustus Caesar Dodge*, 143–151, 196–197, 201, 219–233; Buchanan to J. G. Jones, May 4, 1855, Plitt to Buchanan, Jan. 29, 1855, BJLC; Salter, *Augustus C. Dodge*, 31–32; Savage, *Our Living Representative Men*, 73.

11. May, *Manifest Destiny's Underworld*, 40–42, 47–48; "Revolution in Nicaragua," *North American and United States Gazette* (Philadelphia, PA), Dec. 15, 1853; "Progress of the Revolution," July 3, 1854, "Aid to the Nicaragua, Filibusters," Dec. 29, 1855, *Daily Morning News* (Savannah, GA); "William Walker," *Daily Scioto Gazette* (Chillicothe, OH), June 14, 1854; "From Nicaragua," *Bangor Daily Whig and Courier* (Bangor, ME), Oct. 16, 1855; "Conquest of Nicaragua," *Fayetteville Observer* (Fayetteville, NC), Nov. 8, 1855; "From Nicaragua," Nov. 14, 1855 (quoted), "Nicaragua Affairs," Jan. 4, 1856, *Daily National Intelligencer* (Washington, DC); "More Emigrants for Nicaragua," *Charleston Mercury* (Charleston, SC), Jan. 12, 1856; W. J. Canter to Buchanan, Jan. 16, 1854, BuHSP; Spencer, *Victor and the Spoils*, 358–362, 370–371 (quoted); Belohlavek, *Broken Glass*, 265; Nichols, *Franklin Pierce*, 459; Scroggs, *Filibusters and Financiers*, 9, 12–17, 36–37, 40–48, 92, 101, 108, 117–129.

12. May, *Manifest Destiny's Underworld*, 48, 122; Nichols, *Franklin Pierce*, 459–462; Belohlavek, *Broken Glass*, 256–266; Spencer, *Victor and the Spoils and the Spoils*, 371; Scroggs, *Filibusters and Financiers*, 135–149, 151–156, 165–169, 171–174; "The Administration and the Nicaragua Question," *New York Herald* (New York, NY), May 9, 1856; "Recognition of Nicaragua," *Daily National Intelligencer* (Washington, DC), May 16, 1856; "Our Relations With Nicaragua," *Charleston Mercury* (Charleston, SC); "Pierce's rivals . . .," *Daily Scioto Gazette* (Chillicothe, OH), May 26, 1856.

13. Campbell, *Slave Catchers*, 103; Fehrenbacher, *Slaveholding Republic*, 236.

14. Belohlavek, *Broken Glass*, 3–24; Forney, *Anecdotes of Public Men*, vol. 1, 227; Savage, *Our Living Representative Men*, 143–144; Schimmel, "William H. English," 291; "A Spirited Electioneer Contest . . .," Oct. 28, 1826 (quoted), *New Hampshire Statesman and Concord Register* (Concord, NH).

15. Belohlavek, *Broken Glass*, 43–113; Forney, *Anecdotes of Public Men*, vol. 1, 227; Savage, *Our Living Representative Men*, 145–149; Robert Winthrop to Cushing, Feb. 25, 1836, Cushing to Winthrop, Mar. 1, 1836, CuMHS; *Speech of Mr. Caleb Cushing . . . Delivered in the House of Representatives*, Sept. 25, 1837 (Washington, 1837) found in CuMHS; *Address by Caleb Cushing*, Transactions of the Essex Agricultural Society, for 1850, Published by Order of the Society, December, 1850 (Salem: Printed at Office of Salem Gazette and Essex Co. Mercury, 1850) found in CuMHS; "Letter of Hon. Caleb Cushing," Feb. 15, 1838, "Anti-Slavery, to the People of Massachusetts," Jan. 25, 1839, *Emancipator* (New York, NY).

16. Belohlavek, *Broken Glass*, 123–182; "The Hon. Caleb Cushing," Sept. 20, 1841, "Address of the Hon. Caleb Cushing," Oct. 7, 1841, "Address of the Hon. Caleb Cushing, Editorial," Oct. 7, 1841, "Mr. Caleb Cushing," July 18, 1842,

"Caleb Cushing," Oct. 13, 1842, *Daily Atlas* (Boston, MA); "Rumored Changes in the Cabinet," June 24, 1842, "The Hon. Caleb Cushing . . .," May 23, 1843, *North American and Daily Advertiser* (Philadelphia, PA); "Hon. Caleb Cushing," Oct. 26, 1842, *Fayetteville Observer* (Fayetteville, NC); "The Appointment of Caleb Cushing as Agent of the U. States to China," May 27, 1843, *Daily National Intelligencer* (Washington, DC); Speech, Temple Street Church, Oct. 7, 1842, CuMHS; Savage, *Our Living Representative Men*, 150–151; Forney, *Anecdotes of Public Men*, vol. 1, 227–228; Edward Everett to Cushing, May 18, Aug. 2, 1842, W. W. Irwin to Cushing, Mar. 24, 1843, Daniel Webster to Cushing, Mar. 29, 1843, John Tyler to Hugh Legare, May 16, May 21, 1843, in *Letters and Times of the Tylers*, vol. 3, 100–101, 101–102, 108–110, 110, 111–112, 112–113.

17. Belohlavek, *Broken Glass*, 182–209; Cushing to Pierce, Feb. 25, 1847, PiLC; "The Hon. Caleb Cushing . . .," *Cleveland Herald* (Cleveland, OH), Jan. 22, 1847; "Brig. Gen. Caleb Cushing," *Emancipator* (Jonesborough, TN), June 2, 1847; "Accident to Gen. Caleb Cushing," *Vermont Patriot* (Montpelier, VT), June 3, 1847; "Caleb Cushing Has at Last 'Gone to His Own Place,'" *New Hampshire Statesman*, Nov. 12, 1847.

18. Belohlavek, *Broken Glass*, 209–232, 224 (quoted); "Democratic State Convention," *New York Herald* (New York, NY), Sept. 7, 1848; "Gen. Caleb Cushing," Apr. 25, 1851 (quoted), "The Appointment of the Hon. Caleb Cushing," May 25, 1852, "Hon. Caleb Cushing," July 26, 1853, *Boston Daily Atlas* (Boston, MA); Forney, *Anecdotes of Public Men*, vol. 1, 228; Savage, *Our Living Representative Men*, 151–152; *Oration Delivered by the Hon. Caleb Cushing . . .* (New York, 1858) found in CuMHS; Hoar, *Autobiography of Seventy Years*, 173 (quoted); Henry Wise to Hunter, Apr. 16, 1853, in Hunter, *Correspondence*, 156–157; W. W. H. Davis to Coryell, July 15, 1853, CoHSP; Henry Wise to Pierce, June 22, 1852, in Wise, *Recollections of Thirteen Presidents*, 35–39.

19. Fehrenbacher, *Slaveholding Republic*, 236; Campbell, *Slave Catchers*, 103–105; Savage, *Our Living Representative Men*, 153; Belohlavek, *Broken Glass*, 248–250, 258–159, 263, 265–269; "Letter from Caleb Cushing to Mr. Frothingham," *Weekly Herald* (New York, NY), Nov. 5, 1853 (quoted); *Boston Post*, Sept. 29, 1853, found in Campbell, *Slave Catchers*, 104; Hoar, *Autobiography of Seventy Years*, 173.

20. Campbell, *Slave Catchers*, 103, 105–106, 110–147; Savage, *Our Living Representative Men*, 153; Belohlavek, *Broken Glass*, 273–275; Fehrenbacher, *Slaveholding Republic*, 236–238; "Selections, the Rendition of Anthony Burns," June 16, 1852, "Refuge of Oppression, the Administration and the Fugitive Slave Law," Dec. 2, 1853, *Liberator* (Boston, MA); "Prospect of the Liberation of Anthony Burns," *Boston Daily Atlas* (Boston, MA), Oct. 10, 1854; "The Fugitive Slave Law in Operation," *Daily Cleveland Herald* (Cleveland, OH), Oct. 10, 1853; "Fugitive Slave Law, &c.," Nov. 25, 1853, "Great Excitement—Arrest of a Fugitive Slave!," Mar. 24, 1854, *Frederick Douglass's Paper* (Rochester, NY); "Fugitive Slave, Excitement at Milwaukie," *Daily Morning News* (Savannah, GA), Mar. 21, 1854; Gara, *Presidency of Franklin Pierce*, 107–108; Morris, *Free Men All*, 166.

21. For an outstanding exploration of the impact of the Fugitive Slave Law of 1850 at the local level, see Harrold, *Border War*. Belohlavek, *Broken Glass*, 273; Gara, *Presidency of Franklin Pierce*, 70; Campbell, *Slave Catchers*, 106; Baker, *Rescue of Joshua Glover*, 55–56; Cave Johnson to unknown, Jan. 3, 1854 (quoted), JoNYHS.

22. Belohlavek, *Broken Glass*, 244 (quoted), 273; Campbell, *Slave Catchers*, 106; Walther, *William Lowndes Yancey*, 188–189; Francis Grund to Burke, Aug. 17, 1853, EBLC; McCulloch, *Men and Measures*, 24; Wise, *Recollections of Thirteen Presidents*, 48–49 (quoted); Clay-Clopton, *Belle of the Fifties*, 64.

23. Johannsen, *Douglas*, 239; Potter, *Impeding Crisis*, 74 (quoted); Wallace, *Lew Wallace*, 235.

24. *CG*, 30C-1S, 21 (quoted), 53–56 (quoted); Hinman, *Daniel Dickinson*, 58–59.

25. Klunder, *Lewis Cass*, 168–69; Johannsen, *Stephen A. Douglas*, 239; Holt, *Fate of Their Country*, 131–132 (quoted); "Letter from Gen. Cass," *Dover Gazette and Strafford Advertiser* (Dover, NH), Jan. 8, 1848.

26. Potter, *Impeding Crisis*, 72; *Appendix to the CG*, 31C-1S, 61 (quoted), 58–74 (quoted); Klunder, *Lewis Cass*, 176–179.

27. Klunder, *Lewis Cass*, 176–179; Johannsen, *Stephen A. Douglas*, 241–246, 248.

28. Douglas to Asa Whitney, Oct. 15, 1845, Douglas to Lanphier and George Walker, Sept. 5, 1850, Douglas to J. H. Crane, D. M. Johnson, L. J. Eastin, Dec. 17, 1853, in SDL, 127–133, 194, 268–271; Johannsen, *Stephen A. Douglas*, 304–301, 317–329, 393–394; John McClernand to Lanphier and George Walker, May 30, 1848 (quoted), MiLC.

29. For Douglas's ownership of slaves and a plantation, see the correspondence between Douglas and Ja. S. Strickland and Brander Williams & Co., New Orleans, in DoLPL. Johannsen, *Stephen A. Douglas*, 207–209, 211, 232, 299–300, 337–338; Douglas to Lanphier, Aug. 3, 1850, Douglas to James Sheahan, Mar. 10, 1855, Douglas to editor of the Washington *States*, Jan. 7, 1859, Douglas to James McHatton, April 4, 1861 in SDL, 189–191, 335, 433–434, 508–509. Douglas to Lanphier, Aug. 3, 1850, Feb. 13, 1854, Douglas to the editor of the *Concord State Capitol Reporter*, Feb. 16, 1854, Douglas to Parmenas Turnley, Nov. 30, 1852, in SDL, 189–190, 255–256 (quoted), 283–284, 284–290; "Stephen Douglas and the American Union," University of Chicago Library, http://www.lib.uchicago.edu/e/spcl/excat/douglas2.html.

30. Johannsen, *Stephen A. Douglas*, 390–391, 402; Etcheson, *Bleeding Kansas*, 9; Pierce, First Annual Message, Dec. 5, 1853, http://www.presidency.ucsb.edu/ws/index.php?pid=29494; Richards, *Slave Power*, 184; Douglas to Joel Matteson, Jan. 2, 1854, in SDL, 272–282; *CG*, 33C-1S, 26–27; http://www.senate.gov/artandhistory/history/common/briefing/President_Pro_Tempore.htm#5; Stephens, *Constitutional View*, 1:242 (quoted).

31. Pelzer, *Augustus Caesar Dodge*, 1, 7, 12–33, 37–39, 42–43, 46–61, 72–83, 91, 94–107, 115–119, 128–137; For Dodge's youth among slavery, see Pelzer, *Augustus Caesar Dodge*, 14–39; For Dodge's "mammy," see *Appendix to the CG*, 33C-1S, 381; Salter, *Augustus C. Dodge*, 3–4, 6–21, 25–27; Certificate of Election, 1840, Robert Lucas Letters, NYHS; Dodge to Jesse Williams, Dec. 12, 1842, Dodge to Col. Benton, Nov. 11, 1852, ADDM; Clare Dodge to Dodge, Jan. 9, 1848, ADIC; http://bioguide.congress.gov/scripts/biodisplay.pl?index=D000394; Forney, *Anecdotes of Public Men*, vol. 2, 172; Cook, *Baptism of Fire*, 32.

32. Pelzer, *Augustus Caesar Dodge*, 143–151, 147–148 (quoted), 181; Salter, *Augustus C. Dodge*, 27; Dodge to Rorer, Apr. 18, 1854, David Rorer Letters, Iowa State Library, Iowa City.

33. *CG*, 33C-1S, 28, 115; Salter, *Augustus C. Dodge*, 27; Etcheson, *Bleeding Kansas*, 10–12; Johannsen, *Stephen A. Douglas*, 402–403, 405–408; Pelzer, *Augustus Caesar*

Dodge, 181–182; Nichols, *Franklin Pierce*, 303–304; Stephens, *Constitutional View*, 2:242, 243; Clay-Clopton, *Belle of the Fifties*, 42–43.

34. Etcheson, *Bleeding Kansas*, 12; Johannsen, *Stephen A. Douglas*, 411; Douglas to Turnley, Nov. 30, 1852, in SDL, 255–256.

35. Etcheson, *Bleeding Kansas*, 14; Johannsen, *Stephen A. Douglas*, 413–414; Nichols, *Franklin Pierce*, 321–322; James Bowlin to Buchanan, Apr. 21, 1854, BuHSP.

36. Nichols, *Franklin Pierce*, 322–324; Johannsen, *Stephen A. Douglas*, 414–415; Bowlin to Buchanan, Apr. 21, 1854, BuHSP; Tweed to J. Murphy, Mar. 4, 1854, TwNYHS; Douglas to Lanphier, Feb. 13, 1854, in SDL, 283–284; Marcy to Seymour, Feb. 11, 1854 (quoted), FCNYHS.

37. *CG*, 33C-1S, 221–222, 239 (quoted), 240; Etcheson, *Bleeding Kansas*, 14–15; Johannsen, *Stephen A. Douglas*, 415; Holt, *Fate of Their Country*, 141–144; *Library of Original Sources*, 144–152; Stephens, *Constitutional View*, 2:250–251.

38. *CG*, 33C-1S, 273, 275–282 (quoted); Johannsen, *Stephen A. Douglas*, 419.

39. *CG*, 33C-1S, 288–292; Cooper, *Politics of Slavery*, 341–359; Toombs to W. W. Burwell, Feb. 3, 1854 (quoted), in TSC, 342–343.

40. Toombs to W. W. Burwell, Feb. 3, 1854 (quoted), in TSC, 342–343; Marcy to Seymour, Feb. 11, 1854 (quoted), FCNYHS; *CG*, 33C-1S, 421; Klunder, *Lewis Cass*, 266.

41. *Appendix to the CG*, 33C-1S, 375–383; Pelzer, *Augustus Caesar Dodge*, 185–192; John McQueen to Rhett, Feb. 3, 1854, Robert Barnwell Rhett Papers, South Carolina Historical Society.

42. *Appendix to the CG*, 33C-1S, 247–249.

43. *CG*, 33C-1S, 344, 407, 450–451, 456–458, 474, 457; Douglas to Lanphier, Feb. 13, 1854, in SDL, 283–284.

44. *CG*, 33C-1S, 531–532; Richards, *Slave Power*, 111; Johannsen, *Stephen A. Douglas*, 428–432; Pelzer, *Augustus Caesar Dodge*, 193–194; Van Der Weele, "Jesse David Bright," 143; Campbell to Buchanan, Mar. 16, 1854, BuHSP; Stephens, *Constitutional View*, 2:252; Forney, *Anecdotes of Public Men*, 2:155, 176.

45. Clay-Clopton, *Belle of the Fifties*, 62; Johannsen, *Stephen A. Douglas*, 432; Etcheson, *Bleeding Kansas*, 19; Pierce to Buchanan, Feb. 22 / Mar. 13, 1854, Marcy to Buchanan, Mar. 12, 1854 (quoted), BuHSP; Nichols, *American Leviathan*, 105.

46. Newspaper clipping, in Richardson to unknown, Dec. 30, 1854, RiCHS; Thavenet, "William Alexander Richardson," 2–3, 9–11, 14 (quoted), 12–19, 22–24, 32–33, 41–44, 74; Holt, "Political Career of Richardson," 223–228, 232 (quoted); Johannsen, *Stephen A. Douglas*, 341, 395.

47. Thavenet, "William Alexander Richardson," 51, 53–54, 56, 64–72, 80, 82, 95, 98, 111, 116; Holt, "Political Career of Richardson," 228–232, 234–235; Johannsen, *Stephen A. Douglas*, 189 (quoted), 341; *CG*, 30C-1S, 59; *Quincy Herald*, Sept. 17, 1850, found in Thavenet, "William Alexander Richardson," 111; Account of Leonard Wells Volk, in Wilson, *Intimate Memories of Lincoln*, 243 (quoted); Richards, *Slave Power*, 186.

48. *CG*, 33C-1S, 294–297 (quoted); Nichols, *American Leviathan*, 106; Schimmel, "William H. English," 209, 212, 215.

49. *CG*, 33C-1S, 294–297; Schimmel, "William H. English," 212, 217; Bright to English, Jan. 31, 1854 (quoted), EnIHS.

50. *CG*, 33C-1S, 294–297, 297 (quoted); Schimmel, "William H. English," 210, 217; Nichols, *American Leviathan*, 104–105, 107; Etcheson, *Bleeding Kansas*, 19.

51. Etcheson, *Bleeding Kansas*, 19; Nichols, *American Leviathan*, 105; *CG*, 33C-1S, 442, 482; Potter, *Impeding Crisis*, 156, 166; Nichols, *Franklin Pierce*, 336; Slidell to Buchanan, Mar. 25, 1854 (quoted), Robbins to Buchanan, Mar. 13, 1854, J. D. Andrews to Buchanan, Mar. 21, 1854 (quoted), BuHSP; Johannsen, *Stephen A. Douglas*, 433.

52. *CG*, 33C-1S, 701–703; Nichols, *Franklin Pierce*, 337; Nichols, *American Leviathan*, 107–109; Richards, *Slave Power*, 185–187; Thomas Bayley to Cobb, May 6, 1854, in TSC, 343; Summers, *Plundering Generation*, 210–212.

53. *CG*, 33C-1S, 1128–1133; Stephens to Burwell, May 7, 1854 (quoted), in TSC, 343–344; Nichols, *American Leviathan*, 109–111; Etcheson, *Bleeding Kansas*, 19; Richards, *Slave Power*, 187–188; Holt, "Political Career of Richardson," 235–236; Johannsen, *Stephen A. Douglas*, 433; Schimmel, "William H. English," 234–235; Marcy to Seymour, May 3, 1854, FCNYHS.

54. *CG*, 33C-1S, 1142; *Appendix to the CG*, 33C-1S, 605–610; Schimmel, "William H. English," 236–238, 240; Michael Bright to English, May 30, 1854, EnIHS; Stephens, May 9, 1854, in Johnston and Browne, *Life of Stephens*, 276–277.

55. *CG*, 33C-1S, 1160–1183; Stephens, May 11, 1854 (quoted), in Johnston and Browne, *Life of Stephens*, 277; Johannsen, *Stephen A. Douglas*, 433; Richards, *Slave Power*, 188; Etcheson, *Bleeding Kansas*, 19; Nichols, *American Leviathan*, 111–116; Thavenet, "William Alexander Richardson," 149; Holt, "Political Career of Richardson," 236; "The Crime Is Committed," *Daily Cleveland Herald* (Cleveland, OH), May 26, 1856 (quoted).

56. *Appendix to the CG*, 33C-1S, 794–796; Thavenet, "William Alexander Richardson," 150–151.

57. *CG*, 33C-1S, 1240–1255, 1300–1311, 1321; Stephens, May 23, 1854 (quoted), in Johnston and Browne, *Life of Stephens*, 277; Richards, *Slave Power*, 188; Etcheson, *Bleeding Kansas*, 19–20; Thavenet, "William Alexander Richardson," 152; Holt, "Political Career of Richardson," 236–237; Nichols, *American Leviathan*, 118; Johannsen, *Stephen A. Douglas*, 434; Stephens to J. W. Duncan, May 26, 1854, in TSC, 345; Forney to Buchanan, May 26, 1854, BuHSP; Nichols, *Franklin Pierce*, 338; Stephens, *Constitutional View*, 2:252.

58. Etcheson, *Bleeding Kansas*, 2 (quoted); J. G. Jones to Buchanan, May 18, 1854, Bowlin to Buchanan, Apr. 21, 1854, Forney to Buchanan, May 25, 1854 (quoted), Henry Slicer to Buchanan, June 10, 1854 (quoted), BuHSP; http://www.senate.gov/artandhistory/history/common/briefing/Senate_Chaplain.htm; Stephens to J. W. Duncan, May 26, 1854, in TSC, 345; Nichols, *American Leviathan*, 120.

59. Clay-Clopton, *Belle of the Fifties*, 59; Francis P. Blair to John Dix, in Dix, *Memoirs*, 1:283–284.

Chapter 5

1. Campbell, *Slave Catchers*, 83–84; Giddings, *History of the Rebellion*, 367; John Robbins to Buchanan, Mar. 13, 1854 (quoted), John Forney to Buchanan, Sept. 25, 1854 (quoted), BuHSP.

2. W. Z. Stuart to English, Mar. 13, 1854 (quoted), EnIHS; Gienapp, *Origins of the Republican Party*, 74–76; George Houston to Davis, Aug. 19, 1855 (quoted), DaIHS.

3. Johannsen, *Stephen A. Douglas*, 418, 422, 446; Stephens, *Constitutional View*, 2:248; Gienapp, *Origins of the Republican Party*, 72–74; Giddings, *History of the Rebellion*, 366–367; Potter, *Impeding Crisis*, 162–165, 175; Douglas to editor of the *Concord State Capitol Reporter*, Feb. 16, 1854, Douglas to Edward Coles, Feb. 18, 1854, in SDL, 284–290, 290–298; Campbell, *Slave Catchers*, 86–87.

4. For a comprehensive history of the American Whig Party, see Holt, *American Whig Party*.

5. Anbinder, *Nativism and Slavery*, 3–5, 7, 43, 46, 104–120; Holt, *American Whig Party*, 845–847; Gienapp, *Origins of the Republican Party*, 93–100; Hoar, *Autobiography of Seventy Years*, 188; Forney, *Anecdotes of Public Men*, vol. 1, 132.

6. Anbinder, *Nativism and Slavery*, 12–14, 20–22, 43–50; Gienapp, *Origins of the Republican Party*, 92, 94, 98–99; Jeremiah Black to Buchanan, Feb. 17, 1855, A. L. Hays to Buchanan, May 8, 1854 (quoted), Henry Slicer to Buchanan, June 10, 1854, BuHSP; Julian, *Political Recollections*, 142; Holt, *American Whig Party*, 846, 849.

7. Gienapp, *Origins of the Republican Party*, 78–90, 105, 273–303; Julian, *Political Recollections*, 143–144; John Cadwalader to Buchanan, Sept. 18, 1855 (quoted), Rufus Brown to Buchanan, Feb. 18, 1856, BuHSP.

8. Marcy to Buchanan, Sept. 10, 1855 (quoted), Jenks to Buchanan, Oct. 15, 1855 (quoted), Brown to Buchannan, Feb. 18, 1856, BuHSP; Gienapp, *Origins of the Republican Party*, 103, 125; Holt, *American Whig Party*, 841–845; Etcheson, *Bleeding Kansas*, 24–25; Salmon Chase to Pike, Mar. 22, 1855, in Pike, *First Blows of the Civil War*, 294.

9. Cook, *Baptism of Fire*, 46–51; Holt, *American Whig Party*, 866–868; James Grimes to Pike, Aug. 14, 1854 (quoted), in Pike, *First Blows of the Civil War*, 259; Jesse Bright to Hunter, Sept. 2, 1854, in Hunter, *Correspondence*, 158–159 (quoted); Gienapp, *Origins of the Republican Party*, 121–122; George Jones to William Dawson and Robert Toombs, Apr. 26, 1854, DoIC; Johannsen, *Stephen A. Douglas*, 469.

10. John Wadding to Davis, Apr. 24, 1854, William Kennedy to Davis, July 1, 1854 (quoted), T. A. Hendricks to Davis, June 18, 1855, DaIHS; Hamilton Smith to English, Mar. 15, 1854, J. R. Slack to English, June 30, 1854, J. S. Maughlin to English, no date, EnIHS.

11. Schimmel, "William H. English," 258–260; W. W. Wick to English, June 5, 1854, J. B. Norman to English, Dec. 25, 1855 (quoted), EnIHS; Van Der Weele, "Jesse David Bright," 145–151; Gienapp, *Origins of the Republican Party*, 108; Holt, *American Whig Party*, 863; Thornbrough, *Indiana in the Civil War*, 56–57; W. R. N. to Davis, Apr. 14, 1854, Eckles to Davis, May 16, 1854, Davis to Dr. W. R. Nassinger, July 20, 1854, J. O. Jones to Davis, Dec. 23, 1854, Davis to J. O. Jones, Dec. 28, 1854, Ezra Read to Davis, Dec. 16, 1854, DaIHS; Wallace, *Lew Wallace*, 238.

12. Van Der Weele, "Jesse David Bright," 150–151; Wallace, *Lew Wallace*, 238; Davis to Dr. W. R. Nassinger, July 20, 1854, J. O. Jones to Davis, Dec. 23, 1855, David to J. O. Jones, Dec. 28, 1855, Ezra Read to Davis, Dec. 16, 1854 (quoted), DaIHS; Schimmel, "William II. English," 315; Thornbrough, *Indiana in the Civil War*, 57.

13. Van Der Weele, "Jesse David Bright," 151–153; Schimmel, "William H. English," 261–263, 284; Holt, *American Whig Party*, 862–863; Gienapp, *Origins of the Republican Party*, 109; Anbinder, *Nativism and Slavery*, 71; Julian, *Political Recollections*, 144; William Bryant to Davis, July 19, 1854, DaIHS; William Lee to English, Sept. 11,

1854 ("slaughtered" quote), EnIHS; Graham Fitch to English, July 18, 1854, EnIHS; Thomas Hendricks to F. Hardin, July 14, 1854, F. Hardin to Thomas Hendricks, July 19, 1854 ("fanatics" quote), EnCHS; Wallace, *Lew Wallace*, 235, 237 ("whale" quote); English to John Breckinridge, Aug. 16, 1854, William Brown to Breckinridge, Aug. 21, 1854, BFLC; Bright to Hunter, Sept. 2, 1854 ("afraid" quote), in Hunter, *Correspondence*, 158–159.

14. Schimmel, "William H. English," 159–185, 284–286, 312–315; Van Der Weele, "Jesse David Bright," 151–156; Anbinder, *Nativism and Slavery*, 71–72; B. Laurel to English, July 13, 1854, S. T. Plate to English, Oct. 20, 1854, J. B. Norman to English, Nov. 21, 1854, E. Sugg to English, Jan. 1, 1855, R. W. English to English, Oct. 20, 1854 (quoted), EnIHS; James Vanter to Breckinridge, Dec. 1, 1854 ("regret" quote), BFLC; Thornbrough, *Indiana in the Civil War*, 67; A. W. Lowdermilk to Davis, Sept. 1, 1854, H. W. Daniels to Davis, Oct. 12, 1854, B. H. C. to Davis, Oct. 17, 1854, George Houston to Davis, Aug. 19, 1855, R. Wharry to Davis, Oct. 18, 1854 ("salt creek" quote), DaIHS

15. Van Der Weele, "Jesse David Bright," 181; Schimmel, "William H. English," 313; Thornbrough, *Indiana in the Civil War*, 68; Colfax to Rev. Jackson, Dec. 12, 1854, SCLL; Ballard Smith to English, Jan. 6, 1855, Fred Matthis to English, Jan. 5, 1855, EnIHS; John Law to Davis, Feb. 8, 1855 (quoted), DaIHS.

16. Johannsen, *Stephen A. Douglas*, 439–445, 449–452; Douglas to Edward Coles, Feb. 18, 1854, Douglas to twenty-five Chicago clergymen, Apr. 6, 1854, Douglas to Howell Cobb, Apr. 2, 1854 (quoted), in SDL, 290–298, 300, 300–321; John Robbins to Buchanan, Mar. 13, 1854, BuHSP; Breese to Editor of the *Reporter*, Oct. 28, 1854, SBLPL; Giddings, *History of the Rebellion*, 370; Douglas to Breckinridge, Sept. 14, 1854 (quoted), BFLC.

17. Johannsen, *Stephen A. Douglas*, 445, 447–451, 451 (quoted); James Shields to Lanphier, Jan. 14, 1855, LaLPL; Douglas to James Sheahan, Sept. 14, 1854, Mar. 10, 1855, Douglas to George Buell, Aug. 3, 1855, in SDL, 330, 335, 340; Hansen and Nygard, "Democratic Party in Illinois," 114; Etcheson, *Bleeding Kansas*, 23.

18. Johannsen, *Stephen A. Douglas*, 451–459; Shields to Lanphier, Oct. 25, 1854 (quoted), Jan. 14, 1855, LaLPL; Campbell, *Slave Catchers*, 89; Etcheson, *Bleeding Kansas*, 23; Douglas to Lanphier, Aug. 25, 1865, Douglas to Breckinridge, Sept. 14, 1854, in SDL, 327, 329; T. B. B. to "Dearest Carry," Sept. 2, 1854, Thomas Bryan Letter, CHS; Hansen and Nygard, "Democratic Party in Illinois," 114–115; Walther, *William Lowndes Yancey*, 181 ("Hell" quote).

19. Johannsen, *Stephen A. Douglas*, 448, 451–459; Shields to Lanphier, Oct. 25, 1854, Jan. 14, 1855, LaLPL; Campbell, *Slave Catchers*, 89; Etcheson, *Bleeding Kansas*, 23; Douglas to Lanphier, Aug. 25, 1854, Douglas to Breckinridge, Sept. 14, 1854, in SDL, 327, 329; Breese to unknown, Mar. 20, 1854 (quoted), SBLPL; James Know to Richard Yates, Sept. 4, 1854, ReCHS; Gienapp, *Origins of the Republican Party*, 124.

20. Thavenet, "William Alexander Richardson," 153–157; Count Gurowski to Pike, June 8, 1854, in Pike, *First Blows of the Civil War*, 253–254; Gienapp, *Origins of the Republican Party*, 125–126; James Know to Richards Yates, Sept. 4, 1854, ReCHS; Johannsen, *Stephen A. Douglas*, 450; Hansen and Nygard, "Democratic Party in Illinois," 114; Holt, *American Whig Party*, 870–871; Trumbull to John Palmer, Nov. 23, 1854, in Trumbull, "Letters to Palmer," 20–24.

21. Johannsen, *Stephen A. Douglas*, 460–464; Hansen and Nygard, "Democratic Party in Illinois," 115–117; H. L. Breese to Breese, Sept. 26, 1854 (quoted), SBL PL; Trumbull to Palmer, Nov. 23, 1854 (quoted), Dec. 3, 1855, in Trumbull, "Letters to Palmer," 20–24, 26.

22. Gienapp, *Origins of the Republican Party*, 126–127, 174–175; J. C. Allen to Lanphier, Dec. 5, 1854 ("peril" quote), William Richardson to Lanphier, Dec. 17, 1854, Jan. 12, Jan. 15, Jan. 19, 1855, Shields to Lanphier, Jan. 12, Jan. 15, 1855, LaL PL; Douglas to Lanphier, Dec. 18, 1854, DoL PL; Douglas to James Sheahan, Feb. 6, 1855, in SDL, 333–334.

23. Gienapp, *Origins of the Republican Party*, 139, 173; *New York Tribune*, Mar. 23, 1855, in Pike, *First Blows of the Civil War*, 292–293; Colfax to Rev. Jackson, Dec. 12, 1854, SCLL; Coleman, *Disruption of Pennsylvania Democracy*, 61, 64–66; Anbinder, *Nativism and Slavery*, 30, 53–55, 57; Forney to Breckinridge, Sept. 13, 1854, BFLC; James Reynolds to Buchanan, Oct. 23, 1854, Glancy Jones to Buchanan, July 9, 1854, J. Franklin Reigatt to Buchanan, July 28, 1854, J. S. Black to Buchanan, Feb. 17, 1855, Forney to Buchanan, July 13, 1855, BuHS P; Joseph Thompson to Bigler, Mar. 29, 1852, Col. Hopkins to Bigler, Sept. 10, 1852, Lynde Eliot to Bigler, Sept. 20, 1852, James Campbell to Bigler, Sept. 21, 1852, Peter Wager to Bigler, June 17, 1853, BiHS P.

24. Gienapp, *Origins of the Republican Party*, 139, 143, 173; Coleman, *Disruption of Pennsylvania Democracy*, 61, 64–66, 68–69; Anbinder, *Nativism and Slavery*, 53–55, 57; Forney to Breckinridge, Sept. 13, 1854, BFLC; Reynolds to Buchanan, Oct. 23, 1854, Glancy Jones to Buchanan, July 9, 1854, Reigatt to Buchanan, July 28, 1854, Black to Buchanan, Feb. 17, 1855, Forney to Buchanan, May 25, 1854, July 13, 1855, James Van Dyke to Buchanan, Mar. 22, 1854, George Sanderson to Buchanan, Mar. 10, 1854 (quoted), June 22, 1854 (quoted), Wilson Candless to Buchanan, June 12, 1854, BuHS P.

25. Holt, *American Whig Party*, 881–886; Gienapp, *Origins of the Republican Party*, 140–142, 145; Forney to Buchanan, Mar. 19, May 25, Sept. 25, 1854, Van Dyke to Buchanan, Mar. 22, 1854, John Slidell to Buchanan, Mar. 25, 1854, James Campbell to Buchanan, Mar. 16, 1854, Plitt to Buchanan, Apr. 8, 1854, Slicer to Buchanan, June 10, 1854, Jenks to Buchanan, July 7, Aug. 18, Oct. 13, Oct. 17, Nov. 13 (quoted), 1854, William Hopkins to Buchanan, Sept. 11, 1854, Candless to Buchanan, June 10, 1854, Lewis Clover to Buchanan, June 15, 1854, Sanderson to Buchanan, June 22, Oct. 24, 1854, Reigatt to Buchanan, July 28, 1854, Glancy Jones to Buchanan, July 9, 1854 (quoted), BuHS P; Forney to Bigler, Aug. 11, 1853, "Extract from letter of Mr. Strong under date of Aug. 23rd 1853," BiHS P; Forney to Breckinridge, Sept. 13 (quoted), Oct. 19, 1854, BFLC; Anbinder, *Nativism and Slavery*, 58–60; G. Bailey to Pike, June 6, 1854, in Pike, *First Blows of the Civil War*, 247; Coleman, *Disruption of Pennsylvania Democracy*, 68–70, 74–75; Jones, *J. Glancy Jones*, vol. 1, 260; Buchanan to Glancy Jones, Jan. 11, 1855, BJLC.

26. Gienapp, *Origins of the Republican Party*, 140–142, 145, 173, 208–209; Forney to Buchanan, Mar. 19, May 25, Sept. 25, 1854, Van Dyke to Buchanan, Mar. 22, 1854, Slidell to Buchanan, Mar. 25, 1854, Campbell to Buchanan, Mar. 16, 1854, Plitt to Buchanan, Apr. 8, 1854, Slicer to Buchanan, June 10, 1854, Jenks to Buchanan, Mar. 17, July 7, Aug. 18, Oct. 13, Oct. 17, Nov. 13, 1854, Mar. 6, Oct. 15, 1855, Hopkins to Buchanan, Sept. 11, 1854, Candless to Buchanan, June 10, June 12, 1854, Clover

to Buchanan, June 15, 1854, Sanderson to Buchanan, June 22, Oct. 24, 1854, May 2, 1855 (quoted), Reigatt to Buchanan, July 28, 1854, Glancy Jones to Buchanan, July 9, 1854, Reynolds to Buchanan, Oct. 23, 1854, Black to Buchanan, Feb. 17, 1855, BuHSP; Forney to Breckinridge, Sept. 13, Oct. 19, 1854, BFLC; Anbinder, *Nativism and Slavery*, 58–60, 127, 150–154; Coleman, *Disruption of Pennsylvania Democracy*, 68–70, 74–75, 77–78; Buchanan to Glancy Jones, Jan. 11, May 4 (quoted), 1855, BJLC; Savage, *Our Living Representative Men*, 94–95.

27. Nichols, *Franklin Pierce*, 362–363; Marcy to Horatio Seymour, Aug. 24, Aug. 30 (quoted), 1854, FCNYHS; Clover to Buchanan, June 15, 1854, BuHSP; Gienapp, *Origins of the Republican Party*, 147–149; C. Wheatly to Breckinridge, Feb. 25, 1854 (quoted), BFLC; Johannsen, *Stephen A. Douglas*, 422; Albert Tracy to Tracy, July 3, 1854, TrNYPL.

28. Holt, *American Whig Party*, 894–895, 897; Nichols, *Franklin Pierce*, 363; Dickinson to Mr. Clinton, May 20, 1854, in Dickinson, *Speeches, Correspondence, Etc.*, 484; Savage, *Our Living Representative Men*, 435–436; Marcy to Seymour, Aug. 30, 1854, FCNYHS; Preston King to Tilden, Oct. 13, 1854 (quoted), TiNYPL; Spencer, *Victor and the Spoils*, 328–329; Robert Kelly to Seymour, Oct. 7, 1854, SeNYSL.

29. Gienapp, *Origins of the Republican Party*, 149; Noble Eldokim to Seymour, July 11, 1856, T. S. Laxton to Seymour, Oct. 1, 1855, SeNYSL; Holt, *American Whig Party*, 894–896; Dickinson to Burke, Mar. 23, 1854 ("Old Guard" and "traitors" quote), EBLC.

30. Henry Randall to Seymour, Dec. 22, 1854, SeNYSL; Holt, *American Whig Party*, 900–907; King to Tilden, Oct. 13, 1854, TiNYPL; Anbinder, *Nativism and Slavery*, 78–80, 83–84; Tweed to J. Murphy, Feb. 5, 1855, TwNYHS; George Taylor to Breckinridge, May 24, 1855, BFLC; Savage, *Our Living Representative Men*, 436.

31. Forney to Buchanan, Apr. 3, 1855 ("lava" quote), Cobb to Buchanan, Dec. 5, 1854 ("slaughtered" quote), BuHSP; John Adair to Breckinridge, June 25, 1855, BFLC; Gienapp, *Origins of the Republican Party*, 161, 172; Potter, *Impeding Crisis*, 175; Schimmel, "William H. English," 189; Etcheson, *Bleeding Kansas*, 23; Richards, *Slave Power*, 190–191, 194.

32. Sanderson to Buchanan, May 2, 1855, Jenks to Buchanan, May 14, 1855, BuHSP; Johannsen, *Stephen A. Douglas*, 468–469, 476; Nichols, *Franklin Pierce*, 365, 435, 438–439; William Underwood to Lanphier, Dec. 18, 1854 (quoted), LaLPL; Buchanan to Glancy Jones, May 4, June 1, 1855, BJLC; Klunder, *Lewis Cass*, 271.

33. For Dodge's career and appointment, see Chapter 4; http://bioguide.congress.gov/scripts/biodisplay.pl?index=E000039; George Houston to Davis, Aug. 19, 1855, DaIHS; http://www.senate.gov/artandhistory/history/common/briefing/President_Pro_Tempore.htm#5; Woollen, *Sketches of Early Indiana*, 228; Johannsen, *Stephen A. Douglas*, 402; Van Der Weele, "Jesse David Bright," 130.

34. Jones, *J. Glancy Jones*, vol. 1, 10, 19, 50–55, 58–59, 62–67, 71, 76–79.

35. Jones, *J. Glancy Jones*, vol. 1, 78–109, 111–112, 125, 131, 134–136, 138–139, 141–142, 144–145, 155–156; Buchanan to Glancy Jones, May 21, 1842, Jan. 2, 1844 (quoted), Mar. 30, 1847 (quoted), Mar. 8, 1850, BJLC.

36. Jones, *J. Glancy Jones*, vol. 1, 157–159, 163, 199–203, 209–210, 256–257, 315–322; Buchanan to Glancy Jones, May 14, June 1, June 12, Sept. 10, Oct. 18, Nov. 11, Nov. 17, 1851, Apr. 3, Sept. 10, Nov. 15, Nov. 19, Dec. 7, Dec. 13, Dec. 15. Dec.

21, 1852, Jan. 31, Feb. 18, Feb. 21, Mar. 4 (quoted), Mar. 12, Apr. 26, 1853, Apr. 26, 1854, Jan. 11, 1855, BJLC; Glancy Jones to Buchanan, Mar. 29, July 9, Aug. 14, 1854, May 9, 1855, Jenks to Buchanan, Dec. 10, Dec. 30, 1855, BuHSP; Franklin Pierce to Glancy Jones, Oct. 2, 1855, in Jones, *J. Glancy Jones*, vol. 1, 255–256; Stephens to unknown, Nov. 30, 1855, in Johnston and Browne, *Life of Stephens*, 299.

37. Stephens to unknown, Dec. 2, 1855, in Johnston and Browne, *Life of Stephens*, 299; Jones, *J. Glancy Jones*, vol. 1, 265–266; Schimmel, "William H. English," 340–342; Johannsen, *Stephen A. Douglas*, 488; Gienapp, *Origins of the Republican Party*, 244; Holt, "Political Career of Richardson," 238; A. Gallatin Talbott to Breckinridge, Dec. 2, 1855 (quoted), BFLC.

38. *CG*, 34C-1S, 3–4, 4–5, 6–8, 8–10, 10–17, 20–21, 24–26; Anbinder, *Nativism and Slavery*, 197 (quoted), 197–200; Schimmel, "William H. English," 340–342; Forney to Buchanan, Apr. 3, 1855, John Appleton to Buchanan, Dec. 11, 1855, BuHSP; Giddings, *History of the Rebellion*, 383–388; Jones, *J. Glancy Jones*, vol. 1, 268–315; R. Emmet Monaghan to Buchanan, Dec. 3, 1855, Glancy Jones to Buchanan, Mar. 9, 1856, BuHSP.

39. *CG*, 34C-1S, 27–29, 31–35; 51–73; 77–87, 89–92, 94–95, 99–104, 128–131, 139–149, 159–160, 165–193, 211–221, 229–231, 232–242, 246–247, 250–260, 261–270, 280–283; Schimmel, "William H. English," 342–344, 348–349; Anbinder, *Nativism and Slavery*, 200–201; Giddings, *History of the Rebellion*, 384–389, 387 (quoted); Stephens to unknown, Dec. 11, Dec. 27, Dec. 30, 1855, Jan. 8. 1856 (quoted), Stephens to Linton Stephens, Feb. 1, 1856, Stephens to unknown, Feb. 2, Feb. 4, 1856, in Johnston and Browne, *Life of Stephens*, 300–306; Cobb to wife, Dec. 23, 1855, Feb. 2, 1856, Robert Winthrop to Cobb, Jan. 5, 1856, in TSC, 357–358, 358–359; A. Wheeler to Colfax, Dec. 23, 1855, SCLL; John Dix to Bigelow, Dec. 30, 1855, BiNYPL; J. B. Norman to English, Dec. 25, 1855, Isaac Smith to English, Jan. 22, 1856, A. F. Morrison to English, Jan. 1, 1856, EnIHS; Trumbull to Palmer, Jan. 2, Jan. 24, 1856, in Trumbull, "Letters to Palmer," 26–27, 28–29; Holt, "Political Career of Richardson," 329; Johannsen, *Stephen A. Douglas*, 489; Forney to Buchanan, Dec. 15, 1855, Glancy Jones to Buchanan, Dec. 16, 1855, Jenks to Buchanan, Dec. 30, 1855, Jan. 4, 1856, BuHSP.

40. *CG*, 34C-1S, 294–302, 304–321, 332–343; Schimmel, "William H. English," 343, 348–349; Trumbull to Palmer, Jan. 1856, in Trumbull, "Letters to Palmer," 28–29; Holt, "Political Career of Richardson," 238; Anbinder, *Nativism and Slavery*, 200–201; Stephens to Linton Stephens, Feb. 1, 1856, Stephens to unknown, Feb. 2, Feb. 4, 1856, in Johnston and Browne, *Life of Stephens*, 300–306; Johannsen, *Stephen A. Douglas*, 489; Jenks to Buchanan, Jan. 26, 1856, Forney to Buchanan, Feb. 3, 1856, BuHSP; Giddings, *History of the Rebellion*, 388–389, 388 ("wild excitement" quote); Thomas Harris to Lanphier, Feb. 6, 1856 ("hell" quote), LaLPL; Winthrop to Cobb, Jan. 5, 1856, Cobb to wife, Feb. 2, 1856, Toombs to Thomas Thomas, Feb. 9, 1856 ("dangerous" quote), in TSC, 357–358, 358–359, 359–361.

41. David Atchison to Hunter, Mar. 4, 1855 (quoted), in Hunter, *Correspondence*, 160–161; Etcheson, *Bleeding Kansas*, 29–32, 35–39, 42; Giddings, *History of the Rebellion*, 373; Forney to Buchanan, May 12, 1855, BuHSP.

42. Johannsen, *Stephen A. Douglas*, 468, 473; Etcheson, *Bleeding Kansas*, 53, 55–63, 67; Nichols, *Franklin Pierce*, 407–408, 410–418; Summers, *Plundering Generation*, 153–154; Meerse, "James Buchanan," 134; Glancy Jones to Buchanan, May 9, 1855,

Marcy to Buchanan, June 8, 1855, Forney to Buchanan, Feb. 23, May 12, 1855, Jenks to Buchanan, Aug. 6, 1855, Thomas Stokes to Buchanan, Aug. 28, 1855, BuHSP; Schimmel, "William H. English," 368; Forney, *Anecdotes of Public Men*, vol. 1, 13, 15; W. V. McKean to Breckinridge, May 23, 1855, BFLC; Glancy Jones to A. O. P. Nicholson, Nov. 18, 1855, J. Glancy Jones Letter, NYHS; Thomas to Stephens, Feb. 25, 1856 (quoted), in TSC, 361–362.

43. Etcheson, *Bleeding Kansas*, 69 (quoted), 71–75, 78–87, 91–92; Schimmel, "William H. English," 368–369; Johannsen, *Stephen A. Douglas*, 490–491; Nichols, *Franklin Pierce*, 441, 444; Trumbull to Palmer, Jan. 24, 1856, in Trumbull, "Letters to Palmer," 28–29.

44. Sinha, "Caning of Charles Sumner," 233–262; *New York Tribune*, May 19, May 22, May 23, May 28, 1856, in Pike, *First Blows of the Civil War*, 335–337, 338–339, 339–340, 342–343; Johannsen, *Stephen A. Douglas*, 504; Toombs to George Crawford, May 30, 1856, Junius Hillyer to Cobb, May 28, 1856, in TSC, 365; Schimmel, "William H. English," 385–386, 392–393; Giddings, *History of the Rebellion*, 394–395, 398–399; CG, 34C-1S, 1597, 1613–1614; George Newell to Tilden, May 27, 1856, TiNYPL.

45. Etcheson, *Bleeding Kansas*, 100–105, 107–113; Gienapp, *Origins of the Republican Party*, 297–298; Gara, *Presidency of Franklin Pierce*, 120, 122; Plitt to Buchanan, Jan. 29, 1855 (quoted), BuHSP.

46. H. M. Rice to Breckinridge, May 9, 1855, BFLC; Clay-Clopton, *Belle of the Fifties*, 59–61; Nichols, *Franklin Pierce*, 428, 450; Spencer, *Victor and the Spoils*, 366; S. R. Anderson to A. O. P. Nicholson, Nov. 21, 1855, PiNYHS; N. G. Upham to Buchanan, Apr. 9, July 25, 1855, Forney to Buchanan, July 13, Aug. 12, 1855, Jenks to Buchanan, July 16, 1855, John Houston to Buchanan, Aug. 6, 1855, BuHSP.

47. Nichols, *Franklin Pierce*, 426–428, 450; Forney to Buchanan, Nov. 27, Dec. 5, 1854, July 13, Aug. 12, Oct. 22, Nov. 25, 1855, Jenks to Buchanan, July 16, Dec. 10, 1855, Slidell to Buchanan, Dec. 5, 1854, Glancy Jones to Buchanan, Oct. 12, Nov. 18, Nov. 22, 1855, Plitt to Buchanan, Oct. 16, 1855, Josiah Randall to Buchanan, Nov. 19, 1855, BuHSP; Forney to Breckinridge, Nov. 15, 1855, BFLC; Glancy Jones to Nicholson, Nov. 18, 1855, J. Glancy Jones Letter, NYHS.

48. Nichols, *Franklin Pierce*, 429–435; Trumbull to Palmer, Jan. 2, 1856, in Trumbull, "Letters to Palmer," 26–27; Giddings, *History of the Rebellion*, 386–387, 390; Stephens to unknown, Dec. 30, 1855, in Johnston and Browne, *Life of Stephens*, 300–301; Pierce, Third Annual Message, Dec. 31, 1855, http://www.presidency.ucsb.edu/ws/index.php?pid=29496; Marcy to Buchanan, Dec. 23, 1855, Glancy Jones to Buchanan, Dec. 26, 1855, BuHSP.

49. Clay-Clopton, *Belle of the Fifties*, 59; Trumbull to Palmer, Jan. 2, 1856, in Trumbull, "Letters to Palmer," 26–27; Sickles to Buchanan, Jan. 3, 1856, Forney to Buchanan, Jan. 4, Feb. 3, 1856, Reigart to Buchanan, Jan. 4, 1856, Sanderson to Buchanan, Feb. 1, 1856, BuHSP.

50. Clay-Clopton, *Belle of the Fifties*, 59; Johannsen, *Stephen A. Douglas*, 510; Nichols, *Franklin Pierce*, 451–452; Nichols, *Disruption of American Democracy*, 12; A. Loomis to Seymour, Oct. 6, 1855, SeNYSL; J. Seibels to Buchanan, Oct. 11, Dec. 23, 1855, Jan. 31, 1856 ("bold bid" quote), James Bowlin to Buchanan, Apr. 21, 1854, Slidell to Buchanan, June 17, 1854, Apr. 1855, Dec. 9, 1855, Joseph Wright to Buchanan, Nov. 14, 1854, Robert Tyler to Buchanan, July 23, 1855, Pierre Soule to Buchanan, June

26, 1855 ("harm" quote), John Heist to Forney, Nov. 15, 1855, Sickles to Buchanan, Nov. 25, 1855, Sanderson to Buchanan, Nov. 27, 1855, Van Dyke to Buchanan, Nov. 27, 1855, Jenks to Buchanan, Dec. 10, 1855, Rufus Brown to Buchanan, Feb. 18, 1856, L. K. Bowers to Buchanan, Feb. 24, 1856, Alfred Gilmore to Buchanan, Feb. 26, 1856, Glancy Jones to Buchanan, Mar. 7, 1856, Cobb to Buchanan, Dec. 5, 1854 ("defeat" quote), BuHSP; Stephens to Thomas, June 16, 1856, in TSC, 367–372; Dickinson to Burke, Mar. 20, 1856, EBLC.

51. B. P. Douglas to English, Dec. 9, 1855, EnIHS; Upham to Buchanan, July 25, 1855, BuHSP; H. W. Beers to Breckinridge, Aug. 18, 1855, Charles Wheatly to Breckinridge, Feb. 18, 1855 (quoted), BFLC.

52. Nichols, *Franklin Pierce*, 453–455; Spencer, *Victor and the Spoils*, 367; L. B. Garvin to Seymour, Jan. 3, 1856, FCNYHS; Forney to Buchanan, July 13, 1855, Mar. 3, 1856, Glancy Jones to Buchanan, Nov. 18, Dec. 16, 1855, Feb. 18, Mar. 7, 1856, Sickles to Buchanan, Nov. 25, 1855, Marcy to Buchanan, Jan. 27, 1856, Brown to Buchanan, Feb. 18, 1856, BuHSP; Samuel Staples to Dickinson, Jan. 1, 1855, DiNew; Dickinson to Rogers, Mar. 25, 1855, in Dickinson, *Speeches, Correspondence, Etc.*, 485–486; Dickinson to Burke, Sept. 2, 1855, Mar. 30, 1856, EBLC; Isaac Butts to Tilden, July 6, 1856, TiNYPL.

53. Johannsen, *Stephen A. Douglas*, 507, 509, 510, 514; Halstead and Fisher, *Trimmers, Trucklers, and Temporizers*, 16 (quoted); Wheatly to Breckinridge, Feb. 25, 1855, Forney to Breckinridge, Nov. 15, 1855, BFLC; Plitt to Buchanan, Sept. 24, 1855, BJLC; Thomas Cobb to Cobb, Mar. 4, 1856, in TSC, 362; Francis Mallory to Hunter, Apr. 13, 1856, in Hunter, *Correspondence*, 186–187; S. R. Anderson to Nicholson, Nov. 21, 1855, Mar. 15, 1856, PiNYHS; Plitt to Buchanan, Oct. 16, 1855, Marcy to Buchanan, Oct. 29, 1855, Glancy Jones to Buchanan, Nov. 18, 1855, Albert Ramsey to Buchanan, Nov. 29, 1855, Tyler to Buchanan, Jan. 23, 1856, Forney to Buchanan, Feb. 3, 1856, Bowers to Buchanan, Feb. 24, 1856, John Stuart to Sanderson, Feb. 27, 1856, Upham to Buchanan, Mar. 3, 1856, H. Carver to Buchanan, May 27, 1856, Nathan Clifford to Buchanan, May 27, 1856, Van Dyke to Buchanan, May 30, 1856, BuHSP.

54. Upham to Buchanan, Apr. 9, 1855, Plitt to Buchanan, Apr. 8, 1854 (quoted), Apr. 1855, Hendrick Wright to Buchanan, May 1, 1855, Jenks to Buchanan, July 7, Aug. 18, Nov. 24, 1854, May 14, 1855, Seibels to Buchanan, July 2, Oct. 11, 1855 (quoted), May 8, 1856, John Houston to Buchanan, Aug. 6, 1855, Cobb to Buchanan, Dec. 5, 1854, Clover to Buchanan, June 15, 1854, Joseph Wright to Buchanan, Nov. 14, 1854, Charles Macalester to Buchanan, Jan. 1, 1855, Forney to Buchanan, Mar. 19, 1854 (quoted), Van Dyke to Buchanan, Nov. 11, 1855, Sanderson to Buchanan, Nov. 27, 1855, Sickles to Buchanan, Dec. 16, 1855, Bowers to Buchanan, Feb. 24, 1856, BuHSP; Charles McHatton to Breckinridge, Jan. 24, 1856 (quoted), BFLC; Francis Mallory to Hunter, May 11, 1856, in Hunter, *Correspondence*, 189–191; Halstead and Fisher, *Trimmers, Trucklers, and Temporizers*, 16–17.

55. Upham to Buchanan, Apr. 9, 1855, Plitt to Buchanan, Mar. 3, 1854, Apr. 1855, Hendrick Wright to Buchanan, May 1, 1855, Glancy Jones to Buchanan, May 18, Aug. 14, 1854, Oct. 12, Nov. 18, 1855, Feb. 27, Mar. 9, 1856, Jenks to Buchanan, Dec. 26, 1854, May 14, Sept. 27, Dec. 10, 1855, Robbins to Buchanan, Mar. 13, 1854, Forney to Buchanan, Mar. 19, May 25, 1854, July 13, Aug. 18, Aug. 21, Oct. 22, Nov. 25, 1855, Mar. 11, 1856, Slidell to Buchanan, Oct. 11, 1855, Jan. 17, Jan.

30, 1856, Randall to Buchanan, Nov. 19, 1855, Van Dyke to Buchanan, Nov. 27, 1855, John Barber to Buchanan, Feb. 23, 1856, Tyler to Buchanan, May 24, 1856, BuHSP; Jones, *J. Glancy Jones*, vol. 1, 329–343; *New York Tribune*, May 13, 1856, in Pike, *First Blows of the Civil War*, 323–333; Nichols, *Disruption of American Democracy*, 13; Buchanan to Glancy Jones, Nov. 30, Dec. 7, Dec. 18, 1855, Feb. 19, Mar. 7, Mar. 25, May 1, June 27, 1856, BJLC; Nichols, *Franklin Pierce*, 454–455; Forney, *Anecdotes of Public Men*, vol. 1, 13, 194; W. W. McKean to Breckinridge, Nov. 19, 1855, Forney to Breckinridge, Jan. 1856, Buchanan to Slidell, May 28, 1856 (quoted), BFLC; Johannsen, *Stephen A. Douglas*, 509; Klein, *President James Buchanan*, 251; Recollection of S. M. Barlow, in Curtis, *Life of James Buchanan*, 170–173.

56. Klein, *President James Buchanan*, 251–252; Buchanan to Pierce, Apr. 29, 1856, in Buchanan, *Works*, 78–79; Glancy Jones to Buchanan, May 8, 1854, May 9, 1855, Mar. 7, Mar. 22, Apr. 27, Apr. 28, 1856, Slidell to Buchanan, Oct. 18, 1854, Dec. 9, 1855, Jan. 17, 1856, Plitt to Buchanan, Apr. 1855, Oct. 16, 1855, Sanderson to Buchanan, May 2, 1855, Forney to Buchanan, May 12, 1855, Feb. 3, Apr. 23, 1856, Jenks to Buchanan, May 14, May 27, July 16, Sept. 27, Oct. 15, Dec. 10, 1855, Jan. 18, 1856, Marcy to Buchanan, May 28, 1855, Seibels to Buchanan, July 2, 1855, Wise to Buchanan, Aug. 10, 1855 (quoted), Tyler to Buchanan, Nov. 12, 1855, Jan. 23, May 24, 1856, John Heist to Forney, Nov. 15, 1855, R. Emmet Monaghan to Buchanan, Dec. 3, 1855, Van Dyke to Buchanan, Dec. 3, 1855, Joseph Wright to Buchanan, Jan. 14, 1856, Sickles to Buchanan, Feb. 3, 1856, Sanders to Buchanan, Mar. 25, 1856, John Cook to Buchanan, Apr. 24, 1856, John Appleton to Buchanan, Apr. 26, 1856, Ch. Jas. Faulkner to Buchanan, June 1, 1856, BuHSP; Curtis, *Life of James Buchanan*, 169; Halstead and Fisher, *Trimmers, Trucklers, and Temporizers*, 18.

57. Johannsen, *Stephen A. Douglas*, 478–483; W. D. Leatitrae to Lanphier, Nov. 9, 1855, Robert Smith to Lanphier, Nov. 23, 1855, LaLPL; H. V. Wilson to Breckinridge, Jan. 21, Feb. 3 (quoted), 1856, Douglas to Breckinridge, Sept. 12, Sept. 22, 1855, BFLC; Douglas to James Stone, Sept. 11, 1855, in SDL, 340–341.

58. Johannsen, *Stephen A. Douglas*, 478–483, 507; Slidell to Buchanan, Feb. 7, 1856, Sanders to Buchanan, May 24, 1856, H. Carver to Buchanan, May 27, 1856 (quoted), BuHSP.

59. Johannsen, *Stephen A. Douglas*, 483–484, 491–504, 506–510, 512–513; Douglas to Lanphier and George Walker, Oct. 15, 1855, Douglas to George Jones, Oct. 15, 1855, Douglas to Cobb, Oct. 6, 1855, Jan. 8, 1856 (quoted), Douglas to James Singleton, Mar. 5, Mar. 16, 1856, in SDL, 342–343, 344, 346–347, 349–350, 351.

60. Van Der Weele, "Jesse David Bright," 157–161, 164; Nichols, *Disruption of American Democracy*, 13; Van Dyke to Buchanan, Apr. 12, Nov. 11, 1855, Sickles to Buchanan, Aug. 15, 1854 (quoted), J. Watson Webb to Buchanan, Apr. 27, 1856, Slidell to Buchanan, Feb. 7, Mar. 11 (quoted), 1856, Glancy Jones to Buchanan, Feb. 27, 1856, Tyler to Buchanan, May 24, 1856, Corcoran to Buchanan, May 27, 2856, BuHSP; D. Cooper to Breckinridge, Apr. 16, 1855, Douglas to Breckinridge, May 25, 1855, R. B. Carlton to H. M. Rice, Aug. 6, 1855, Bright to Breckinridge, Oct. 30, 1854, Oct. 5, 1855, William Newton to Breckinridge, Sept. 11, Oct. 10, 1855, Richardson to Breckinridge, Nov. 2, 1855, BFLC; Bright to Hunter, Sept. 2, 1854, July 29, 1855, John Dawson to Hunter, June 2, Aug. 10, Aug. 25, Aug. 26, 1855, in Hunter, *Correspondence*, 158–59, 163–64, 168, 168–69, 169–70, 170–71;

Douglas to Breckinridge, Sept. 7, 1854, in SDL, 328–329; Johannsen, *Stephen A. Douglas*, 510; Forney, *Anecdotes of Public Men*, vol. 1, 19.

61. Van Der Weele, "Jesse David Bright," 164–171; Douglas to James Sheahan, Feb. 6, 1855, in SDL, 333–334; Schimmel, "William H. English," 356–360, 401–402; Johannsen, *Stephen A. Douglas*, 510; Klein, *President James Buchanan*, 225; Isaac Smith to English, Jan. 22, 1856, P. M. Kent to English, Mar. 7, Mar. 9, 1856, J. B. W. to English, May 23, 1856, H. to English, June 13, 1856, J. A. Cravens to English, June 13, 1856, EnIHS; Halstead and Fisher, *Trimmers, Trucklers, and Temporizers*, 45; Wallace, *Lew Wallace*, 236, 248–250; Thornbrough, *Indiana in the Civil War*, 71; Van Dyke to Buchanan, Nov. 27, 1855, Joseph Wright to Buchanan, Jan. 14 (quoted), May 26, 1856, BuHSP.

Chapter 6

1. John Slidell to Buchanan, Oct. 18, 1854, May 2, May 24, 1856, Alfred Gilmore to Buchanan, Feb. 26, 1856, John Forney to Buchanan, May 2, 1856, William Corcoran to Buchanan, May 27, 1856, BuHSP; James Bayard to Corcoran, July 10, 1848, CoLC; Van Der Weele, "Jesse David Bright," 172–173; Johannsen, *Stephen A. Douglas*, 515; Klein, *President James Buchanan*, 255; Recollection of S. M. Barlow, in Curtis, *Life of James Buchanan*, 170–173; Nichols, *Disruption of American Democracy*, 3–5, 12.

2. Van Der Weele, "Jesse David Bright," 174–175; Nichols, *Disruption of American Democracy*, 3–4, 14–15, 17; Recollection of S. M. Barlow, in Curtis, *Life of James Buchanan*, 170–172; Johannsen, *Stephen A. Douglas*, 515; Klein, *President James Buchanan*, 225; Isaac Butts to Tilden, July 6, 1856, TiNYPL; James C. Van Dyke to Buchanan, May 23, May 30, 1856, Daniel Sickles to Buchanan, May 24, 1856, Telegram, May 30, 1856, Forney to Buchanan, May 26, 1856, Slidell to Buchanan, May 26, 1856, Corcoran to Buchanan, May 27, 1856, Robert Tyler to Buchanan, Telegram, May 30, 1856, Henry Magraw to Buchanan, May 31, 1856, BuHSP.

3. Van Der Weele, "Jesse David Bright," 175–176; Schimmel, "William H. English," 399–400, 402–403; Nichols, *Disruption of American Democracy*, 15; Thornbrough, *Indiana in the Civil War*, 71; William Richardson to Douglas, June 1, 1856 (quoted), Stephen Douglas Papers found in Van Der Weele, "Jesse David Bright," 176; Corcoran to Buchanan, May 31, 1856, Jonathan Folts to Buchanan, June 2, 1856, BuHSP.

4. Nichols, *Franklin Pierce*, 467; Halstead and Fisher, *Trimmers, Trucklers, and Temporizers*, 42, 45; Johannsen, *Stephen A. Douglas*, 515–517; Thavenet, "William Alexander Richardson," 178; Unknown to Buchanan, May 31, 1856, BuHSP.

5. Halstead and Fisher, *Trimmers, Trucklers, and Temporizers*, 23; H. M. Rice to John Breckinridge, Feb. 12, 1856, BFLC; Toombs to T. Lomax, June 6, 1855 (quoted), in TSC, 351–353; Colfax to C. G. Powell, Oct. 24, 1855, SCLL; Glancy Jones to Buchanan, Mar. 7 (quoted), May 30, 1856, Hendrick Wright to Buchanan, May 28, 1856, Van Dyke to Buchanan, May 30, 1856, George Martin to Buchanan, May 31, 1856, BuHSP.

6. Democratic Party, *Official Proceedings, 1856*, 3, 13–15; Halstead and Fisher, *Trimmers, Trucklers, and Temporizers*, 25–27, 30; Van Der Weele, "Jesse David Bright," 177–178; Johannsen, *Stephen A. Douglas*, 517; Thavenet, "William Alexander Richardson," 178–179; Curtis, *Life of James Buchanan*, 171.

7. Democratic Party, *Official Proceedings, 1856*, 15–18; Johannsen, *Stephen A. Douglas*, 517; G. R. Barrett to Buchanan, June 2, 1856, William Bigler, Telegram to Buchanan, June 2, 1856, BuHSP; Halstead and Fisher, *Trimmers, Trucklers, and Temporizers*, 31–32, 35, 42; John Ward to Cobb, June 3, 1856 (quoted), in TSC, 367; Jones, *J. Glancy Jones*, vol. 1, 347.

8. Johannsen, *Stephen A. Douglas*, 517; Halstead and Fisher, *Trimmers, Trucklers, and Temporizers*, 33–41, 39 (quoted); Douglas to Richardson, June 3, 1856, in SDL, 361; Schimmel, "William H. English," 405–406; Democratic Party, *Official Proceedings, 1856*, 23–30; Nichols, *Disruption of American Democracy*, 49; Walther, *William Lowndes Yancey*, 127.

9. Democratic Party, *Official Proceedings, 1856*, 34–43; Van Der Weele, "Jesse David Bright," 177–178; Halstead and Fisher, *Trimmers, Trucklers, and Temporizers*, 46–49; Recollection of S. M. Barlow, in Curtis, *Life of James Buchanan*, 171–172; Johannsen, *Stephen A. Douglas*, 518; Schimmel, "William H. English," 407.

10. Van Der Weele, "Jesse David Bright," 177–178; Johannsen, *Stephen A. Douglas*, 518–519; Nichols, *Disruption of American Democracy*, 17; Democratic Party, *Official Proceedings, 1856*, 44–45, 45–58, 60–61; Halstead and Fisher, *Trimmers, Trucklers, and Temporizers*, 50–53, 56; Schimmel, "William H. English," 407; Thavenet, "William Alexander Richardson," 180–181; Holt, "Political Career of Richardson," 240; Douglas to Richardson, June 3 ("withdrawal" quote), June 5, 1856, in SDL, 361, 362.

11. Democratic Party, *Official Proceedings, 1856*, 46–58, 60–63, 66–67; Van Der Weele, "Jesse David Bright," 177–178; Schimmel, "William H. English," 407; Halstead and Fisher, *Trimmers, Trucklers, and Temporizers*, 53, 56, 59–61; Slidell to Breckinridge, June 17, 1856, BFLC; Johannsen, *Stephen A. Douglas*, 519; Nichols, *Disruption of American Democracy*, 17.

12. Archibald Dixon to Breckinridge, June 9, 1856, BFLC; Anbinder, *Nativism and Slavery*, 202–209; Finkelman, *Millard Fillmore*, 133–134; Nichols, *Disruption of American Democracy*, 19–20, 41; Julian, *Political Recollections*, 145, 152–154, 153 (quoted).

13. Julian, *Political Recollections*, 152–154; Holt, "Another Look," in Birkner, *James Buchanan*, 42–44; Isaac Holmes to A. P. Butler, Mar. 17, 1856, in Hunter, *Correspondence*, 182–183; A. M. Marinad to William Holman, Sept. 4, 1856, Holman Papers, Lilly Library; Stephens to unknown, Aug. 12, 1856, in Johnston and Browne, *Life of Stephens*, 314–315; Cobb to Buchanan, Aug. 3, 1856 (quoted), in TSC, 378–379; James Guthrie to Breckinridge, July 3, 1856, BFLC.

14. Buchanan to Nahum Capen, Aug. 27, 1856, in Buchanan, *Works*, 88; Gienapp, *Origins of the Republican Party*, 348–351; "The Cogitations of a Traveler in the Eastern States to His Friend in Washington," Oct. 1, 1855 (quoted), MaNYSL; Wise, *Recollections of Thirteen Presidents*, 53; Julian, *Political Recollections*, 152–153.

15. Julian, *Political Recollections*, 152–153; Klein, *President James Buchanan*, 257–258; Nichols, *Disruption of American Democracy*, 43; Summers, *Plundering Generation*, 240; Pierce to Breckinridge, July 22, 1856, BFLC; Anbinder, *Nativism and Slavery*, 224–226; Holt, "Another Look," in Birkner, *James Buchanan*, 45.

16. Benjamin Taylor to Corcoran, Sept. 27, 1856, CoLC; Klein, *President James Buchanan*, 257–258; "Speech at Wheatland," Nov. 6, 1856, in Buchanan, *Works*, 96–97; Buchanan to Glancy Jones, June 29, 1856 (quoted), BJLC; Sinha, *Counterrevolution of Slavery*, 189–190; Buchanan to Capen, Aug. 27, 1856 (quoted), in Curtis, *Life of*

James Buchanan, 180; Nichols, *Disruption of American Democracy*, 42–43; Julian, *Political Recollections*, 152; Democratic State Committee to Tilden, Sept. 15, 1856, TiNYPL.

17. Klein, *President James Buchanan*, 259; Nichols, *Disruption of American Democracy*, 44; I. Chadbourne to Horatio Seymour, Sept. 15, 1856, SeNYSL; Horace Greeley to Pike, Sept. 21, 1856, in Pike, *First Blows of the Civil War*, 348; Stephens to Thomas Thomas, June 16, 1856, James Branham to Cobb, Sept. 15, 1856 (quoted), in TSC, 367–372, 381–382; Stampp, *America in 1857*, 9; Buchanan to William Reed, Sept. 14, 1856, in Buchanan, *Works*, 91–92.

18. *Indianapolis Daily Sentinel*, July 16, 1856, found in Thornbrough, *Indiana in the Civil War*, 75; Schimmel, "William H. English," 396–399, 408, 438–439; Bright to Burke, Nov. 12, Dec. 23, 1856, EBLC; Summers, *Plundering Generation*, 241.

19. Bright to Burke, Nov. 12, Dec. 23, 1856, EBLC; Bright to Corcoran, Oct. 12 ("confident" quote), Oct. 25 ("clinch" quote), 1856, CoLC; Bright to Breckinridge, Oct. 20, 1856, BFLC.

20. Thornbrough, *Indiana in the Civil War*, 76–78; Schimmel, "William H. English," 409–456; Anbinder, *Nativism and Slavery*, 241; Bright to English, Oct. 20, 1856 (quoted), P. M. Kent to English, Mar. 7, Mar. 9, July 1, July 5, 1856, W. C. K. to English, June 12, 1856, J. A. Cravens to English, June 13, June 25, 1856, H. Commingore to English, June 13, 1856, EnIHS; Certificate of Election, State of Indiana, Dec. 31, 1856, EnISL; Van Der Weele, "Jesse David Bright," 190–191.

21. S. B. Jewett to Breckinridge, Aug. 2, 1856, John Taylor to Breckinridge, Nov. 12, 1856 (quoted), A. Birdsall to Breckinridge, Aug. 19, 1856, BFLC; Hinman, *Daniel Dickinson*, 143; Horace Greeley to Pike, Aug. 6, 1856, Charles Dana to Pike, July 24, 1856 (quoted), in Pike, *First Blows of the Civil War*, 346–347; Nichols, *Disruption of American Democracy*, 45–46; Meerse, "James Buchanan," 21; Summers, *Plundering Generation*, 240.

22. Birdsall to Breckinridge, Aug. 19, 1856, Buchanan to Breckinridge, Sept. 2 (quoted), Sept. 25, 1856, BFLC; Klein, *President James Buchanan*, 259; Curtis, *Life of James Buchanan*, 174; Cobb to Buchanan, July 27, 1856 (quoted), in TSC, 377–378; Anbinder, *Nativism and Slavery*, 238–239, 242; Richard Brodhead to Coryell, Sept. 24, 1856, CoHSP; Coleman, *Disruption of Pennsylvania Democracy*, 88–89, 92, 95–96; Buchanan to Capen, Aug. 27, 1856, in Curtis, *Life of James Buchanan*, 180; Buchanan to Glancy Jones, July 6, July 11, July 24, July 29, 1856, BJLC; Glancy Jones to A. O. P. Nicholson, Nov. 18, 1855, J. Glancy Jones Letter, NYHS; Jones, *J. Glancy Jones*, vol. 1, 344–345, 347; Forney, *Anecdotes of Public Men*, vol. 2, 237–240; Nichols, *Disruption of American Democracy*, 47; Dusinberre, *Civil War Issues in Philadelphia*, 27–28, 30; Meerse, "James Buchanan," 99; Forney to John Dix, Sept. 11, 1856, Dix to Forney, Sept. 15, 1856, in Dix, *Memoirs*, 2:321; Summers, *Plundering Generation*, 241; Buchanan to William Reed, Sept. 14, 1856, in Curtis, *Life of James Buchanan*, 182.

23. Buchanan to Breckinridge, Sept. 25, 1856, William Preston to Breckinridge, Oct. 11, 1856 (quoted), Glancy Jones to Breckinridge, Nov. 17, 1856, BFLC; Nichols, *Disruption of American Democracy*, 46–47; Coleman, *Disruption of Pennsylvania Democracy*, 90–101; Meerse, "James Buchanan," 21; Forney, *Anecdotes of Public Men*, vol. 2, 240 (quoted); Dusinberre, *Civil War Issues in Philadelphia*, 31–32, 41–42; Curtis, *Life of James Buchanan*, 175; Jones, *J. Glancy Jones*, vol. 1, 345, 347; Glancy Jones to W. Grandin, Oct. 31, 1856, HGUVA; W. Grandin to Hunter, Oct. 18, 1856 (quoted), in Hunter, *Correspondence*, 199–200.

24. Johannsen, *Stephen A. Douglas*, 522–523, 533–534; Douglas to James Sheahan, July 9, 1856 (quoted), in SDL, 365–366; Hansen and Nygard, "Democratic Party in Illinois," 116–118; Trumbull to Palmer, May 21, July 31, Aug. 3, 1856, in Trumbull, "Letters to Palmer," 30–33; Thavenet, "William Alexander Richardson," 175–176.

25. Johannsen, *Stephen A. Douglas*, 535–538; Trumbull to Palmer, July 31, Aug. 3, 1856, in Trumbull, "Letters to Palmer," 31–33; Douglas to Buchanan, Sept. 29, 1856 (quoted), Douglas to Sheahan, Oct. 6, 1856, in SDL, 367–368, 368–369; Thavenet, "William Alexander Richardson," 185–186, 188, 193; Holt, "Political Career of Richardson," 241–242; Hansen and Nygard, "Democratic Party in Illinois," 119; H. M. Rice to Breckinridge, Nov. 16, 1856, BFLC; Richard Yates to Logan Reavis, Nov. 29, 1856 (quoted), ReCHS.

26. Buchanan to Joshua Bates, Nov. 6, 1856 (quoted), in Buchanan, *Works*, 98–99; Julian, *Political Recollections*, 154–155; Anbinder, *Nativism and Slavery*, 243; Holt, "Another Look," in Birkner, *James Buchanan*, 39; Stampp, *America in 1857*, 28; Stephens, *Constitutional View*, 2:257; Curtis, *Life of James Buchanan*, 177; John Taylor to Breckinridge, Nov. 12, 1856 (quoted), BFLC; Millard Fillmore to Corcoran, Nov. 10, 1856, CoLC; Johannsen, *Stephen A. Douglas*, 537; Forney, *Anecdotes of Public Men*, vol. 2, 238; Nichols, *Disruption of American Democracy*, 48; Bright to Burke, Nov. 12, 1856 (quoted), EBLC.

27. Julian, *Political Recollections*, 156; Nichols, *Disruption of American Democracy*, 48; Trumbull to Palmer, Dec. 2, 1856 (quoted), in Trumbull, "Letters to Palmer," 33–34; Johannsen, *Stephen A. Douglas*, 538; Stampp, *America in 1857*, 11, 28.

28. John Cunningham to Breckinridge, Nov. 7, 1856 (quoted), BFLC; http://bioguide.congress.gov/scripts/biodisplay.pl?index=B000459; http://www.portal.state.pa.us/portal/server.pt/community/1790-1879/4283/william_bigler/444242; "Longstreth and Bigler Most Popular in Quakerdom," *New York Herald* (New York, NY), July 20, 1848; George Plitt to Buchanan, Oct. 2, 1851, BJLC; "Democratic State Convention—Bigler Nominated," June 6, 1851, "Governor Bigler," June 3, 1854, *North American and United States Gazette* (Philadelphia, PA); "Hon. Wm. Bigler," *Daily South Carolinian* (Columbia, SC), Jan. 25, 1856; William Denlinger to Bigler, Mar. 18, 1850, Glancy Jones to Bigler, May 22, June 10, Aug. 21, 1850, Oct. 18, Oct. 31, 1851, A. Boyd Hamilton to Bigler, June 26, 1850, Morris Longsheth to Bigler, Aug. 15, 1850, J. G. McKinly to George Sanderson, Aug. 17, 1850, Sanderson to Bigler, Aug. 20, 1850, Buchanan to Bigler, Mar. 24, Oct. 18, 1851, A. Beaumont to Bigler, Oct. 24, 1851, T. M. Pettit to Bigler, Oct. 22, 1851, Bigler to Buchanan, Oct. 28, 1851, BiHSP; Daniel Jenks to Buchanan, July 7, Oct. 3, Oct. 13, Oct. 17, 1854, Sanderson to Buchanan, June 22, Oct. 24, 1854, Forney to Buchanan, Mar. 19, May 25, 1854, Jan. 3, 1856, Van Dyke to Buchanan, Mar. 22, 1854, Slidell to Buchanan, Mar. 25, 1854, Jan. 3, 1856, Plitt to Buchanan, Apr. 8, 1854, J. Franklin Reigatt to Buchanan, July 28, 1854, BuHSP; Meerse, "James Buchanan," 93.

29. Jenks to Buchanan, Oct. 17, Dec. 26, 1854, Mar. 6, Apr. 17, Dec. 30, 1855, Jan. 4 (quoted), Jan. 18, 1856, Sanderson to Buchanan, Oct. 24, 1854 (quoted), Nov. 27, 1855, Feb. 1, 1856, Van Dyke to Buchanan, Apr. 15, Nov. 11, Nov. 27, 1855, Jan. 18, 1856, Forney to Buchanan, Oct. 29, Nov. 25, 1855, Glancy Jones to Buchanan, Feb. 4, 1856, BuHSP; http://bioguide.congress.gov/scripts/biodisplay.pl?index=B000459.

30. Glancy Jones to Buchanan, Feb. 27, Mar. 22, 1856, Van Dyke to Buchanan, Mar. 9, 1856, Forney to Buchanan, Mar. 11, 1856, Slidell to Buchanan, Mar. 11, 1856, Victor Piollet to Buchanan, Mar. 1856, Bigler to Buchanan, Jan. 19, 1856, Jenks to Buchanan, Jan. 26, 1856, BuHSP; draft of speech on the inferiority of blacks and the righteousness of slavery (quoted), draft of speech supporting the Fugitive Slave Law, BiHSP; "Colonel Bigler," July 29, 1851, "Bigler and the Abolitionists," Oct. 11, 1851, *North American and United States Gazette* (Philadelphia, PA); "Hon. Wm. Bigler," *Daily South Carolinian* (Columbia, SC), Jan. 25, 1856.

31. Van Der Weele, "Jesse David Bright," 192, 194; Murphy, *Political Career of Bright*, 126–127; Thornbrough, *Indiana in the Civil War*, 78; Nichols, *Disruption of American Democracy*, 88; Meerse, "James Buchanan," 114; Schimmel, "William H. English," 462; Bright to Corcoran, Jan. 27, 1857, CoLC.

32. http://bioguide.congress.gov/scripts/biodisplay.pl?index=F000158; Graham Fitch to Lanman, Biographical sketch, 1858, LaIHS; Biographical sketch of Graham Newell Fitch, P. M. Kent to English, Jan. 23, 1857, EnIHS; Schimmel, "William H. English," 462 (quoted); Julian, *Political Recollections*, 117; Colfax to Pratt, Mar. 26, 1849, July 12, 1851, Daniel Pratt Papers, ISL; Bright to Corcoran, Jan. 15 (quoted), Jan. 16, Jan. 27, 1857, CoLC.

33. Schimmel, "William H. English," 462–463; Meerse, "James Buchanan," 114–115; Van Der Weele, "Jesse David Bright," 194–197; Murphy, *Political Career of Jesse Bright*, 127; Aquilla Jones to Davis, Feb. 20, 1857, Thomas Clark to Davis, Feb. 20, 1857, A. M. Pratt to Davis, Feb. 25, 1857, Lee Woods to Davis, Mar. 4, 1857, Caucus agreement signed by twenty members (quoted), DaIHS; W. F. Sherrod to English, Jan. 30, 1857, EnIHS; Bright to Corcoran, Jan. 30, 1857 (quoted), CoLC.

34. Murphy, *Political Career of Jesse Bright*, 127–128; Van Der Weele, "Jesse David Bright," 197–200, 207; Woollen, *Sketches of Early Indiana*, 227; Fitch to Breckinridge, Feb. 4, 1857, BFLC; S. S. Crow to English, Feb. 5, 1857, EnIHS; Chauncey Carter to Davis, Dec. 2, 1857, John Defrees to Davis, Oct. 30, 1858, Austin Brown to Davis, Dec. 23, 1857 (quoted), May 13, 1858, David Gooding to Davis, Dec. 19, 1857, A. C. Pepper to Davis, Feb. 17, 1857, A. Sovering to Davis, May 2, 1858, DaIHS; Bright to Corcoran, Feb. 4, 1857 (quoted), Samuel Barlow to Corcoran, Feb. 11, 1857, CoLC; *CG*, 34C-3S, 626.

35. Van Der Weele, "Jesse David Bright," 209–211, 216 (quoted); *CG*, 35C-1S, 1659; Nichols, *Disruption of American Democracy*, 176; Murphy, *Political Career of Jesse Bright*, 128–130; Woollen, *Sketches of Early Indiana*, 227–228; Defrees to Davis, Oct. 30, 1858, DaIHS.

36. Nichols, *Disruption of American Democracy*, 52; Stampp, *America in 1857*, 48–49; Van Dyke to Buchanan, Feb. 23, 1855, BuHSP; Toombs to Stephens, Dec. 1, 1856 (quoted), in TSC, 383–384.

37. Nichols, *Disruption of American Democracy*, 54–56; James Buchanan Henry to George Curtis, in Curtis, *Life of James Buchanan*, 187; Klein, *President James Buchanan*, 264–265; Stampp, *America in 1857*, 57; Dickinson to Brown, Jan. 24, 1857, in Dickinson, *Speeches, Correspondence, Etc.*, 500; Buchanan to Glancy Jones, Dec. 8, 1856, BJLC; Toombs to Thomas, Feb. 5, 1857, in TSC, 394–395; Schimmel, "William H. English," 264–265; Murphy, *Political Career of Jesse Bright*, 130; S. S. Crow to English, Feb. 5, 1857, Bright to English, Apr. 16, 1857, EnIHS; Bright to Corcoran, Jan. 16, Jan. 27 (quoted), 1857, CoLC; Van Der Weele, "Jesse David Bright," 202.

38. Nichols, *Disruption of American Democracy*, 56–57; Stampp, *America in 1857*, 51, 57–58, 76; Cobb to wife, Jan. 6, 1857, Robert McLane to Cobb, Feb. 14, 1857, Forney to Cobb, Feb. 18, 1857, Toombs to Stephens, Feb. 24, 1857, in TSC, 389, 395–396, 396–397, 397–398; Meerse, "James Buchanan," 176–180; Dickinson to Rogers, Dec. 25, 1856, Dickinson to Brown, Jan. 24, 1857, in Dickinson, *Speeches, Correspondence, Etc.*, 499–500, 500; Isaiah Rynders to Buchanan, Feb. 5, 1855, BuHSP; Hinman, *Daniel Dickinson*, 145, 147; Buchanan to Glancy Jones, Dec. 8, 1856 (quoted), Buchanan to Henry Wise, Dec. 26, 1856 (quoted), BJLC.

39. Nichols, *Disruption of American Democracy*, 58, 62–63; Thomas Harris to Lanphier, Jan. 7, 1857, LaLPL; Stampp, *America in 1857*, 58–60; Johannsen, *Stephen A. Douglas*, 551–552; Douglas to Samuel Treat, Dec. 20, 1856, Feb. 5, 1857, in SDL, 369–370, 372; Meerse, "James Buchanan," 130; Meerse, "Origins of Buchanan-Douglas Feud," 159–160; Klunder, *Lewis Cass*, 285–286; Buchanan to Lord Clarendon, Feb. 23, 1857, in Buchanan, *Works*, 102–03; Gienapp, "Leadership," in Birkner, *James Buchanan*, 101; C. W. C. Dunnington to Hunter, July 25, 1857, in Hunter, *Correspondence*, 213–214.

40. Van Der Weele, "Jesse David Bright," 204–205; Schimmel, "William H. English," 468–469; Nichols, *Disruption of American Democracy*, 66; Klein, *President James Buchanan*, 267; Bright to Breckinridge, Mar. 30, 1857, BFLC; Robert McLane to Cobb, Feb. 14, 1857, in TSC, 395–396; Thomas Clark to Davis, Feb. 20, 1857 (quoted), Aquilla Jones to Davis, Feb. 20, 1857, Pratt to Davis, Feb. 25, 1857, Carter to Davis, June 26, 1857, DaIHS; Meerse, "James Buchanan," 115, 217; C. W. C. Dunnington to Hunter, July 25, 1857, in Hunter, *Correspondence*, 213–214; Joseph Wright to Allen Hamilton, Sept 26, 1857, Holman Misc., Lilly Library; Marcy to Robert McClelland, Apr. 6, 1857, Diary entry, Apr. 9, 1857, in Marcy, "Diary and Memoranda," 649–650, 650; Klunder, *Lewis Cass*, 286–287.

41. Marcy to McClelland, Apr. 6, 1857, Apr. 9, 1857, in Marcy, "Diary and Memoranda," 649–650, 650; Klunder, *Lewis Cass*, 286–287; Buchanan to Lord Clarendon, Feb. 23, 1857, Lord Clarendon to Buchanan, Mar. 13, 1857, in Buchanan, *Works*, 102–103, 114–115; Lewis Cass to Belmont, Mar. 9, 1857, BeNYPL.

42. Nichols, *Disruption of American Democracy*, 67, 72, 77–79; Stampp, *America in 1857*, 52, 61–62; Curtis, *Life of James Buchanan*, 193–194, 211; Coleman, *Disruption of Pennsylvania Democracy*, 103, 105; Mar. 4, Mar. 20, 1857, in Marcy, "Diary and Memoranda," 641–62, 644–645; Buchanan to Cobb, Feb. 21, 1857, Toombs to Stephens, Feb. 24, 1857, in TSC, 397, 397–398; Bigler to Buchanan, Feb. 17, 1857, John Cochrane to Glancy Jones, Feb. 18, 1857, Henry May to Glancy Jones, Feb. 25, 1857, in Jones, *J. Glancy Jones*, vol. 1, 349, 357, 367–369; Buchanan to Jeremiah Black, Mar. 6, 1857, in Buchanan, *Works*, 114; Buchanan to Glancy Jones, Nov. 29, 1856, Feb. 17, Feb. 22, Feb. 28, July 28, 1857, BJLC; William Ludlow to Tilden, July 1857, TiNYPL; Gienapp, "Leadership," in Birkner, *James Buchanan*, 98, 101–102; Harris to Lanphier, Jan. 3, 1857, LaLPL; Douglas to Treat, Feb. 5, 1857 (quoted), in SDL, 372.

43. Nichols, *Disruption of American Democracy*, 60; Fehrenbacher, *Dred Scott Case*, 307.

44. Allen, *Origins of Dred Scott Case*, 140–152; Fehrenbacher, *Dred Scott Case*, 194–195, 264–265, 267–276, 279–280, 286, 290, 305.

45. John Catron to Buchanan, Feb. 6, Feb. 10, 1857, BuHSP; Nichols, *Disruption of American Democracy*, 64; Fehrenbacher, *Dred Scott Case*, 307.

46. Legal historian Austin Allen downplays Buchanan's role and contends that the broad *Scott* ruling was shaped more by the court's previous rulings than by partisan politics. Allen, *Origins of Dred Scott Case*, 152–159; Catron to Buchanan, Feb. 19, Feb. 23, 1857, Robert Grier to Buchanan, Feb. 23, 1857, BuHSP; Nichols, *Disruption of American Democracy*, 64–66; Fehrenbacher, *Dred Scott Case*, 234, 307–312; Johannsen, *Stephen A. Douglas*, 547; Forney, *Anecdotes of Public Men*, vol. 2, 227, 230.

47. Nichols, *Disruption of American Democracy*, 68–69, 76–77; Klein, *President James Buchanan*, 269–270; James Buchanan Henry to Curtis, in Curtis, *Life of James Buchanan*, 187; Foote, *Casket of Reminiscences*, 111–112; Wise, *Recollections of Thirteen Presidents*, 60–61.

48. Klein, *President James Buchanan*, 271; Johannsen, *Stephen A. Douglas*, 545; Fehrenbacher, *Dred Scott Case*, 312; Clay-Clopton, *Belle of the Fifties*, 63.

49. Nichols, *Disruption of American Democracy*, 71; Klein, *President James Buchanan*, 271–272; Fehrenbacher, *Dred Scott Case*, 313–314; James Buchanan Henry to Curtis, in Curtis, *Life of James Buchanan*, 187–193; Foote, *Casket of Reminiscences*, 111 (quoted); Hunt, *Inaugural Addresses*, 176–178 (quoted); "The Triumph of Slavery," *New York Tribune*, Mar. 5, 1857, in Pike, *First Blows of the Civil War*, 365–367.

50. Klein, *President James Buchanan*, 278–280; Meerse, "James Buchanan," 22, 55–63, 78, 180; Van Dyke to Buchanan, Feb. 23, 1855, BuHSP; Buchanan to John Y. Mason, Dec. 29, 1856, in Buchanan, *Works*, 100–101; F. Bigger to English, Mar. 30, 1857, EnIHS; Mar. 17, Mar. 24, Mar. 25, Apr. 4, 1857, Marcy to McClelland, Apr. 6, 1857, Unknown to Marcy, Mar. 27, 1857 (quoted), in Marcy, "Diary and Memoranda," 642–643, 645–646, 646–47, 647, 648–49, 649–650; Glancy Jones to Burke, Feb. 9, 1857, EBLC; Black to Breese, Aug. 7, 1858, J. Cook to Breese, Sept. 21, 1858, SBLPL; Summers, *Plundering Generation*, 27–28.

51. Meerse, "James Buchanan," 56–63, 65–67, 122–138; Summers, *Plundering Generation*, 27–28, 239, 242–248; Buchanan to John Y. Mason, Dec. 29, 1856, in Buchanan, *Works*, 100–101; Bigger to English, Mar. 30, 1857, EnIHS; Klein, *President James Buchanan*, 280–281, 284; Mar. 17 (quoted), Mar. 24 (quoted) 1857, Unknown to Marcy, Mar. 27, 1857, in Marcy, "Diary and Memoranda," 647; Nichols, *Disruption of American Democracy*, 83–85, 91; Johannsen, *Stephen A. Douglas*, 550, 554–555; Douglas to Treat, Feb. 5, 1857, in SDL, 372; Buchanan to Wise, Dec. 26, 1856, BJLC; Dix, *Memoirs*, 2:327; W. B. Maclay to Burke, Dec. 16, 1856, EBLC; Gienapp, "Leadership," in Birkner, *James Buchanan*, 102–103; Stephen Dillaye to Cobb, June 8, 1858 (quoted), in TSC, 439; W. M. Corry to Hammond, Nov. 11, 1858 (quoted), HaLC; "Ruin of the Democratic Party."

52. For a recent and comprehensive study of the Taney Court, see Allen, *Origins of Dred Scott Case*. Fehrenbacher, *Dred Scott Case*, 1–3, 226–227, 234, 315–321, 323; http://www.aoc.gov/cc/capitol/oscc.cfm; Julian, *Political Recollections*, 158–159; Forney, *Anecdotes of Public Men*, vol. 2, 226–227 (quoted); Johannsen, *Stephen A. Douglas*, 548–549; "Decision of the Supreme Court," *New York Tribune*, Mar. 8, 1857 (quoted), in Pike, *First Blows of the Civil War*, 367–370; Allen, *Origins of Dred Scott Case*, 1–2, 134, 160–169, 178–187, 192.

53. For outstanding discussions of slavery and the Constitution, see Finkelman, *Slavery and the Founders* and Cooper, *Liberty and Slavery*. Allen, *Origins of Dred Scott Case*, 134–135, 202; Fehrenbacher, *Dred Scott Case*, 3; Julian, *Political Recollections*, 159 (quoted); "Decision of the Supreme Court," *New York Tribune*, Mar. 8, 1857, in

Pike, *First Blows of the Civil War*, 367–370; Giddings, *History of the Rebellion*, 403–404 (quoted).

54. For explanation of the connections between the *Scott* ruling and the economic crisis, see Jenny Wahl, "*Dred*, Panic, War: How a Slave Case Triggered Financial Crisis and Civil Disunion," in Finkelman and Kennon, *Congress and Crisis*, 159–202; Stampp, *America in 1857*, 223–230; Cobb to Buchanan, Aug. 4, 1858, Cobb to Stephens, Oct. 9, 1857 (quoted), in TSC, 440–441, 424–425; Bigelow to Bryant, Oct. 12 (quoted), Dec. 28, 1857, BiNY PL; Buchanan, First Annual Message, http://www.presidency.ucsb.edu/ws/index.php?pid=29498; Klein, *President James Buchanan*, 314–315.

55. *Inaugural Addresses*, 183; Nichols, *Disruption of American Democracy*, 52–53; Klein, *President James Buchanan*, 317; Curtis, *Life of James Buchanan*, 211–212; May, "Invasions," in Birkner, *James Buchanan*, 124; Klunder, *Lewis Cass*, 288.

56. Klein, *President James Buchanan*, 317; Buchanan, First Annual Message, http://www.presidency.ucsb.edu/ws/index.php?pid=29498 (quoted); "The Southern Convention," *New York Times* (New York, NY), Dec. 15, 1856; "Southern Convention—Knoxville, Ten.," July 7, 1857, "Southern Commercial Conventions," Aug. 3, 1857, *Daily National Intelligencer* (Washington, DC).

57. Buchanan, First Annual Message, http://www.presidency.ucsb.edu/ws/index.php?pid=29498; May, "Invasions," in Birkner, *James Buchanan*, 126–127, 130–131; Klein, *President James Buchanan*, 319–320; May, *Manifest Destiny's Underworld*, 43–45, 49; Scroggs, *Filibusters and Financiers*, 286–307, 308–323, 337–341; Stephens to Linton Stephens, Jan. 3, 1858 (quoted), in Johnston and Browne, *Life of Stephens*, 328; Giddings, *History of the Rebellion*, 414; Bigelow to Bryant, Dec. 28, 1857 (quoted), BiNY PL.

58. May, *Manifest Destiny's Underworld*, 50–51, 53, 66–67, 75–76, 160; Scroggs, *Filibusters and Financiers*, 319, 325–327, 338–339, 341–347, 368, 390–391; May, "Invasions," in Birkner, *James Buchanan*, 128–130; Klein, *President James Buchanan*, 319–320; Giddings, *History of the Rebellion*, 414–416; Stephens to Linton Stephens, Jan. 3, Jan. 20, 1858, in Johnston and Browne, *Life of Stephens*, 328, 328–329; Buchanan, Message to the Senate, Jan. 7, 1858, in Buchanan, *Works*, 171–175; Bigelow to Bryant, Dec. 28, 1857, BiNY PL.

59. Klein, *President James Buchanan*, 320–324; Buchanan, Second Annual Message, http://www.presidency.ucsb.edu/ws/index.php?pid=29499 (quoted); Buchanan, "Message on the Protection of Isthmian Routes," Feb. 18, 1859, "Message on a Treaty with Nicaragua," Dec. 19, 1859, in Buchanan, *Works*, 296–299, 371–372; Klunder, *Lewis Cass*, 290, 292; Curtis, *Life of James Buchanan*, 219–222.

60. Klein, *President James Buchanan*, 321–322, 324–325; Buchanan to Christopher Fallon, Dec. 14, 1857, in Buchanan, *Works*, 165; Fehrenbacher, *Slaveholding Republic*, 130–131; Dodge to Cass, Nov. 10, 1858 (quoted), United States Legation notes, Aug. 1857, DoIC; Klunder, *Lewis Cass*, 289–290; Buchanan, First Annual Message, http://www.presidency.ucsb.edu/ws/index.php?pid=29498; Buchanan, Second Annual Message, http://www.presidency.ucsb.edu/ws/index.php?pid=29499 (quoted).

61. Sinha, *Counterrevolution of Slavery*, 125–152; "Flourishing Condition of the African Slave Trade," *Liberator* (Boston, MA), Jan. 1, 1858; Curtis, *Life of James Buchanan*, 213–214; "The Slave Trade—Piracy," *Charleston Mercury* (Charleston, SC),

May 22, 1858; Stephens to unknown, in Johnston and Browne, *Life of Stephens*, 336; Fehrenbacher, *Slaveholding Republic*, 184–186; "The Duty of Our Government," *Mississippian and State Gazette* (Jackson, MS), June 16, 1858; "What Should Be Done about the 'British Outrages," May 18, 1858, "The Right of Search in Parliament," June 20, 1858, "The Right of Search, Important Debate on the African Slave Trade," Aug. 7, 1858, *New York Herald* (New York, NY); "Activity of the Slave Trade," *New York Tribune*, Feb. 16, 1860, in Pike, *First Blows of the Civil War*, 491–493.

Chapter 7

1. William Miles to Hammond, Nov. 10, 1858, HaLC; Etcheson, *Bleeding Kansas*, 113; Nichols, *Disruption of American Democracy*, 53.

2. Etcheson, *Bleeding Kansas*, 91–92, 112–115, 118, 131; Nichols, *Franklin Pierce*, 441–444, 473–475, 478, 481–483; Pierce, Fourth Annual Message, http://www.presidency.ucsb.edu/ws/index.php?pid=29497.

3. John Geary to Pierce, Dec. 22, 1856 (quoted), Jan. 12, 1857 (quoted), PiLC; Etcheson, *Bleeding Kansas*, 131, 136–137, 139–141, 143–144; Trumbull to Palmer, Dec. 2, 1856, in Trumbull, "Letters to Palmer," 33–34; Nichols, *Franklin Pierce*, 486; Pierce, Fourth Annual Message, http://www.presidency.ucsb.edu/ws/index.php?pid=29497; Klein, *President James Buchanan*, 291.

4. Etcheson, *Bleeding Kansas*, 143–144; Klein, *President James Buchanan*, 291; Foote, *Casket of Reminiscences*, 110.

5. For the extent of proslavery voter fraud in Kansas, see Summers, *Plundering Generation*, 248–251; Etcheson, *Bleeding Kansas*, 141–158; Klein, *President James Buchanan*, 291, 296–297; Republican Congressional Committee, 1857–1859, "Ruin of the Democratic Party," 6–7.

6. Klein, *President James Buchanan*, 293, 300, 309; Meerse, "James Buchanan," 285–286; Julian, *Political Recollections*, 162; Norman Eddy to Davis, Nov. 26, 1857 ("swindle" quote), A. J. Smedley to Davis, Feb. 5, 1858, J. B. Otey to Davis, Feb. 7, 1858, DaIHS; "Ruin of the Democratic Party," 6 (Walker quote), 8 ("grand fraud" quote); Etcheson, *Bleeding Kansas*, 158–159; Thomas Thomas to Stephens, June 15, 1857 (quoted), Feb. 7, 1858, Joseph Brown to Stephens, Feb. 9, 1858, Cobb to Stephens, June 18, 1857, Toombs to W. W. Burwell, July 11, 1857, in TSC, 400–401, 429–431, 431–432, 402–403, 403–404; Sinha, *Counterrevolution of Slavery*, 192; Hunter to Shelton Leake, Oct. 16, 1857 (quoted), in Hunter, *Correspondence*, 237–241; Foote, *Casket of Reminiscences*, 114–115; Buchanan to James Denver, Mar. 27, 1858, in Buchanan, *Works*, 200–201; Douglas to Robert Walker, July 21, 1857, in SDL, 386–387; Howell Cobb to unknown Southern Democrat, July 27, 1857, WaNYHS.

7. Klein, *President James Buchanan*, 293–294 (quoted), 295 (quoted); Cobb to Stephens, June 18, July 21, Sept. 12, Sept. 19, Oct. 9, 1857, Toombs to Burwell, July 11, 1857, in TSC, 402–403, 406–407, 422–423, 423–424, 424–425, 403–404; Cobb to unknown Southern Democrat, July 27, 1857, Douglas to Walker, July 21, 1857, WaNYHS; Foote, *Casket of Reminiscences*, 118; "Ruin of the Democratic Party," 8; William Miles to Hammond, Nov. 10, 1858, HaLC.

8. Klein, *President James Buchanan*, 300–301; Etcheson, *Bleeding Kansas*, 156–157, 159; Nichols, *Disruption of American Democracy*, 154; Johannsen, *Stephen A. Douglas*, 581, 586.

9. Johannsen, *Stephen A. Douglas*, 582–583; Thomas Harris to Lanphier, Dec. 1, 1857 (quoted), LaL PL.

10. Johannsen, *Stephen A. Douglas*, 586; Etcheson, *Bleeding Kansas*, 160; Harris to Lanphier, Dec. 3, 1857 (quoted), LaL PL; Smith Miller to English, Dec. 28, 1857, EnIHS; Douglas to Lanphier, Dec. 6, 1857 (quoted), in SDL, 405.

11. *CG*, 35C-1S, 4–5; *Appendix to the CG*, 35C-1S, 1–7; Buchanan, First Annual Message, http://www.presidency.ucsb.edu/ws/index.php?pid=29498; Etcheson, *Bleeding Kansas*, 159; Klein, *President James Buchanan*, 301; Nichols, *Disruption of American Democracy*, 150, 153; Johannsen, *Stephen A. Douglas*, 589; Giddings, *History of the Rebellion*, 405 (quoted); Julian, *Political Recollections*, 161 (quoted).

12. *CG*, 35C-1S, 5, 14–22.

13. Klein, *President James Buchanan*, 300; J. B. Norman to English, Dec. 30, 1857, EnIHS; James Hood to Davis, Dec. 11, 1857, Michael Shannon to Davis, Dec. 15, 1857, H. K. Wilson to Davis, Dec. 15, 1857 ("woeful" quote), B. H. Cornwell to Davis, Dec. 16, 1857, David Gooding to Davis, Dec. 19, 1857, Austin Brown to Davis, Dec. 20, 1857, Gordon Tanner to Davis, Dec. 22, 1857, James Hood to Davis, Dec. 26, 1857, J. L. Benson to Davis, Jan. 1, 1858, Daniel F. to Davis, Jan. 1, 1858, Jerry Smith to Davis, Jan. 1, 1858, A. G. Porter to Davis, Jan. 2, 1858, Ezra Read to Davis, Dec. 28, 1857, Jan. 4, 1858, George Sample to Davis, Dec. 21, 1857, Norman Eddy to Davis, Dec. 24, 1857 ("cannot" quote), DaIHS.

14. "Memorandum of Interview, Burlingame and Colfax with Douglas, at his residence, Dec 14, 1857, 8:30–11:30pm," SCISL; Klein, *President James Buchanan*, 302; George Ashman to Walker, Dec. 1, 1857, WaNYHS; Etcheson, *Bleeding Kansas*, 160; Nichols, *Disruption of American Democracy*, 154; Douglas to Walker, July 21, 1857, in SDL, 386–387; Douglas to McClernand, Nov. 23, 1857, McCL PL; Bigelow to Bryant, Dec. 28, 1857, BiNY PL.

15. *CG*, 35C-1S, 47–52 (quoted).

16. *CG*, 35C-1S, 113–118, 119–121; Harris to Lanphier, Dec. 21, 1857, LaL PL.

17. *CG*, 35C-1S, 137–140.

18. Etcheson, *Bleeding Kansas*, 165–166; Douglas to John Forney et al., Feb. 6, 1858 (quoted), Feb. 15, 1858 (quoted), in SDL, 408–410, 413; *CG*, 35C-1S, 570–571; Johannsen, *Stephen A. Douglas*, 605.

19. *CG*, 35C-1S, 919–920; *Appendix to the CG*, 35C-1S, 87, 96, 112–115; Johannsen, *Stephen A. Douglas*, 606–607.

20. *Appendix to the CG*, 35C-1S, 163–166; Van Der Weele, "Jesse David Bright," 218–219.

21. *Appendix to the CG*, 35C-1S, 194–201; Johannsen, *Stephen A. Douglas*, 607; *CG*, 35C-1S, 1264–1265; Etcheson, *Bleeding Kansas*, 174.

22. Etcheson, *Bleeding Kansas*, 175; Klein, *President James Buchanan*, 308–310; Van Der Weele, "Jesse David Bright," 217–218; Stephens to Linton Stephens, Jan. 3, 1858, Jan. 20, 1858 (quoted), in Johnston and Browne, *Life of Stephens*, 328, 328–329; Harris to Lanphier, Jan. 21, Jan. 28, Feb. 9, 1858, LaL PL; James Hood to Davis, Dec. 11, 1857, Michael Shannon to Davis, Dec. 15, 1857, DaIHS; Buchanan to Joseph Baker, Jan. 11, 1858 (quoted), in Buchanan, *Works*, 176–177.

23. Cox and Northrup, *Life of Cox*, 5, 29–31, 33–36, 38, 40–62, 70–72; Wells, "Political Career of Cox," 1–2; Lindsey, *"Sunset" Cox*, 3–7.

24. Cox and Northrup, *Life of Cox*, 61–62, 67, 69–72, 77; Lindsey, *"Sunset" Cox*, 7–11, 14–15; Forney, *Anecdotes of Public Men*, vol. 1, 283; Cox, *Buckeye Abroad*; Wells, "Political Career of Cox," 4–5.

25. Wells, "Political Career of Cox," 1, 5–6, 7, 8–10; Lindsey, *"Sunset" Cox*, 15 (quoted), 16, 18; Cox and Northrup, *Life of Cox*, 77, 79–80; Forney, *Anecdotes of Public Men*, vol. 1, 283; Cox, *Eight Years in Congress*, 13.

26. Cox and Northrup, *Life of Cox*, 80–81; *CG*, 35C-1S, 53–57; Lindsey, *"Sunset" Cox*, 22–23; Cox, *Eight Years in Congress*, 14; Wells, "Political Career of Cox," 13.

27. Cox, *Eight Years in Congress*, 14; "Ruin of the Democratic Party," 12; Johannsen, *Stephen A. Douglas*, 604; Cox and Northrup, *Life of Cox*, 81; Wells, "Political Career of Cox," 13; Meerse, "James Buchanan," 309; Giddings, *History of the Rebellion*, 408; Harris to Lanphier, Dec. 3, Dec. 21, 1857, Jan. 21 (quoted), Jan. 28, Feb. 9, 1858, LaL PL; Forney, *Anecdotes of Public Men*, vol. 2, 247; Trumbull to Palmer, May 20, 1858 (quoted), in Trumbull, "Letters to Palmer," 36–38; Bigelow to Bryant, Feb. 11, 1858 (quoted), BiNY PL.

28. Nichols, *Disruption of American Democracy*, 157–158; Wells, "Political Career of Cox," 19–20.

29. *CG*, 35C-1S, 533–535; Klein, *President James Buchanan*, 309–310; Johannsen, *Stephen A. Douglas*, 604; Buchanan, *Mr. Buchanan's Administration*, 33, 42; "Message on the Constitution of Kansas," Feb. 2, 1858, in Buchanan, *Works*, 179–192; Stephens to Linton Stephens, Feb. 3, 1858, in Johnston and Browne, *Life of Stephens*, 329; Edmund Burke to Bright, Feb. 18, 1858 (quoted), in Van Der Weele, "Jesse David Bright," 217; A. J. Smedley to Davis, Feb. 5, 1858 (quoted), DaIHS; Etcheson, *Bleeding Kansas*, 169.

30. Stephens to Linton Stephens, Feb. 5, 1858 (quoted), in Johnston and Browne, *Life of Stephens*, 329–330; *CG*, 35C-1S, 596–606; Etcheson, *Bleeding Kansas*, 169; Nichols, *Disruption of American Democracy*, 159–160; Klein, *President James Buchanan*, 310; "Grow on Keitt," *New York Tribune*, Feb. 6, 1858, in Pike, *First Blows of the Civil War*, 379–380.

31. Nichols, *Disruption of American Democracy*, 160–162; Bigelow to Bryant, Feb. 11, 1858, BiNY PL; *CG*, 35C-1S, 621–622; Klein, *President James Buchanan*, 310.

32. Joseph Brown to Stephens, Feb. 9 (quoted), Mar. 26, 1858, in TSC, 431–432, 432–433; Harris to Lanphier, Feb. 10, 1858 (quoted), MiLC; Harris to McClernand, Feb. 16, 1858, McCL PL; Eddy to Davis, Nov. 27, 1857, DaIHS; James Givry to English, Mar. 24, 1858 (quoted), EnIHS; Colfax to Powell, Feb. 17, 1858, SCISL.

33. Ezra Read to Davis, Dec. 28, 1857, A. Severing to Davis, Feb. 7, 1858, DaIHS; George McConnell to Lanphier, Dec. 1857 / Jan. 1858 (quoted), LaL PL; Summers, *Plundering Generation*, 252; Etcheson, *Bleeding Kansas*, 169–170; Johannsen, *Stephen A. Douglas*, 602; Meerse, "James Buchanan," 313, 316; Douglas to Sam Treat, Feb. 28, 1858, in SDL, 418; Summers, "Press," in Birkner, *James Buchanan*, 83–84; "Ruin of the Democratic Party," 9–10.

34. "Ruin of the Democratic Party," 9–14 (quoted); Summers, "Press," in Birkner, *James Buchanan*, 81, 86; Summers, *Plundering Generation*, 45; Etcheson, *Bleeding Kansas*, 170; Coleman, *Disruption of Pennsylvania Democracy*, 105, 113–114; Douglas to McClernand, Feb. 21, 1858, McCL PL; Douglas to Treat, Feb. 28, 1858 (quoted), in SDL, 418; Meerse, "James Buchanan," 298–299; Forney, *Anecdotes of Public Men*, vol. 1, 13 (quoted), 15; Forney, *Anecdotes of Public Men*, vol. 2, 86, 247; Buchanan to Joseph Baker, Jan. 11, 1858, in Buchanan, *Works*, 376–377.

35. A. M. P. to Davis, Jan. 18, 1858, Eli Davis to Davis, Jan. 18, 1858, Harry Wilson to Davis, Jan. 30, 1858, M. McKee to Davis, Feb. 10, 1858, DaIHS; Thornbrough, *Indiana in the Civil War*, 80–81; Schimmel, "William H. English," 540–541, 543; Meerse, "James Buchanan," 321, 333–33; Summers, *Plundering Generation*, 252; Cox and Northrup, *Life of Cox*, 83; Wells, "Political Career of Cox," 22; Lindsey, *"Sunset" Cox*, 26; "Ruin of the Democratic Party," 12; Cox, *Eight Years in Congress*, 14.

36. Stephens to Linton Stephens, Mar. 1858 (quoted), Mar. 11, Mar. 12, 1858, in Johnston and Browne, *Life of Stephens*, 330–331; Douglas to New York Anti-Lecomptonites, Feb. 11, 1858 (quoted), in SDL, 411–412.

37. Nichols, *Disruption of American Democracy*, 166; Schimmel, "William H. English," 1–16, 18–20, 29, 36–38, 43–52, 66–67; English to Holman, Aug. 1850, Holman Papers, Lilly Library; Bright to English, Nov. 8, 1842, Apr. 21, 1843, EnIHS.

38. Schimmel, "William H. English," 61, 64–67, 78–79, 87–89, 93, 99–101, 117, 122; English to Holman, Aug. 1850, Holman Papers, Lilly Library; Bright to English, Oct. 14, Dec. 21, Dec. 23, 1850, Dec. 16, 1851, Jan. 26, Feb. 10, Feb. 16, May 15, Aug. 22, Nov. 21 (quoted), Dec. 5, 1852, Jan. 25, 1853, EnIHS; Johannsen, *Stephen A. Douglas*, 356.

39. Schimmel, "William H. English," 127–149, 164–166, 184–185, 188–189, 204–251, 266; Certificate of Election, State of Indiana, Oct. 12, 1852, Bright to English, Jan. 31, 1854 (quoted), EnIHS.

40. Schimmel, "William H. English," 281–287, 292–293, 372–380, 385–386, 392, 403, 458; E. Sugg to English, Jan. 1, 1855, P. M. Kent to English, Mar. 7, Mar. 9, 1856, Bright to English, Oct. 20, 1856, EnIHS; *Appendix to the CG*, 34C-1S, 289; *CG*, 35C-1S, 1016; Certificate of Election, State of Indiana, Oct. 1856, EnIHS.

41. Schimmel, "William H. English," 473–482, 536–537; *Appendix to the CG*, 34C-3S, 105–108; J. A. Cravens to English, Jan. 24, 1858, W. W. Wick to English, Feb. 8, Mar. 6, 1858, J. B. Norman to English, Mar. 5, 1858, EnIHS.

42. A. Severing to Davis, Feb. 7, 1858 (quoted), DaIHS; J. B. Norman to English, Dec. 30, 1857, Feb. 7, 1858, EnIHS; Schimmel, "William H. English," 545–554; *CG*, 35C-1S, 1013–1017 (quoted).

43. Schimmel, "William H. English," 558–560, 564–565; Van Der Weele, "Jesse David Bright," 219–220; Joseph Low to English, Mar. 10, 1858, A. Sovering to English, Mar. 21, 1858, J. A. Cravens to English, Mar. 21, 1858, L. G. Matthews to English, Mar. 21, Mar. 29, 1858, John S. to English, Mar. 26, 1858, James Givry to English, Mar. 24, 1858, Aswill Woolley to English, Mar. 29, 1858, M. C. Kerr to English, Mar. 27, 1858 (quoted), Bright to English, Mar. 9, 1858 (quoted), EnIHS.

44. L. G. Matthews to English, Mar. 29, 1858, Buchanan to Cobb, Mar. 31, 1858, EnIHS; Schimmel, "William H. English," 569–570 (quoted), 572–574.

45. Schimmel, "William H. English," 574, 576–578, 580–581; Etcheson, *Bleeding Kansas*, 176; Buchanan to Cobb, Mar. 31, 1858 (quoted), EnIHS.

46. *CG*, 35C-1S, 1435–1438; Stephens to Linton Stephens, Apr. 2, 1858, in Johnston and Browne, *Life of Stephens*, 332; Schimmel, "William H. English," 581–582, 616; Wells, "Political Career of Cox," 23, 25; Lindsey, *"Sunset" Cox*, 27; Cox and Northrup, *Life of Cox*, 83; "Ruin of the Democratic Party," 12; Cox, *Eight Years in Congress*, 15 (quoted); A. Lovering to Davis, Apr. 1858 (quoted), DaIHS; S. S. Marshall to Lanphier, Apr. 1, 1858 (quoted), LaLPL; Colfax to unknown, Apr. 10, 1858, SCISL.

47. *CG*, 35C-1S, 1557–1559, 1589–1590; Eddy to Davis, Apr. 15, 1858, DaIHS; Schimmel, "William H. English," 583–584, 586; Stephens to Linton Stephens, Apr. 7, 1858, in Johnston and Browne, *Life of Stephens*, 332; Meerse, "James Buchanan," 321–353; Summers, *Plundering Generation*, 252–254; Richards, *Slave Power*, 205.

48. *CG*, 35C-1S, 1627; Stephens to R. M. J., Apr. 17, 1858, in Johnston and Browne, *Life of Stephens*, 332; Schimmel, "William H. English," 591–594; Owen Lovejoy to Pike, Apr. 20, 1858 (quoted), in Pike, *First Blows of the Civil War*, 417.

49. Nichols, *Disruption of American Democracy*, 170–171; Toombs to Buchanan, Apr. 18, 1858 (quoted), in TSC, 433; Julian, *Political Recollections*, 162.

50. Schimmel, "William H. English," 596–598, 601–603; Nichols, *Disruption of American Democracy*, 171–172; Julian, *Political Recollections*, 162; Eddy to Davis, Apr. 27, 1858 (quoted), Unknown Hoosier to Davis, May 1, 1858 (quoted), DaIHS; *CG*, 35C-1S, 1743.

51. *CG*, 35C-1S, 1765, 1766 ("expedients" quote); Schimmel, "William H. English," 604–605.

52. *CG*, 35C-1S, 1765–1767, 1812; Schimmel, "William H. English," 605–615; W. W. Wick to Davis, Apr. 25, 1858, DaIHS; Stephens to R. M. J., Apr. 29, 1858 ("tide" quote), in Johnston and Browne, *Life of Stephens*, 333; Harris to Lanphier, Apr. 29, 1858 ("miserable" quote), LaLPL.

53. *CG*, 35C-1S, 1880–1882, 1905 (quoted); Schimmel, "William H. English," 616–617; Wells, "Political Career of Cox," 25.

54. *CG*, 35C-1S, 1897, 1899, 1904–1906; Schimmel, "William H. English," 624; Wells, "Political Career of Cox," 31–32; Etcheson, *Bleeding Kansas*, 181; Buchanan, *Mr. Buchanan's Administration*, 45; Meerse, "James Buchanan," 354–356; "Ruin of the Democratic Party," 10 (quoted), 12–13; Harris to Lanphier, Apr. 30, 1858 (quoted), LaLPL; Ezra Read to Davis, May 2, 1858 (quoted), H. H. Gifford to Davis, May 15, 1858, DaIHS.

55. Lindsey, *"Sunset" Cox*, 27–28; Cox, *Eight Years in Congress*, 13; Cox, *Union-Disunion-Reunion*, 55–59; Buchanan to English, May 22, July 2 (quoted), 1858, S. S. English to English, May 4, 1858 (quoted), EnIHS.

56. *CG*, 35C-1S, 19–22, 1766.

57. *CG*, 35C-1S, 4–5, 138; *Appendix to the CG*, 35C-1S, 1–5; Etcheson, *Bleeding Kansas*, 141–152.

58. *CG*, 35C-1S, 137–138.

59. *Appendix to the CG*, 35C-1S, 163–166.

60. *Appendix to the CG*, 35C-1S, 163–166.

61. Jones, *J. Glancy Jones*, vol. 2, 18; Schimmel, "William H. English," 624–625 ("bad men" quote); Curtis, *Life of James Buchanan*, vol. 2, 207; David Provencel to English, May 21, 1858, EnIHS; Phillips, *Life of Robert Toombs*, 130 ("rejoice" quote); Joseph Brown to Stephens, May 7, 1858 ("forbear" quote), in TSC, 434.

62. Etcheson, *Bleeding Kansas*, 182; A. Sovering to Davis, May 2, 1858 (quoted), DaIHS.

Chapter 8

1. Colfax to Powell, Feb. 17, 1858 (quoted), SCISL.

2. J. L. Benson to Davis, Jan. 1, 1858, Daniel F. to Davis, Jan. 1, 1858, G. M. E. Griffith to Davis, Jan. 11, 1858, J. W. Osborn to Davis, Jan. 13, 1858, John McNaman to Davis, Jan. 19, Feb. 11, 1858, Soloman Akers to Davis, Jan. 25, 1858, Michael Branson to Davis, Feb. 1, 1858, James Lucas to Davis, Mar. 28, 1858, James Hood to Davis, Apr. 12, 1858, A. Sovering to Davis, May 2, 1858, Norman Eddy to Davis, Apr. 27, 1858 (quoted), S. H. Buskirk to Davis, Feb. 3, 1858 (quoted), unknown Hoosier to Davis, May 1, 1858, Ezra Read to Davis, Feb. 17, 1858 (quoted), A. B. Conduitt to Davis, Feb. 1, 1858, DaIHS.

3. Thornbrough, *Indiana in the Civil War*, 81; Jerry Smith to Davis, Jan. 1, 1858 ("vampires" quote), A. M. P. to Davis, Jan. 18, 1858, J. A. Wright to Davis, Jan. 21, 1858, J. B. Otey to Davis, Jan. 21, 1858 ("misrepresent" quote), A. J. Smedley to Davis, Feb. 5, 1858, James M. to Davis, Feb. 6, 1858, M. McKee to Davis, Feb. 10, 1858, S. A. Hall to Davis, Feb. 13, 1858, Ezra Read to Davis, Jan. 4 ("rascality" quote), Feb. 17, 1858, W. D. Greencastle to Davis, Feb. 16, 1858, B. J. Clark to Davis, Feb. 19, 1858, Milt Osborne to Davis, Feb. 21, 1858, Henry Brenan to Davis, Feb. 26, 1858, J. H. Crooks to Davis, Mar. 22, 1858, C. Carter to Davis, Apr. 26, 1858, DaIHS; Colfax to Stailey et al., June 8, 1858, SCISL; M. C. Kerr to English, Jan. 23, 1858, J. B. Norman to English, Jan. 24, Feb. 7, 1858, Horace H. to English, Jan. 30, 1858, James Morrison to English, Feb. 16, 1858, James Mitchell to English, Apr. 22, 1858 ("presume" quote), EnIHS; Van Der Weele, "Jesse David Bright," 220.

4. Thornbrough, *Indiana in the Civil War*, 81; Van Der Weele, "Jesse David Bright," 226–228; J. B. Norman to English, Jan. 24, Mar. 5, 1858, W. W. Wick to English, Jan. 26, Mar. 13, 1858, Unknown to English, Mar. 22, 1858, EnIHS; D. E. Williamson to Davis, Jan. 12, 1858 ("defiance" quote), A. M. P. to Davis, Jan. 18, 1858, Eli Davis to Davis, Jan. 18, 1858 ("Bright & Fitch" quote), Soloman Akers to Davis, Jan. 25, 1858, James Hood to Davis, Jan. 25, Mar. 2, 1858, Harry Wilson to Davis, Jan. 30, 1858, A. B. Conduitt to Davis, Feb. 1, 1858, C. B. Goodnight to Davis, Feb. 1, 1858, A. J. Smedley to Davis, Feb. 4, 1858, M. McKee to Davis, Feb. 10, 1858, Milt Osborne to Davis, Feb. 21, May 22, 1858, J. B. Otey to Davis, Feb. 25, 1858, George Sample to Davis, Mar. 1, 1858, Solomon Garrigus to Davis, Mar. 13, 1858, Samuel Fisher to Davis, Mar. 16, 1858, Norman Eddy to Davis, Apr. 25, 1858, Austin Brown to Davis, May 13, 1858, H. H. Gifford to Davis, May 15, 1858, W. H. Sibley to Davis, June 16, 1858, W. D. Shepherd to Davis, Oct. 13, 1858, William Daily to Davis, Nov. 22, 1858, DaIHS.

5. A. Sevring to Davis, Feb. 7, 1858, A. Lovering to Davis, Mar. 1858 ("Judas" quote), C. Carter to Davis, Apr. 26, 1858, Ezra Read to Davis, May 2, 1858 (quoted), Solomon Akers to Davis, July 8, 1858, W. D. Shepherd to Davis, Oct. 13, 1858, J. B. Ryan to Davis, Oct. 14, 1858, Winston Pierce to Davis, Oct. 21, 1858, George Sample to Davis, Nov. 9, 1858, Austin Brown to Davis, Jan. 16, 1859, DaIHS; John Bekin et al. to Thompson, Aug. 23, 1858, ThISL; Schimmel, "William H. English," 633, 635–636, 642–645, 648–650, 664–667, 671–673; J. Merriwether to English, Mar. 20, 1858, P. M. Kent to English, Mar. 20, Apr. 22,

1858, W. M. French to English, Apr. 7, 1858, W. C. D. P. to English, Apr. 8, 1858, H. Heffren to English, May 15, 1858, J. B. Norman to English, May 21, 1858, James Buchanan to English, July 2, 1858, H. Comingore to English, July 12, 1858, W. W. Wick to English, Aug. 3, 1858, H. F. Feeney to English, Aug. 5, 1858, Certificate of Election, State of Indiana, Oct. 28, 1858, Lewis Jordan to English, Nov. 3, 1858, EnIHS; Nichols, *Disruption of American Democracy*, 219; Van Der Weele, "Jesse David Bright," 230; Thornbrough, *Indiana in the Civil War*, 82–83; Colfax to Kline, Oct. 18, 1858, SCISL.

6. Davis to Coryell, June 7, 1858 (quoted), CoHSP; Bigler to Unknown, May 10, 1859, BiHSP; Nichols, *Disruption of American Democracy*, 204–207; Summers, *Plundering Generation*, 255; Coleman, *Disruption of Pennsylvania Democracy*, 113–116; Dusinberre, *Civil War Issues in Philadelphia*, 78.

7. Coleman, *Disruption of Pennsylvania Democracy*, 116–117; Dusinberre, *Civil War Issues in Philadelphia*, 79; Buchanan to Harriet Lane, Oct. 15, 1858 (quoted), BJLC; Klein, *President James Buchanan*, 330; Forney, *Anecdotes of Public Men*, vol. 1, 120; Jones, *J. Glancy Jones*, vol. 2, 80, 86, 88, 91; Glancy Jones, 1858 speech (quoted), in Jones, *J. Glancy Jones*, vol. 2, 81–82.

8. Gideon Tucker to Burke, Mar. 16, 1859, EBLC; Peter Cagger to Tilden, Sept. 28, 1858, TiNYPL; Mushkat, *Fernando Wood*, 80–83, 83 (quoted); J. W. Byrdsall to Hammond, Nov. 13, 1858, HaLC.

9. Mushkat, *Fernando Wood*, 85–88; Nichols, *Disruption of American Democracy*, 207–208, 220; J. W. Byrdsall to Hammond, Nov. 13, 1858 (quoted), HaLC; Richards, *Slave Power*, 210; Horace Greeley to Pike, July 7, 1858, in Pike, *First Blows of the Civil War*, 422.

10. Pelzer, *Augustus Caesar Dodge*, 227–233, 237–238, 240–241, 248; Henry Dean to Bailey, June 12, 1858, Jan. 1859, BaDM; Dean to George Jones, Feb. 2, 1859, DeDM; Cook, *Baptism of Fire*, 111; Nichols, *Disruption of American Democracy*, 209–210, 219; Cox and Northrup, *Life of Cox*, 84–85.

11. George Jones to Hammond, Nov. 19, 1858 (quoted), HaLC; Douglas to Jacob Brown, Aug. 29, 1858 (quoted), DoLPL; Thavenet, "William Alexander Richardson," 212.

12. Johannsen, *Stephen A. Douglas*, 621–624, 627, 647; J. W. S. to Charles Lanphier, May 23, 1858, Thomas Harris to Lanphier, May 27, 1858, MiLC; William Wick to Davis, Apr. 25, 1858, DaIHS; Dean to Henry Wise, Nov. 11, 1858, DeCHS; Jeremiah Black to Breese, Apr. 7, Sept. 17, 1858, Philip Hoyne to Breese, Aug. 23, 1858, Isaac Cook to Breese, Aug. 27, Sept. 13, Sept. 21 (quoted), 1858, James Clarkson to Breese, Aug. 30, Sept. 9, 1858, A. G. Herndon to Breese, Sept. 13, 1858, SBLPL; Cobb to Stephens, Sept. 8, 1858, in TSC, 442–444; Thomas Harris to Lanphier, May 8, 1858 (quoted), LaLPL; Foote, *Casket of Reminiscences*, 121; Fehrenbacher, *Prelude to Greatness*, 112–113; Summers, *Plundering Generation*, 254–255; Thavenet, "William Alexander Richardson," 212; Trumbull to Palmer, June 19, 1858, in Trumbull, "Letters to Palmer," 38–40; Douglas to McClernand, Oct. 1, 1859, Lanphier to McClernand, Jan. 10, 1860, McCLPL; Buchanan to Joseph Holt, Aug. 4, 1859, in Buchanan, *Works*, 329.

13. Johannsen, *Stephen A. Douglas*, 624–631; Nichols, *Disruption of American Democracy*, 212–213, 215 (quoted); Klein, *President James Buchanan*, 328–329; Trumbull to Palmer, June 19, 1858, in Trumbull, "Letters to Palmer," 38–40.

14. Johannsen, *Stephen A. Douglas*, 619–620, 635–636; Douglas to James Cutts, June 22, 1858, in SDL, 422–423; Mushkat, *Fernando Wood*, 87; Richards, *Slave Power*, 209–210; Foote, *Casket of Reminiscences*, 121, 134–135; Fehrenbacher, *Prelude to Greatness*, 112–113; Dean to Henry Wise, Nov. 11, 1858 (quoted), DeCHS.

15. Johannsen, *Stephen A. Douglas*, 639–640; Fehrenbacher, *Prelude to Greatness*, 70–83; W. P. Boyd to John Crittenden, July 17, 1858, MiLC.

16. Nichols, *Disruption of American Democracy*, 214–215; Fehrenbacher, *Prelude to Greatness*, 99, 113–114; Johannsen, *Stephen A. Douglas*, 641–644, 648–649; Klein, *President James Buchanan*, 329; Dean to Henry Wise, Nov. 11, 1858 ("decapitated" quote), DeCHS; Douglas to Usher Linder, Aug. 1858 ("hounds" quote), in SDL, 427; Foote, *Casket of Reminiscences*, 135; Cox, *Eight Years in Congress*, 20 ("tiger" quote).

17. Douglas to the editor of the *Washington States*, Jan. 7, 1859, in SDL, 433–434; Cobb to Stephens, Sept. 8, 1858 (quoted), in TSC, 442–444; John Breckinridge to John Moore, Oct. 5, 1858, MiLC.

18. Johannsen, *Stephen A. Douglas*, 645, 648–649, 654, 656, 658, 664–666, 670; Allen, *Origins of Dred Scott Case*, 213–217; Cobb to Stephens, Sept. 8, 1858 (quoted), in TSC, 442–444; Fehrenbacher, *Prelude to Greatness*, 97–98, 101, 108, 112–113, 121–122; Douglas to Abraham Lincoln, July 24, July 30, 1858, in SDL, 423–424, 424–425; "Second Debate with Stephen A. Douglas at Freeport, Illinois," Aug. 27, 1858, in Lincoln, *Collected Works*, 38–76 (quoted).

19. Johannsen, *Stephen A. Douglas*, 666, 669, 677; Fehrenbacher, *Prelude to Greatness*, 107–108, 114–116; Amos Nourse to Pike, Jan. 25, 1859, in Pike, *First Blows of the Civil War*, 430–431; Douglas to Wise, Nov. 7, 1858, in SDL, 429; Lincoln to Henry Asbury, Nov. 19, 1858, Lincoln to Anson Miller, Nov. 19, 1858, in Lincoln, *Collected Works*, 339, 340; A. B. Florer to Davis, Nov. 10, 1858 (quoted), W. A. Gorman to Davis, Nov. 13, 1858 (quoted), DaIHS.

20. Schimmel, "William H. English," 674; Johannsen, *Stephen A. Douglas*, 680–681; Richards, *Slave Power*, 208, 211; Summers, *Plundering Generation*, 31; Nichols, *Disruption of American Democracy*, 219–221; John Tucker to Hunter, Nov. 6, 1858 (quoted), in Hunter, *Correspondence*, 269.

21. Johannsen, *Stephen A. Douglas*, 685–687, 694; Clay-Clopton, *Belle of the Fifties*, 138 (quoted); Davis to Miss Davis, Dec. 16, 1858 (quoted), DaIHS; Trumbull to Palmer, Dec. 19, 1858, in Trumbull, "Letters to Palmer," 41; S. S. Marshall to Lanphier, Dec. 9, 1858 (quoted), J. C. Allen to Lanphier, Dec. 13, 1858, LaLPL; Foote, *Casket of Reminiscences*, 136 (quoted); Douglas to Graham Fitch, Jan. 21, Jan. 22, 1859, in SDL, 435, 435–436.

22. Singleton to Douglas, Feb. 25, 1859, SiLPL; J. C. Allen to Lanphier, Dec. 13, 1858 (quoted), LaLPL; F. H. Keith to Davis, Jan. 2, 1859, DaIHS.

23. Buchanan, "Message, on the Death of the Postmaster-General," Mar. 9, 1859, in Buchanan, *Works*, 314; B. F. Hallett to Coryell, Mar. 8, 1859, CoHSP; Nichols, *Disruption of American Democracy*, 243–244, 246–247; "Incendiarism," Dec. 13, 1859, "Holt & Co. vs. Civilization," Dec. 27, 1859, "Incendiaries—Worse and Worse," Jan. 9, 1860, *New York Tribune*, in Pike, *First Blows of the Civil War*, 452–54, 455–56, 464–65; J. L. M. Curry to Burke, Jan. 13, 1860, EBLC; Dean to Henry Wise, Nov. 11, 1858 (quoted), DeCHS.

24. Mushkat, *Fernando Wood*, 87–90; Wood to Wise, Apr. 11, 1859, WoNYHS; Reverdy Johnson to Dickinson, Sept. 15, 1859, in Dickinson, *Speeches, Correspondence,*

Etc., 521–522; Gideon Tucker to Burke, Mar. 16, 1859, EBLC; Johannsen, *Stephen A. Douglas*, 702, 738.

25. Reverdy Johnson to Dickinson, Sept. 15, 1859, Judge Allen to Dickinson, Sept. 16, 1859, Dickinson to Mr. Rogers, Apr. 12, 1860, in Dickinson, *Speeches, Correspondence, Etc.*, 521–522, 531–533; Mushkat, *Fernando Wood*, 90–91; *Proceedings of the Democratic State Convention Held at Syracuse, N.Y., September 14 and 15, 1859* (Albany, 1859) found in MaNYSL; Johannsen, *Stephen A. Douglas*, 738–739; Hinman, *Daniel Dickinson*, 151–152; G. Hughes to Dickinson, Dec. 11, 1858, Wilbur Haywood to Dickinson, June 12, 1859, DiNew.

26. Johannsen, *Stephen A. Douglas*, 701–703; Egerton, *Year of Meteors*, 56; Bigler to unknown, May 10, 1859, Bigler Letters, NYHS; Buchanan to M. Johnson, Sept. 19, 1859 (quoted), BuNYHS; Singleton to Douglas, Feb. 25, 1859, SiLPL; Lincoln to Trumbull, Dec. 11, 1858, in Lincoln, *Collected Works*, 344–345.

27. Johannsen, *Stephen A. Douglas*, 702–704, 741; Douglas to Pierre Soulé, Dec. 1858, in Douglas, *Letters of Stephen A. Douglas*, 430; Venable, "Conflict between Douglas and Yancey," 231–232; John Forsyth to Douglas, May 9, 1860, DoLPL; Burnett, *Pen Makes a Good Sword*, 97–98, 100–107.

28. Venable, "Conflict between Douglas and Yancey," 232; A. C. Scott to Davis, Jan. 1, 1859 (quoted), DaIHS; Johannsen, *Stephen A. Douglas*, 703–704; Singleton to Douglas, Feb. 25, 1859, SiLPL; Douglas to Singleton, Mar. 31, 1859 (quoted), DoLPL.

29. Douglas to James Scofield, Mar. 1859, Douglas to J. B. Dorr, June 22, 1859, Douglas to the editors of the *San Francisco National*, Aug. 16, 1859, Douglas to Henry McCoy, Sept. 27, 1859, in SDL, 440, 446–447, 453–466, 468–469; Nichols, *Disruption of American Democracy*, 260; Johannsen, *Stephen A. Douglas*, 704.

30. Douglas to William Dunbar, Aug. 31, 1859, Douglas to Reverdy Johnson, Oct. 21, 1859, Douglas to Henry Raymond, Aug. 24, 1859, in SDL, 466–467, 477–478, 478; Johannsen, *Stephen A. Douglas*, 707–713; Douglas to Dickinson, Oct. 1, 1859 (quoted), in Dickinson, *Speeches, Correspondence, Etc.*, 523; Douglas to Peter Cagger, Feb. 19, 1860 (quoted), Douglas to William Seaver, July 17, 1859, DoLPL; Cobb to Buchanan, Nov. 14, 1859, Toombs to Stephens, Dec. 26, 1859, in TSC, 448–449, 451–452; Stephen Douglas, "The Dividing Line between Federal and Local Authority: Popular Sovereignty in the Territories," *Harper's Magazine*, Sept. 1859, http://harpers.org/archive/1859/09/.

31. Etcheson, *Bleeding Kansas*, 208–213; "John Brown," Oct. 29, 1859, *New York Tribune*, in Pike, *First Blows of the Civil War*, 449–450; Buchanan, *Mr. Buchanan's Administration*, 62; Giddings, *History of the Rebellion*, 424–425; Dusinberre, *Civil War Issues in Philadelphia*, 84–86; Horatio Seymour to J. V. L. Pruyn, Jan. 10, 1860 (quoted), GoNYSL; Sinha, *Counterrevolution of Slavery*, 207–208; Johannsen, *Stephen A. Douglas*, 716; John Letcher to Hunter, Dec. 9, 1859 (quoted), in Hunter, *Correspondence*, 274–275; Cobb to Buchanan, Nov. 14, 1859, in TSC, 448–449.

32. Sinha, *Counterrevolution of Slavery*, 208–209; Dusinberre, *Civil War Issues in Philadelphia*, 84; Giddings, *History of the Rebellion*, 425–426; Johannsen, *Stephen A. Douglas*, 716; Schimmel, "William H. English," 755–758; Wooster Sherman to Hunter, Dec. 10, 1859 (quoted), in Hunter, *Correspondence*, 277–278; Dickinson to Samuel Barlow, Dec. 17, 1859 (quoted), in Dickinson, *Speeches, Correspondence, Etc.*, 526–530; Coleman, *Disruption of Pennsylvania Democracy*, 119; Cobb to Buchanan, Nov. 14, 1859, in TSC, 448–449.

33. *CG*, 36C-1S, 1, 5–15; Toombs to Stephens, Dec. 26, 1859 (quoted), in TSC, 451–452; Johannsen, *Stephen A. Douglas*, 716, 722; Julian, *Political Recollections*, 168; Holman to Allen Hamilton, Dec. 28, 1859, Holman Papers, Lilly Library.

34. Johannsen, *Stephen A. Douglas*, 717–718; Schimmel, "William H. English," 751–753; McClernand to John Henry, Jan. 14, 1860, McCLPL; Giddings, *History of the Rebellion*, 428.

35. For a comprehensive examination of Hinton Helper and his work, see Brown, *Southern Outcast*. *CG*, 36C-1S, 2–5, 21, 52, 86–87, 152, 158, 160–161, 165, 170, 175, 188; Toombs to Stephens, Dec. 28, 1859, in TSC, 452–453; Thomas Kidd to Mc-Clernand, Dec. 16, 1859, McCLPL; Holman to Allen Hamilton, Dec. 28, 1859, Holman Papers, Lilly Library; Giddings, *History of the Rebellion*, 427–429; Julian, *Political Recollections*, 171–172; Helper, *Impending Crisis of the South*; Johannsen, *Stephen A. Douglas*, 718; Buchanan, *Mr. Buchanan's Administration*, 59 (quoted); Brown, *Southern Outcast*, 2–4, 8, 69, 72–80, 82–88, 91–107, 115–118, 124–126, 153–175, 179–182; "The Helper Book," Jan. 12, 1860, *New York Tribune* (quoted), in Pike, *First Blows of the Civil War*, 469–470.

36. *CG*, 36C-1S, 188, 189, 197, 198, 209, 219, 220, 235, 247, 256, 269, 274; Sinha, *Counterrevolution of Slavery*, 209–210; Johannsen, *Stephen A. Douglas*, 720; Trumbull to Richard Yates, Nov. 2, 1859, ReCHS; Toombs to Stephens, Dec. 26 (quoted), Dec. 28 (quoted), 1859, in TSC, 451–452; Buchanan, "Third Annual Message, Dec. 19, 1859" (quoted), in Buchanan, *Works*, 339–370; Josiah Robinson to Davis, Jan. 9, 1860, Davis to daughter, Jan. 10, 1860, DaIHS; Lanphier to McClernand, Dec. 27, 1859 (quoted), O. B. Ficklin to McClernand, Mar. 19, 1860, McCLPL; Mc-Clernand to Lanphier, Dec. 22, Dec. 27, Dec. 30 (quoted), 1859, Jan. 3, Jan. 14, 1860, LaLPL.

37. *CG*, 36C-1S, 312–317 (quoted); Schimmel, "William H. English," 761–765; McClernand to Lanphier, Feb. 11, 1860, LaLPL; McClernand to John Henry, Jan. 14, 1860, McCLPL.

38. *CG*, 36C-1S, 409–413, 587, 603, 607, 634, 650, 662; Toombs to Stephens, Jan. 31, 1860, in TSC, 458–459; Johannsen, *Stephen A. Douglas*, 720; Giddings, *History of the Rebellion*, 435; McClernand to Lanphier, Feb. 11, 1860, LaLPL.

39. *CG*, 36C-1S, 379–385, 420–426, 658–659 (quoted), 915–920; McClernand to Lanphier, Feb. 23, 1860, LaLPL; Johannsen, *Stephen A. Douglas*, 723–730; Sinha, *Counterrevolution of Slavery*, 194.

40. Sinha, *Counterrevolution of Slavery*, 194; Johannsen, *Stephen A. Douglas*, 730–731; Toombs to Stephens, Dec. 26, 1859, Feb. 10, 1860, in TSC, 451–452, 460–462; Phillips, *Life of Robert Toombs*, 183–184; *CG*, 36C-1S, 935; Holman to C. O'Brien, Feb. 15, 1860 (quoted), HOBIHS; "The Assault on Mr. Hickman," Feb. 13, 1860, *New York Tribune*, in Pike, *First Blows of the Civil War*, 486–489; Clay-Clopton, *Belle of the Fifties*, 142 (quoted); Cox, *Eight Years in Congress*, 17; McClernand to Lanphier, Apr. 4, 1860 (quoted), LaLPL.

41. *CG*, 36C-1S, 997–998; "Ruin of the Democratic Party," 10 ("object" quote), 4 ("drag" quote), 9–14; Summers, *Plundering Generation*, 257–259; Curtis, *Life of James*, vol. 2, 246–261; Coleman, *Disruption of Pennsylvania Democracy*, 122–123; Buchanan, "Message, on the Covode Investigation," Mar. 28, June 22, 1860, Buchanan to Mr. Stanton, June 10, 1860, Buchanan to James Bennett, June 18, 1860, in Buchanan, *Works*, 399–405, 433, 434, 435–443.

42. Thornbrough, *Indiana in the Civil War*, 88; Venable, "Conflict between Douglas and Yancey," 235; J. S. France to McClernand, Jan. 13, 1860, McCLPL; Van Der Weele, "Jesse David Bright," 230–232; William Daily to Davis, Nov. 22, Dec. 16 ("overthrow" quote), 1859, James Vawter to Davis, Dec. 7, 1858, David Snyder to Davis, Mar. 24, 1860, DaIHS.

43. Ezra Read to Davis, Jan. 16, 1860, Smith Jones to Davis, Feb. 11, 1860 (quoted), DaIHS; Van Der Weele, "Jesse David Bright," 232–235; Murphy, *Political Career of Bright*, 133–134; Holt, "Political Career of Richardson," 246; J. B. Norman to English, Jan. 20, 1860, J. A. Cravens to English, Jan. 31, 1860, EnIHS; Tredway, *Democratic Opposition to Lincoln*, 159; Johannsen, *Stephen A. Douglas*, 738; Holman to O'Brien, Jan. 25, 1860, HOBIHS.

44. Johannsen, *Stephen A. Douglas*, 732–734, 737–739; Buchanan to Arnold Plumer, Apr. 14, 1860, in Curtis, *Life of James Buchanan*, vol. 2, 286–287; Buchanan to J. L. Baker, July 25, 1859, in Buchanan, *Works*, 327–328, 393; Douglas to James Sheahan, Apr. 18, 1859, in SDL, 443–444; Sheahan, *Life of Stephen A. Douglas*; Thavenet, "William Alexander Richardson," 217–219; Holt, "Political Career of Richardson," 246–247; McClernand to Lanphier, Mar. 28, Mar. 30, 1860, LaLPL; Venable, "Conflict between Douglas and Yancey," 235; Douglas to Henry Cleveland, Mar. 31, 1860 (quoted), DoNYHS; Roger Pryor to Hammond, Oct. 13, 1858 (quoted), HaLC.

45. Johannsen, *Stephen A. Douglas*, 737–744; Halstead and Hesseltine, *Three against Lincoln*, 12; Coleman, *Disruption of Pennsylvania Democracy*, 118, 123–125; Holman to O'Brien, Mar. 2, 1860, HOBIHS; James Lucas to Davis, Mar. 9, 1860, DaIHS; McClernand to Lanphier, Mar. 2, 1860, LaLPL; Benjamin Brewster to Hunter, Mar. 5, 1860, in Hunter, *Correspondence*, 299–300; Murray McConnell to Douglas, Apr. 22, 1860 (quoted), DoLPL.

46. Davis to "My Dear Child," Apr. 19, 1860, Davis to wife, May 6, 1860 (quoted), James Lucas to Davis, Mar. 9, Apr. 16, 1860, James Stewart to Davis, Mar. 15, 1860, J. B. Otey to Davis, Mar. 16, 1860, Isaac Elston to Davis, Mar. 17, 1860, David Snyder to Davis, Mar. 24, Apr. 16, 1860, DaIHS; Taylor, *Destruction and Reconstruction*, 3; Sinha, *Counterrevolution of Slavery*, 200; Halstead, *Three against Lincoln*, 8, 41; Lanphier to McClernand, Mar. 15, 1860 (quoted), McCLPL.

47. Halstead, *Three against Lincoln*, 7–9, 9 (quoted), 13, 15; Johannsen, *Stephen A. Douglas*, 748–750; Holt, "Political Career of Richardson," 246–247; O. B. Ficklin to McClernand, Mar. 19, 1860, McCLPL; Walther, *William Lowndes Yancey*, 240, 329; Taylor, *Destruction and Reconstruction*, 3.

48. Halstead, *Three against Lincoln*, 10, 16–18, 17 (quoted); Taylor, *Destruction and Reconstruction*, 5; Johannsen, *Stephen A. Douglas*, 751; Van Der Weele, "Jesse David Bright," 240–241; James Seddon to Hunter, Dec. 26, 1859, in Hunter, *Correspondence*, 280–284; Hinman, *Daniel Dickinson*, 155–157, 159–160; Breckinridge to Dickinson, June 19, 1860, Bright to Dickinson, July 19, 1860 (quoted), DiNew; Austin King to Douglas, Apr. 15, 1860, DoLPL.

49. Van Der Weele, "Jesse David Bright," 241; Walther, *William Lowndes Yancey*, 237–239; Venable, "Conflict between Douglas and Yancey," 236–237, 230–231; P. S. Cornelius to Davis, Jan. 31, 1860, DaIHS; Sinha, *Counterrevolution of Slavery*, 197–198; Johannsen, *Stephen A. Douglas*, 750; Halstead, *Three against Lincoln*, 11; Taylor, *Destruction and Reconstruction*, 4–5.

50. Halstead, *Three against Lincoln*, 40; O. B. Ficklin to McClernand, Mar. 19, 1860 (quoted), McCLPL; Ficklin, *Genealogical*, 42; Venable, "Conflict between Douglas and Yancey," 226; Walther, *William Lowndes Yancey*, 244.

Chapter 9

1. Buchanan, *Mr. Buchanan's Administration*, 66; Halstead and Hesseltine, *Three against Lincoln*, 7, 18–21, 26; Parkhurst, *Official Proceedings*, 3–9; Johannsen, *Stephen A. Douglas*, 749, 751; Nichols, *Disruption of American Democracy*, 296–297; Van Der Weele, "Jesse David Bright," 241–242.

2. Parkhurst, *Official Proceedings*, 9–10, 16, 20–21; Halstead and Hesseltine, *Three against Lincoln*, 25, 27, 31; Belohlavek, *Broken Glass*, 295–299, 302, 305–307; Taylor, *Destruction and Reconstruction*, 4; Venable, "Conflict between Douglas and Yancey," 238–239; Johannsen, *Stephen A. Douglas*, 751–752.

3. Parkhurst, *Official Proceedings*, 21, 24–26, 31–35; Halstead and Hesseltine, *Three against Lincoln*, 32, 37–39, 42–44; Telegram, Thomas Bocock to Hunter, Apr. 25, 1860 (quoted), Telegram, Thomas Bocock to William Miles, Apr. 25, 1860, in Hunter, *Correspondence*, 320.

4. Parkhurst, *Official Proceedings*, 35, 37–40; Halstead and Hesseltine, *Three against Lincoln*, 45–56; Sinha, *Counterrevolution of Slavery*, 201; Walther, *William Lowndes Yancey*, 240–242; C. P. Culver to Douglas, Apr. 28, 1860, Stephen Douglas Letters, Lincoln Presidential Library; William Wick to Hunter, Apr. 27, in Hunter, *Correspondence*, 321–322.

5. Halstead and Hesseltine, *Three against Lincoln*, 57–59, 62–64; Toombs to Stephens, May 5, May 12, 1860, in TSC, 468–469, 477–478; Burnett, *Pen Makes a Good Sword*, 109; C. P. Culver to Douglas, Apr. 28, 1860 (quoted), DoLPL; Parkhurst, *Official Proceedings*, 41–42, 44, 46–50; Johannsen, *Stephen A. Douglas*, 754; Note with newspaper clipping, "Bigler Resolution at Charleston," BiHSP.

6. Halstead and Hesseltine, *Three against Lincoln*, 64–65; Egerton, *Year of Meteors*, 75; Walther, *William Lowndes Yancey*, 243; Charles Mason to Hunter, Apr. 30, 1860, in Hunter, *Correspondence*, 322–323; Venable, "Conflict between Douglas and Yancey," 239; Toombs to Stephens, May 5, 1860, in TSC, 468–469.

7. Halstead and Hesseltine, *Three against Lincoln*, 66–74, 79–85, 80 ("bridegroom" quote); Parkhurst, *Official Proceedings*, 50, 52, 55–65; Johannsen, *Stephen A. Douglas*, 755–756; Holt, "Political Career of Richardson," 249; Walther, *William Lowndes Yancey*, 243–244, 244; Sinha, *Counterrevolution of Slavery*, 201–202 ("Gulf squadron" quote).

8. Halstead and Hesseltine, *Three against Lincoln*, 85–86, 93–95, 111–113, 115; Sinha, *Counterrevolution of Slavery*, 202; Walther, *William Lowndes Yancey*, 244–245.

9. Halstead and Hesseltine, *Three against Lincoln*, 88–90, 96, 98–104, 106–109; Parkhurst, *Official Proceedings*, 66–67, 72–91; Belohlavek, *Broken Glass*, 308; Schimmel, "William H. English," 814–822; Davis to wife, May 7, 1860, DaIHS.

10. John Millero to Davis, May 12, 1860 (quoted), A. M. Puett to Davis, May 28, 1860, DaIHS; Toombs to Stephens, May 7, 1860, in TSC, 469–470; Stephens, *Constitutional View*, 2:273; Walther, *William Lowndes Yancey*, 245–248; Johannsen, *Stephen A. Douglas*, 759; Van Der Weele, "Jesse David Bright," 244, 246; Stephens to R. M. J., May 6, 1860 (quoted), in Johnston and Browne, *Life of Stephens*, 355.

11. Johannsen, *Stephen A. Douglas*, 759–762; J. Travis Rosser to Douglas, June 5, 1860, Samuel Bridge to Douglas, Apr. 11, 1860, George Cravens to Douglas, May 5, 1860, John Forsyth to Douglas, May 9, 1860, DoLPL; William Wick to Hunter, May 6, 1860 (quoted), in Hunter, *Correspondence*, 323–325; Johnston and Browne, *Life of Stephens*, 353; Walther, *William Lowndes Yancey*, 249; Burnett, *Pen Makes a Good Sword*, 99–109, 111–112.

12. Cobb to Buchanan, Nov. 14, 1859, Toombs to Stephens, Jan. 11, Feb. 10 (quoted), May 16, June 9, 1860, Toombs to Robert Collins, et al., May 10, 1860, Cobb to John Lamar, May 22, 1860, in TSC, 448–449, 455–456, 460–462, 475–477, 478–479, 479–480, 481; Bigler to Robert Tyler, May 15, 1860, Bigler Letters, NYHS; Charles Russell to Hunter, May 13, May 29, 1860, John Letcher to Hunter, June 4, 1860 (quoted), in Hunter, *Correspondence*, 325–336, 330–331, 331–332; Johannsen, *Stephen A. Douglas*, 763; Bright to Burke, May 14, 1860, EBLC; Buchanan to Robert Tyler, June 13, 1860, Buchanan Letters, BuLPL; A. M. Puett to Davis, May 28, 1860, DaIHS.

13. Johannsen, *Stephen A. Douglas*, 763–764; Buchanan, *Mr. Buchanan's Administration*, 78; Halstead and Hesseltine, *Three against Lincoln*, 186; Dickinson to Mr. Rogers, Apr. 12, 1860, in Dickinson, *Speeches, Correspondence, Etc.*, 531–533; James Guthrie to Tilden, May 21, 1860, Samuel Barlow to Tilden, June 1860, TiNYPL; Nichols, *Disruption of American Democracy*, 312; Bright to Dickinson, June 30, 1860 ("anxious" quote); John Dix to Buchanan, May 9, 1860, in Curtis, *Life of James Buchanan*, vol. 2, 288n; Horatio Seymour to Samuel Barlow, May 15 ("responsibility" quote), June 8, 1860, FCNYHS.

14. Summers, *Plundering Generation*, 30; Horatio Seymour to Samuel Barlow, May 15 (quoted), June 8, 1860, FCNYHS; Bright to Dickinson, July 19, 1860, DiNew; William Richardson to Douglas, May 13, 1860, DoLPL; Winston Pierce to Davis, May 28, 1860, John Tyler to Davis, June 9, 1860, DaIHS; Dix, *Memoirs*, 1:327; J. A. Logan to McClernand, June 2, 1860 (quoted), McCLPL; Buchanan to Robert Tyler, June 13, 1860 (quoted), Buchanan Letters, LPL.

15. Johannsen, *Stephen A. Douglas*, 762–763, 767; Egerton, *Year of Meteors*, 155–157; J. B. Otey to Davis, June 18, 1860, DaIHS; Van Der Weele, "Jesse David Bright," 248–250; Sinha, *Counterrevolution of Slavery*, 206; Halstead and Hesseltine, *Three against Lincoln*, 185, 261; Foote, *Casket of Reminiscences*, 121; Stephens to unknown, June 19, 1860 (quoted), in Johnston and Browne, *Life of Stephens*, 365; Walther, *William Lowndes Yancey*, 249; Stephens to J. Henley Smith, June 17, 1860, in TSC, 481–482.

16. Halstead and Hesseltine, *Three against Lincoln*, 185, 190–221; Parkhurst, *Official Proceedings*, 93, 97–111, 113–125; Belohlavek, *Broken Glass*, 309–310; Johannsen, *Stephen A. Douglas*, 768–769; Burnett, *Pen Makes a Good Sword*, 112; John Cobb to John Lamar, June 20, 1860, in TSC, 482–483.

17. Halstead and Hesseltine, *Three against Lincoln*, 223–230; Parkhurst, *Official Proceedings*, 125, 133–142; James Mason to Dickinson, June 22, 1860 (quoted), DiNew; Johannsen, *Stephen A. Douglas*, 769–770; Burnett, *Pen Makes a Good Sword*, 112–113; Thavenet, "William Alexander Richardson," 227.

18. Douglas to Richardson, June 20, 1860, Douglas to Dean Richmond, June 22, 1860, in SDL, 492–493, 493–494; Halstead and Hesseltine, *Three against Lincoln*, 230–237, 262–263; Burnett, *Pen Makes a Good Sword*, 112–113; Johannsen, *Stephen A.*

Douglas, 769–771; Thavenet, "William Alexander Richardson," 227; Holt, "Political Career of Richardson," 250; Parkhurst, *Official Proceedings*, 142–152, 144 (quoted).

19. Halstead and Hesseltine, *Three against Lincoln*, 238 (Gaulden quote), 237 (Moffat quote), 248 (Flournoy quote).

20. Halstead and Hesseltine, *Three against Lincoln*, 241–245, 249, 251–252, 256; Parkhurst, *Official Proceedings*, 152–157, 163, 168–169, 172–174; Belohlavek, *Broken Glass*, 310–311; Stephens to J. Henley Smith, July 2, Sept. 12, 1860, in TSC, 483–486, 494–496; Johnston and Browne, *Life of Stephens*, 353; Johannsen, *Stephen A. Douglas*, 771–772; Stephens, *Constitutional View*, 2:274; Burnett, *Pen Makes a Good Sword*, 113–114.

21. Halstead and Hesseltine, *Three against Lincoln*, 265, 267–269, 271–276; Sinha, *Counterrevolution of Slavery*, 206–207; Buchanan, *Mr. Buchanan's Administration*, 82; Hinman, *Daniel Dickinson*, 262; John Breckinridge to Dickinson, June 29, 1860, in Dickinson, *Speeches, Correspondence, Etc.*, 535; Austin King to Douglas, Apr. 15, 1860, DoL PL; Stephens, *Constitutional View*, 2:274 (quoted); Cobb to John Lamar, May 22, 1860 (quoted), in TSC, 479–480; James Foley to English, Aug. 11, 1859, EnIHS; Walther, *William Lowndes Yancey*, 250–251; "Speech of the Hon. Wm. L. Yancey," June 27, 1860, *Constitution* (Washington, DC) ("arch-enemy" quote).

22. "Last Night of the Democratic Party," June 23, 1860, *New York Tribune*, in Pike, *First Blows of the Civil War*, 520–524; Stephens to J. Henley Smith, July 2, 1860, in TSC, 483–486; Halstead and Hesseltine, *Three against Lincoln*, 118–140, 144–177; Fehrenbacher, *Prelude to Greatness*, 154–159; Edward Everett to Corcoran, June 6, 1860, CoLC; Stephens, *Constitutional View*, 2:275.

23. Knupfer, "1860," in Birkner, *James Buchanan*, 146; Buchanan, *Mr. Buchanan's Administration*, 81.

24. Halstead and Hesseltine, *Three against Lincoln*, 254–255; Parkhurst, *Official Proceedings*, 175–176, 184–185; Stephens, *Constitutional View*, 2:275; Burnett, *Pen Makes a Good Sword*, 113–114; Buchanan, *Mr. Buchanan's Administration*, 82; Julian, *Political Recollections*, 175.

25. Douglas to William Ludlow, et al., June 27, 1860, in SDL, 494–496; Johannsen, *Stephen A. Douglas*, 776, 785.

26. Hinman, *Daniel Dickinson*, 164; Halstead and Hesseltine, *Three against Lincoln*, 12; Curtis, *Life of James Buchanan*, vol. 2, 289; Buchanan to C. Comstock, July 5, 1860, Buchanan, Speech at the White House, July 9, 1860, in Curtis, *Life of James Buchanan*, vol. 2, 289–290, 290–295; Johannsen, *Stephen A. Douglas*, 777; Thavenet, "William Alexander Richardson," 229, 232; Douglas to Nathaniel Paschall, July 4, 1860, Douglas to Charles Lanphier, July 5, 1860 (quoted), in SDL, 497, 497–498.

27. Stephens, *Constitutional View*, 2:275; J. C. Van Dyke to Bigler, June 26, 1860, James McFarland to Bigler, June 28, 1860, G. W. Smith to Bigler, July 23, 1860, Jacob Thompson to Bigler, July 24, 1860, A. P. Whitaker to Bigler, July 31, 1860, BiHSP; Belohlavek, *Broken Glass*, 311–312; Isaac Stevens to Burke, Aug. 23, 1860, EBLC; Breckinridge to Dickinson, June 29, 1860, in Dickinson, *Speeches, Correspondence, Etc.*, 535; Schimmel, "William H. English," 829–830.

28. Stephens, *Constitutional View*, 2:276; Buchanan to Coryell, Sept. 26, 1860 (quoted), CoHSP.

29. Johannsen, *Stephen A. Douglas*, 778–801, 805; Egerton, *Year of Meteors*, 199–202; Burnett, *Pen Makes a Good Sword*, 114–115; Daniels to Mother, Oct. 21, 1860,

George Daniels Letters, NYHS; Douglas to James Sheridan, Aug. 22, 1860, in SDL, 499; Speech excerpt in Cox, *Union-Disunion-Reunion*, 58.

30. J. Lawrence Getz to Bigler, June 21, 1860, D. S. Koons to Bigler, July 16, 1860, W. G. Murray to Bigler, July 23, 1860, A. Iverson to Bigler, July 23, 1860, Isaac Stevens to Bigler, July 24, Aug. 5, 1860, A. P. Whitaker to Bigler, July 31, 1860, J. E. Coulter to Bigler, Aug. 4, 1860, James MacFarland to Bigler, Aug. 6, 1860, John McKiernan to Bigler, Aug. 21, 1860, BiHSP; Coleman, *Disruption of Pennsylvania Democracy*, 123, 127–128, 137–138, 140; "Veto of the Homestead Bill," June 22, 1860, in Buchanan, *Works*, 443–451; Dusinberre, *Civil War Issues in Philadelphia*, 96–97, 101; Sam Bridges to Coryell, July 17, 1860, CoHSP; Vaux to Douglas, Sept. 5, 1860 (quoted), Richard Vaux Letters, CHS; Buchanan to Coryell, Sept. 26, 1860, CoHSP.

31. Van Der Weele, "Jesse David Bright," 250–251, 254–258; Thornbrough, *Indiana in the Civil War*, 89; Woollen, *Sketches of Early Indiana*, 230; Tredway, *Democratic Opposition to Lincoln*, 144; Bright to English, Sept. 23, 1860, EnIHS; Bright to Dickinson, June 30, 1860 (quoted), DiNew.

32. Van Der Weele, "Jesse David Bright," 261–264; Thornbrough, *Indiana in the Civil War*, 93, 95–96; Bright to English, Sept. 23, 1860, English to N. Caper, Feb. 1, 1860 (quoted), J. A. Cravens to English, Oct. 21, Nov. 25, 1860, EnIHS; Schimmel, "William H. English," 829–832, 847–849, 869; A. Wheeler to Colfax, May 27, 1860 (quoted), SCISL.

33. August Belmont to Tilden, Aug. 1860, Belmont et al. to Tilden, Aug. 2, 1860 (quoted), William Kelly to Tilden, Aug. 16, 1860, Ransom Gillet to Tilden, Oct. 20, 1860 (quoted), Peter Cagger to Tilden, Oct. 22, 1860, TiNYPL; Nichols, *Disruption of American Democracy*, 343–344, 364–365; Breckinridge to Dickinson, June 29, 1860, in Dickinson, *Speeches, Correspondence, Etc.*, 535; Bright to Dickinson, June 30, 1860, DiNew; Johannsen, *Stephen A. Douglas*, 792, 797; Chairman, National Democratic Executive Committee to "The Friends of Breckinridge & Lane," New York City, July 1860, BiHSP; Stephens to J. Henly Smith, Oct. 13, 1860, in TSC, 500–502.

34. William Yancey to Burke, Oct. 14, 1860, EBLC; Joshua Henry to Tilden, Sept. 17, Sept. 19, 1860, Peter Cagger to Tilden, Sept. 29, 1860, Theodore Miller to Tilden, Oct. 21, 1860, TiNYPL; Dickinson to Mr. Rogers, Oct. 15, 1860 (quoted), in Dickinson, *Speeches, Correspondence, Etc.*, 538; Bright to Dickinson, July 19, 1860, DiNew; Johannsen, *Stephen A. Douglas*, 781–782; Douglas to James Cutts, June 30, 1860, in SDL, 496.

35. Egerton, *Year of Meteors*, 192, 196–197; William Fessenden to Pike, Sept. 12, 1860, in Pike, *First Blows of the Civil War*, 525–526; Fehrenbacher, *Prelude to Greatness*, 159–160; Coleman, *Disruption of Pennsylvania Democracy*, 140; Dusinberre, *Civil War Issues in Philadelphia*, 101; Stephens, *Constitutional View*, 2:277 (quoted); Winfield Scott to Buchanan, "Views," Oct. 29, 1860, CoLC.

36. Summers, *Plundering Generation*, 51–52; Coleman, *Disruption of Pennsylvania Democracy*, 141; H. Quigley to McClernand, Dec. 8, 1860 (quoted), McCLPL; Fehrenbacher, *Prelude to Greatness*, 159–160, 160 (quoted); Johannsen, *Stephen A. Douglas*, 803–804; Buchanan, *Mr. Buchanan's Administration*, 84; Schimmel, "William H. English," 849.

37. Cobb to Robert Collins et al., May 9, 1860, in TSC, 471–474.

38. Dickinson to Henry Orr, Sept. 13, 1853 (quoted), in Dickinson, *Speeches, Correspondence, Etc.*, 476–481; CG, 31C-1S, 956.

39. Bright to English, Oct. 8, Nov. 3, Dec. 27, 1861, Jan. 7, Nov. 22, 1862, EnIHS; Van Der Weele, "Jesse David Bright," 294–305; Murphy, *Political Career of Jesse Bright*, 138–145; Thornbrough, *Indiana in the Civil War*, 115–116.

40. Thavenet, "William Alexander Richardson," 233–301; "Richardson, William Alexander, (1811–1875)," *Biographical Directory of the United States Congress*, http:// bioguide.congress.gov/scripts/biodisplay.pl?index=R000228; Holt, "Political Career of Richardson," 252–262.

41. Buchanan to Rev. D. Schaff, Oct. 17, 1861 (quoted), Buchanan to J. Glancy Jones, July 1, 1867 (quoted), BJLC; Buchanan, *Mr. Buchanan's Administration*; "Buchanan, James, (1791–1868)," *Biographical Directory of the United States Congress*, http:// bioguide.congress.gov/scripts/biodisplay.pl?index=B001005.

42. Jones, *J. Glancy Jones*, vol. 2, 122, 126–130, 131, 135–138, 139–149, 149–155.

43. Bright to English, Mar. 31, Apr. 14, July 7, 1861, EnIHS; Schimmel, "William H. English," 863–867, 869, 878–890.

44. Nichols, *Franklin Pierce*, 507–532.

45. Hinman, *Daniel Dickinson*, 167–209; Breckinridge to Dickinson, June 29, 1860, Dickinson to H. S. Randall, Dec. 7, 1860, Dickinson to James Mason and Robert Hunter, Jan. 4, 1861, John Mason to Dickinson, Jan. 12, 1861, Dickinson to James Eldridge, May 1, 1861, Dickinson to Mr. Spencer, May 7, 1861, Mr. Porter to Dickinson, Aug. 23, 1861, Dickinson to Mr. Spencer, Aug. 28, 1861, H. W. Rogers to Dickinson, Aug. 31, 1861, Dickinson to Mrs. Mygatt, Sept. 2, 1861, William Nagle to Dickinson, Sept. 13, 1861, Noah Davis, et al. to Dickinson, Sept. 19, 1861, Dickinson to Noah Davis, et al., Oct. 17, 1861, William Seward to Dickinson, Oct. 31, 1861, Dr. N. Niles to Dickinson, Nov. 6, 1861, Dickinson to Mr. Spencer, Nov. 25, 1861, Dickinson to "A Friend in New York," Sept 21, 1862, Dickinson to Col. N. E. Paine, Jan. 7, 1863, "Mr. Dickinson Declining Renomination as Attorney General," Aug. 24, 1863, Dickinson to Mr. Rogers, July 31, 1864, Dickinson to William Seward, July 4, 1864, Dickinson to Lewis Cass, Sept. 26, 1864, in Dickinson, *Speeches, Correspondence, Etc.*, 535, 538–539, 539–542, 544–545, 549–550, 550–551, 553–554, 554, 554–555, 555–556, 557, 558, 559, 560–561, 562–563, 585–586, 599–600, 623–625, 650–653, 654, 658–659; Dickinson, "Speech of the Hon. Daniel Dickinson, of New York, Delivered at the Cooper Institute, New York, July 18, 1860." Breckinridge and Lane Campaign Documents, no. 6 (Washington City, 1860); Dickinson to D. D. T. Cowen, May/June 4, 1863 (quoted), Dickinson Papers, NYHS.

46. Johannsen, *Stephen A. Douglas*, 808–872.

47. Buchanan to Marcy, Nov. 21, 1850 (quoted), MaLC.

BIBLIOGRAPHY

Primary Sources

Gideon Bailey Papers, Iowa State Library, Des Moines
August Belmont Papers, New York Public Library
John Bigelow Papers, New York Public Library
William Bigler Collection, Pennsylvania Historical Commission
William Bigler Letters, New-York Historical Society
William Bigler Papers, Historical Society of Pennsylvania
Breckinridge Family Papers, Library of Congress
Sidney Breese Papers, Abraham Lincoln Presidential Library
Jesse Bright Letters, Chicago Historical Society
Jesse Bright Letters, Indiana State Library
Thomas Bryan Letter, Chicago Historical Society
James Buchanan Collection, New-York Historical Society
James Buchanan Letters, Abraham Lincoln Presidential Library
James Buchanan Papers, Historical Society of Pennsylvania
James Buchanan Papers, Library of Congress
James Buchanan and Harriet Lane Johnston Papers, Library of Congress
Edmund Burke Letter, New-York Historical Society
Edmund Burke Papers, Library of Congress
Schuyler Colfax Papers, Indiana State Library
Schuyler Colfax Papers, Lilly Library, Indiana University
William Corcoran Papers, Library of Congress
Lewis Coryell Papers, Historical Society of Pennsylvania
Cushing Family Papers, Massachusetts Historical Society
Cushing Speeches Collection, Massachusetts Historical Society
George Daniels Letters, New-York Historical Society
John Davis Papers, Indiana Historical Society
Henry Dean Papers, Chicago Historical Society
Henry Dean Papers, Iowa State Library, Des Moines
Daniel Dickinson Papers, Newberry Library
Daniel Dickinson Papers, New-York Historical Society
Augustus Caesar Dodge Papers, Iowa State Library, Des Moines
Augustus Caesar Dodge Papers, Iowa State Library, Iowa City
Augustus Caesar Dodge Papers, University of Iowa Library, Iowa City
Stephen Douglas Letters, New-York Historical Society
Stephen Douglas Papers, Abraham Lincoln Presidential Library
William English Papers, Chicago Historical Society
William English Papers, Indiana Historical Society

William English Papers, Indiana State Library
Fairchild Collection, New-York Historical Society
William Gorham Papers, New York State Library
John Graham Letters, Indiana State Library
James Henry Hammond Papers, Library of Congress
William Holman Papers, Lilly Library, Indiana University
William Holman Papers, Lilly Library, Iowa University
Holman-O'Brien Papers, Indiana Historical Society
Hunter-Garnett Papers, University of Virginia
Cave Johnson Letters, New-York Historical Society
J. Glancy Jones Letter, New-York Historical Society
John Ketcham Papers, Indiana Historical Society
Charles Lanman Collection, Indiana Historical Society
Charles Lanphier Papers, Abraham Lincoln Presidential Library
Harlow Lindley Collection, Indiana Historical Society
Robert Lucas Letters, New-York Historical Society
William Marcy Papers, Library of Congress
William Marcy Papers, New York State Library
John McClernand Papers, Abraham Lincoln Presidential Library
George Fort Milton Papers, Library of Congress
Franklin Pierce Letters, New-York Historical Society
Franklin Pierce Papers, Library of Congress
Francis Pollard Letter, Indiana Historical Society
Daniel Pratt Papers, Indiana State Library
Logan Reavis Papers, Chicago Historical Society
Robert Barnwell Rhett Papers, South Carolina Historical Society
William Richardson Papers, Abraham Lincoln Presidential Library
William Richardson Papers, Chicago Historical Society
David Rorer Letters, Iowa State Library, Iowa City
Horatio Seymour Collection, New York State Library
Horatio Seymour Papers, New-York Historical Society
James Singleton Papers, Abraham Lincoln Presidential Library
Caleb Blood Smith Papers, Library of Congress
Richard Thompson Papers, Indiana State Library
Samuel Tilden Papers, New York Public Library
Albert Tracy Papers, New York Public Library
William Tweed Letters, New-York Historical Society
Richard Vaux Letters, Chicago Historical Society
Robert Walker Papers, New-York Historical Society
Mike Walsh Papers, New-York Historical Society
Daniel Webster Papers, New-York Historical Society
Fernando Wood Papers, New-York Historical Society

Published Primary Sources

Benton, Thomas Hart. *Thirty Years View; or, A History of the Workings of American Government for Thirty Years, from 1820 to 1850.* Vol. 2. New York: D. Appleton, 1854.

Buchanan, James. *Mr. Buchanan's Administration on the Eve of the Rebellion.* New York: D. Appleton, 1866.

———. *The Works of James Buchanan, Comprising His Speeches, State Papers, and Private Correspondence.* Vol. 10. Edited by John Moore. Philadelphia: J. B. Lippincott, 1910.

Clay-Clopton, Virginia. *A Belle of the Fifties: Memoirs of Mrs. Clay, of Alabama, Covering Social and Political Life in Washington in the South, 1853–66.* London: Wm. Heinemann, 1905.

Congressional Address. An Address to the People of the United States, and Particularly to the People of the States Which Adhere to the Federal Government. Washington, DC, 1864.

Congressional Globe. Library of Congress. http://memory.loc.gov/ammem/amlaw/lwcg.html.

Copperhead Minstrel: A Choice Collection of Democratic Poems and Songs, for the Use of Political Clubs and the Social Circle. New York: Feeks and Bancker, 1863.

Cox, Samuel. *A Buckeye Abroad; or, Wanderings in Europe, and in the Orient.* New York: George P. Putnam, 1852.

———. *Eight Years in Congress, from 1857 to 1865: Memoir and Speeches.* New York: D. Appleton, 1865.

———. *Union-Disunion-Reunion: Three Decades of Federal Legislation, 1855 to 1885.* Providence, RI: J. A. and R. A. Reid, 1885.

Democratic Party. *Official Proceedings of the National Democratic Convention, Held in Cincinnati, June 2–6, 1856.* Cincinnati: Enquirer Company Steam Printing Establishment, 1856.

———. *Official Proceedings of the Democratic National Convention, Held in 1864 at Chicago.* Chicago: Times Steam Book and Job Printing House, 1864.

Dickinson, Daniel. *Speech of the Hon. Daniel Dickinson, of New York, Delivered at the Cooper Institute, New York, July 18, 1860.* Breckinridge and Lane Campaign Documents, no. 6. Washington City: National Democratic Executive Committee, 1860.

Dickinson, Daniel, and John R. Dickinson. *Speeches, Correspondence, Etc., of the Late Daniel S. Dickinson of New York Including, Addresses on Important Public Topics, Speeches in the State and United States Senate, and in Support of the Government during the Rebellion, Correspondence Private and Political (Collected and Arranged by Mrs. Dickinson), Poems (Collected and Arranged by Mrs. Mygatt), Etc.* New York: G. P. Putnam and Sons, 1867.

Dix, Morgan. *Memoirs of John Adams Dix.* 2 vols. New York: Harper and Brothers, 1883.

Douglas, Stephen. *The Letters of Stephen A. Douglas.* Edited by Robert Johannsen. Urbana: University of Illinois Press, 1961.

Foote, Henry. *Casket of Reminiscences.* Washington, DC: Chronicle, 1874.

Forney, John. *Anecdotes of Public Men.* Vol. 1. New York: Harper and Brothers, 1873.

———. *Anecdotes of Public Men.* Vol. 2. New York: Harper and Brothers, 1881.

Giddings, Joshua. *The History of the Rebellion: Its Authors and Causes.* New York: Follett, Foster, 1864.

Halstead, Murat, and Rex Fisher. *Trimmers, Trucklers, and Temporizers.* Madison: State Historical Society of Wisconsin, 1961.

Halstead, Murat, and William Hesseltine. *Three against Lincoln: Murat Halstead Reports the Caucuses of 1860*. Baton Rouge: Louisiana State University Press, 1960.

Helper, Hinton. *The Impending Crisis of the South: How to Meet It*. New York: A. B. Burdick, 1860.

Hincks, William, and F. H. Smith, eds. *Proceedings of the Democratic National Convention Held at Baltimore, June, 1852*. Washington, DC: Buell and Blanchard, 1852.

Hoar, George Frisbie. *Autobiography of Seventy Years*. Vol. 1. New York: C. Scribner's Sons, 1903.

Hunt, John Gabriel, ed. *The Inaugural Addresses of the Presidents*. New York: Gramercy Books, 1995.

Hunter, Robert M. T. *Correspondence of Robert M. T. Hunter, 1826–1867*. Edited by Charles Henry Ambler. New York: Da Capo Press, 1971.

Julian, George. *Political Recollections, 1840–1872*. Chicago: Jansen, McClurg, 1884.

The Letters and Times of the Tylers. Vol. 3. Edited by Lyon Gardiner Tyler. Williamsburg, VA: 1896.

The Library of Original Sources, Editors Edition. Edited by Oliver Thatcher. New York: University Research Extension, 1907.

Lincoln, Abraham. *The Collected Works of Abraham Lincoln*. Vol. 3. Edited by Roy P. Basler. New Brunswick, NJ: Rutgers University Press, 1953.

Marcy, William. "Diary and Memoranda of William L. Marcy, 1857." *American Historical Review* 24 (July 1919): 641–653.

McCulloch, Hugh. *Men and Measures of Half a Century: Sketches and Comments*. New York: C. Scribner's Sons, 1888.

Miscegenation: The Theory of the Blending of the Races, Applied to the American White Man and Negro. London: Trubner, 1864.

Parkhurst, John. *Official Proceedings of the Democratic National Convention, Held in 1860, at Charleston and Baltimore*. Cleveland, OH: Nevins' Print, 1860.

Phillips, Ulrich. *The Life of Robert Toombs*. New York: Macmillan, 1913.

Pike, James. *First Blows of the Civil War: The Ten Years of Preliminary Conflict in the United States; From 1850 to 1860*. New York: American News, 1879.

Ritchie, Thomas. "Ritchie Letters." *John P. Branch Historical Papers of Randolph-Macon College* 4, no. 1 (1913) (Richmond, VA: Richmond Press).

"The Ruin of the Democratic Party: Reports of the Covode and Other Committees." Published by Republican Congressional Committee. N.d.

Sheahan, James. *The Life of Stephen A. Douglas*. New York: Harper and Brothers, 1860.

Stephens, Alexander. *A Constitutional View of the Late War between the States; Its Causes, Character, Conduct, and Results*. Vol. 1. Philadelphia: National, 1867.

——. *A Constitutional View of the Late War between the States; Its Causes, Character, Conduct, and Results*. Vol. 2. Philadelphia: National, 1868–1870.

Taylor, Richard. *Destruction and Reconstruction: Personal Experiences of the Late War in the United States*. London: William Blackwood and Sons, 1879.

Tilden, Samuel. *The Writings and Speeches of Samuel J. Tilden*. Vol. 1. Edited by John Bigelow. New York: Harper and Brothers, 1885.

Toombs, Robert, Alexander Stephens, and Howell Cobb. *The Correspondence of Robert Toombs, Alexander H. Stephens, and Howell Cobb.* Edited by Ulrich Bonnell Phillips. Annual Report of the American Historical Association for the Year 1911, vol. 2. Washington, 1913.

Tredway, G. R. *Democratic Opposition to the Lincoln Administration in Indiana.* Indianapolis: Indiana Historical Bureau, 1973.

Trumbull, Lyman. "Collection of Letters from Lyman Trumbull to John Palmer, 1854–1858." *Illinois State Historical Society Journal* 16 (1923): 20–41.

Vallandigham, Clement. *Speeches, Arguments, Addresses, and Letters of Clement L. Vallandigham.* New York: J. Walter, 1864.

Wallace, Lew. *Lew Wallace: An Autobiography.* Vol. 1. New York: Harper and Brothers, 1906.

Wilson, Rufus. *Intimate Memories of Lincoln.* Elmira, NY: Primavera Press, 1945.

Wise, John. *Recollections of Thirteen Presidents.* New York: Doubleday, Page, 1906.

Woollen, William Wesley. *Biographical and Historical Sketches of Early Indiana.* Indianapolis: Hammond, 1883.

Newspapers

Arkansas State Democrat (Little Rock, AR)
Bangor Daily Whig and Courier (Bangor, ME)
Boston Daily Advertiser (Boston, MA)
Boston Daily Atlas (Boston, MA)
Charleston Mercury (Charleston, SC)
Cleveland Herald (Cleveland, OH)
Daily Atlas (Boston, MA)
Daily Cleveland Herald (Cleveland, OH)
Daily Morning News (Savannah, GA)
Daily National Intelligencer (Washington, DC)
Daily Register (Raleigh, NC)
Daily Scioto Gazette (Chillicothe, OH)
Daily South Carolinian (Columbia, SC)
Dover Gazette and Strafford Advertiser (Dover, NH)
The Emancipator (New York, NY)
Fayetteville Observer (Fayetteville, NC)
Frederick Douglass's Paper (Rochester, NY)
The Liberator (Boston, MA)
Lowell Daily Citizen and News (Lowell, MA)
Mississippi Free Trader and Natchez Gazette (Natchez, MS)
Mississippian and State Gazette (Jackson, MS)
New Hampshire Statesman and Concord Register (Concord, NH)
New York Daily Times (New York, NY)
New York Herald (New York, NY)
New York Times (New York, NY)
North American and United States Gazette (Philadelphia, PA)

Vermont Patriot (Montpelier, VT)
Weekly Herald (New York, NY)

Unpublished Theses and Dissertations

Ferree, Walter. "The New York Democracy: Division and Reunion, 1847–1852." Ph.D. diss., University of Pennsylvania, 1953.
Meerse, David. "James Buchanan, the Patronage, and the Northern Democratic Party, 1857–1858." Ph.D. diss., University of Illinois, 1969.
Schimmel, Elliot L. "William H. English and the Politics of Self-Deception, 1845–1861." Ph.D. diss., Florida State University, 1986.
Thavenet, Dennis. "William Alexander Richardson, 1811–1875." Ph.D. diss., University of Nebraska, 1967.
Van Der Weele, Wayne J. "Jesse David Bright: Master Politician from the Old Northwest." Ph.D. diss., Indiana University, 1958.
Wells, Edward. "The Political Career of Samuel Sullivan Cox during the Ohio Phase." M.A. thesis, Ohio State University, 1935.

Published Secondary Sources

Allen, Austin. *Origins of the Dred Scott Case: Jacksonian Jurisprudence and the Supreme Court, 1837–1857.* Athens, GA: University of Georgia Press, 2006.
Anbinder, Tyler. *Nativism and Slavery: The Northern Know Nothings and the Politics of the 1850s.* New York: Oxford University Press, 1992.
Baker, H. Robert. *The Rescue of Joshua Glover: A Fugitive Slave, the Constitution, and the Coming of the Civil War.* Athens: Ohio University Press, 2006.
Baker, Jean. *Affairs of Party: The Political Culture of Northern Democrats in the Mid-nineteenth Century.* New York: Fordham University Press, 1983.
Barnwell, John. *Love of Order: South Carolina's First Secession Crisis.* Chapel Hill: University of North Carolina Press, 1982.
Bauer, K. Jack. *Zachary Taylor: Soldier, Planter, Statesman of the Old Southwest.* Baton Rouge: Louisiana State University Press, 1985.
Beckert, Sven. *The Monied Metropolis: New York City and the Consolidation of the American Bourgeoisie, 1850–1896.* New York: Cambridge University Press, 2001.
Belohlavek, John. *Broken Glass: Caleb Cushing and the Shattering of the Union.* Kent, OH: Kent State University Press, 2005.
Binder, Frederick Moore. *James Buchanan and the American Empire.* Cranbury, NJ: Associated University Presses, 1994.
Birkner, Michael, ed. *James Buchanan and the Political Crisis of the 1850s.* Selinsgrove, PA: Susquehanna University Press, 1996.
Brown, David. *Southern Outcast: Hinton Rowan Helper and the Impending Crisis of the South.* Baton Rouge: Louisiana State University Press, 2006.
Burnett, Lonnie A. *The Pen Makes a Good Sword: John Forsyth of the Mobile Register.* Tuscaloosa: University of Alabama Press, 2006.
Campbell, Stephen. *The Slave Catchers: Enforcement of the Fugitive Slave Law, 1850–1860.* Chapel Hill: University of North Carolina Press, 1970.

Clary, David. *Eagles and Empire: The United States, Mexico, and the Struggle for a Continent*. New York: Bantam Books, 2009.

Coleman, John F. *The Disruption of the Pennsylvania Democracy, 1848–1860*. Harrisburg, PA: Pennsylvania Historical and Museum Commission, 1975.

Cook, Robert. *Baptism of Fire: The Republican Party in Iowa, 1838–1878*. Ames: Iowa State University Press, 1994.

Cooper, William J., Jr. *Liberty and Slavery: Southern Politics to 1860*. Columbus, OH: McGraw-Hill, 1983.

——. *The South and the Politics of Slavery, 1828–1856*. Baton Rouge: Louisiana State University Press, 1978.

Cox, William, and Milton Northrup. *Life of Samuel Sullivan Cox*. Syracuse, NY: M. H. Northrup, 1899.

Craven, Avery. *The Coming of the Civil War*. Chicago: University of Chicago Press, 1957.

Curtis, George. *Life of James Buchanan: Fifteenth President of the United States*. Vol. 2. New York: Harper and Brothers, 1883.

Davis, William. *Rhett: The Turbulent Life and Times of a Fire-Eater*. Columbia: University of South Carolina Press, 2001.

Dusinberre, William. *Civil War Issues in Philadelphia, 1856–1865*. Philadelphia: University of Pennsylvania Press, 1965.

Egerton, Douglas. *Year of Meteors: Stephen Douglas, Abraham Lincoln, and the Election That Brought on the Civil War*. New York: Bloomsbury Press, 2010.

Etcheson, Nicole. *Bleeding Kansas: Contested Liberty in the Civil War Era*. Lawrence: University Press of Kansas, 2004.

Eyal, Yonatan. *The Young America Movement and the Transformation of the Democratic Party, 1828–1861*. Cambridge, UK: Cambridge University Press, 2007.

Fehrenbacher, Don. *The Dred Scott Case: Its Significance in American Law and Politics*. New York: Oxford University Press, 1978.

——. *Prelude to Greatness: Lincoln in the 1850's*. Stanford: Stanford University Press, 1962.

——. *The Slaveholding Republic: An Account of the United States Government's Relations to Slavery*. New York: Oxford University Press, 2001.

Ficklin, Walter. *A Genealogical History of the Ficklin Family*. Denver, CO: W. H. Kistler Press, 1912.

Finkelman, Paul. *Millard Fillmore*. New York: Times Books, 2011.

——. *Slavery and the Founders: Race and Liberty in the Age of Jefferson*. Armonk, NY: M. E. Sharpe, 1996.

Finkelman, Paul, and Donald Kennon, eds. *Congress and the Crisis of the 1850s*. Athens: Ohio University Press, 2012.

Gara, Larry. *The Presidency of Franklin Pierce*. Lawrence: University of Kansas Press, 1991.

Gienapp, William. *The Origins of the Republican Party, 1852–1856*. New York: Oxford University Press, 1987.

Hamilton, Holman. *Prologue to Conflict: The Crisis and Compromises of 1850*. Lexington: University of Kentucky Press, 1964.

Hansen, Stephen, and Paul Nygard. "Stephen A. Douglas, the Know-Nothings, and the Democratic Party in Illinois, 1854–1858." *Illinois Historical Journal* 87, no. 2. (1994): 109–130.

Harrold, Stanley. *Border War: Fighting over Slavery before the Civil War*. Chapel Hill: University of North Carolina Press, 2010.

Hickman, George. *The Life of General Lewis Cass, with His Letters and Speeches on Various Subjects.* Baltimore: N. Hickman, 1848.

Hinman, Marjory. *Daniel Dickinson: Defender of the Constitution.* Windsor, NY: Published by the author, 1987.

Holt, Michael. *The Fate of Their Country: Politicians, Slavery Extension, and the Coming of the Civil War.* New York: Hill and Wang, 2004.

———. *The Political Crisis of the 1850s.* New York: Wiley, 1978.

———. *The Rise and Fall of the American Whig Party: Jacksonian Politics and the Onset of the Civil War.* New York: Oxford University Press, 1999.

Holt, Robert. "The Political Career of William A. Richardson." *Journal of the Illinois State Historical Society* 20 (June 1933): 222–269.

Huston, James. *Stephen A. Douglas and the Dilemmas of Democratic Equality.* New York: Rowman and Littlefield, 2006.

Jennings, Thelma. *The Nashville Convention: Southern Movement for Unity, 1848–1851.* Memphis: Memphis State University Press, 1980.

Johannsen, Robert. *Stephen A. Douglas.* New York: Oxford University Press, 1973.

Johnston, Richard, and William Brown. *Life of Alexander H. Stephens.* Philadelphia: J. B. Lippincott, 1883.

Jones, Charles. *The Life and Public Services of J. Glancy Jones.* 2 vols. Philadelphia: J. B. Lippincott, 1910.

Klein, Philip. *President James Buchanan: A Biography.* University Park: Pennsylvania State University Press, 1962.

Klement, Frank. "'Brick' Pomeroy: Copperhead and Curmudgeon." *Wisconsin Magazine of History* 35, no. 2 (1951): 106–113, 156–157.

Klunder, Willard. *Lewis Cass and the Politics of Moderation.* Kent, OH: Kent State University Press, 1996.

Lindsey, David. *"Sunset" Cox: Irrepressible Democrat.* Detroit: Wayne State University Press, 1959.

Lucas, David. *Nicaragua: War of the Filibusters.* Richmond, VA: B. F. Johnson, 1896.

May, Robert. *John A. Quitman: Old South Crusader.* Baton Rouge: Louisiana State University Press, 1985.

———. *Manifest Destiny's Underworld: Filibustering in Antebellum America.* Chapel Hill: University of North Carolina Press, 2002.

McPherson, James. *Battle Cry of Freedom: The Civil War Era.* New York: Oxford University Press, 1988.

Meerse, David. "Origins of the Buchanan-Douglas Feud Reconsidered." *Journal of the Illinois State Historical Society* 67, no. 2 (1974): 154–174.

Moore, Glover. *The Missouri Controversy.* Lexington: University of Kentucky Press, 1953.

Morris, Thomas. *Free Men All: The Personal Liberty Laws of the North, 1780–1861.* Baltimore: Johns Hopkins University Press, 1974.

Murphy, Charles. *The Political Career of Jesse Bright.* Indiana Historical Society Publications, vol. 10, no. 3. Indianapolis: Printed for the Society, 1931.

Mushkat, Jerome. *Fernando Wood: A Political Biography.* Kent, OH: Kent State University Press, 1990.

———. *The Reconstruction of the New York Democracy, 1861–1874.* Rutherford, NJ: Fairleigh Dickinson University Press, 1981.

———. *Tammany: The Evolution of a Political Machine, 1789–1865.* Syracuse, NY: Syracuse University Press, 1971.

Neely, Mark. *The Union Divided: Party Conflict in the Civil War North.* Cambridge, MA: Harvard University Press, 2002.

Nichols, Roy F. *American Leviathan: The Evolution and Process of Self-Government in the United States.* New York: Harper and Row, 1963.

———. *The Democratic Machine, 1850–1854.* New York: AMS Press, 1967.

———. *The Disruption of the American Democracy.* New York: Macmillan, 1948.

———. *Franklin Pierce: Young Hickory of the Granite Hills.* Philadelphia: University of Pennsylvania Press, 1931, 1967.

Pelzer, Louis. *Augustus Caesar Dodge.* Iowa Biographical Series. Iowa City: State Historical Society of Iowa, 1908.

Peterson, Merrill. *The Great Triumverate: Webster, Clay, and Calhoun.* New York: Oxford University Press, 1987.

Philips, Ulrich. *The Life of Robert Toombs.* New York: Macmillan, 1913.

Potter, David. *The Impeding Crisis, 1848–1861.* New York: Harper and Row, 1976.

Proctor, L. B. *Lives of Eminent Lawyers and Statesmen of the State of New York with Notes of Cases Tried by Them, Speeches, Anecdotes, and Incidents in Their Lives.* Vol. 2. New York: S. S. Peloubet, 1882.

Richards, Leonard. *The Slave Power: The Free North and Southern Domination, 1780–1860.* Baton Rouge: Louisiana State University Press, 2000.

Salter, William. *Augustus C. Dodge, Senator of the United States from Iowa.* Iowa City: State Historical Society of Iowa, 1887.

Savage, John. *Our Living Representative Men: From Official and Original Sources.* Philadelphia: Childs and Peterson, 1860.

Scroggs, William. *Filibusters and Financiers: The Story of William Walker and His Associates.* New York: Macmillan, 1916.

Sewell, Richard. *John P. Hale and the Politics of Abolition.* Cambridge, MA: Harvard University Press, 1965.

Silbey, Joel. *A Respectable Minority: The Democratic Party in the Civil War Era, 1860–1868.* New York: W. W. Norton, 1977.

Sinha, Manisha. "The Caning of Charles Sumner: Slavery, Race, and Ideology in the Age of the Civil War." *Journal of the Early Republic* 23, no. 2 (2003): 233–262.

———. *The Counterrevolution of Slavery: Politics and Ideology in Antebellum South Carolina.* Chapel Hill: University of North Carolina Press, 2000.

Smith, Elbert. *The Presidency of James Buchanan.* Lawrence: University Press of Kansas, 1975.

Spencer, Ivor D. *The Victor and the Spoils: A Life of William L. Marcy.* Providence, RI: Brown University Press, 1959.

Stampp, Kenneth. *America in 1857: A Nation on the Brink.* New York: Oxford University Press, 1990.

Stegmaier, Mark. *Texas, New Mexico, and the Compromise of 1850.* Kent, OH: Kent State University Press, 1996.

Stiles, T. J. *The First Tycoon: The Epic Life of Cornelius Vanderbilt.* New York: Vintage Books, 2009.

Streeter, Floyd. *Political Parties in Michigan, 1837–1860.* Lansing: Michigan Historical Commission, 1918.

Summers, Mark. *The Plundering Generation: Corruption and the Crisis of the Union, 1849–1861.* New York: Oxford University Press, 1987.

Thornbrough, Emma Lou. *Indiana in the Civil War Era, 1850–1880.* The History of Indiana, vol. 3. Indianapolis: Indiana Historical Bureau, 1965.

Venable, Austin. "The Conflict between the Douglas and Yancey Forces in the Charleston Convention." *Journal of Southern History* 8, no. 2 (1942): 226–241.

Vorenberg, Michael. *Final Freedom: The Civil War, the Abolition of Slavery, and the Thirteenth Amendment.* Cambridge, UK: Cambridge University Press, 2001.

Walther, Eric. *William Lowndes Yancey and the Coming of the Civil War.* Chapel Hill: University of North Carolina Press, 2006.

Weber, Jennifer. *Copperheads: The Rise and Fall of Lincoln's Opponents in the North.* New York: Oxford University Press, 2006.

Wilson, Rufus. *Intimate Memories of Lincoln.* Elmira, NY: Primavera Press, 1945.

Wood, Forrest W. *Black Scare: The Racist Response to Emancipation and Reconstruction.* Berkeley: University of California Press, 1968.

Wood, Nicholas. "John Randolph of Roanoke and the Politics of Slavery in the Early Republic." *Virginia Magazine of History and Biography* 120 (Summer 2012): 106–143.

Websites

The American Presidency Project. State of the Union Addresses and Messages. http://www.presidency.ucsb.edu/sou.php#axzz1IVmtGPlj

Architect of the Capitol. "The Old Supreme Court Chamber." http://www.aoc.gov/cc/capitol/oscc.cfm

Biographical Directory of the United States Congress. http://bioguide.congress.gov/scripts/biodisplay.pl?index=B000789

Maryland Institute College of Art. http://www.mica.edu/About_MICA/Facts_and_History/Historical_Timeline/1847-1878_Renewal_and_Expansion_in_the_Industrial_Age.html.

Pennsylvania Historical and Museum Commission. "Governor William Bigler." http://www.portal.state.pa.us/portal/server.pt/community/1790-1879/4283/william_bigler/444242.

United States Senate. "President Pro Tempore." http://www.senate.gov/artandhistory/history/common/briefing/President_Pro_Tempore.htm#5.

——. "Senate Chaplain." http://www.senate.gov/artandhistory/history/common/briefing/Senate_Chaplain.htm.

University of Chicago Library. "Stephen Douglas and the American Union." http://www.lib.uchicago.edu/e/spcl/excat/douglas2.html.

INDEX